READING
FOR
RECOGNITION

READING

FOR

RECOGNITION

RUTH F. EISENBERG
Pace College Westchester

CAROL J. SWIDORSKI
Westchester Community College

HOLT, RINEHART AND WINSTON, INC.
NEW YORK CHICAGO SAN FRANCISCO ATLANTA DALLAS

TO OUR PARENTS
with love and recognition

TO THE TEACHER

What does the college freshman want to read in a collection of essays? What does the English teacher hope to achieve with the student in his reading? These are the two basic questions the editors of this collection used to govern their choices and to govern their approaches to the material once it had been chosen.

Cynics may answer the first question negatively. We disagree. We feel the student wants to read material with a high interest factor, material that communicates a sense of immediacy, and material that makes him more conversant with some of the great and important names and issues.

To this general end, we have chosen essays that apply to or comment on problems of the contemporary world, but are not so of-the-moment that they immediately date themselves. The hippie movement is passé now, and Haight-Ashbury just another problem neighborhood; race and violence are basic issues in our society.

To engage interest, we have used much humor; about twenty percent of the articles fall into the wide range of humorous writing. Almost one-quarter of the contents utilize literary illustration or narrative because they are highly readable. Many of the articles are brief; they make their succinct point and quit. Finally, the list of authors is, we think, impressive, and we invite you to look over the Contents.

The second question—what English teachers hope to achieve—is more complex than the mere enjoyment of a text. Better reading, better thinking, and better writing are usually the ultimate goals; the apparatus that accompanies the articles is geared to those ends.

The purpose of each introduction is to supply the reader with an orientation and a perspective. Each gives some pertinent data on the writer, while some indicate the source of the material. "To the Reader" offers hints so the student can read more rapidly and with fuller comprehension because he will have some idea of what to read for.

While the questions are intended to help the reader, they may also be used to guide class discussion. In almost every essay, the first question seeks the theme since it is the conviction of the editors that reading for the main idea is the most important kind of reading. The questions that follow help reveal the thinking of the essayist in the development of his main points. The final questions point up the form, technique, and style of the essay or essayist. The student is asked to find, recognize, and sometimes analyze rhetorical or stylistic devices.

To aid vocabulary development, two techniques have been employed. There is a vocabulary list at the end of each essay that requires such a list. More significantly perhaps, throughout the essay, any word that seemed critical to an intelligent reading is defined in a footnote.

Following the questions and vocabulary are discussion and writing topics that may be used in the classroom or as broad starting points for themes. Some topics allow personal reflection; others require research.

"Cross References" leads the student to other essays in the collection that deal with related subject matter. "Recommended Reading" refers the interested student to related essays, books, and plays beyond the collection.

Though the book has been planned as a unit from Prologue to Epilogue, it need not be used that way. To facilitate handling, we have devised a double Contents. The thematic approach is described in the foreword "To The Student." The Rhetorical

Contents is primarily for the teacher's use. There is occasionally overlapping and duplication in distribution of the titles; that is because some pieces fill more than one category. For example, Schwartz can be taught, rhetorically, for analysis, classification, or tone; Kennedy, for argument or diction. Sometimes, too, an argumentative piece is developed largely via a particular expository technique. If, at times, you disagree with the editors and want to argue their decision, that is quite okay; we argued between ourselves often.

Good writers and good writing: these are what the book presents. Reading for enjoyment, stimulation, and emulation is what we hope it will accomplish.

White Plains, N.Y.
Yonkers, N.Y.

January 1969

Ruth F. Eisenberg
Carol J. Swidorski

TO THE STUDENT

The student on the brink of recognition of himself and the world is the individual to whom this book is addressed. Faced with responsibility, the need for achievement, and desire for commitment, he is apt to find the world large and chaotic — in many ways overwhelming.

This book will not bring total recognition, but it will heighten individual awareness. It offers material through which the student can gain a broader perspective of the world, a world that surely needs improvement. Self-understanding and the understanding of other people are two basic ingredients to any betterment. This is basic to the view of Eric Sevareid's essay "The Dark of the Moon," which has provided the theme for this book.

The collection opens with "Public Issues," essays that examine our world and a few of its problems: what it is to be a man and an American; what it is to face the dilemmas of democracy, race, violence, dope, individualism. While all the problems are serious, not all the material is; laughter sometimes brings special insights.

The second section, "The Heart of Man," introduces some people, well-known and unknown, who make up our world — the lives of some of whom have, directly or indirectly, affected ours, whether or not we realize it.

The third section of the book, "Controlling the Earth from the Earth," explores man's mind: the mechanics of thinking; the relation of words to thought; the expansion of man's capacity to think and feel by the creative use of his mind, his talents, and his leisure.

With this broader perspective, the serious student is often spurred to look more deeply at particularly bothersome problems. Two of the most pressing problems of our time, both personal and public, are dissent and violence. Each of these issues is explored in "Two Private Issues" via historical commentary and contemporary thought. Then particular dilemmas are argued: dissent — how much free speech is too much? violence — how violent is our society?

The book closes with "The Hope and the Reassurance," six essays of idealism. Each is by a man whose thinking has profoundly affected the world. Each man, in turn, reflects optimism about the innate capacity of mankind for moral achievement, responsible action, and love — collectively, the highest realizations of awareness or self-recognition.

White Plains, N. Y.   Ruth F. Eisenberg
Yonkers, N. Y.   Carol J. Swidorski

January 1969

ACKNOWLEDGMENTS

The authors would like to express another kind of recognition: that acknowledging the many people who aided and encouraged us, one way or another, in putting this book together:

To our chairmen and colleagues: particularly Barbara Cole, Robert Dell, Alberta Avery, and Kay McKemy for suggestions and comments.

To the library staffs at Pace College Westchester under the direction of Maryvie Cramblitt and Westchester Community College under John Kager.

To Eileen Johnsmeyer, guardian of the key to the Xerox.

To the editorial staff at Holt, particularly Phillip Leininger, our patient editor; Richard Beal, our consultant critic; Kenney Withers, who signed us on; and Jane Ross, who guided us through *all* those permissions.

To many of our authors whose personal notes were very kind.

To friends like Harold Kalvin, Arthur Eisenberg, James Oest, Bernadette Coomaraswamy, and Maureen Jedlicka for their interest in the whole project.

And lastly and most importantly, to June Richardson, Jay and Steve Eisenberg, and Allen Bachrach—people closest to us—whose constant support, active participation, and loving endurance cheered us on from the beginning.

Thank you.

CONTENTS

iii

CONTROLLING THE EARTH FROM THE EARTH   133

The Workings of the Mind   135

Some Thoughts on Words   193

The Uses of Leisure

RHETORICAL CONTENTS

EXPOSITORY

PROSE

Definition

Illustration

Comparison and Contrast

Classification

Analysis

NARRATIVE
PROSE

DESCRIPTIVE
PROSE

ARGUMENTATIVE
PROSE

Diction

Diction

Tone

ERIC SEVAREID

"THE DARK OF THE MOON"

INTRODUCTION

Eric Sevareid (1912–   ) is known to all Americans who listen to the CBS television evening news program. His calm and measured tones reflect his calm and measured thinking as he analyzes and comments on the news. Mr. Sevareid joined CBS in 1939 after eight years of newspaper work. He has written many magazine articles and several books including his autobiography, *Not So Wild a Dream* (1946), and his most recent collection of essays, *This Is Eric Sevareid*, published in 1964.

TO THE READER

Until recently, the dark side of the moon was an undiscovered mystery. As you read through the essary, consider the parallel Sevareid is drawing between the dark of the moon and the dark of man.

Your immediate reaction may be that Sevareid is antiscience. This is not true; what he is for is more significant than what he is against.

This, thank goodness, is the first warm and balmy night of the year in these parts: the first frogs are singing. Altogether this is hardly the night for whispering sweet sentiments about the reciprocal trade act, the extension thereof. But since we are confined, by tradition, to the contemplation of public themes and issues, let us contemplate the moon. The lovely and luminous moon has become a public issue. For quite a few thousand years it was a private issue; it figured in purely bilateral negotiations between lovers, in the incantations of jungle witch doctors and Indian corn planters. Poets from attic windows issued the statements about the moon, and they made better reading than the Mimeographed handouts now being issued by assistant secretaries of defense.

[2]   The moon was always measured in terms of hope and reassurance and the heart pangs of youth on such a night as this; it is now measured in terms of mileage and foot-pounds of rocket thrust. Children sent sharp, sweet wishes to the moon; now they dream of bluntnosed missiles.

[3]   There must come a time, in every generation, when those who are older secretly get off the train of progress, willing to walk back to where they came from, if they can find the way. We're afraid we're getting off now. Cheer, if you wish, the first general or Ph.D. who splatters something on the kindly face of the moon. We shall grieve for him, for ourself, for the young lovers and poets and dreamers to come, because the ancient moon will never be the same again. Therefore, we suspect, the heart of man will never be the same.

[4]   We find it very easy to wait for the first photographs of the other side of the moon, for we have not yet seen the other side of Lake Louise or the Blue Ridge peak that shows through the cabin window.

[5]   We find ourself quite undisturbed about the frontpage talk of "controlling the earth from the moon," because we do not believe it. If neither men nor gadgets nor both combined can control the earth from the earth, we fail to see how they will do so from the moon.

[6]   It is exciting talk, indeed, the talk of man's advance toward space. But one little step in man's advance toward man — that, we think, would be truly exciting. Let those who wish try to discover the composition of a lunar crater; we would settle for discovering the true mind of a Russian commissar or the inner heart of a delinquent child.

[7]   There is, after all, another side — a dark side — to the human spirit, too. Men have hardly begun to explore these regions; and it is going to be a very great pity if we advance upon the bright side of the moon with the dark side of ourselves, if the cargo in the first rockets to reach there consists of fear and chauvinism[1] and suspicion. Surely we ought to have our credentials in order, our hands very clean and perhaps a prayer for forgiveness on our lips as we prepare to open the ancient vault of the shining moon.

---

[1]excessive devotion to any cause, especially zealous and belligerent patriotism or blind enthusiasm for military glory

EXERCISES

Questions

1. Paragraphs 1 and 7 present the theme of the essay. Draw them together and state the thesis.
2. Why is the essay's title appropriate? How does it relate to the theme?
3. What is Sevareid's attitude toward the moon and romance and toward the moon and science?
4. What would he rather see than a landing on the moon? Which would you rather see?
5. Note Sevareid's use of phrases like "bilateral negotiations between lovers," "Mimeographed handouts," "get off the train of progress." How does the tone implied in these phrases serve the essay's theme?
6. Notice the structure of paragraph 2. In each sentence, the old and the new are contrasted. Notice also the specific details he uses. Examine paragraph 6 for structure and detail. Is it like paragraph 2?

Vocabulary

reciprocal
incantations
credentials

POSTSCRIPT TO THE READER

This essay serves as the theme for the entire book. The editors feel that young people in a technological world face the very situation that Mr. Sevareid presents. This book reflects the essay's philosophy; the divisions of the book are even called by names taken from the essay.

i

Public Issues

MY PARENTS
SPEAK OF OUR
GENERATION
AS IF THEY
HAD NOTHING
TO DO
WITH IT—

Washington Star Syndicate, Inc.

5-23 BRICKMAN

The Washington Star Syndicate, Inc.

E. B. WHITE

"THE MEANING
OF DEMOCRACY"

INTRODUCTION

E. B. White (1899–   ) was born in Mt. Vernon, a suburb of New York City,
an appropriate birthplace for a man who later became an editor of *The New
Yorker* magazine, one of the most influential literary magazines in America.
A master stylist, White is known for his wit and his keen observing eye. A few
months before his death, President Kennedy presented White with the Presidential Medal of Freedom for his contribution to "the quality of American
life." Among his many books are *One Man's Meat* (1942), *Here Is New York*
(1949), and *The Elements of Style* (1952) with William Strunk, Jr.

TO THE READER

White believes that words are important, and democracy is one of our most
important words. His approach is informal, yet highly serious.
　　Compare White's images with your ideas of democracy.

July 3, 1943

　　We received a letter from the Writers' War Board the other day
asking for a statement on "The Meaning of Democracy." It presumably is

our duty to comply with such a request, and it is certainly our pleasure. [2] Surely the Board knows what democracy is. It is the line that forms on the right. It is the don't in don't shove. It is the hole in the stuffed shirt through which the sawdust slowly trickles; it is the dent in the high hat. Democracy is the recurrent suspicion that more than half of the people are right more than half of the time. It is the feeling of privacy in the voting booths, the feeling of communion in the libraries, the feeling of vitality everywhere. Democracy is a letter to the editor. Democracy is the score at the beginning of the ninth. It is an idea that hasn't been disproved yet, a song the words of which have not gone bad. It's the mustard on the hot dog and the cream in the rationed coffee. Democracy is a request from a War Board, in the middle of a morning in the middle of a war, wanting to know what democracy is.

EXERCISES

Questions

1. According to White, what is democracy?
2. Examine the statements, "Democracy is the score at the beginning of the ninth," or "It's the mustard on the hot dog." What exactly does each one say about democracy?
3. White defines via imagery. In what way is it more effective to say, "Democracy is a letter to the editor," than to say, "Democracy is the freedom to express and publish your opinion on almost any matter"?
4. Study White's sentences. How does he avoid monotony? How does he use repetition?
5. Discuss the tone of the second paragraph. Justify the gentle irony of the last sentence.

For Discussion and Writing

1. Take any of White's statements; use it as a theme sentence and amplify it.
2. Define any of the following in White's manner: freedom, justice, tyranny, dictatorship, woman, man. After you write your theme, check the word in a standard dictionary.

CROSS REFERENCES

COOKE: "It's a Democracy, Isn't It?"
COUSINS: "The Environment of Language"
KENNEDY: "Inaugural Address"
KING: "I Have a Dream"

ALISTAIR COOKE

"IT'S A DEMOCRACY, ISN'T IT?"

INTRODUCTION

Alistair Cooke (1908–   ), English born and Cambridge educated, at one time served as the host of one of America's prestige television shows, *Omnibus*. As such, he became known to millions of Americans previously unaware of his existence as a leading correspondent, journalist, film critic, and commentator on American affairs. He writes for the *Manchester Guardian,* one of England's leading papers, as its chief United States correspondent. In addition, he has written several books, *Douglas Fairbanks* (1940), *A Generation on Trial* (1950), and *One Man's America* (1952), from which this excerpt was taken.

TO THE READER

Cooke defines democracy in terms of privacy and intrusion. He concludes that Americans and Britons view privacy differently.

I was standing on the corner of Lexington Avenue on a Sunday in May waiting for a bus. It was a gorgeous day, hot and golden, and there were not many people around. Sunday is more than a bearable day in New York because for one thing there are about a million less cars than usual. No trucks. Surburbanites in for the day pointing up and down and walking with their feet out. A couple of cabs parked outside a lunch-room, the drivers gone in for a beer. A family or two hand in hand, taking the children off to the park. A well-dressed upper-crust couple coming across from Park Avenue also hand in hand—a very common sight in New York, for Americans are not much concerned in such matters with what looks proper or what the neighbors will think. A good day—the sort of day when, for all the panicky newspaper headlines, your faith in people, and their needs and inclinations, is restored.

[2] Suddenly, I heard a ghost. It was a familiar ghost, an invisible man somewhere in mid-air saying in a brisk monotone—"Strike. The count is two and two. Runners on first and third." This lingo, or the language of which this is a snatch, is something you would hear in a hundred places—homes, cafes, saloons, cars—from then till the end of the first week in October. It is a radio sports announcer covering a ball game—a ball game being, as you probably know, a baseball game.

[3] The voice was coming from nowhere. A young Negro couple, arm in arm, was ambling towards me. But the man's free arm carried a little box. Of course, it was a portable radio. They went down the subway steps, and as they pattered down into the darkness the voice went on floating up, more excited now: "A base hit to left field. Fuselli's in, Rodgers coming into third." Nobody else on the street seemed to notice or to care. But if you had cared, and wanted for one day to get away from radio, I don't know where you could have gone. Out on Coney Island, thousands of bodies would be lying in close proximity not only to thousands of other bodies but to hundreds of other little boxes, tuned high. And the air would be so full of "He's out" and "The bases are loaded" and "Full count," that you'd have had quite a time knowing what the wild waves were saying.

[4] This little picture is meant to produce a shudder in you. If it doesn't, then Britons are not what they used to be, and their passion for privacy, and what's more, for respecting the next man's privacy, is dead and gone. Don't misunderstand me. I approve myself very strongly of this feeling. I share it. But it makes me all the less of an American. Only a week ago, I heard a plonking sound, allied to music, quite faint, coming up through the living-room floor. It was a neighbor in our apartment house who is either six years of age and a promising pianist or forty years of age and a dope . . . because she—why do I say "she," I wonder—has been stuck on that same piece for a month or two now. I grumbled about the sameness of her repertory, and my twelve-year-old daughter, idling over a book, said, "Relax, Pop, you don't have to hear it if you don't want to."

[5] By this simple remark my daughter didn't mean that I could get up and go downstairs and start a riot, or that I could call the police or take out an

injunction. She simply meant I should shut my mind to the sound. I made sure this is what she meant, because when I played aloud with the idea of strangling our tinkling neighbor, she said, "I don't think that's very nice. She paid *her* rent too, you know."

[6]   Now, I should like to say that I am proud of my daughter and usually turn to her for a response that is commonsensical and unshocked (by, so far as I can make out, anything in life). But I wasn't aware she had acquired so young a fundamental mood or attitude of what Americans call democracy. In Britain, one of the minor duties of good citizenship is not to disturb the private life of other citizens. In this country, it's the other way around — not to disturb other citizens who are enjoying their private life in public. That, as you see, is a heavily loaded interpretation of an attitude that is universal among Americans. And there are limits. Just the same, the decision of a Washington court of appeal not to let advertisers broadcast in public buses only shows how far you can go in America without being stopped.

[7]   Americans regard most of us born in Britain as dull, decent, amiable people but given to being rather testy about our rights. So "Relax, Pop," says my daughter and goes back to reading her book with one third of her mind, listening to the pianist downstairs with another lobe, and at the same time dreaming on all cylinders about some absent male of the species. Quite aside from the principle involved, this attitude entails a considerable physical feat. It is the ability not to hear what you don't want to hear, what the most famous radio critic in America calls "selective deafness." He says it is a faculty essential to an enjoyment of American radio, and it is a faculty that most visiting Britons would rather not develop. Because they soon learn, as Mr. Crosby — John, not Bing — remarks, that the advertising people are aware of this conditioned reflex and so from year to year, like drug addicts, they increase the dose of the sales talk they cut into the programs. Still, nobody hearing his favorite comedian or forum discussion or symphony concert bothers to turn off the "plug." He lets it chatter on about some soap that "atomizes dirt" or a toothpaste that is "kind to gums but murder on film." And then the ecstatic announcer stops, and so back to Bob Hope or "Whither Europe?" or the Second Symphony of Beethoven.

[8]   To watch an American on a beach, or crowding into a subway, or buying a theater ticket, or sitting at home with his radio on, tells you something about one aspect of the American character: the capacity to withstand a great deal of outside interference, so to speak; a willing acceptance of frenzy which, though it's never self-conscious, amounts to a willingness to let other people have and assert their own lively, and even offensive, character. They are a tough race in this. You are expected — far beyond what other peoples would say were the restraints of manners — to assume that one man's opinion is as good as another's. The expert is an American idol, but only in certain understood fields. He is safe from contradiction if his expertness is in a science — in medicine, technology, industrial research, or in making some-

thing with his hands (better, if he uses somebody else's hands, because that shows he has mastered a process which can be left to drones): such things as an automobile, a waterproof watch, or a non-riding girdle. But when it comes to ideas about life and love and religion and education and architecture and painting and music, indeed all forms of pleasure, there is a national conviction that an expert is a phony, or "wants to be different," and that what matters is you should know what you like and—this is a democracy, isn't it?—speak up and say your piece. It may well be born from generations of living close to many races and many prejudices and temperaments and having to strike a livable compromise that may not be as smooth as some other societies; but at least it is a society, a going concern, which had to be built not out of a theory but out of the urgent practical need to get along at all.

[9] At any rate, if you want to live here in any spiritual comfort you have to allow for a wide variety of temperament in your friends and neighbors and approve a sharp clash of tastes. An insistence on privacy in such a society looks, as it would not look in Britain, like a form of conceit or neurosis, a refusal to admit the status quo by which you all live. So if the issue ever came up in argument, I think most Americans would say that it is merely elementary good manners and good citizenship to look on yourself as only one member of the community, whether that community is a town, a party, or a family.

EXERCISES

Questions

1. The theme of this essay is expressed in paragraph 8. According to Cooke, what is unique about the American character? Why do Americans "assume that one man's opinion is as good as another's." How does Cooke connect these two ideas? What do you think of them?

2. In paragraph 1, Cooke observes several couples holding hands and generalizes about Americans. Why is this an appropriate beginning for this essay? How is this further developed in paragraph 6?

3. "This little picture is meant to produce a shudder in you" begins paragraph 4 which is addressed to Britons. Need it apply only to Britons? How did you feel about the street scene Cooke presented? Is a lack of respect for privacy an American characteristic?

4. What is "selective deafness"? What are some of its advantages? disadvantages? How do you practice it in your own life?

5. How does Cooke define British democracy and American democracy with respect to privacy? Compare these with White's definition of democracy.

6. What are "good manners": respecting other people's privacy or tolerating other people's lack of privacy?

7. Note Cooke's humor via his use of slang (dope, paragraph 4) or his remark about his daughter's three brain lobes, or his kidding about com-
   mercials. How does humor serve the purpose of the essay?
8. Paragraph 1 contains many sentence fragments. Find them. What is the
   effect of the use of the fragments?
9. Cooke uses a variety of levels of diction in this piece. Find sentences
   which illustrate the use of slang, informal language, and formal language.

For Discussion and Writing

1. To whom does America listen:
   —the police chief or the criminologist on crime prevention
   —the lovelorn columnist or the psychologist on marriage affairs
   —the taxpayers' association or the urbanologist on slum clearance
   —the next-door neighbor or the critic on a "good film"
2. Intruders on privacy:
   —the transistor radio
   —billboard advertising
   —piped in music
   —paper-thin apartment walls
3. "Tuning out" into alienation
4. "Tuning out" to a cry for help

CROSS REFERENCES

WHITE: "The Meaning of Democracy"
STEINBECK: "America and the Americans"

JAMES WILLIAM FULBRIGHT

"THE COLD WAR
IN AMERICAN LIFE"

INTRODUCTION

James William Fulbright (1907–   ), Democratic Senator from Arkansas, is Chairman of the Senate Foreign Relations Committee. Senator Fulbright became a controversial figure because of his outspoken and spirited opposition to President Johnson's policy on Viet Nam. Although he is most widely recognized domestically for his knowledge and grasp of American history and politics, his name is known around the world for his support of education. The scholarships established in his name and supported by Congress have aided graduate students in such fields as history, literature, and art to further their studies abroad. Senator Fulbright is a fairly prolific writer, two of his more recent books being *Old Myths and New Realities* (1964), from which this abridged essay is taken, and *The Arrogance of Power* (1967).

TO THE READER

The Senator attacks some generally held ideas about American policy, with two of them his two chief targets.

The essay has four sections: part one states the problem; part two shows the causes of the problem and where the money is going; part three shows where it is *not* going; and part four shows where it should be going. After reading each section, write a caption stating the main idea or ideas discussed.

See if you can find where Fulbright supplies political arguments to bolster Sevareid's point of view.

The Constitution of the United States, in the words of its preamble, was established, among other reasons, in order to "provide for the common defense, promote the general welfare, and secure the blessings of liberty. . . ." In the past generation the emphasis of our public policy has been heavily weighted on measures for the common defense to the considerable neglect of programs for promoting the liberty and welfare of our people. The reason for this, of course, has been the exacting demands of two World Wars and an intractable cold war, which have wrought vast changes in the character of American life.

[2]   Of all the changes in American life wrought by the cold war, the most important by far, in my opinion, has been the massive diversion of energy and resources from the creative pursuits of civilized society to the conduct of a costly and interminable struggle for world power. We have been compelled, or have felt ourselves compelled, to reverse the traditional order of our national priorities, relegating individual and community life to places on the scale below the enormously expensive military and space activities that constitute our program of national security. Thus, we work ourselves into a fearful state of alarm over every incident on the Berlin access routes while blandly ignoring the increase of crime and violence in our great cities; we regard ourselves as gravely threatened by the rantings of a Cuban demagogue while taking little notice of the social disintegration caused by chronic unemployment; we undertake a $20-billion crash program to be first on the moon in order to avoid a possible blow to our pride while refusing to spend even a fraction of that amount for urgently needed federal aid to public education.

[3]   These of course are not the only effects of the continued world crisis on American life. There have been many others, some most welcome and constructive. Directly or indirectly, the world struggle with communism has stimulated economic and industrial expansion, accelerated the pace of intellectual inquiry and scientific discovery, broken the shell of American isolation, and greatly increased public knowledge and awareness of the world outside the United States. At the same time, the continuing world conflict has cast a shadow on the tone of American life by introducing a strand of apprehension and tension into a national style which has traditionally been one of buoyant optimism. . . .

[4]   Overriding all these changes, however, good and bad, has been the massive diversion of wealth and talent from individual and community life for the increasingly complex and costly effort of maintaining a minimum level of national security in a world in which no nation can be immune from the threat of sudden catastrophe. We have had to turn away from our hopes in order to concentrate on our fears, and the result has been accumulating neglect of those things which bring happiness and beauty and fulfillment into our lives. The "public happiness," in August Heckscher's term, has become a luxury to be postponed to some distant day when the dangers that now beset us will have disappeared.

[5]   This inversion[1] of priorities, I think, is the real meaning of the cold war in American life. It has consumed money and time and talent that could otherwise have been used to build schools and homes and hospitals, to re-move the blight of ugliness that is spreading over the cities and highways of America, and to overcome the poverty and hopelessness that afflict the lives of one-fifth of the people in an otherwise affluent society. It has put a high premium on avoiding innovation at home, because new programs involve controversy as well as expense and it is felt that we cannot afford domestic divisions at a time when external challenges require us to maintain the highest possible degree of national unity. Far more pervasively than the United Nations or the Atlantic community could ever do, the cold war has encroached upon our sovereignty; it has given the Russians the major voice in determining what proportion of our federal budget must be allocated to the military and what proportion, therefore, cannot be made available for domestic social and economic projects. This is the price that we have been paying for the cold war, and it has been a high price indeed.

[6]   At least as striking as the inversion of priorities which the cold war has enforced upon American life is the apparent readiness with which the Amer-ican people have consented to defer programs for their welfare and happi-ness in favor of costly military and space programs. Indeed, if the Congress accurately reflects the temper of the country, then the American people are not only willing, they are eager, to sacrifice education and urban renewal and public health programs—to say nothing of foreign aid—to the require-ments of the armed forces and the space agency. There is indeed a most striking paradox in the fact that military budgets of more than $50 billion are adopted by the Congress after only perfunctory debate, while domestic education and welfare programs involving sums which are mere fractions of the military budget are painstakingly examined and then either consider-ably reduced or rejected outright. I sometimes suspect that in its zeal for armaments at the expense of education and welfare, the Congress tends to overrepresent those of our citizens who are extraordinarily agitated about national security and extraordinarily vigorous about making their agitation known.

[1]reversing in position, direction, or relationship

[7]   It may be that the people and their representatives are making a carefully reasoned sacrifice of welfare to security. It may be, but I doubt it. The sacrifice is made so eagerly as to cause one to suspect that it is fairly painless, that indeed the American people prefer military rockets to public schools, and flights to the moon to urban renewal. In a perverse way, we have grown rather attached to the cold war. It occupies us with a seemingly clear and simple challenge from outside and diverts us from problems here at home which many Americans would rather not try to solve, some because they are genuinely and deeply preoccupied with foreign affairs, others because they find domestic problems tedious and pedestrian, others because they genuinely believe these problems to be personal rather than public, others because they are unwilling to be drawn into an abrasive national debate as to whether poverty, unemployment, and inadequate education are in fact national rather than local or individual concerns.

[8]   We have been preoccupied with foreign affairs for twenty-five years, and while striking progress has nonetheless been made in certain areas of our domestic life, the overall agenda of neglect has grown steadily longer. We can no longer afford to defer problems of slums and crime and poverty and inadequate education. In the long run, the solution of these problems has as vital a bearing on the success of our foreign policies as on the public happiness at home. We must therefore reassess the priorities of our public policy, with a view to redressing the disproportion between our military and space efforts on the one hand, and our education and human welfare programs on the other. We must overcome the "cold war" mentality that has persuaded millions of sensible and intelligent citizens that the prosecution of the cold war is our only truly essential national responsibility, that missiles and nuclear armaments and space flights are so vital to the safety of the nation that it is almost unpatriotic to question their cost and their proliferation, and that in the face of these necessities the internal requirements of the country, with respect to its schools and cities and public services, must be left for action at some remote time in the future — as if these requirements were not themselves vital to the national security, and as if, indeed, our generation is likely to know more tranquil days.

[9]   In the 1830s Alexis de Tocqueville[2] saw America as a nation with a passion for peace, one in which the "principle of equality," which made it possible for a man to improve his status rapidly in civilian life, made it most unlikely that many Americans would ever be drawn to form a professional military caste. In 1961, President Eisenhower warned the nation of the pervasive and growing power of a "military-industrial complex." Tocqueville was quite right in his judgment that the United States was unlikely to be-

---

[2]A French statesman and author who visited America in 1831 and 1832. His observations, published in *Democracy in America*, are well-known for their keen insight into the American character.

come a *militarist* society. We have, however, as a result of world-wide involvements and responsibilities, become a great *military* power, with a vast military establishment that absorbs over half of our federal budget, profoundly influences the nation's economy, and exercises a gradually expanding influence on public attitudes and policies.

[10] Without becoming militarist in the sense of committing themselves to the military virtues as standards of personal behavior, the American people have nonetheless come to place great — and, in my opinion, excessive — faith in military solutions to political problems. Many Americans have come to regard our defense establishment as the heart and soul of our foreign policy, rather than as one of a number of instruments of foreign policy whose effectiveness depends, not only on its size and variety, but also on the skill, and restraint, with which it is used.

[11] Our faith in the military is akin to our faith in technology. We are a people more comfortable with machines than with intellectual abstractions. The military establishment is a vast and enormously complex machine, a tribute to the technological genius of the American people; foreign policy is an abstract and esoteric art, widely regarded as a highly specialized occupation of "eastern intellectuals," but not truly an "American" occupation. Our easy reliance on the military establishment as the foundation of our foreign policy is not unlike the reliance which we place on automobiles, televisions, and refrigerators: they work in a predictable and controllable manner, and on the rare occasions when they break down, any good mechanic can put them back in working order.

[12] The trouble with the American technological bias is that it can conceal but not eliminate the ultimate importance of human judgment. Like any other piece of machinery, our military establishment can be no better than the judgment of those who control it. In a democracy, control is intended to be exercised by the people and their elected representatives. To a very considerable extent the American people are not now exercising effective control over the armed forces; nor indeed is the Congress, despite its Constitutional responsibilities in this field. Partly because of anxieties about the cold war, partly because of our natural technological bias, which leads us to place extraordinary faith in the ability of "technicians" to deal with matters that we ourselves find incomprehensible, and partly because of the vested interests of the "military-industrial complex," we are permitting the vast military establishment largely to run itself, to determine its own needs, and to tell us what sacrifices are expected of us to sustain the national arsenal of weapons.

[13] The abnegation[3] of responsibility by the Congress in this field is strikingly illustrated by its debates — or, more accurately, "nondebates" — on the defense budget. When, for example, Senator McGovern of South Dakota

---

[3]relinquishing, giving up

suggested in September, 1963, that defense spending might be reduced by 5 percent, the Senate, with virtually no discussion, voted the McGovern amendment down by a vote of 70 to 2 and proceeded, after an afternoon of desultory discussion, to enact the whole defense appropriation bill. When later that fall I had the dubious honor of managing the foreign aid bill on the Senate floor through three weeks of extremely contentious debate, I could not help noting how astonishingly the forces of "economy" had picked up strength between the debate on the $50 billion defense appropriation and the $4 billion foreign aid bill.

[14] In 1964, for example, both Houses enacted a military procurement authorization bill of more than $17 billion within less than two months of the opening of the Congressional session. The only controversial item in the bill was an amendment authorizing $52 million for development of a new strategic manned bomber, which was adopted by both Houses despite the firm opposition of the Secretary of Defense. In the course of this debate, Senator Nelson of Wisconsin posed a most pertinent question. "I am questioning," he said, "what is apparently an established tradition — perhaps a national attitude — which holds that a bill to spend billions of dollars for the machinery of war must be rushed through the House and the Senate in a matter of hours, while a treaty to advance the cause of peace, or a program to help the underdeveloped nations of the world, or a bill to guarantee the rights of all our citizens, or a bill to advance the interests of the poor, must be scrutinized and debated and amended and thrashed over for weeks and perhaps months."*

[15] The ease with which defense budgets are enacted by Congress is due in no small degree to the enormous importance of defense spending for the economy. Defense contractors and great numbers of workers all over the country have a vested interest in a high level of defense spending. It is the beneficiaries of the jobs and profits that defense spending creates, along with the generals and admirals, who constitute the formidable "military-industrial complex." And because of the jobs and profits stimulated by defense, Members of Congress have taken a benign attitude toward waste and duplication in the defense budget that is nothing less than amazing by contrast with the deeply held convictions about economy that influence their attitude toward education, urban renewal, or foreign aid.

[16] The uncritical acceptance of astronomical military expenditures by millions of Americans is matched by a similar extravagance with respect to space flights, and particularly the project for landing an American on the moon by 1970, at a cost of something between $20 and $30 billion.

[17] The question is not whether we should or should not send a manned rocket ship to the moon, but whether the project is so vital and so urgent as to warrant the indefinite postponement of other national efforts. This question has been debated at length, both in the Congress and in various publi-

*Congressional Record, February 26, 1964, p. 3584.

cations. I have heard nothing to persuade me that it would be a national calamity if the landing on the moon were delayed until 1980 or 1990. I have
heard and seen a great deal which persuades me that our continuing neglect
of deteriorating schools and rising unemployment *would* be a national
calamity.

[18] The argument most frequently heard in support of Project Apollo, the
moon shot program, is that if we do not pursue a crash program in space the
Russians will get to the moon ahead of us. This argument can be challenged
on two grounds: first, it is not at all clear that the Russians are *trying* to beat
us to the moon; secondly — and more important — it is even less clear that it
would be an irretrievable disaster if they did.

[19] The issue between freedom and dictatorship is a great deal more than a
competition in technological stunts. The real competition is between two
conflicting concepts of man and of his life in organized societies. Does it not
follow that our success has a great deal to do with our capacity to employ
and educate our people to create the conditions for human happiness and
individual fulfillment in a free society? If, at the end of this decade, the Russians should have reached the moon and we should not, but have instead
succeeded in building the best system of public education in the world, in
the renovation of our cities and transport, in the virtual elimination of slums
and crime, in the alleviation of poverty and disease, whose prestige would
be higher, who would then be ahead in the world-wide struggle for the
minds of men?

[20] It is frequently said that we did not provide adequate funds for education and other vital domestic needs before we had a space program and that
there is no assurance that we would increase our efforts in these areas if the
space program were abandoned or reduced. This, I am bound to concede,·
may well be true, although the Congress has come close several times to
adopting a meaningful general program of federal aid to education, and it
is possible that the reduction of our space expenditures would provide the
impetus for the enactment of a general education bill. In any case, I see little merit in the view that since we will not spend money anyway on things
we urgently need, we might as well spend it on things we do not need. If it
comes to that, I for one would rather not spend the money at all.

[21] There is a real danger that our national programs in defense and space
will become a drain on the civilian economy and will jeopardize our position
in world trade. At present only 25 percent of our total national research and
development spending are going into industrial research for civilian purposes. Western European countries are spending twice as large a proportion
of their gross national products as the United States for civilian research and
development. The Japanese, largely as a result of progress through civilian
research, have introduced the first transistorized television sets into the
United States, are getting twice our rate of production from textile machinery,
and are turning out automated ships that can carry more cargo than our ships
with smaller crews.

[22] Equally alarming is the prospective diversion of scientists and engineers from careers in university teaching. In the next decade there will be a great increase in our college population. If the present teacher-student ratio is to be maintained, the universities in the next several years will have to retain two thirds of their current output of new Ph.D.s instead of the present one third. Thus, the current flow of graduate research scholars to government and industry would have to be cut in half. It is just at this critical point that the demand for scientific talent for the space program is rapidly rising. It is increasingly clear that the supply of scientists and engineers in the present decade will not be sufficient to meet the demands of a mushrooming space program, a rapidly expanding college population, and all the other needs of the civilian economy.

[23] These are only some of the compelling reasons for bringing our space program into a more realistic relationship to pressing national needs. In the face of all the unsolved problems of our country — problems of inadequate education, racial tensions, rising unemployment, of urban blight and rising crime — I cannot bring myself to believe that landing an American on the moon represents the most urgent need, the most compelling challenge, or the most promising opportunity before the American people in this decade.

[24] Many Americans may regard huge military and space programs as the only truly urgent requirements on our national agenda, but it is difficult to believe that this enthusiasm is shared by the 4.2 million Americans who are unemployed or by the 30 million Americans who have incomes of less than $3,000 a year.

[25] While the cold war and our enormously costly national security programs pre-empt so much of our time and attention and national wealth, the most important resources of our country — its human resources — are being extravagantly wasted and neglected. As the President's *Manpower Report,* issued early in 1964, points out, unemployment in 1963 increased to 5.7 percent of the labor force despite major advances in production and employment; unemployment of young workers, between the ages of 16 and 19, reached 17 percent in 1963 while unemployment among nonwhite Americans stood at 11 percent; despite an unemployment rate twice as high for school dropouts as for high-school graduates, 30 percent of all young people continue to end their education before completing high school; despite the decline in unskilled jobs and the expanding demand for professional, technical, clerical, and service workers — for workers, that is, with at least high-school education and specialized training — nearly a million young people are leaving school every year without having completed elementary or secondary school.

[26] The statistics of poverty, though striking, are antiseptic compared to the actual misery and hopelessness of being poor. The real meaning of poverty is not just loss of learning and productivity, but thousands of angry and dispossessed teen-agers who make our city streets dangerous for "respectable"

citizens; 350,000 youngsters across the nation who form what the Secretary of Labor has described as an "outlaw pack," because they have stopped looking for work, are unemployed today, and will remain so for the rest of their lives; children in a blighted mining town in eastern Kentucky who are potbellied and anemic from lack of food; share-croppers, white as well as black, living in squalid shacks and working for a few dollars a day—when they can find work at all—anywhere in a crescent of rural poverty that extends from Virginia southward across Georgia and Alabama into the Mississippi delta and the Ozarks.

[27] Poverty in America has a racially different moral connotation from poverty in underdeveloped nations. The poor countries of the world have the excuse, for what it is worth, that the means of feeding, housing, and educating their people simply do not exist. In America the means do exist; the failure is essentially one of distribution. The children who go to bed hungry in a Harlem slum or a West Virginia mining town are not being deprived because no food can be found to give them; they are going to bed hungry because, despite all our miracles of invention and production, we have not yet found a way to make the necessities of life available to all of our citizens —including those whose failure is not a lack of personal industry or initiative, but only an unwise choice of parents. What is to be done?

[28] . . . I think that we must face up to the need for major new legislation in the field of education regardless of the partisan divisions which it may provoke. We must do so if we truly mean to alleviate the scourge of poverty in American life. And although it is clear that there is no simple dollar-for-dollar relationship between savings in the defense and space budgets and Congressional willingness to appropriate money for education, it seems to me quite possible that the elimination of superfluous defense and space expenditures would help overcome the reluctance to support education legislation of certain Members of Congress whose concern with economy is genuine and strong.

[29] As a result of the rapidly spreading automation of the American economy, the traditional mechanism of distributing purchasing power through employment and income is breaking down. In essence, our ability to generate economic demands is falling steadily behind our ability to increase the supply of purchasable goods and services. It may be that the growing disequilibrium is so profound as to be irreversible by government policies in support of education, economic growth, and full employment. If so, we shall eventually have to devise new ways of providing income to those who cannot be put to gainful work.

[30] Whether truly radical measures will be required or not, there is no question that if our national war on poverty is to come anywhere near the goal of "total victory" proclaimed by President Johnson, it will require enormous public effort and a great deal of public money. To those who shrink from such a commitment in the name of economy, I would emphasize that the elimination of poverty and the improvement of education are at

least as important to the security of our country in the long run as the maintenance of a strong defense establishment, and a good deal more important than a voyage to the moon.

[31] These questions of education, employment, and poverty have a profound bearing on the Negro movement for equal rights and opportunity. They are in fact the heart and core of the civil-rights issue, which, far from being a separate and distinct national problem, is bound up with these broader problems both in its causes and in its prospective resolution. " . . . the Negro," writes Joseph P. Lyford, an executive of the Center for the Study of Democratic Institutions and former staff director for New York City's Public Education Association, "has done a great deal more than expose the contradictions between the actual and professed beliefs of the American citizen. His battle for freedom has established the fact that the Negro cannot win equality of opportunity until American society as a whole develops some way of dealing with the rise of mass unemployment and the growing ineffectiveness of our political and educational system. What we call the 'Negro revolution' is a preview of a much bigger crisis to come; it is forcing us to take a closer look at certain extremely unpleasant developments that are going to transform or destroy the traditional institutions and habits of all of us, black and white."*

[32] It seems clear that even the strongest civil-rights legislation can have only a marginal effect in advancing the hopes of the Negro for a fair and decent status in American society. Unaccompanied by major national efforts in the fields of education and employment, civil-rights legislation can have little more than symbolic value. At most, it can vindicate a principle without significantly alleviating the *conditions* of poverty and undereducation which are the core of the problem.

[33] If there is a solution to the problem of racial discrimination in our society — and I believe there is — it lies in a direct assault on the national conditions which foster and sustain it. These conditions are poverty, unemployment, and inadequate education. The entry of a pair of Negro children into an all-white school in Birmingham may vindicate a principle, but it has little bearing on the needs of millions of children all over the nation, white as well as Negro, who are being denied adequate education in overcrowded schools staffed by inadequate numbers of underpaid and undertrained teachers. Forcing open a construction union in New York to a few Negro apprentices may be regarded as a victory for equal opportunity, but, as Mr. Lyford writes, "it has almost no bearing on the employment prospects of hundreds of thousands of teen-agers and millions of adults — white and Negro — who are sinking to the bottom of a society that may very well have 14 million unemployed by 1960."†

*Joseph P. Lyford, "Proposal for a Revolution — Part 1," *The Saturday Review,* October 19, 1963, p. 19.
†Ibid., p. 29.

[34] Despite notable advances in the formal rights of Negroes since the Supreme Court decision of 1954, employment prospects for Negroes are actually declining, and declining at an accelerating rate. The causes of this are inadequate education and the spread of automation. Factory and service jobs, which have been the principal source of Negro employment, are being eliminated by automation at rates estimated to be anywhere from 17,000 to 40,000 a week.

[35] The point which I wish to emphasize is that the overriding economic and social problems of America — poverty, race relations, unemployment, and defective education — are profoundly related to each other and to our position in the world as well, and that there can be no resolution of any one of these problems in the absence of a national effort to resolve all of them.

[36] The time for such an effort is long overdue. We have allowed these problems to fester and grow during the long years of our preoccupation with crises and challenges abroad. To neglect them further is not to accept conditions as they now exist, but to acquiesce in the slow but relentless disintegration of our free society. The cold war, as David Riesman has written, "is a distraction from serious thought about man's condition on the planet."* My own belief is that the prevailing conditions of our foreign relations are favorable to a refocusing of our efforts on problems here at home, but even if they are not, it would still be essential to revise our priorities, because the success of our foreign policy depends ultimately on the strength and character of our society, which in turn depend on our success in resolving the great social and economic issues of American life.

[37] Of all the requirements on our national agenda, none warrants higher priority than the need to turn some part of our thoughts and our creative energies away from the cold war back in on America itself. If we do so, and if we sustain the effort, we may find that the most vital assets of our nation, for its public happiness and its security as well, remain locked within our own frontiers, in our cities and in our countryside, in our work and in our leisure, in the hearts and minds of our people.

EXERCISES

Questions

1. Fulbright states his theme in paragraphs 2 and 35. How do the fifth and eighth paragraphs reinforce and amplify the thesis? Where else does he state his thesis? Restate his primary concern in your own words.
2. How has the cold war paradoxically given the Russians the major voice in determining our federal budget?
3. Distinguish between a militarist and a military society. In what ways have we become a military power?
4. In paragraphs 16 and 17, Fulbright discusses space and defense in re-

lation to our national security and says that the education of our people is far more important for that security. Where does he support this contention? What events have occurred since 1964, when this was published, to support Fulbright's arguments?

5. How significant is it that the Russians may conquer space ahead of us?

6. Is the cost of these programs the only factor to be considered? What three other problems stem from our "inversion of priorities"? What resources of our nation are not developed when we spend huge sums on defense? Compare Fulbright's position here to Sevareid's position.

7. How are civil rights and economic opportunity joined in the last section? What does Fulbright say about "token integration"? What examples does he give? Can you name any others?

8. Notice how the first sentences of paragraphs 2, 4, 5, and 6 are tied together by repetition of or changes in key terms. Read the first sentences of paragraphs 9, 10, 11, and 12. How are they tied together? Can you find other examples of these helpful transitional devices?

9. Fulbright uses various means to support his reasoning. In paragraphs 3 and 9, he calls on experts. What do you know of these men? How many others has he mentioned? In the second section, what statistics does Fulbright employ to support his position? Where does he use illustration? How does the use of these devices aid the impact of his essay?

10. In paragraph 11, Fulbright uses an analogy to explain some American viewpoints. Is the analogy valid?

Vocabulary

intractable	esoteric
demagogue	fatuity
buoyant	desultory
scapegoats	venal
pervasively	scourge
abrasive	parsimony

For Discussion and Writing

1. Military solutions to nonmilitary problems
2. How to promote "the general welfare" of the American people
3. America as "a people more comfortable with machines than with intellectual abstractions"
4. Justifying space research

CROSS REFERENCES

SEVAREID: "The Dark of the Moon"
SCHLESINGER: "A Note on Language"
SORENSON: "The Looking Glass War of Words"
KING: "I Have a Dream"
STEINBECK: "America and the Americans"

HORACE MINER

"BODY RITUAL AMONG THE NACIREMA"

INTRODUCTION

Horace Miner (1912–   ) is an anthropologist — a specialist in the cultures of primitive peoples. He is particularly interested in those societies in our time that are still closely tied to the earth. In the foreword of the essay that follows, Dr. Miner tells something of the job and the scientific attitude a worker in anthropology must have. In 1955, he earned his doctorate at the University of Chicago. Since then he has taught at Chicago, at other universities in the United States, and on a Fulbright Fellowship, at a college in Uganda. He has also worked elsewhere in Africa, and in South America. He has published several books; two of them are *Culture and Agriculture* (1949), and *City in Modern Africa* (1967).

TO THE READER

Compare the rituals of the Nacirema to your own.

As part of his preparation for the study of other cultures, the anthropologist attempts to divest himself of his ethnocentrism.[1] Insofar as he is successful, he is enabled to report objectively, without surprise, shock, or undue value judgments, even such extreme practices as those reported here.

From *American Anthropologist*, Vol. 58, 1956, pp. 503–507. Used with permission of the American Anthropological Association and the author.
[1]the belief in the inherent superiority of one's own group or culture accompanied by a feeling of contempt for other groups and cultures

The anthropologist has become so familiar with the diversity of ways in which different peoples behave in similar situations that he is not apt to be surprised by even the most exotic customs. In fact, if all of the logically possible combinations of behavior have not been found somewhere in the world, he is apt to suspect that they must be present in some yet undescribed tribe. This point has, in fact, been expressed with respect to clan organization by Murdock (1949:71). In this light, the magical beliefs and practices of the Nacirema present such unusual aspects that it seems desirable to describe them as an example of the extremes to which human behavior can go.

[2] Professor Linton first brought the ritual of the Nacirema to the attention of anthropologists twenty years ago (1936:326), but the culture of this people is still very poorly understood. They are a North American group living in the territory between the Canadian Cree, the Yaqui and Tarahumare of Mexico, and the Carib and Arawak of the Antilles. Little is known of their origin, although tradition states that they came from the east. According to Nacirema mythology, their nation was originated by a culture hero, Notgnihsaw, who is otherwise known for two great feats of strength—the throwing of a piece of wampum across the river Pa-To-Mac and the chopping down of a cherry tree in which the Spirit of Truth resided.

[3] Nacirema culture is characterized by a highly developed market economy which has evolved in a rich natural habitat. While much of the people's time is devoted to economic pursuits, a large part of the fruits of these labors and a considerable portion of the day are spent in ritual activity. The focus of this activity is the human body, the appearance and health of which loom as a dominant concern in the ethos[2] of the people. While such a concern is certainly not unusual, its ceremonial aspects and associated philosophy are unique.

[4] The fundamental belief underlying the whole system appears to be that the human body is ugly and that its natural tendency is to debility and disease. Incarcerated in such a body, man's only hope is to avert these characteristics through the use of the powerful influences of ritual and ceremony. Every household has one or more shrines devoted to this purpose. The more powerful individuals in the society have several shrines in their houses and, in fact, the opulence of a house is often referred to in terms of the number of such ritual centers it possesses. Most houses are of wattle and daub construction, but the shrine rooms of the more wealthy are walled with stone. Poorer families imitate the rich by applying pottery plaques to their shrine walls.

[5] While each family has at least one such shrine, the rituals associated with it are not family ceremonies but are private and secret. The rites are normally only discussed with children, and then only during the period

---

[2]the underlying sentiment that shapes the beliefs, customs, or practices of a group or society

when they are being initiated into these mysteries. I was able, however, to establish sufficient rapport with the natives to examine these shrines and to have the rituals described to me.

[6] The focal point of the shrine is a box or chest which is built into the wall. In this chest are kept the many charms and magical potions without which no native believes he could live. These preparations are secured from a variety of specialized practitioners. The most powerful of these are the medicine men, whose assistance must be rewarded with substantial gifts. However, the medicine men do not provide the curative potions for their clients, but decide what the ingredients should be and then write them down in an ancient and secret language. This writing is understood only by the medicine men and by the herbalists who, for another gift, provide the required charm.

[7] The charm is not disposed of after it has served its purpose, but is placed in the charm-box of the household shrine. As these magical materials are specific for certain ills, and the real or imagined maladies of the people are many, the charm-box is usually full to overflowing. The magical packets are so numerous that people forget what their purposes were and fear to use them again. While the natives are very vague on this point, we can only assume that the idea in retaining all the old magical materials is that their presence in the charm-box, before which the body rituals are conducted, will in some way protect the worshiper.

[8] Beneath the charm-box is a small font. Each day every member of the family, in succession, enters the shrine room, bows his head before the charm-box, mingles different sorts of holy water in the font, and proceeds with a brief rite of ablution. The holy waters are secured from the Water Temple of the community, where the priests conduct elaborate ceremonies to make the liquid ritually pure.

[9] In the hierarchy of magical practitioners, and below the medicine men in prestige, are specialists whose designation is best translated "holy-mouth-men." The Nacirema have an almost pathological horror of and fascination with the mouth, the condition of which is believed to have a supernatural influence on all social relationships. Were it not for the rituals of the mouth, they believe that their teeth would fall out, their gums bleed, their jaws shrink, their friends desert them, and their lovers reject them. They also believe that a strong relationship exists between oral and moral characteristics. For example, there is a ritual ablution of the mouth for children which is supposed to improve their moral fiber.

[10] The daily body ritual performed by everyone includes a mouth-rite. Despite the fact that these people are so punctilious about care of the mouth, this rite involves a practice which strikes the uninitiated stranger as revolting. It was reported to me that the ritual consists of inserting a small bundle of hog hairs into the mouth, along with certain magical powders, and then moving the bundle in a highly formalized series of gestures.

[11] In addition to the private mouth-rite, the people seek out a holy-mouth-man once or twice a year. These practitioners have an impressive set of paraphernalia, consisting of a variety of augers, awls, probes, and prods. The use of these objects in the exorcism of the evils of the mouth involves almost unbelievable ritual torture of the client. The holy-mouth-man opens the client's mouth and, using the above mentioned tools, enlarges any holes which decay may have created in the teeth. Magical materials are put into these holes. If there are no naturally occurring holes in the teeth, large sections of one or more teeth are gouged out so that the supernatural substance can be applied. In the client's view, the purpose of these ministrations is to arrest decay and to draw friends. The extremely sacred and traditional character of the rite is evident in the fact that the natives return to the holy-mouth-men year after year, despite the fact that their teeth continue to decay.

[12] It is to be hoped that, when a thorough study of the Nacirema is made, there will be careful inquiry into the personality structure of these people. One has but to watch the gleam in the eye of a holy-mouth-man, as he jabs an awl into an exposed nerve, to suspect that a certain amount of sadism is involved. If this can be established, a very interesting pattern emerges, for most of the population shows definite masochistic tendencies. It was to these that Professor Linton referred in discussing a distinctive part of the daily body ritual which is performed only by men. This part of the rite involves scraping and lacerating the surface of the face with a sharp instrument. Special women's rites are performed only four times during each lunar month, but what they lack in frequency is made up in barbarity. As part of this ceremony, women bake their heads in small ovens for about an hour. The theoretically interesting point is that what seems to be a preponderantly masochistic[3] people have developed sadistic specialists.

[13] The medicine men have an imposing temple, or *latipso,* in every community of any size. The more elaborate ceremonies required to treat very sick patients can only be performed at this temple. These ceremonies involve not only the thaumaturge[4] but a permanent group of vestal maidens who move sedately about the temple chambers in distinctive costume and headdress.

[14] The *latipso* ceremonies are so harsh that it is phenomenal that a fair proportion of the really sick natives who enter the temple ever recover. Small children whose indoctrination is still incomplete have been known to resist attempts to take them to the temple because "that is where you go to die." Despite this fact, sick adults are not only willing but eager to undergo the protracted ritual purification, if they can afford to do so. No matter how ill the supplicant or how grave the emergency, the guardians of many temples will not admit a client if he cannot give a rich gift to the custodian. Even

---

[3]people who gain gratification from pain, deprivation, and so forth, inflicted on themselves

[4]a worker of wonders or miracles

after one has gained admission and survived the ceremonies, the guardians will not permit the neophyte to leave until he makes still another gift.

[15] The supplicant entering the temple is first stripped of all his or her clothes. In every-day life the Nacirema avoids exposure of his body and its natural functions. Bathing and excretory acts are performed only in the secrecy of the household shrine, where they are ritualized as part of the body-rites. Psychological shock results from the fact that body secrecy is suddenly lost upon entry into the *latipso*. A man, whose own wife has never seen him in an excretory act, suddenly finds himself naked and assisted by a vestal maiden while he performs his natural functions into a sacred vessel. This sort of ceremonial treatment is necessitated by the fact that the excreta are used by a diviner to ascertain the course and nature of the client's sickness. Female clients, on the other hand, find their naked bodies are subjected to the scrutiny, manipulation and prodding of the medicine men.

[16] Few supplicants in the temple are well enough to do anything but lie on their hard beds. The daily ceremonies, like the rites of the holy-mouth-men, involve discomfort and torture. With ritual precision, the vestals awaken their miserable charges each dawn and roll them about on their beds of pain while performing ablutions, in the formal movements of which the maidens are highly trained. At other times they insert magic wands in the supplicant's mouth and force him to eat substances which are supposed to be healing. From time to time the medicine men come to their clients and jab magically treated needles into their flesh. The fact that these temple ceremonies may not cure, and may even kill the neophyte, in no way decreases the people's faith in the medicine men.

[17] There remains one other kind of practitioner, known as a "listener." This witch-doctor has the power to exorcise the devils that lodge in the heads of people who have been bewitched. The Nacirema believe that parents bewitch their own children. Mothers are particularly suspected of putting a curse on children while teaching them the secret body rituals. The counter-magic of the witch-doctor is unusual in its lack of ritual. The patient simply tells the "listener" all his troubles and fears, beginning with the earliest difficulties he can remember. The memory displayed by the Nacirema in these exorcism sessions is truly remarkable. It is not uncommon for the patient to bemoan the rejection he felt upon being weaned as a babe, and a few individuals even see their troubles going back to the traumatic effects of their own birth.

[18] In conclusion, mention must be made of certain practices which have their base in native esthetics but which depend upon the pervasive aversion to the natural body and its functions. There are ritual fasts to make fat people thin and ceremonial feasts to make thin people fat. Still other rites are used to make women's breasts larger if they are small, and smaller if they are large. General dissatisfaction with breast shape is symbolized in the fact that the ideal form is virtually outside the range of human variation. A few women

afflicted with almost inhuman hypermammary development are so idolized that they make a handsome living by simply going from village to village and permitting the natives to stare at them for a fee.

[19] Reference has already been made to the fact that excretory functions are ritualized, routinized, and relegated to secrecy. Natural reproductive functions are similarly distorted. Intercourse is taboo as a topic and scheduled as an act. Efforts are made to avoid pregnancy by the use of magical materials or by limiting intercourse to certain phases of the moon. Conception is actually very infrequent. When pregnant, women dress so as to hide their condition. Parturition takes place in secret, without friends or relatives to assist, and the majority of women do not nurse their infants.

[20] Our review of the ritual life of the Nacirema has certainly shown them to be a magic-ridden people. It is hard to understand how they have managed to exist so long under the burdens which they have imposed upon themselves. But even such exotic customs as these take on real meaning when they are viewed with the insight provided by Malinowski when he wrote (1948:70):

> Looking from far and above, from our high places of safety in the developed civilization, it is easy to see all the crudity and irrelevance of magic. But without its power and guidance early man could not have mastered his practical difficulties as he has done, nor could man have advanced to the higher stages of civilization.

References Cited

LINTON, RALPH
     1936   The Study of Man. New York, D. Appleton-Century Co.
MALINOWSKI, BRONISLAW
     1948   Magic, Science, and Religion. Glencoe, The Free Press.
MURDOCK, GEORGE P.
     1949   Social Structure. New York, The Macmillan Co.

EXERCISES

Questions

1. The theme of Miner's essay is partially expressed in his first and last paragraphs. Couple this with the real identity of the Nacirema. What then is his theme?

2. At what point did you realize this was a satire on America? Was your attitude resentful or amused? In either case, why?

3. What does the article reveal about America's health habits? Why is it significant that the author described the activities in terms of religious ritual?

4.   What does the article reveal about America's attitude toward the human body? toward sex? Evaluate.
5.   The chief interest and humor of this piece derives from the fact that Miner is viewing us as an objective outsider might view us. Is he completely objective? When has he been prejudiced in his presentation?
6.   Examine your own charm box (paragraph 7). Is it accurately described by Miner?
7.   Miner used three descriptive techniques for referring to common items: literal description—a "chest . . . built into a wall," and a "bundle of hog hairs"; words spelled backwards—*notgnihsaw* and *latipso*; and descriptions in terms of religious rituals—"holy-mouth-men" and "maidens" who "roll (their patients) about on their beds of pain." What is the effect of this renaming?

Vocabulary

debility
ablution
punctilious
vestal
neophyte
traumatic

For Discussion and Writing

1.   Sadism and masochism in beauty care
2.   Sweet breath, sex and the road to happiness—advertising style
3.   The sex symbol, male and female, in our society
4.   Is cleanliness next to godliness?
5.   When disinfectants are more dangerous than dirt
6.   American dating patterns as "religious ritual"

CROSS REFERENCES

STEINBECK: "America and the Americans"
KNIGHT: "The Eucalyptic Dream"
SWIFT: "A Modest Proposal"

RECOMMENDED READING

SWIFT, JONATHAN: *Gulliver's Travels*
MEAD, MARGARET: *Coming of Age in Samoa*

TOM WOLFE

"CLEAN FUN AT RIVERHEAD"

INTRODUCTION

Tom Wolfe (1931–   ) is a Ph.D. (Yale, 1957) who writes a mod, pop
English that is strictly nonacademic. He has been called the "poet laureate
of pop," and he himself describes his writing as having a "wowie" style.
Mr. Wolfe worked several years as a reporter writing for such prestigious
papers as the *Washington Post* and the greatly missed *New York Herald
Tribune*. He has also been a contributor to such magazines as *Esquire* and
Harpers Bazaar. Seeing the automobile as the central symbol of modern
American culture, he has incorporated it into the title of his book, *The
Kandy Kolored Tangerine-Flake Streamline Baby*, 1963, from which this
essay is taken. A more recent book is *The Electric Kool-Aid Acid Test, 1968*.

TO THE READER

The title implies the tone of the essay. In a sprightly way, Wolfe is very
negative about his subject matter.
    Discover in what sense the fun is "clean."

The inspiration for the demolition derby came to Lawrence Mendelsohn one night in 1958 when he was nothing but a spare-ribbed twenty-

eight-year-old stock-car driver halfway through his 10th lap around the Islip, L.I., Speedway and taking a curve too wide. A lubberly young man with a Chicago boxcar haircut came up on the inside in a 1949 Ford and caromed him 12 rows up into the grandstand, but Lawrence Mendelsohn and his entire car did not hit one spectator.

[2] "That was what got me," he said, "I remember I was hanging upside down from my seat belt like a side of Jersey bacon and wondering why no one was sitting where I hit. 'Lousy promotion,' I said to myself.

[3] "Not only that, but everybody who *was* in the stands forgot about the race and came running over to look at me giftwrapped upside down in a fresh pile of junk."

[4] At that moment occurred the transformation of Lawrence Mendelsohn, racing driver, into Lawrence Mendelsohn, promoter, and, a few transactions later, owner of the Islip Speedway, where he kept seeing more of this same underside of stock car racing that everyone in the industry avoids putting into words. Namely, that for every purist who comes to see the fine points of the race, such as who is going to win, there are probably five waiting for the wrecks to which stock car racing is so gloriously prone.

[5] The pack will be going into a curve when suddenly two cars, three cars, four cars tangle, spinning and splattering all over each other and the retaining walls, upside down, right side up, inside out and in pieces, with the seams bursting open and discs, rods, wires and gasoline spewing out and yards of sheet metal shearing off like Reynolds Wrap and crumpling into the most baroque shapes, after which an ash-blue smoke starts seeping up from the ruins and a thrill begins to spread over the stands like Newburg sauce.

[6] So why put up with the monotony between crashes?

[7] Such, in brief, is the early history of what is culturally the most important sport ever originated in the United States, a sport that ranks with the gladiatorial games of Rome as a piece of national symbolism. Lawrence Mendelsohn had a vision of an automobile sport that would be all crashes. Not two cars, not three cars, not four cars, but 100 cars would be out in an arena doing nothing but smashing each other into shrapnel. The car that outrammed and outdodged all the rest, the last car that could still move amid the smoking heap, would take the prize money.

[8] So at 8:15 at night at the Riverhead Raceway, just west of Riverhead, L.I., on Route 25, amid the quaint tranquility of the duck and turkey farm flatlands of eastern Long Island, Lawrence Mendelsohn stood up on the back of a flat truck in his red neon warmup jacket and lectured his 100 drivers on the rules and niceties of the new game, the "demolition derby." And so at 8:30 the first 25 cars moved out onto the raceway's quarter-mile stock car track. There was not enough room for 100 cars to mangle each other. Lawrence Mendelsohn's dream would require four heats. Now the 25 cars were placed at intervals all about the circumference of the track,

making flatulent revving noises, all headed not around the track but toward a point in the center of the infield.

[9]   Then the entire crowd, about 4,000, started chanting a countdown, "Ten, nine, eight, seven, six, five, four, three, two," but it was impossible to hear the rest, because right after "two" half the crowd went into a strange whinnying wail. The starter's flag went up, and the 25 cars took off, roaring into second gear with no mufflers, all headed toward that same point in the center of the infield, converging nose on nose.

[10] The effect was exactly what one expects that many simultaneous crashes to produce: the unmistakable tympany of automobiles colliding and cheap-gauge sheet metal buckling; front ends folding together at the same cockeyed angles police photographs of night-time wreck scenes capture so well on grainy paper; smoke pouring from under the hoods and hanging over the infield like a howitzer cloud; a few of the surviving cars lurching eccentrically on bent axles. At last, after four heats, there were only two cars moving through the junk, a 1953 Chrysler and a 1958 Cadillac. In the Chrysler a small fascia of muscles named Spider Ligon, who smoked a cigar while he drove, had the Cadillac cornered up against a guard rail in front of the main grandstand. He dispatched it by swinging around and backing full throttle through the left side of its grille and radiator.

[11] By now the crowd was quite beside itself. Spectators broke through a gate in the retaining screen. Some rushed to Spider Ligon's car, hoisted him to their shoulders and marched off the field, howling. Others clambered over the stricken cars of the defeated, enjoying the details of their ruin, and howling. The good, full cry of triumph and annihilation rose from Riverhead Raceway, and the demolition derby was over.

[12] That was the 154th demolition derby in two years. Since Lawrence Mendelsohn staged the first one at Islip Speedway in 1961, they have been held throughout the United States at the rate of one every five days, resulting in the destruction of about 15,000 cars. The figures alone indicate a gluttonous appetite for the sport. Sports writers, of course, have managed to ignore demolition derbies even more successfully than they have ignored stock car racing and drag racing. All in all, the new automobile sports have shown that the sports pages, which on the surface appear to hum with life and earthiness, are at bottom pillars of gentility. This drag racing and demolition derbies and things, well, there are too many kids in it with sideburns, tight Levis and winkle-picker boots.

[13] Yet the demolition derbies keep growing on word-of-mouth publicity. The "nationals" were held last month at Langhorne, Pa., with 50 cars in the finals, and demolition derby fans everywhere know that Don McTavish, of Dover, Mass., is the new world's champion. About 1,250,000 spectators have come to the 154 contests held so far. More than 75 per cent of the derbies have drawn full houses.

[14] The nature of their appeal is clear enough. Since the onset of the

Christian era, i.e., since about 500 A.D., no game has come along to fill the gap left by the abolition of the purest of all sports, gladiatorial combat. As late as 300 A.D. these bloody duels, usually between men but sometimes between women and dwarfs, were enormously popular not only in Rome but throughout the Roman Empire. Since then no game, not even boxing, has successfully acted out the underlying motifs of most sport, that is, aggression and destruction.

[15] Boxing, of course, is an aggressive sport, but one contestant has actually destroyed the other in a relatively small percentage of matches. Other games are progressively more sublimated[1] forms of sport. Often, as in the case of football, they are encrusted with oddments of passive theology and metaphysics to the effect that the real purpose of the game is to foster character, teamwork, stamina, physical fitness and the ability to "give-and-take."

[16] But not even those wonderful clergymen who pray in behalf of Congress, expressway ribbon-cuttings, urban renewal projects and testimonial dinners for ethnic aldermen would pray for a demolition derby. The demolition derby is, pure and simple, a form of gladiatorial combat for our times.

[17] As hand-to-hand combat has gradually disappeared from our civilization, even in wartime, and competition has become more and more sophisticated and abstract, Americans have turned to the automobile to satisfy their love of direct aggression. The mild-mannered man who turns into a bear behind the wheel of a car—i.e., who finds in the power of the automobile a vehicle for the release of his inhibitions—is part of American folklore. Among teen-agers the automobile has become the symbol, and in part the physical means, of triumph over family and community restrictions. Seventy-five per cent of all car thefts in the United States are by teen-agers out for "joy rides."

[18] The symbolic meaning of the automobile tones down but by no means vanishes in adulthood. Police traffic investigators have long been convinced that far more accidents are purposeful crashes by belligerent drivers than they could ever prove. One of the heroes of the era was the Middle Eastern diplomat who rammed a magazine writer's car from behind in the Kalorama embassy district of Washington two years ago. When the American bellowed out the window at him, he backed up and smashed his car again. When the fellow leaped out of his car to pick a fight, he backed up and smashed his car a third time, then drove off. He was recalled home for having "gone native."

[19] The unabashed, undisguised, quite purposeful sense of destruction

---

[1]the diversion of the energy of an impulse from its immediate goal to one of a higher social, moral or esthetic nature or use; nobler or purer

of the demolition derby is its unique contribution. The aggression, the battering, the ruination are there to be enjoyed. The crowd at a demolition derby seldom gasps and often laughs. It enjoys the same full-throated participation as Romans at the Colosseum. After each trail or heat at a demolition derby, two drivers go into the finals. One is the driver whose car was still going at the end. The other is the driver the crowd selects from among the 24 vanquished on the basis of his courage, showmanship or simply the awesomeness of his crashes. The numbers of the cars are read over loudspeakers, and the crowd chooses one with its cheers. By the same token, the crowd may force a driver out of competition if he appears cowardly or merely cunning. This is the sort of driver who drifts around the edge of the battle avoiding crashes with the hope that the other cars will eliminate one another. The umpire waves a yellow flag at him and he must crash into someone within 30 seconds or run the risk of being booed off the field in dishonor and disgrace.

[20] The frank relish of the crowd is nothing, however, compared to the kick the contestants get out of the game. It costs a man an average of $50 to retrieve a car from a junk yard and get it running for a derby. He will only get his money back—$50—for winning a heat. The chance of being smashed up in the madhouse first 30 seconds of a round are so great, even the best of drivers faces long odds in his shot at the $500 first prize. None of that matters to them.

[21] Tommy Fox, who is nineteen, said he entered the demolition derby because, "You know, it's fun. I like it. You know what I mean?" What was fun about it? Tommy Fox had a way of speaking that was much like the early Marlon Brando. Much of what he had to say came from the trapezii,[2] which he rolled quite a bit, and the forehead, which he cocked, and the eyebrows, which he could bring together expressively from time to time. "Well," he said, "you know, like when you hit'em, and all that. It's fun."

[22] Tommy Fox had a lot of fun in the first heat. Nobody was bashing around quite like he was in his old green Hudson. He did not win, chiefly because he took too many chances, but the crowd voted him into the finals as the best showman.

[23] "I got my brother," said Tommy. "I came in from the side and he didn't even see me."

[24] His brother is Don Fox, thirty-two, who owns the junk yard where they both got their cars. Don likes to hit them, too, only he likes it almost too much. Don drives with such abandon, smashing into the first car he can get a shot at and leaving himself wide open, he does not stand much chance of finishing the first three minutes.

[2]muscles of the shoulders and neck

[25] For years now sociologists have been calling upon one another to undertake a serious study of America's "car culture." No small part of it is the way the automobile has, for one very large segment of the population, become the focus of the same sort of quasi-religious dedication as art is currently for another large segment of a higher social order. Tommy Fox is unemployed, Don Fox runs a junk yard, Spider Ligon is a maintenance man for Brookhaven Naval Laboratory, but to categorize them as such is getting no closer to the truth than to have categorized William Faulkner in 1926 as a clerk at Lord & Taylor, although he was.

[26] Tommy Fox, Don Fox and Spider Ligon are acolytes[3] of the car culture, an often esoteric[4] world of arts and sciences that came into its own after World War II and now has believers of two generations. Charlie Turbush, thirty-five, and his son, Buddy, seventeen, were two more contestants, and by no stretch of the imagination can they be characterized as bizarre figures or cultists of the death wish. As for the dangers of driving in a demolition derby, they are quite real by all physical laws. The drivers are protected only by crash helmets, seat belts and the fact that all glass, interior handles, knobs and fixtures have been removed. Yet Lawrence Mendelsohn claims that there have been no serious injuries in 154 demolition derbies and now gets his insurance at a rate below that of stock car racing.

[27] The sport's future may depend in part on word getting around about its relative safety. Already it is beginning to draw contestants here and there from social levels that could give the demolition derby the cachet of respectability. In eastern derbies so far two doctors and three young men of more than passable connections in eastern society have entered under whimsical *noms de combat* and emerged neither scarred nor victorious. Bull fighting had to win the same social combat.

[28] All of which brings to mind that fine afternoon when some high-born Roman women were out in Nero's box at the Colosseum watching this sexy Thracian carve an ugly little Samnite up into prime cuts, and one said, darling, she had an inspiration, and Nero, needless to say, was all for it. Thus began the new vogue of Roman socialites fighting as gladiators themselves, for kicks. By the second century A.D. even the Emperor Commodus was out there with a tiger's head as a helmet hacking away at some poor dazed fall guy. He did a lot for the sport. Arenas sprang up all over the empire like shopping center bowling alleys.

[29] The future of the demolition derby, then, stretches out over the face of America. The sport draws no lines of gender, and post-debs may reach Lawrence Mendelsohn at his office in Deer Park.

[3]altar boys
[4]understood by or meant for only the select few who have special knowledge or interest

EXERCISES

Questions

1. Wolfe's theme is not expressed but rather implied by the tone of the article. What is Wolfe's attitude toward demolition derbies? Cite specific references to support your answer.
2. In what terms does Wolfe define the demolition derby? Why? What does he say it is *not*? Why not?
3. What unpleasant realization was the motive behind Mendelsohn's organizing the first demolition derby? How does knowledge of this motivation prepare you for the author's other comments about derby fans? Notice the various descriptions of audience reaction. See especially paragraphs 3, 5, 11, and 19. Can you generalize about their reactions?
4. The idea of the gladiators in the Colosseum runs like a unifying thread through the essay. What is this concept's chief contribution to the content of the essay?
5. How does Wolfe define "sport"? What is your reaction to this definition?
6. What is the symbolic meaning of the automobile?
7. What does the conversation with Tommy Fox reveal about him? Since he was selected as representative of derby participants, what is Wolfe implying?
8. In paragraph 28, in describing the Roman ladies, Wolfe implies not only a prediction but a comment on our society. State both. How valid are they?
9. Wolfe obviously attended a derby. Check paragraph 5 to see how he uses detail to record what he saw. What is the impact of his two similes? Make a list of all words ending in "ing." What do they reveal?
10. Examine the description of the wrecking of the cars in the first sentence of paragraph 10. Which words were chosen to appeal to the senses? What are the images created?
11. Comment on the first sentence in paragraph 7. What is the potential danger of demolition derbies? What does Wolfe imply this reflects about our national culture?
12. Would you describe Wolfe's style as conversational? If so, why? If not, how would you describe it?
13. Other than the title, what examples of irony can you find in the essay? How, other than ironic, would you describe the tone of this essay?

Vocabulary

lubberly
baroque

flatulent
fascia
oddments
ethnic
cachet

For Discussion and Writing

1.   Psychological tests for drivers
2.   Automobile Racing: Sport or Insanity
3.   Sadism and Football
4.   Is there a car cult in America?
5.   My car: My master
6.   The enjoyment of violence

CROSS REFERENCES

STEINBECK: "America and the Americans"
MINER: "Body Ritual Among the Nacirema"
WERTHAM: "Epilogue" from *A Show of Violence*
WOODWARD: "America: Part of an International Culture of Violence"
HARRINGTON: "The American Experience: Historically Violent"

J. H. PLUMB

"A DRUG IS A DRINK IS A SMOKE"

INTRODUCTION

J. H. Plumb (1911–   ) is a professor of English History and Chairman of the History Department at Cambridge University. Editor of the projected twenty-five volume *History of Human Society*, of which the first five volumes have been published, writer of two major histories, *Men and Centuries* and *The Growth of Political Stability: England 1675–1725*, he is also a biographer, a critic, and a reviewer. The essay that follows came from Professor Plumb's monthly contribution to the *Saturday Review* under the heading "Perspective."

TO THE READER

Watch how Professor Plumb sets up some of our favorite ideas about drugs and then proceeds to upset them.

The essay strives to support the equation illustrated by his title. Ask yourself, how many drugs am I addicted to?

Bear in mind that perspective means the faculty of seeing all the relevant data in a meaningful relationship.

Reprinted from the *Saturday Review*, May 27, 1967, with the permission of the author and the *Saturday Review*.

New York, vital, beautiful, opulent, is smeared with slime — poverty, decadence, decay, and drugs. Amidst the power and glittering riches there are pools of human débris, lives broken by abundance as well as by poverty. Who can ever forget the haunting story of young Friede, crawling the gutters of the Lower East Side in a hired car with his girl dead in its trunk, wandering aimlessly like some mindless, battered insect, stopping and starting, remembering and forgetting, caring and not caring? Wealthy, well-educated, replete with advantages that would have seemed paradisaical to the hungry and ambitious adolescents of Latin America or Africa, he and his girl had frittered their lives away with dope. Dick Schaap in a piece of effective reportage, *Tuned On* (New American Library, $4.95), brings back the sad, gray story, nauseating in its futility and witlessness. At the thought of such young wasted lives the bile rises: surely the Narcotics Bureau should be strengthened; surely the penalties imposed on pushers and traders should become really punitive.

[2]   The Friede case was but one sensational event in what is rapidly becoming a flowing tide that will engulf more and more of the younger generation in drugs. Universities are particularly prone: Oxford and Cambridge, Harvard, Yale, and Berkeley acquire increasing numbers of addicts, as well as experimenters playing, it is true, mainly with hemp and LSD rather than with heroin. What the youth of America and England do today, the youth of Europe, East and West, will do tomorrow or the day after. There will be other sensations, other Friede cases, perhaps even more terrible and more haunting: personal tragedy will sear homes from which want, disease, and cruelty have been banished. Why can this be?

[3]   The spread of drugs gives the castigators[1] of our civilization a wonderful time. They trot out all the old clichés about youth's loss of Christian morality, about the breakdown of the family and marriage, the artificiality of modern life with its emotional emptiness and boredom in an age of machines, the lack of those deep satisfactions felt by the peasant and craftsman, hungry and downtrodden though they were. Is the very affluence that gives youth much leisure but too little work, much security but too little direction the key to its wantonness?[2] If the bread line were just around the corner would the desire for dope vanish? After all, the youth of Athens and Cairo are not riding high on LSD, amphetamines, heroin, and the like. Few Jeremiahs[3] have had it so good as those who prophesy the doom, and revel at the decadence, of today's Western youth. And too many, far too many, ordinary decent liberals go along with them, at least half the way. Where drugs are concerned, much of the adult population suffers a semantic block-

---

[1]people who punish or criticize severely
[2]carelessness or recklessness without regard for what is just or humane
[3]a prophet in the Old Testament

age and, as ever, they rarely think historically. It is hard to get drugs into perspective.

[4]   What society in recorded history, save perhaps a few of the most aboriginal,[4] has not tolerated, indeed sometimes welcomed, the use of stimulants or drugs? None that I know. Once invented — maybe very, very early in the Neolithic revolution — the use of alcohol by kings, priests, and people spread like a bush fire. The earliest farmers in England were buried with their beer beakers, presumably to enable them to wassail through eternity. And peasant societies do not just take alcohol; they get drunk. Look at Brueghel's pictures, or at films of festivals in Nepal or the Andes or wherever primitive agrarian production is the dominant way of life. In industrial society, of course, millions of men and women get high on alcohol week in and week out. The mutilated and lifeless bodies that result from automobile accidents by drivers overdrugged with alcohol are the price society seems willing to pay for its addiction to drink. Add to the wrecked cars the broken homes of alcoholics, their self-destruction, the huge waste of social capital invested in human lives that drink brings about year after year.

[5]   Yet temperance is akin to crankiness. Without alcohol, magazines as well as men would wilt. I am addicted enough to loathe the prospect of a world without wine. We accept alcohol, we have socialized it, and we have shut our eyes to the immense damage that total addiction causes because we handle our own addiction competently, well within the tolerance that our temperaments and physiques permit. But let us be honest: we need a chorous of Gertrude Steins [5] chiming in our ears, "A drink is a drug is a drug is a drink is a drug."

[6]   "What about Islam?" one may inquire. "There, surely, is freedom from alcohol." Yes, but not from hashish, which is as common in Islam as drink in the West. In most Oriental and Near Eastern societies as well as in Mexico, the Caribbean, and Central America, marihuana has been socialized as alcohol has been by us, although almost certainly at a lower cost in human wastage. Addiction is less, the results physically not so destructive. That is why *The Marihuana Papers*, edited by David Solomon (Bobbs-Merrill, $10), should be carefully studied by anyone concerned over the growing spread of reefer smoking in North America and Europe. What is regarded as perfectly normal and respectable in Karachi, Cairo, or Algiers is antisocial and illegal in San Francisco, Boston, and New York.

[7]   The outlawing of marihuana makes odd reading. Way back in the Thirties Fiorello La Guardia set up a highpowered commission of doctors, biologists, educators, and sociologists. They found that marihuana was not being peddled in high schools, that it was not breaking up families, plunging adolescents into degradation, or inflicting physical or mental breakdown

---

[4]primitive

[5]Miss Stein was an American expatriate writer whose Paris salon during the twenties was a meeting place of artists and writers. Her best-known remark is, "A rose is a rose is a rose."

on its users. Indeed, on the face of this evidence, reefers would seem to be far less harmful than not only alcohol but also tobacco — another killing drug that we permit, knowing its evil, long-term effects on the human body. But as yet no government in the world, whether bright red or deep blue, whether dictatorial or democratic, has made anything but token gestures to reduce or suppress tobacco addiction. Once more let us have a chant by the Gertrude Stein chorus, "A drug is a drink is a smoke is a drug is a drink."

[8]   James I hated tobacco — a beastly, filthy habit that he naturally associated with subversives as well as decadents. New drugs to those who do not use them always seem the peculiar prerogative of subversives. When James I's grandson, Charles II, came to the English throne, he grew very apprehensive about the spread of coffee-drinking and particularly coffee-houses, where he felt opponents of his régime came together not only to indulge in the brew, but to breed sedition. [6] He subjected them to rigorous control, even thought of suppressing cafés altogether, but again the frug won. As did tea. Tea was initially regarded as such an effeminate drink that the heavy manual worker sneeringly stuck to his early morning beer; however, once his prejudices were overcome, he found a deep reddish brown brew of Indian tea to be a more effective stimulant. In fact, energized by tea, he was a better worker. But still a drugged one — as are the caffeine addicts of America or Europe.

[9]   Drugs everywhere abound. And when anything abounds there is investment, private and public. Vast fortunes can be, indeed are being made from alcohol and nicotine, caffeine, and the host of minor drugs and sedatives and stimulants that we all use. Because of these strongly vested interests there is always resistance to anything that will cut sharply into profits. Thus, whatever their drain on human life, nicotine and alcohol are not going to be added to the Narcotics Bureau's list. Moreover, human beings are odd, curiously persistent, and often very lawless where legal restriction cuts across their needs: if the industrial West wants to adopt marihuana, or anything else for that matter, punitive actions will be as useless as Prohibition was in the Twenties.

[10] It should be realized that drugs become less harmful when socialized; if alcohol could be purchased only in the company of alcoholics it would be infinitely more dangerous. With technological advance more drugs will become easily available; like most human addictions, they need long, dispassionate, [7] and scientific appraisal. Perhaps sensible permission is indicated rather than punitive prohibition. For a society that bans marihuana and permits alcohol is ripe for the satire of a Swift. However, we are not alone in our folly; after all, Islam permits marihuana and bans alcohol. Will mankind ever be truly conscious of its absurdities? To that question the historical perspective gives a gloomy answer.

[6]incitement of discontent or rebellion against one's government
[7]free from passion, personal feeling or bias; impartial

EXERCISES

Questions

1. What is the significance of the title and the Gertrude Stein-like song? How is a drink like a smoke, etc.? How is it not?
2. Why are coffee and tea drugs? Why is tobacco? On the basis of their similarities, what suggestion does Plumb make concerning the socializing of their use? What is the effect of socializing alcohol? hashish? other drugs?
3. How does Plumb discount the popular explanation that the current spread of drugs is the result of the emptiness of modern life?
4. What evidence is presented that alcohol is a dangerous drug? Why then does western man refuse to give it up? Is the defense of drinking logical or emotional? How comparable are attitudes toward drinking with attitudes toward other drugs like marijuana.
5. Professor Plumb mentions the belief of James I that people who smoked tobacco were subversive and a generalized belief that users of new drugs "to those who do not use them" are subversive. Can you supply any evidence to support or attack his statements?
6. Plumb uses a variety of sources in paragraph 4 to support his theme sentence that nearly all societies have tolerated or welcomed stimulants or drugs. Comment on the effectiveness of these authorities. Where else does he do this?
7. Note how Professor Plumb structures his essay. He goes from the drug we fear most (marijuana) to the one we fear least (tea). What explanation can you offer for this?

For Discussion and Writing

1. Addiction vs. moderation in drugs
2. Prohibition: Why it failed. Why all "Prohibitions" must fail
3. The use of alcohol among Jews and Mormons
4. Minimum ages for smoking, drinking, using coffee and tea, using marijuana
5. The slang of marijuana—what it reveals about attitudes

CROSS REFERENCE

ASIMOV: "Matter Over Mind"

JOHN CIARDI

"I MET A MAN"

INTRODUCTION

John Ciardi (1916–   ) is a poet, a teacher, and an editor. He is also a director of one of the best-known writer's conferences in the United States, the annual Breadloaf Conference in Vermont. Ciardi has published many volumes of verse, among them *Homeward to America* (1940) and *I Marry You* (1955). His translation of Dante's *Inferno* is considered one of the best of modern times. In addition, he is the Poetry Editor of the *Saturday Review*. He uses his column to publish his verse, comment on his life as a poet, and observe the American scene. Sometimes he publicly answers his mail; the following essay is a sample.

TO THE READER

Remember your Dick and Jane, "Run, Spot, Run," books from first grade as you read this essay and try to analyze why Ciardi has used this simple style.

The following two letters arrived from Minnesota in the same envelope and are here faithfully transcribed:

Reprinted from the *Saturday Review*, February 26, 1966, where it originally appeared under the title "Mailbag" on Mr. Ciardi's "Manner of Speaking" page. Used with the permission of the *Saturday Review* and the author.

To John Ciardi

[2]   John Ciardi your writing is very bad in the book I Met a Man because you do not put periords. On pages 1-2-3-4-6-9-10-11-12-14 and all the rest of the pages I do not understand because you did not put a period. On page 62 sentences 1-4 and 8, I do not understand because you put commas instead of periords. So copy the book over please because I love it.

From Kathy K [no periord]

Sir:

[3]   My daughter is eight years old and reads constantly.

Please understand, in her letter she could not realize the form of the poems in your charming book, I Met a Man, but she is quite sensitive to the sentence structure in the majority of childrens books & could not help but notice the change.

I do not expect you to interrupt your busy schedule with a detailed explanation but it is so important to her, I'm sure you understand my concern.

Thank you again, from Kathy and:

Mrs. J. K.

[4]   Look, Kathy. Look.
See the poet.
The poet is fat.
He is fifty.
He is dull.
He is sitting at his desk writing a book.
Has he written a lot of books at his desk?
He has written twenty-five of them.

[5]   The desk is not tidy.
Make him tidy it.
It is a mess.
It is covered with all the periods he did not put in his books.
Make him put in the periods.

[6]   Where shall he put the periods?
Shall he put them after the titles of poems?
It is not necessary to put periods after the titles of poems.
Shall he put them at the end of every line?
It is not necessary to put a period at the end of every line of a poem.
Where shall he put them?
Don't you know?
Ask Mommy.
Doesn't Mommy know?
Make him put them in anyway.
Look, Kathy. Look.
See the little girl.

She is pretty.
What is the little girl doing?
She is reading the book.
Why is she frowning?
She is frowning because she does not understand.
When the fat, dull, fifty-year-old poet does something the little girl does not understand, the fat, dull, fifty-year-old poet is wrong.
Make him copy it over.

[7]   Look, Kathy. Look.
See the mommy.
What is the mommy doing?
She is being concerned.
She is understanding the little girl.
She is making sure the little girl expresses herself.
The mommy does not wish to confuse the little girl with information.
It is more important that the little girl be understood.
It is more important that the little girl express herself.
The little girl is sweet.
The mommy loves her and does not wish to confuse her.
Does the fat, dull fifty-year-old poet love her, too?
Yes, he does, but he has children of his own to fight free of.
Does he understand his children?
He relentlessly refuses to understand them.
Does he make sure his children express themselves?
He is unable to stop them but he tries.
Does he scold his children?
Yes. Hopefully. But he is afraid it is a lost cause.
Is he going to scold the little girl?
No, he is scolding the mommy.
Why is he scolding the mommy?
He is scolding her for spoiling the little girl.
He doesn't care whether or not the little girl is entirely understood.
He says *he* has been waiting fifty years to be understood.
He says the little girl can wait.
He says the little girl has more time than he has.
He does not want to copy the book over.
He says he wrote it right the first time and he is working on another book and needs his time for that.
He says he wants the mommy to copy the book over.
He wants her to copy it over a hundred times on the blackboard.
Why must mommy copy the book over?
She must copy it over for not explaining to the little girl.
What does he want her to explain to the little girl?

He wants the mommy to explain that the poet is fat, dull, fifty, and much smarter than the little girl.

He wants the mommy to tell the little girl that the fat, dull, old poet knows a lot more about periods than the little girl does.

He wants the mommy to explain that it is only wilfully cute to tell the fat, dull, old poet to copy the book over.

He wants the mommy to explain the difference between a title and a sentence.

He wants the mommy to explain the difference between a line of poetry and a sentence.

Doesn't the fat, dull, old poet care whether or not the little girl is understood?

He does care, but only within limits.

He says *he* wants to be understood.

Doesn't the fat, dull, old poet care whether or not the little girl expresses herself?

He does care, but only within limits.

He says *he* wants to express himself.

What? At fifty!

That is much too old for being understood!

That is much too old for expressing oneself!

That is ridiculous!

What a fat, dull, old poet!

What a pretty, bright-eyed, understood, self-expressing, little girl!

What a silly mommy!

Copy all of them over.

EXERCISES

Questions

1. Why did Ciardi write this piece? Did he accomplish his purpose?
2. Why has Ciardi made this letter public? Why is this more than a private matter? Why has he used "Dick and Jane" prose to write to Kathy's mother?
3. How does Ciardi analyze the relationship between the reader and the writer?
4. What does the letter reveal about parental attitudes toward children? Readers' attitudes toward poets or other writers? What does the exchange reveal about attitudes toward language, particularly grammar and punctuation?
5. Note how the content and the tone, which is satiric, are related. How does the tone reinforce the poet's position? Will Kathy be able to understand this? What does this reveal about the relationship between meaning and structure?

6. Is it significant that the word "period" is sometimes spelled correctly, sometimes misspelled in Kathy's letter? What other grammatical mistakes can you find in Kathy's letter? What errors are there in Mrs. J. K.'s letter? How do these errors actually reinforce Ciardi's viewpoint?

7. Why does he say he "relentlessly refuses" to understand his children and that "he has children of his own to fight free of"?

8. Is there any implicit criticism in this essay of America being a child-oriented society? Is there any relationship between this idea and anti-intellectualism?

9. Notice that Ciardi begins with 2, 3, and 4-word sentences, and ends with equally short sentences. The climax, however, contains five, long, nearly parallel, fairly complex sentences. Why are these different?

10. What is the effect of using simple sentences with almost identical word order? What does it reveal of his opinion of Mrs. K. and Kathy?

For Discussion and Writing
1. What the reader owes the writer
2. What the writer owes the reader
3. Should there be limits on children's self-expression?
4. The creative child
5. The creative adult

CROSS REFERENCES

HIGHET: "What Use Is Poetry?"
STEINBECK: "America and Americans"
WODEHOUSE: "William Shakespeare and Me"

MORTON FRIED

"A FOUR-LETTER WORD
THAT HURTS"

INTRODUCTION

Morton Fried (1923–   ) holds his Ph.D. in anthropology from Columbia University where he currently teaches. His area of specialization is the Chinese and through various research grants, he has studied the people of Taiwan. His publications include many articles and books on the Chinese, their family structure, and culture. He also served as editor for the two-volume *Readings in Anthropology* (1967), and *War: An Anthology of Armed Conflict and Aggression* (1968).

TO THE READER

Work out a definition of race for yourself and see how Dr. Fried treats it.
     Look for racially-oriented concepts or expressions you have been taught to believe or may use, and reconsider their accuracy in the light of Dr. Fried's evidence.

Taking the great white race away from today's racists is like taking candy from a baby. There are sure to be shrieks and howls of outrage. But

Reprinted from the *Saturday Review*, Vol. 48, October 2, 1965. Used with permission of the author and the *Saturday Review*.

it will be very hard to take away this piece of candy, because, to drop the metaphor, nothing is harder to expunge than an idea. The white race is not a real, hard fact of nature; it is an idea.

[2]   In 1959 a young anthropologist named Philip Newman walked into the very remote village of Miruma in the upper Asaro Valley of New Guinea to make a field study of the Gururumba. It was late that first afternoon when it began to dawn upon his native hosts that he had made no move to leave. Finally a man of some rank plucked up his courage and said, "How long will you stay, red man?"

[3]   Most people are probably amused, but a few will be puzzled and chagrined to know that what passes in our own culture as a member of the great white race is considered red by some New Guineans. But when did anyone ever really see a *white* white man? Most so-called white men are turned by wind, rain, and certain kinds of lotion to various shades of brown, although they would probably prefer to be thought bronze. Even the stay-in who shuns the sun and despises cosmetics would rarely be able to be considered white in terms of the minimal standards set on television by our leading laundry detergents. His color would likely be a shade of the pink that is a basic tint for all Caucasoids. (That, like "Caucasian," is another foolish word in the service of this concept of race. The Caucasus region, as far as we know, played no significant role in human evolution and certainly was not the cradle of any significant human variety.)

[4]   Actually, even the generalization about pink as a basic skin tint has to be explained and qualified. In some people the tint of the skin is in substantial measure the result of chemical coloring matter in the epidermis; in others there is no such coloring matter, or very little, and tinting then depends on many factors, including the color of the blood in the tiny capillaries of the dermis. Statistically, there is a continuous grading of human skin color from light to dark. There are no sharp breaks, no breaks at all. Since nobody is really white and since color is a trait that varies without significant interruption, I think the most sensible statement that can be made on the subject is that there is no white race. To make this just as true and outrageous as I can, let me immediately add that there never *was* a white race.

[5]   While at it, I might as well go on to deny the existence of a red race, although noting that if there was such a thing as the white race it would be at least esthetically more correct to call it the red race. Also, there is not now and never has been either a black race or a yellow race.

[6]   To deny that there are differences between individuals and between populations is ridiculous. The New Guineans spotted Dr. Newman as an off-beat intruder as soon as they clapped eyes on him. Of course, they were noticing other things as well and some of those other things certainly helped to make distinctions sharper. After all, Newman was relatively clean, he had clothes on, and, furthermore, he didn't carry himself at all like a Gururumba — that is to say like a human being. I was spotted as an alien the first time I

showed up in the small city of Ch'uhsien, in Anhwei province, China, back
in 1947. Even after more than a year in that place, there was no question
about my standing out as a strange physical type. During the hot summer,
peasants who had never seen anything like me before were particularly
fascinated by my arms protruding from my short-sleeved shirt, and I almost
had to stop patronizing the local bath house. I am not a hirsute fellow for
someone of my type, but in Ch'uhsien I looked like a shaggy dog, and farmers deftly plucked my hairs and escaped with souvenirs. Another time, a
charming young lady of three scrambled into my lap when I offered to tell
her a story; she looked into my eyes just as I began and leaped off with a
scream. It was some time before I saw her again, and in the interval I learned
that in this area the worst, bloodthirsty, child-eating demons can be identi-
fied by their blue eyes.

[7]   Individual differences are obvious, even to a child. Unfortunately,
race is not to be confused with such differences, though almost everybody
sees them and some people act toward others on the basis of them. I say
"unfortunately," because the confusion seems so deeply embedded as to
make anyone despair of rooting it out.

[8]   Most laymen of my acquaintance, whether tolerant or bigoted, are
frankly puzzled when they are told that race is an idea. It seems to them that
it is something very real that they experience every day; one might as well
deny the existence of different makes and models of automobiles. The answer to that analogy is easy: cars don't breed. Apart from what the kids
conjure up by raiding automobile graveyards, and putting the parts together to get a monster, there are no real intergrades in machinery of this
kind. To get a car you manufacture parts and put them together. To get our
kind of biological organism you start with two fully formed specimens, one
of each sex, and if they are attracted to each other, they may replicate.
Their replication can never be more than approximate as far as either of
them, the parents, is concerned, because, as we so well know, each con-
tributes only and exactly one-half of the genetic material to the offspring.
We also know that some of the genetic material each transmits may not be
apparent in his or her own makeup, so that it is fully possible for a child to
be completely legitimate without resembling either side of the family,
although he may remind a very old aunt of her grandfather.

[9]   The phenomenon of genetic inheritance is completely neutral with
regard to race and racial formation. Given a high degree of isolation,
different populations might develop to the point of being clearly distinguishable while they remained capable of producing fertile hybrids. There
would, however, be few if any hybrids because of geographical isolation,
and the result would be a neat and consistent system.

[10]   Much too neat and consistent for man. Never in the history of this
globe has there been any species with so little *sitzfleisch*. Even during the
middle of the Pleistocene, way down in the Lower Paleolithic, 300,000 or

more years ago, our ancestors were continent-hoppers. That is the only reasonable interpretation of the fact that very similar remains of the middle Pleistocene fossil *Homo erectus* are found in Africa, Europe, and Asia. Since that time movement has accelerated and now there is no major region of this planet without its human population, even if it is a small, artificially maintained, nonreproductive population of scientists in Antarctica.

[11] The mobility so characteristic of our genus, Homo, has unavoidable implications, for where man moves, man mates. (Antarctica, devoid of indigenous population, is perhaps the only exception.) This is not a recent phenomenon, but has been going on for one or two million years, or longer than the period since man became recognizable. We know of this mobility not only from evidence of the spread of our genus and species throughout the world, but also because the fossils of man collected from one locality and representing a single relatively synchronic population sometimes show extraordinary variation among themselves. Some years ago a population was found in Tabun Cave, near Mt. Carmel, in Israel. The physical anthropologists Ashley Montagu and C. Loring Brace describe it as "showing every possible combination of the features of Neanderthal with those of modern man." At Chouk'outien, a limestone quarry not too far from Peking, in a cave that was naturally open toward the close of the Pleistocene geological period, about 20,000 years ago, there lived a population of diverse physical types. While some physical anthropologists minimize them, those who have actually pored over the remains describe differences as great as those separating modern Chinese from Eskimos on one hand and Melanesians on the other. All of this, of course, without any direct evidence of the skin color of the fossils concerned. We never have found fossilized human skin and therefore can speak of the skin colors of our ancestors of tens of thousands of years ago only through extrapolation, by assuming continuity, and by assuming the applicability of such zoological rules as Gloger's, which was developed to explain the distribution of differently pigmented birds and mammals.

[12] The evidence that our Pleistocene ancestors got around goes beyond their own physical remains and includes exotic shells, stones, and other materials in strange places which these objects could have reached only by being passed from hand to hand or being carried great distances. If our ancestors moved about that much, they also spread their genes, to put it euphemistically. Incidentally, they could have accomplished this spreading of genes whether they reacted to alien populations peacefully or hostilely; wars, including those in our own time, have always been a major means of speeding up hybridization.

[13] Even phrasing the matter this way, and allowing for a goodly amount of gene flow between existing racial populations through hundreds of thousands of years of evolution, the resulting image of race is incredibly wrong, a fantasy with hardly any connection to reality. What is wrong is

our way of creating and relying upon archetypes.[1] Just as we persist in thinking that there is a typical American town (rarely our own), a typical middle-class housewife (never our wife), a typical American male ("not me!") so we think of races in terms of typical, archetypical, individuals who probably do not exist. When it is pointed out that there are hundreds of thousands or millions of living people who fall between the classified races, the frequently heard rejoinder is that this is so now, but it is a sign of our decadent times. Those fond of arguing this way usually go on to assert that it was not so in the past, that the races were formerly discrete.

[14] In a startlingly large number of views, including those shared by informed and tolerant people, there was a time when there was a pure white race, a pure black race, etc., etc., depending upon how many races they recognize. There is not a shred of scientifically respectable evidence to support such a view. Whatever evidence we have contradicts it. In addition to the evidence of Chouk'outien and Tabun mentioned above, there are many other fossils whose morphological characteristics, primitivity to one side, are not in keeping with those of the present inhabitants of the same region.

[15] Part of the explanation of the layman's belief in pure ancestral races is to be found in the intellectually lazy trait of stereotyping which is applied not only to man's ancestry but to landscape and climate through time as well. Few parts of the world today look quite the way they did 15,000 years ago, much less 150,000 years ago. Yet I have found it a commonplace among students that they visualize the world of ages ago as it appears today. The Sahara is always a great desert, the Rockies a great mountain chain, and England separated from France by the Channel. Sometimes I ask a class, after we have talked about the famous Java fossil *Pithecanthropus erectus,* how the devil do they suppose he ever got there, Java being an island? Usually the students are dumbfounded by the question, until they are relieved to discover Java wasn't always cut off from the Asian mainland. Given their initial attitudes and lack of information, it is not surprising that so many people imagine a beautiful Nordic Cro-Magnon, archetypical White, ranging a great Wagnerian forest looking for bestial Neanderthalers to exterminate.

[16] Once again, there is no evidence whatsover to support the lurid nightmare of genocide that early *Homo sapiens* is supposed to have wreaked upon the bumbling and grotesque Neanderthals. None either for William Golding's literary view of the extirpation of primitive innocence and goodness. The interpretation that in my view does least damage to the evidence is that which recognizes the differences between contemporary forms of so-called Neanderthals and other fossil *Homo sapiens* of 25,000 to 100,000 years ago to have been very little more or no greater than those between two

[1]the original pattern or model after which a thing is made

variant populations of our own century. Furthermore, the same evidence indicates that the Neanderthals did not vanish suddenly but probably were slowly submerged in the populations that surrounded them, so that their genetic materials form part of our own inheritance today.

[17] Then, it may be asked, where did the story come from that tells of the struggle of these populations and the extinction of one? It is a relatively fresh tale, actually invented in the nineteenth century, for before that time there was no suspicion of such creatures as Neanderthals. The nineteenth century, however, discovered the fossils of what has been called "Darwin's first witness." After some debate, the fossil remains were accepted as some primitive precursor of man and then chopped off the family tree. The model for this imaginary genealogical pruning was easily come by in a century that had witnessed the hunting and killing of native populations like game beasts, as in Tasmania, in the Malay peninsula, and elsewhere. Such episodes and continuation of slavery and the slave trade made genocide[2] as real a phenomenon as the demand for laissez-faire and the Acts of Combination. It was precisely in this crucible[3] that modern racism was born and to which most of our twentieth-century mythology about race can be traced.

[18] In the vocabulary of the layman the word "race" is a nonsense term, one without a fixed, reliable meaning, and, as Alice pointed out to Humpty Dumpty, the use of words with idiosyncratic meanings is not conducive to communication. Yet I am sure that many who read these words will think that it is the writer who is twisting meaning and destroying a useful, common-sense concept. Far from it. One of the most respected and highly regarded volumes to have yet been published in the field of physical anthropology is *Human Biology,* by four British scientists, Harrison, Weiner, Tanner, and Barnicot (Oxford University Press, 1964). These distinguished authors jointly eschewed the word "race" on the ground that it was poorly defined even in zoology, *i.e.,* when applied to animals other than man, and because of its history of misunderstanding, confusion, and worse, when applied to humans.

[19] Similar views have been held for some time and are familiar in the professional literature. Ashley Montagu, for example, has been in the vanguard of the movement to drop the concept of human race on scientific grounds for twenty-five years. His most recent work on the subject is a collation of critical essays from many specialists, *The Concept of Race* (Free Press, 1964). Frank B. Livingstone, a physical anthropologist at the University of Michigan, has spoken out "On the Non-existence of Human Races" (*Current Anthropology,* 3:3, 1962). In the subsequent debate, opinions divided rather along generational lines. The older scientists preferred to cling to the concept of race while freely complaining about its shortcomings. The younger scientists showed impatience with the concept and wished to drop it and get on with important work that the concept obstructed.

[2]the deliberate and systematic extermination of a national or racial group
[3]a severe, searching test

[20] Quite specifically, there are many things wrong with the concept of race. As generally employed, it is sometimes based on biological character- istics but sometimes on cultural features, and when it is based on biological traits the traits in question usually have the most obscure genetic back- grounds. The use of cultural criteria is best exemplified in such untenable racial constructs as the "Anglo-Saxon race," or the "German race" or the "Jewish race." Under no scientifically uttered definition known to me can these aggregates be called races. The first is a linguistic designation per- taining to the Germanic dialects or languages spoken by the people who about 1,500 years ago invaded the British Isles from what is now Schleswig- Holstein and the adjacent portion of Denmark. The invaders were in no sig- nificant way physically distinct from their neighbors who spoke other languages, and in any case they mated and blended with the indigenous population they encountered. Even their language was substantially altered by diffusion so that today a reference to English as an Anglo-Saxon lan- guage is quaint and less than correct. As for the hyperbolic[4] extension of the designation to some of the people who live in England and the United States, it is meaningless in racial terms — just as meaningless as extending the term to cover a nation of heterogeneous origin and flexible boundaries, such as Germany or France or Italy or any other country. As for the moribund[5] con- cept of a "Jewish race," this is simply funny, considering the extraordinary diversity of the physical types that have embraced this religion, and the large number that have relinquished it and entered other faiths.

[21] The use of cultural criteria to identify individuals with racial categories does not stop with nationality, language, or religion. Such traits as posture, facial expression, musical tastes, and even modes of dress have been used to sort people into spurious[6] racial groups. But even when biological criteria have been used, they have rarely been employed in a scientifically defensible way. One of the first questions to arise, for example, is what kind of criteria shall be used to sort people into racial categories. Following immediately upon this is another query: how many criteria should be used? With regard to the first, science is still in conflict. The new physical anthropologists whose overriding concern is to unravel the many remaining mysteries in human evolution and to understand the role that heredity will play in con- tinuing and future evolution are impatient with any but strictly genetic characters, preferably those that can be linked to relatively few gene loci. They prefer the rapidly mounting blood factors, not only the ABO, Rh, MNS, and other well-known series, but such things as Duffy, Henshaw, Hunter, Kell, and Kidd (limited distribution blood groups named for the first person found to have carried them). Such work has one consistent by-product: the resultant classifications tend to cross-cut and obliterate conventional racial

[4]exaggerated
[5]dying
[6]not genuine

lines so that such constructs as the white race disappear as useful taxonomic units.

[22] Some scientists argue that a classification based on only one criterion is not a very useful instrument. On the other hand, the more criteria that are added, the more abstract the racial construct becomes as fewer individuals can be discovered with all the necessary characteristics and more individuals are found to be in between. The end result is that the typical person is completely atypical; if race makes sense, so does this.

[23] That racial classification is really nonsense can be demonstrated with ease merely by comparing some of the most usual conceptions of white and Negro. What degree of black African ancestry establishes a person as a Negro? Is 51 per cent or 50.1 per cent or some other slight statistical preponderance necessary? The question is ridiculous; we have no means of discriminating quantities of inherited materials in percentage terms. In that case can we turn to ancestry and legislate that anyone with a Negro parent is a Negro? Simple, but totally ineffective and inapplicable: how was the racial identity of each parent established? It is precisely at this point that anthropologists raise the question of assigning specific individuals to racial categories. At best, a racial category is a statistical abstraction based upon certain frequencies of genetic characters observed in small samples of much larger populations. A frequency of genetic characters is something that can be displayed by a population, but it cannot be displayed by an individual, any more than one voter can represent the proportion of votes cast by his party.

[24] The great fallacy of racial classification is revealed by reflecting on popular applications in real situations. Some of our outstanding "Negro" citizens have almost no phenotypic resemblance to the stereotyped "Negro." It requires their acts of self-identification to place them. Simultaneously, tens of thousands of persons of slightly darker skin color, broader nasal wings, more everted lips, less straight hair, etc., are considered as "white" without question, in the South as well as the North, and in all socioeconomic strata. Conversely, some of our best known and noisiest Southern politicians undoubtedly have some "Negro" genes in their makeup.

[25] Why is it so hard to give up this miserable little four-letter word that of all four-letter words has done the most damage? This is a good question for a scientific linguist or a semanticist. After all, the word refers to nothing more than a transitory statistical abstraction. But the question can also be put to an anthropologist. His answer might be, and mine is, that the word "race" expresses a certain kind of unresolved social conflict that thrives on divisions and invidious distinctions. It can thrive in the total absence of genetic differences in a single homogeneous population of common ancestry. That is the case, for example, with the relations between the Japanese and that portion of themselves they know as the Eta.[7]

[7](in Japan) an outcast class

[26] In a truly great society it may be that the kinds of fear and rivalry that generate racism will be overcome. This can be done without the kind of millenarian reform that would be necessary to banish all conflict, for only certain kinds of hostilities generate racism although any kind can be channeled into an already raging racial bigotry. Great areas of the earth's surface have been totally devoid of racism for long periods of time and such a situation may return again, although under altered circumstances. If and when it does, the word "race" may drop from our vocabulary and scholars will desperately scrutinize our remains and the remains of our civilization, trying to discover what we were so disturbed about.

EXERCISES

Questions

1. Paragraph 25 states the theme. How does the title relate to the theme? Restate the theme in your words in the light of Fried's definition of race.
2. Essentially the essay shows the use of definition. What are the origins of race myths? Why is the word race a misnomer? Compare the customary use of race with Dr. Fried's definition. What is race *not*?
3. While denying the existence of races, does Fried deny the existence of differences among people? How is the variation among people different from the variation among cars?
4. Can you guess about the origin of the tale of "blue-eyed demons" which frightened the child in paragraph 6?
5. Our tendency to create archetypes creates a fantasy today as well as a fantasy about our distant ancestors. Why?
6. What fallacies of race, such as the sudden disappearance of Neanderthal man and the existence of "the German race," does the essay reveal? What evidence is introduced to disprove these myths?
7. What does Fried reveal about the classification or the establishment of criteria for distinguishing racial groups? How does he show these attempts to be meaningless or false?
8. What is Fried's hope concerning race?
9. Comment on Fried's introductory analogy. Is it appropriate?
10. The essay uses illustration to demonstrate many of its points (as in paragraphs 2, 3 and 6) about color and hairiness. What other uses of illustration can you find? What point does each serve to clarify?
11. What is the effect of Fried's use of such expressions as "an off-beat intruder," "clapped eyes on her," "scrambled into my lap," "the kids conjure up," "*sitzfleisch*," "chopped off the family tree?"
12. Note Fried's use of authority, especially in paragraphs 18 and 19. How does the author establish the authenticity of his specialists for the uninformed reader?

Vocabulary

bigoted
eschewed
esthetically
euphemistically
everted
expunge
extrapolation
hirsute
indigenous
millenarian
morphological
replicate
semantics
sitzfleisch
synchronic
taxonomic

For Discussion and Writing

1. Define and evaluate "Negro" as it is used in this country. Check the Census Bureau's definition of "Negro" and "white."
2. Examine for their accuracy, popular stereotypes like: all Germans are stubborn; the English lack a sense of humor; Orientals are inscrutable; Italians are hot-tempered.
3. Stereotypes: how they are useful and how they are harmful
4. Examine your own family background. See how far back national origins can be traced. Type yourself and your classmates; how possible is it to do so? How *valid* is it to do so?

CROSS REFERENCES

COUSINS: "The Environment of Language"
HONWANA: "The Hands of the Blacks"
KING: "I Have a Dream"
STEINBECK: "America and Americans"

RECOMMENDED READING

Montagu, Ashley: *Man's Most Dangerous Myth: The Fallacy of Race* (Harper & Row: 1952)

LUIS BERNADO HONWANA

"THE HANDS OF THE BLACKS"

INTRODUCTION

Luis B. Honwana (1942–   ) was born in Mozambique, Portuguese East Africa, where he has also been imprisoned since 1966 for what is described as "political subversive activities." Prior to his jailing, he worked as a cartographer and a journalist and published one book of short stories written in Portuguese but translated into English. The story reprinted here was sent to the London Bureau of the *New York Times* by Nadine Gordimer, one of the leading writers of South Africa.

TO THE READER

Although this sounds like a child's fable, read it for a deeper significance.

I don't remember now how we got on to the subject, but one day teacher said that the palms of the blacks' hands were much lighter than the rest of their bodies because only a few centuries ago they walked around on all fours, like wild animals, so their palms weren't exposed to the sun, which went on darkening the rest of their bodies. I thought of this when

Senhor Padre told us after catechism that we were absolutely hopeless, and that even the blacks were better than we were, and he went back to this thing about their hands being lighter, saying it was like that because they always went about with their hands folded together, praying in secret.

[2]   I thought this was so funny, this thing of the blacks' hands being lighter, that you should just see me now — I don't let go of anybody, whoever they are, until they tell me why they think that the palms of their hands are lighter. Dona Dores, for instance, told me that God made their hands lighter like that so they wouldn't dirty the food they made for their masters, or anything else they were ordered to do that should be kept quite clean.

[3]   Senhor Antunes, the Coca-Cola man, who only comes to the village now and again when all the Cokes in the *cantinas* have been sold, said to me that everything I had been told was a lot of baloney. Of course I don't know if it was really, but he assured me it was. After I said yes, all right, it was baloney, then he told me what he knew about this thing of the blacks' hands. It was like this: "Long ago, many years ago, God, our Lord Jesus Christ, the Virgin Mary, St. Peter, many other saints, all the angels that were in heaven then, and some of the people who had died and gone to heaven — they all had a meeting and decided to make blacks. Do you know how? They got hold of some clay and pressed it into second-hand molds. And to bake the clay of the creatures they took them to the heavenly kilns. Because they were in a hurry and there was no room next to the fire, they hung them in the chimneys. Smoke, smoke, smoke — and there you have them, black as coals. And now do you want to know why their hands stayed white? Well, didn't they have to hold on while their clay baked?"

[4]   When he had told me this Senhor Antunes and the other men who were around us all burst out laughing, they were so pleased.

[5]   That very same day Senhor Frias called me after Senhor Antunes had gone away, and told me that everything I had heard from them there had been just one big pack of lies. Really and truly, what he knew about the blacks' hands was right — that God finished making men and told them to bathe in a lake in heaven. After bathing the people were nice and white. The blacks, well, they were made very early in the morning, and at this hour the water in the lake was very cold, so they only wet the palms of their hands and the soles of their feet before dressing and coming into the world.

[6]   But I read in a book that happened to mention it that the blacks have hands lighter like this because they spent all their days bent over, gathering the white cotton in Virginia and I don't know where else. Of course, Dona Estefania didn't agree when I told her this. According to her it's only because their hands became bleached with all that washing.

[7]   Well, I don't know what you'll think about all this, but the truth is that however calloused and cracked they may be, a black's hands are always lighter than the rest of him. And that's that!

[8]   My mother is the only one who must be right about this question of a black's hands being lighter than the rest of his body. On the day that we were talking about this, us two, I was telling her what I already knew about the matter, and she just couldn't stop laughing. What I found strange was that she didn't tell me at once what she thought about all this, and she only answered me when she was sure I wouldn't get tired of bothering her about it. And even then she was crying and clutching herself around the stomach as if she had laughed so much she couldn't bear it. What she said was more or less this:

> [9]   "God made blacks because they had to be. They had to be, my son, He thought they really had to be. . . . Afterward, He regretted having made them because the other men laughed at them and took them off to their homes and put them to serve as slaves or not much better. But because He couldn't make them all turn white, for those who were used to seeing them black would complain, He made it so that the palms of their hands would be exactly like the palms of other men's hands. And do you know why that was? Of course you don't know, and it's not surprising, because many, many people don't know. Well listen: it was to show that what men do is only the work of men. . . . That what men do is done by hands that are the same—hands of people who, if they had any sense, would know that before everything else they are men. He must have been thinking of this when He made it so that the hands of the blacks would be the same as the hands of all those men who thank God they're not black."

[10]   After telling me this, my mother kissed my hands.
[11]   As I ran off into the yard to play ball, I thought to myself that I had never seen her cry so much when nobody had even hit her or anything.

EXERCISES

Questions

1. Honwana is writing about more than hands. He presents seven stories of why the palms of Negroes are light; six of them bolster the idea of racial superiority. What is the point of the seventh? What is his theme?
2. Note the sources of the stories: a teacher, a "Senhor Padre" or priest, a lady, the Coca-Cola man, etc. What do their stories reveal about them? What point do you infer from Honwana's choices of these particular people?
3. Why did Honwana's mother laugh as she listened to the stories? Why did she then cry?
4. Can you see any reason why the author pretended the narrator was a child?

For Discussion and Writing

How does this illustrative piece support the viewpoint of Dr. Fried in the essay "A Four-Letter Word That Hurts"?

CROSS REFERENCES

COUSINS: "The Environment of Language"
FRIED: "A Four-Letter Word That Hurts"
SAMUELS: "A Statistic Named Mary"

JAMES THURBER

"THE TROUBLE WITH MAN IS MAN"

INTRODUCTION

James Thurber (1894–1961) was a humorist who was serious and a cartoonist who couldn't draw. Nevertheless, he succeeded at both. Drawn in a wavery pen line, his sad floppy dogs and his Walter Mitty-like men who endlessly battle their overpowering wives, are readily recognizable and generally loved. His book, *The Thurber Carnival* (1945), was made into a musical review. With Elliot Nugent he wrote the famous play about college life, *The Male Animal*. Some of his other books are *Is Sex Necessary?*, written with E. B. White (1929); *The Owl in the Attic* (1931); *Fables for Our Time* (1940); *The Wonderful O* (1959); and several books for children.

TO THE READER

Thurber is playing word games with clichés (worn out expressions, used up metaphors). See how many you recognize, how many you use, and how many others you can think of.

The thesis is in the first and the last two paragraphs; the rest of the essay serves as illustration.

Man has gone long enough, or even too long, without being man enough to face the simple truth that the trouble with Man is Man. For nearly three thousand years, or since the time of Aesop, he has blamed his frailties and defects on the birds, the beasts, and the insects. It is an immemorial[1] convention of the writer of fables to invest the lower animals with the darker traits of human beings, so that, by age-old habit, Man has come to blame his faults and flaws on the other creatures in this least possible of all worlds.

[2]   The human being says that the beast in him has been aroused, when what he actually means is that the human being in him has been aroused. A person is not pigeon-toed, either, but person-toed, and what the lady has are not crow's-feet but woman-wrinkles. It is our species, and not any other, that goes out on wildcat strikes, plays the badger game, weeps crocodile tears, sets up kangaroo courts. It is the man, and not the shark, that becomes the loan shark; the cat burglar, when caught, turns out not to be a cat but a man; the cock-and-bull story was not invented by the cock and the bull; and the male of our species, at the height of his arrogant certainties, is mansure and not cocksure, just as, at his most put-upon, he is woman-nagged and not hen-pecked.

[3]   It is interesting to find in one dictionary that "cowed" does not come from "cow" but means, literally, "with the tail between the legs." I had naturally assumed, too, that Man blamed his quailing, or shrinking with fear, on the quail, but the dictionary claims that the origin of the verb "to quail" is uncertain. It is nice to know that "duck" meaning to avoid an unpleasant task, does not derive from our web-footed friend but from the German verb "tauchen," meaning "to dive." We blame our cowardice, though, on poultry, when we say of a cringing man that he "chickened out."

[4]   Lest I be suspected by friends and colleagues, as well as by the F.B.I. and the American Legion, of wearing fur or feathers under my clothing, and acting as a spy in the midst of a species that is as nervous as a man and not as a cat, I shall set down here some of the comparatively few laudatory phrases about the other animals that have passed into general usage. We say, then, that a man has dogged determination, bulldog tenacity, and is the watchdog of this or that public office, usually the Treasury. We call him lionhearted, or as brave as a lion, as proud as a peacock, as lively as a cricket, as graceful as a swan, as busy as a bee, as gentle as a lamb, and we sometimes observe that he has the memory of an elephant and works like a beaver. (Why this should make him dog-tired instead of beaver-tired I don't know.)

[5]   As I sit here, I suddenly, in my fevered fancy, get a man's-eye view,

---

[1]extending back beyond memory, record, or knowledge

not a bird's-eye view, of a police detective snooping about a brownstone house, back in the prohibition days. He has been tipped off that the place is a blind tiger that sells white mule, or tiger sweat, and he will not believe the denials of the proprietor, one Joe, whose story sounds fishy. The detective smells a rat and begins pussy-footing around. He is sure that this is a joint in which a man can drink like a fish and get as drunk as a monkey. The proprietor may be as wise as an owl and as slippery as an eel, but the detective is confident that he can outfox him.

[6]   "Don't hound me. You're on a wild-goose chase," insists Joe, who has butterflies in his stomach, and gooseflesh. (The goose has been terribly maligned by the human being, who has even gone so far as to pretend that the German jack-boot strut is the goose step. Surely only the dog, the cat, and the bug are more derogated than the goose.) "You're as crazy as a loon," Joe quavers.

[7]   "Don't bug me," says the cop, and the bloodhound continues his search. Suddenly he flings open a door, and there stands the proprietor's current mouse, a soiled dove, as naked as a jay bird. But the detective has now ferreted out a secret panel and a cache of currency. "There must be ten thousand clams here," he says. "If you made all this fish legitimately, why do you hide it? And don't try to weasel out."

[8]   "In this rat race it's dog eat dog," the proprietor says, as he either is led off to jail or pays off the cop.

[9]   The English and American vocabularies have been vastly enlarged and, I suppose, enriched by the multitudinous figures of speech that slander and libel the lower animals, but the result has been the further inflation of the already inflated human ego by easy denigration of the other species. We have a thousand disparaging nouns applicable only to human beings, such as scoundrel, rascal, villain, scalawag, varlet, curmudgeon, and the like, but an angry person is much more apt to use, instead of one of these, such words as jackal, jackass, ape, baboon, gorilla, skunk, black sheep, louse, worm, lobster, crab, or shrimp. Incidentally, the word "curmudgeon" seems to derive from the French "cœur méchant," so that an old curmudgeon is nothing worse than an old naughty heart.

[10] The female of our species comes out of slight, slur, insult, and contumely wearing more unfavorable tags and labels than the male. The fishwife, for example, has no fishhusband. The word "shrew" derives from the name of a small furred mammal with a malignant reputation, based on an old, mistaken notion that it is venomous. Shrews are, to be sure, made up of both males and females, but the word is applied only to the female human being. Similarly, "vixen," meaning an ill-tempered person, was originally applied to both sexes (of human beings, not of foxes), but it is now aimed only at the woman. When a man, especially a general or other leader, is called a fox, the word is usually employed in a favorable sense.

[11] Both "shrew" and "vixen" are rarely used any more in domestic

altercations.² For one thing, neither implies mental imbalance, and our species is fond of epithets and invective implying insanity. The list of such slings and arrows in *Roget's Thesaurus*³ contains, of course, such expressions as "off one's rocker" and "off one's trolley," but once again the lower forms of life are accused of being "disturbed," as in "mad as a March hare," "bats," "batty," "bats in the belfry," "crazier than a bedbug," and so on. (My favorite phrase in this Roget category gets away from bugs and bats, and rockers and trolleys; it is "balmy in the crumpet.")

[12] Every younger generation, in its time and turn, adds to our animalistic vocabulary of disparagement. A lone male at a dance is no longer a stag turned wolf when he dogs the steps of a girl; he's a bird dog. And if the young lady turns on him, she no longer snaps, "Get lost!" or "Drop dead!" but, I am told, "Clean out your cage!" Since I heard about this two years ago, however, it may well be old hat by now, having given way to something like "Put your foot back in the trap!" or "Go hide under your rock!" or "Crawl back into the woodwork!"

[13] I am afraid that nothing I can say will prevent mankind from being unkind to catkind, dogkind, and bugkind. I find no record of any cat that was killed by care. There are no dogs where a man goes when he goes to the dogs. The bugs that a man gets out of his mechanisms, if he does get them out, are not bugs but defects caused by the ineptitude, haste, or oversight of men.

[14] Let us all go back to counting sheep. I think that the reason for the prevalent sleeplessness of Americans must be that we are no longer counting sheep but men.

EXERCISES

Questions

1. How many clichés can you count in the second paragraph? Define the terms "kangaroo court," "badger game," "wildcat strikes."
2. Why should Thurber be afraid of the F.B.I. and the American Legion?
3. What is the purpose of the little narrative in paragraphs 5–8? Define "blind tiger" and "tiger sweat." How many other slang expressions in the essay have gone out of date? What problem does this suggest concerning the use of slang?
4. Paragraph 10 deals, to a large extent, with connotation. Can you think of other favorable terms for men (like tiger) or unfavorable terms for women (like minx)? Can you give an explanation why the female is less favorably tagged than the male?

²heated or angry disputes
³a dictionary of synonyms and antonyms

5.   What does Thurber mean by his last paragraph? What is his implied criticism of Americans?

Vocabulary

cache
contumely
denigration
derogated
disparaging
epithets
malign

For Discussion and Writing

1.   Take your favorite slang expression; define it; compare it with the dictionary's handling of the words; check the derivation as well.
2.   Draw up a list of slang expressions and clichés. Analyze the list to see what it reveals about our society.

CROSS REFERENCES

COUSINS: "The Environment of Language"
SCHLESINGER: "A Note on Language"

RECOMMENDED READING

Frank Sullivan's essay: "The Cliché Expert Testifies on . . . ," from *The Night the Old Nostalgia Burned Down* (Little, Brown & Co.: 1953)

ii

The Heart of Man

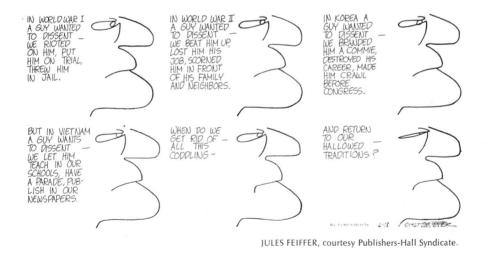

IN WORLD WAR I A GUY WANTED TO DISSENT — WE RIOTED ON HIM, PUT HIM ON TRIAL, THREW HIM IN JAIL.

IN WORLD WAR II A GUY WANTED TO DISSENT — WE BEAT HIM UP, LOST HIM HIS JOB, SCORNED HIM IN FRONT OF HIS FAMILY AND NEIGHBORS.

IN KOREA A GUY WANTED TO DISSENT — WE BRANDED HIM A COMMIE, DESTROYED HIS CAREER, MADE HIM CRAWL BEFORE CONGRESS.

BUT IN VIETNAM A GUY WANTS TO DISSENT — WE LET HIM TEACH IN OUR SCHOOLS, HAVE A PARADE, PUBLISH IN OUR NEWSPAPERS.

WHEN DO WE GET RID OF — ALL THIS CODDLING —

AND RETURN TO OUR HALLOWED — TRADITIONS ?

JULES FEIFFER, courtesy Publishers-Hall Syndicate.

JOHN DOS PASSOS

"TIN LIZZIE"

INTRODUCTION

John Dos Passos (1896–   ) is a writer whose subject matter has been American history and culture and whose chief contribution to the development of American literature is his radical approach to style. His experimentation with writing styles violated old rules but gave a new fluidity to language. He has read and written about the history of our country and used both the history shapers and the man in the street as his subject matter. His major work is *U.S.A.*, a trilogy. The three novels were published between 1930 and 1936 and came out as one volume in 1938. In addition to many other novels, in 1953 he wrote a biography of Jefferson, *The Head and Heart of Thomas Jefferson*. His most recent book is a memoir of his youthful writing days in Paris, *The Best Times* (1966).

TO THE READER

"Tin Lizzie" is a chapter from *The Big Money*, the third book of *U.S.A.* It is one of the several biographical sketches Dos Passos worked into his novel.

As you read this, see if you can detect a shift in the tone as the author's attitude toward Ford is gradually revealed.

*"***M***r. Ford the automobileer,"* the featurewriter wrote in 1900, *"Mr. Ford the automobileer began by giving his steed three or four*

sharp jerks with the lever at the righthand side of the seat; that is, he pulled the lever up and down sharply in order, as he said, to mix air with gasoline and drive the charge into the exploding cylinder. . . . Mr. Ford slipped a small electric switch handle and there followed a puff, puff, puff. . . . The puffing of the machine assumed a higher key. . . . She was flying along about eight miles an hour. The ruts in the road were deep, but the machine certainly went with a dreamlike smoothness. There was none of the bumping common even to a streetcar. . . . By this time the boulevard had been reached, and the automobileer, letting a lever fall a little, let her out. Whiz! She picked up speed with infinite rapidity. As she ran on there was a clattering behind, the new noise of the automobile."

[2]   For twenty years or more,

ever since he'd left his father's farm when he was sixteen to get a job in a Detroit machineshop, Henry Ford had been nuts about machinery. First it was watches, then he designed a steamtractor, then he built a horseless carriage with an engine adapted from the Otto gasengine he'd read about in *The World of Science,* then a mechanical buggy with a one cylinder fourcycle motor, that would run forward but not back;

at last, in ninetyeight, he felt he was far enough along to risk throwing up his job with the Detroit Edison Company, where he'd worked his way up from night fireman to chief engineer, to put all his time into working on a new gasoline engine,

(in the late eighties he'd met Edison at a meeting of electriclight employees in Atlantic City. He'd gone up to Edison after Edison had delivered an address and asked him if he thought gasoline was practical as a motor fuel. Edison had said yes. If Edison said it, it was true. Edison was the great admiration of Henry Ford's life);

and in driving his mechanical buggy, sitting there at the lever jauntily dressed in a tightbuttoned jacket and a high collar and a derby hat, back and forth over the level illpaved streets of Detroit,

scaring the big brewery horses and the skinny trotting horses and the sleekrumped pacers with the motor's loud explosions,

looking for men scatterbrained enough to invest money in a factory for building automobiles.

He was the eldest son of an Irish immigrant who during the Civil War had married the daughter of a prosperous Pennsylvania Dutch farmer and settled down to farming near Dearborn in Wayne County, Michigan;

like plenty of other Americans, young Henry grew up hating the endless sogging through the mud about the chores, the hauling and pitching manure, the kerosene lamps to clean, the irk and sweat and solitude of the farm.

[3]   He was a slender, active youngster, a good skater, clever with his hands; what he liked was to tend the machinery and let the others do the

heavy work. His mother had told him not to drink, smoke, gamble, or go into debt, and he never did.

When he was in his early twenties his father tried to get him back from Detroit, where he was working as mechanic and repairman for the Drydock Engine Company that built engines for steamboats, by giving him forty acres of land.

Young Henry built himself an uptodate square white dwellinghouse with a false mansard roof and married and settled down on the farm,

but he let the hired men do the farming;

he bought himself a buzzsaw and rented a stationary engine and cut the timber off the woodlots.

He was a thrifty young man who never drank or smoked or gambled or coveted his neighbor's wife, but he couldn't stand living on the farm.

He moved to Detroit, and in the brick barn behind his house tinkered for years in his spare time with a mechanical buggy that would be light enough to run over the clayey wagonroads of Wayne County, Michigan.

By 1900 he had a practicable car to promote.

[4]   He was forty years old before the Ford Motor Company was started and production began to move.

Speed was the first thing the early automobile manufacturers went after. Races advertised the makes of cars.

Henry Ford himself hung up several records at the track at Grosse Pointe and on the ice on Lake St. Clair. In his .999 he did the mile in thirty-nine and fourfifths seconds.

But it had always been his custom to hire others to do the heavy work. The speed he was busy with was speed in production, the records, records in efficient output. He hired Barney Oldfield, a stunt bicyclerider from Salt Lake City, to do the racing for him.

[5]   Henry Ford had ideas about other things than the designing of motors, carburetors, magnetos, jigs and fixtures, punches and dies; he had ideas about sales;

that the big money was in economical quantity production, quick turnover, cheap interchangeable easilyreplaced standardized parts;

it wasn't until 1909, after years of arguing with his partners, that Ford put out the first Model T.

[6]   Henry Ford was right.

That season he sold more than ten thousand tin lizzies, ten years later he was selling almost a million a year.

In these years the Taylor Plan was stirring up plantmanagers and manufacturers all over the country. Efficiency was the word. The same ingenuity that went into improving the performance of a machine could go into improving the performance of the workmen producing the machine.

In 1913 they established the assemblyline at Ford's. That season the profits were something like twentyfive million dollars, but they had trouble in keeping the men on the job, machinists didn't seem to like it at Ford's.

[7] Henry Ford had ideas about other things than production.

He was the largest automobile manufacturer in the world; he paid high wages; maybe if the steady workers thought they were getting a cut (a very small cut) in the profits, it would give trained men an inducement to stick to their jobs,

wellpaid workers might save enough money to buy a tin lizzie; the first day Ford's announced that cleancut properly-married American workers who wanted jobs had a chance to make five bucks a day (of course it turned out that there were strings to it; always there were strings to it)

such an enormous crowd waited outside the Highland Park plant

all through the zero January night

that there was a riot when the gates were opened; cops broke heads, jobhunters threw bricks; property, Henry Ford's own property, was destroyed. The company dicks had to turn on the firehose to beat back the crowd.

[8] The American Plan; automotive prosperity seeping down from above; it turned out there were strings to it.

But that five dollars a day

paid to good, clean American workmen

who didn't drink or smoke cigarettes or read or think,

and who didn't commit adultery

and whose wives didn't take in boarders,

made America once more the Yukon of the sweated workers of the world;

made all the tin lizzies and the automotive age, and incidentally,

made Henry Ford the automobileer, the admirer of Edison, the birdlover,

the great American of his time.

[9] But Henry Ford had ideas about other things besides assemblylines and the livinghabits of his employees. He was full of ideas. Instead of going to the city to make his fortune, here was a country boy who'd made his fortune by bringing the city out to the farm. The precepts he'd learned out of McGuffey's Reader,[1] his mother's prejudices and preconceptions, he had preserved clean and unworn as freshprinted bills in the safe in a bank.

He wanted people to know about his ideas, so he bought the *Dearborn Independent* and started a campaign against cigarettesmoking.

When war broke out in Europe, he had ideas about that too. (Suspicion of armymen and soldiering were part of the Mid-West farm tradition, like

---

[1] a grade school reader full of moral teachings used by many generations of nineteenth- and twentieth-century school children

thrift, stickativeness, temperance, and sharp practice in money matters.) Any intelligent American mechanic could see that if the Europeans hadn't been a lot of ignorant underpaid foreigners who drank, smoked, were loose about women, and wasteful in their methods of production, the war could never have happened.

When Rosika Schwimmer broke through the stockade of secretaries and servicemen who surrounded Henry Ford and suggested to him that he could stop the war,

he said sure they'd hire a ship and go over and get the boys out of the trenches by Christmas.

He hired a steamboat, the *Oscar II,* and filled it up with pacifists and socialworkers,

to go over to explain to the princelings of Europe

that what they were doing was vicious and silly.

It wasn't his fault that Poor Richard's commonsense no longer rules the world and that most of the pacifists were nuts,

goofy with headlines.

When William Jennings Bryan[2] went over to Hoboken to see him off, somebody handed William Jennings Bryan a squirrel in a cage; William Jennings Bryan made a speech with the squirrel under his arm. Henry Ford threw American Beauty roses to the crowd. The band played *I Didn't Raise My Boy to Be a Soldier.* Practical jokers let loose more squirrels. An eloping couple was married by a platoon of ministers in the saloon, and Mr. Zero, the flophouse humanitarian, who reached the dock too late to sail,

dove into the North River and swam after the boat.

The *Oscar II* was described as a floating Chautauqua;[3] Henry Ford said it felt like a Middle-Western village, but by the time they reached Christiansand in Norway, the reporters had kidded him so that he had gotten cold feet and gone to bed. The world was too crazy outside of Wayne County, Michigan. Mrs. Ford and the management sent an Episcopal dean after him who brought him home under wraps,

and the pacifists had to speechify without him.

Two years later Ford's was manufacturing munitions, Eagle boats; Henry Ford was planning oneman tanks, and oneman submarines like the one tried out in the Revolutionary War. He announced to the press that he'd turn over his war profits to the government,

but there's no record that he ever did.

One thing he brought back from his trip

was the Protocols of the Elders of Zion.[4]

[2] In 1896, his passionate speech for Free Silver which ended with the sentence, "You shall not crucify mankind upon a cross of gold," won Bryan the nomination for the Presidency. He lost the election. Before his death in 1925, he became a spokesman for the anti-Darwin forces in the famous Scopes, or "monkey," trial.

[3] a summer educational center in New York that also sent out speakers, artists, etc. on circuit lecture tours

[4] a notoriously anti-Semitic document used all over the world to stir hatred against the Jews

He started a campaign to enlighten the world in the *Dearborn Independent;* the Jews were why the world wasn't like Wayne County, Michigan, in the old horse-and-buggy days;

the Jews had started the war, Bolshevism, Darwinism, Marxism, Nietzsche, short skirts and lipstick. They were behind Wall Street and the international bankers, and the white-slave traffic and the movies and the Supreme Court and ragtime and the illegal liquor business.

Henry Ford denounced the Jews and ran for Senator and sued the *Chicago Tribune* for libel,

and was the laughingstock of the kept metropolitan press;

but when the metropolitan bankers tried to horn in on his business he thoroughly outsmarted them.

[10] In 1918 he had borrowed on notes to buy out his minority stockholders for the picayune sum of seventyfive million dollars.

In February, 1920, he needed cash to pay off some of these notes that were coming due. A banker is supposed to have called on him and offered him every facility if the bankers' representative could be made a member of the board of directors. Henry Ford handed the banker his hat,

and went about raising the money in his own way:

he shipped every car and part he had in his plant to his dealers and demanded immediate cash payment. Let the other fellow do the borrowing had always been a cardinal principle. He shut down production and canceled all orders from the supplyfirms. Many dealers were ruined, many supplyfirms failed, but when he reopened his plant,

he owned it absolutely,

the way a man owns an unmortgaged farm with the taxes paid up.

In 1922 there started the Ford boom for President (high wages, waterpower, industry scattered to the small towns) that was skillfully pricked behind the scenes

by another crackerbarrel philosopher,

Calvin Coolidge;

but in 1922 Henry Ford sold one million three hundred and thirtytwo thousand two hundred and nine tin lizzies; he was the richest man in the world.

Good roads had followed the narrow ruts made in the mud by the Model T. The great automotive boom was on. At Ford's production was improving all the time; less waste, more spotters, strawbosses, stoolpigeons (fifteen minutes for lunch, three minutes to go to the toilet, the Taylorized speedup everywhere, reachunder, adjustwasher, screwdown bolt, shove in cotterpin, reachunder, adjustwasher, screwdown bolt, reachunderadjustscrewdownreachunderadjust, until every ounce of life was sucked off into production and at night the workmen went home gray shaking husks).

Ford owned every detail of the process from the ore in the hills until the car rolled off the end of the assemblyline under its own power; the plants were rationalized to the last tenthousandth of an inch as measured by the Johansen scale;

in 1926 the production cycle was reduced to eightyone hours from the ore in the mine to the finished salable car proceeding under its own power,

but the Model T was obsolete.

[11] New Era prosperity and the American Plan
(there were strings to it, always there were strings to it)
had killed Tin Lizzie.
Ford's was just one of many automobile plants.
When the stockmarket bubble burst,
Mr. Ford the crackerbarrel philosopher said jubilantly,
"I told you so.
Serves you right for gambling and getting in debt.
The country is sound."
But when the country on cracked shoes, in frayed trousers, belts tightened over hollow bellies,
idle hands cracked and chapped with the cold of that coldest March day of 1932,
started marching from Detroit to Dearborn, asking for work and the American Plan, all they could think of at Ford's was machineguns.
The country was sound, but they mowed the marchers down.
They shot four of them dead.

[12] Henry Ford as an old man
is a passionate antiquarian
(lives beseiged on his father's farm embedded in an estate of thousands of millionaire acres, protected by an army of servicemen, secretaries, secret agents, dicks under orders of an English exprizefighter,
always afraid of the feet in broken shoes on the roads, afraid the gangs will kidnap his grandchildren,
that a crank will shoot him,
that Change and the idle hands out of work will break through the gates and the high fences;
protected by a private army against
the new America of starved children and hollow bellies and cracked shoes stamping on souplines,
that has swallowed up the old thrifty farmlands
of Wayne County, Michigan,
as if they had never been).
Henry Ford as an old man

is a passionate antiquarian.

He rebuilt his father's farmhouse and put it back exactly in the state he remembered it in as a boy. He built a village of museums for buggies, sleighs, coaches, old plows, waterwheels, obsolete models of motorcars. He scoured the country for fiddlers to play oldfashioned squaredances.

Even old taverns he bought and put back into their original shape, as well as Thomas Edison's early laboratories.

When he bought the Wayside Inn near Sudbury, Massachusetts, he had the new highway where the newmodel cars roared and slithered and hissed oilily past *(the new noise of the automobile)*

moved away from the door,
put back the old bad road,
so that everything might be
the way it used to be,
in the days of horses and buggies

EXERCISES

Questions

1.   What has been the effect of the development and production of the Tin Lizzie on America? In your own words, summarize this portrait of Ford as Dos Passos has revealed him. To do so, examine the last paragraph carefully.
2.   The idea of improving the workmen producing the machine as part of mechanized production is one key to Ford's success. What is Dos Passos' attitude toward the mechanizing of man?
3.   What is the overall function of Henry Ford's mother's injunction that he should not smoke, drink, gamble, or go into debt? Notice that the expression is used several times, slightly changed. What is implied about the nature of morality here? How does this function as a measure of the total morality of his life?
4.   What are the implied "strings" attached to Ford's offer of a cut in the profits? How much of the workingman's interest seems to be behind the offer? Where does Dos Passos show Ford's self-interest?
5.   What were Ford's greatest hypocrisies?
6.   What is the significance of Ford's return to the past? How is the last paragraph ironic?
7.   In what ways was Henry Ford both a success and a failure? Support your answer by specific references to the text.
8.   Examine paragraph 10 which begins, "In 1918 he had borrowed on notes . . . ," and discuss its style, i.e. the single sentence or fragment "paragraphs," the piled up succession of nouns and the assembly line

description. How do form and content tie together? Discuss the success of the technique in convoying so much information in so few words.

9. What details can you find in paragraphs 3 and 4 to picture the pre-automotive age; to describe the youth of Henry Ford?

10. The most notable aspect of Dos Passos' style is his use of what appears to be incomplete sentences, beginning with small letters. With a few exceptions, though, they are complete sentences; he has merely put separate clauses or phrases on separate lines. What is the effect of this? How does his sentence structure relate to his content? Does it aid the reader? Does it impede reading or understanding? Explain.

11. In the middle of paragraph 9, Dos Passos repeats "William Jennings Bryan" three times. What is the effect of this repetition? How many other specific references to people, places, events and dates can you find in paragraph 9?

For Discussion and Writing

1. Myths versus historical accuracy: Lincoln, Poe, Marilyn Monroe
2. The folk "hero": Davy Crockett and Paul Bunyan. Are there other folk heroes perhaps more recent?
3. The image-makers in politics today
4. Automating the assembly line
5. The impact of the automobile on America

CROSS REFERENCES

ROVERE: "The Most Gifted and Successful Demagogue This Country Has Ever Known"
SAMUELS: "A Statistic Named Mary"
WOLFE: "Clean Fun at Riverhead"

RECOMMENDED READING

HUXLEY, ALDOUS: *Brave New World* (Harper & Row: 1932)

RICHARD ROVERE

"THE MOST GIFTED AND SUCCESSFUL DEMAGOGUE THIS COUNTRY HAS EVER KNOWN"

INTRODUCTION

Richard Rovere (1915–   ) is best known to some people as the man who introduced the concept of the "establishment" into American thinking. His book, *The American Establishment*, published in 1962, was the result of many years of observation as a staff writer, editor, or contributing editor to some of the nation's leading magazines: *The Nation, Harpers,* and *The New Yorker.* Mr. Rovere is a prolific writer on the Washington scene; some of his more recent books are *The Eisenhower Years* (1956); *Senator Joe McCarthy* (1959); and *The Goldwater Caper* (1965). His latest book is *Waist Deep in the Big Muddy* (1968), about Vietnam.

TO THE READER

Look for ways in which McCarthy was not a typical demagogue.

Condensed from an article which appeared in *The New York Times Magazine,* April 30, 1967. © 1967 by The New York Times Company. Reprinted by permission of the author and The New York Times Company.

Senator Joe McCarthy (R., Wis.) died 10 years ago, on May 2, 1957, of causes never fully explained, though evidently connected with an ailment of the liver. While not the work of his own hand or that of any other man, his death has been called suicide by some, murder by others. Those who say suicide maintain that he allowed and even encouraged life to slip away, that he deliberately chose not to do what his doctors insisted that he do in order to live. Those who say murder mostly agree with the late George Sokolsky, who wrote: "He was hounded to death by those who could not forget and would not forgive." There is probably a bit of truth in both contentions.

[2]   He was 48 when he died. However, his career as perhaps the most gifted and successful demagogue[1] this country has ever known had come to an end two and a half years earlier, when, on Dec. 2, 1954, the Senate voted, 67 to 22, to censure[2] him for various offenses committed against the presumed dignity of the institution and the self-esteem of its members. And that vote took place less than five years after he had broken out of obscurity by waving before an audience in Wheeling, W. Va., a piece of paper that he said was a "list" of Communists "working and making policy" in the State Department and "known to the Secretary of State" to be conscious agents of the Soviet Union. Before that day—Feb. 9, 1950—he was unknown outside Washington and Wisconsin and not very well known in either the capital or the state whose voters had absent-mindedly sent him to the Senate and were, he had reason to believe, getting ready to retire him in 1952. But a few months after the Wheeling speech he was known throughout the country and around the world, and he was a great power in American politics. He was probably the first American ever to be feared and actively hated on every continent. What he stood for—or was thought to stand for—seemed so ominous to Europeans that Winston Churchill felt constrained to work an anti-McCarthy passage into Elizabeth II's Coronation speech, and The Times of London observed that "the fears and suspicions which center around the personality of Senator McCarthy are now real enough to count as an essential factor in policy making for the West."

[3]   At home, he was greatly feared and greatly admired. From the President on down, no prudent member of the Truman Administration in its last two years, or of the Eisenhower Administration in its first two, took any important decision without calculating the likely response of Joe McCarthy. After a bitter wrangle with McCarthy over the Senate's confirmation of Charles E. Bohlen, today our Ambassador to France, as Ambassador to the Soviet Union, Robert A. Taft, the leader of the Republican majority in the Senate, told President Eisenhower that he would not again do battle in behalf of anyone McCarthy opposed.

[4]   During the months in which the first Republican Administration in 20 years was setting itself up in business, McCarthy held a veto power over appointments.

[1]a person, especially a political leader, who gains power and popularity by arousing the emotions, passions, and prejudices of the people

[2]to criticize or reproach in a harsh or vehement manner

[5]   Many of his colleagues in the Senate convinced themselves that he could determine the outcome of elections. On this the evidence was inconclusive; the chances are that his powers were somewhat overrated.

[6]   It was nevertheless a fact that in the elections of 1950 some Senators who had been critical of McCarthy lost their seats, and for the next four years there was scarcely any senatorial criticism of him. Few spoke well of him, but fewer still spoke ill of him—until at last the day came when the President of the United States decided that McCarthy threatened the morale of the United States Army and gave the first signal for resistance.

[7]   Whatever his impact on elections, he enjoyed, throughout this period, an astonishing and alarming amount of approbation[3] in the country at large. Although his personal following—those who were pleased to think of themselves as "McCarthyites," those who, like William F. Buckley Jr., could hold that "McCarthyism . . . is a movement around which men of good will and stern morality can close ranks"—was never large enough to seem menacing, it was found by the Gallup Poll early in 1954 that 50 per cent of Americans held a "favorable opinion" of him, while only 29 per cent held an "unfavorable opinion." By early 1954, it should be noted, he had accused the Administrations of both Truman and Eisenhower of "treason." And he had said of General of the Army George Catlett Marshall, who up to that moment had seemed the least assailable American of his time, that he was "a man steeped in falsehood . . . who has recourse to the lie whenever it suits his convenience," that he was part of "a conspiracy so infamous, so immense and an infamy so black as to dwarf any previous venture in the history of man," and that he "would sell his grandmother for any advantage." Millions loved it and cried for more.

[8]   In "Orestes," Euripides says of the demagogue that he is "a man of loose tongue, intemperate, trusting in tumult, leading the populace to mischief with empty words." McCarthy was all of this. But he differed from the classic model in some striking and important ways. Throughout history, the demagogue's empty words have conveyed empty promises. What demagogues promise and cannot deliver is a future more desirable than the present. The range is from amelioration[4] at one end of the scale to glory at the other. Some offer both and a bit of everything in between. Hitler promised the Germans an improvement in their individual lives and high adventure and conquest as citizens of his Reich. In this country, Huey Long promised to "share the wealth"—when there was little wealth to share—and thereby to make "every man a king."

[9]   Demagogy almost always involves the exploitation of desires for at least a somewhat better life and of dreams of downright grandeur. But McCarthy promised no one anything. . . . He offered nothing. He had no destination. He was not going anywhere. He was not going anywhere. He had no program of any kind.

[10] He exploited only fears. All demagogues, of course, do this—it is in-

[3]approval, commendation, sanction
[4]improvement

separable from their exploitation of hopes. Like most 20th century dema-gogues (except, of course, such as Stalin and Mao Tse-tung and Castro) Mc-Carthy seized on the fear of Communism. But he did not do it in the usual way. He never dealt with Communism as revolution, as a threat to American society. . . .

[11] McCarthy's interests lay elsewhere. They lay, to be specific, in foreign policy. From the day he stood up in Wheeling until the day he was put down in the Senate, he had nothing to say except that Communists were, as he had charged in Wheeling, "making policy" in those agencies of government that were primarily responsible for our undertakings abroad—the Departments of State and Defense, the United States Information Service, the Central Intelligence Agency. Here, of course, was pay dirt. The cold war was three years old. Four months after Wheeling, our troops were locked in battle with a Communist army in Korea. . . . This was a very edgy country before McCarthy came along to make it edgier still. If he was going to have but a single string to his demagogic bow, he had chosen the best one.

[12] Nevertheless, it seems to me that the fact of the single string is central to any examination of McCarthy's failures as well as his successes, his weak-ness as well as his strength in the practice of demagogy. For purposes of ex-amination, I will assume that the end sought by any demagogue—or any politician, for that matter—is power, by which is meant the ability to control people or events or both. In McCarthy's case, I am not sure that this was ever true. If he had personal ambitions of any kind—to be President of the United States, for example—he never did anything to advance them. His friend and lawyer, Edward Bennett Williams, always insisted that he sought not power but glory. I doubt this too. I think that he wanted little more than to be able to stand back and look upon the mischief and tumult and confusion that were his own handiwork, that he was really a rebel with-out a cause. But he operated within the framework of power, and he used the instruments of power, or at least some of them. His collapse after the Senate censure of 1954 was, I think, a consequence of his failure to ex-ploit hopes and dreams as well as fears and suspicions.

[13] McCarthy was a leader who had a following but not a movement. . . . It would have been impossible to organize around the single proposition that agents of a foreign power should not be making American policy and that they should, as McCarthy kept saying, be "ferreted out." Ferreting of that sort is a job for Government itself, for the President, for the F.B.I. There is no way for the mass to participate in such a purge.

[14] Had he really wished to build a movement, he might have tied anti-Communism to other issues of a more traditional sort. He could, for instance, have argued that the Communist conspiracy to infiltrate the Government threatened the livelihood of every non-Communist civil servant. He could have made himself the letter-carrier's friend, the Government clerk's pro-tector. There was a good deal of McCarthyism in some parts of the labor movement; he might have sought allies in the trade unions. Since he had no

ideological commitments, he could have moved in almost any direction. Though many people today think of him as having been a rightist, an early Bircher, he was in fact nothing of the sort; on domestic issues he voted with the liberals as often as with the conservatives. Had he chosen to do so, he could easily have cooked up some kind of scheme that would have nourished the hopes and the egos of those who accepted his leadership.

[15] If he had done anything of this sort, he would, I feel sure, have survived the Senate's censure and made great capital of it. It is not characteristic of demagogues to collapse when they are rebuffed by the Establishment. All that McCarthy had lost, really, was the chairmanship of the Committee on Government Operations. That had been an important source of his power for two of the years in which he had been a great force in American politics. But he had ascended the heights two years before attaining that chairmanship, when he was just one Senator in 96 and at that a member of the minority party and very low in seniority. Had he ever built a real movement, he could have fired the energies of its members with this new grievance and have threatened his fellow Senators as he had done when he had no powers except those of his loose tongue. Instead he went into retirement and talked about moving to Arizona and ending his days with a country law practice and a small ranch.

[16] In his failure to trade on hopes as well as on fears lay his weakness as a demagogue. But the fatal weakness enables us to take the measure of his remarkable gifts. For it must be remembered that he was by no means the first American who had tried to build a large reputation on anti-Communism. The Russian Revolution was in its infancy when politicians in this and other countries began to see the possibilities in Red-hunting. Hamilton Fish, a former Congressman from New York, had a go at it in the early twenties. The House Committee on Un-American Activities had its greatest days under the leadership of Martin Dies in the late thirties and early forties. McCarthy never had the field to himself. Yet he played it as no one else ever did. With his one-stringed bow, he became a national and an international figure. He gave his name to an "ism" which even today is often as solemnly discussed and analyzed as Marxism-Leninism or Maoism.

. . . .

[17] Beyond any doubt he was a product of the times. What man is not? But I persist in the belief that he helped to make the times what they were, that without his singular presence they would have been different. He was an innovator.[5] Perhaps his largest contribution to demagogy was what I, writing about him in *The New Yorker* not long after his Wheeling speech, called the technique of the Multiple Untruth. Hitler had instructed the world in the uses of the Big Lie. The Big Lie can be put across in a closed society, but in an open society, with a free press and legislative investigations of

[5] one who introduces something new

the kind that not even McCarthy could completely compromise or corrupt, it is difficult to sustain. McCarthy discovered the value of numbers. Had he said in Wheeling or at any point during his career that there was one Communist or two or even five or six, in this or that agency, his bluff could quite easily have been called. But he used large figures and kept changing them. After his Wheeling speech, of which no transcript was ever found, there was some dispute over the number of Communists he had said were on his "list" — it turned out not to be a list but a copy of an old letter from a former Secretary of State to a Congressman — but the highest figure he used was 205, the lowest 57. These were numbers with built-in safety. Showing him to be wrong about three or four of them proved little — what of the other 200 or so, what of the remaining 50-odd?

[18] No one could ever say that he was altogether wrong, or even mostly wrong. Within what appeared to be the Multiple Untruth there might have been — there probably were — some bits and pieces of truth. The Multiple Untruth places an unbearable burden of disproof on the challenger. The work of refutation is always inconclusive, confusing, and — most important of all perhaps — boring to the public. A profusion of names and accusations is exciting. It can be grasped in a single newspaper story. But a hundred newspaper stories, a hundred counteraccusations are simply tiresome, soporific and unconvincing.

[19] In his promulgation of the Multiple Untruth, McCarthy used, to great and at times quite amusing effect, many of the trappings of scholarship, of research. The bulging briefcase was his symbol. He was rarely seen without one. Inside were photostats, transcripts, clippings, copies of other people's correspondence, and assorted "documents." I met him for the first time a year or so before his rise to fame, and he was trying to persuade me of the soundness of the stand he was taking on a matter that had nothing to do with Communism. In his office, he produced for my enlightenment great stacks of papers. No enlightenment ever came. As I examined the papers he handed me, I grew more and more confused. I could not see their relevance; as he talked, I began to lose the thread of his argument. There was, of course, no thread to find, but it took me hours to discover this. I thought at first that I must be at fault and missing his points. It did not occur to me that a man would surround himself with so much paper, with so many photostats, with trays of index cards unless it all meant something. It took me hours to learn that I had been had — that he was passing off as "research" a mere mess of paper that he or someone else had stacked up so that its sheer existence, its bulk, looked impressive. In time, he was to con half the country as, for a time that day, he had conned me.

[20] There was, to my mind, a kind of genius in this. He saw in total irresponsibility and the hocus-pocus of "documentation" possibilities that no one before him had seen, or at any rate put to such effective use. In the long run, the technique may turn out to be his most enduring and his

most lamentable contribution to American life. He developed a style of discourse, or pseudo discourse, that others are using today and with a degree of success approaching his. The American public has in recent years been offered as serious political commentary several books—on President Kennedy, for example, and on President Johnson; and, most notably, on the Warren Commission and Kennedy's assassination—that exemplify as well as any McCarthy speech the uses of the Multiple Untruth and spurious research tricked up to look like the real thing. . . . The first book of this sort that I know of is "McCarthyism: The Fight for America," by Senator Joe McCarthy, a preposterous apologia with more than three footnotes per page citing sources which are mostly nonsources.

[21] There was more to his individual style than his technique for misleading by means of the Multiple Untruth. He deliberately created about his own person an atmosphere of violence, of ugliness, of threat. He shrewdly saw that while Americans like to think of themselves as being imbued with a sense of fair play, there exists among us also a sneaking admiration for the "dirty player." . . . He never bothered to deny that he had let Robert T. Stevens, Eisenhower's Secretary of the Army, know that he would "kick his brains out" if Stevens failed to get in line. He once said to a crowd in Wisconsin, "If you will get me a slippery-elm club and put me aboard Adlai Stevenson's campaign train, I will use it on some of his advisers and perhaps make a good American of him."

[22] "Nice guys finish last," Leo Durocher had said. Many politicians acted on this doctrine long before Durocher's terse formulation of it. But no one ever went so far as McCarthy in letting the public know that he did not consider himself a nice guy, in cultivating the image of himself as the dirty player. Many people are persuaded that this was what finally led to his downfall. For 35 days, or a total of 187 hours, in the late spring of 1954, he played the heavy on network television in what came to be known as the "Army-McCarthy hearings"—a marathon of accusation and counteraccusation on the question, which was more often than not lost sight of, of whether McCarthy and one of his aides, Roy Cohn, had been blackmailing the Army in order to force favors for Pvt. David Schine, a former aide and a friend of Cohn's who, despite all kinds of finagling by members of McCarthy's staff, had been caught up in the draft. He glowered through all his hours on camera. He was abusive, threatening, defiant, disorderly. He denounced the President, the Army, the State Department, and at one time or another every one of the Senators who were sitting in judgment upon him.

[23] The generally accepted view ever since has been that this astonishing performance was his undoing. It was estimated the audience before which he played was seldom smaller than 20 million and that just about every American, except for a few hermits and expatriates, caught the act at one time or another. The great majority were repelled by it. But before it can

be said that this was what finished him it must be acknowledged that Mc-Carthy wasn't running for office and that few demagogues ever worry much about being liked. Fear can serve them as well as favor. There has never been any evidence to suggest that his behavior at the Army-McCarthy hearings lost him any of his real followers. Most of them sat before their television sets and were thrilled as he shouted and screamed and denounced constituted authority. . . .

[24] McCarthy took it lying down. He felt he had lost out in the Army-McCarthy hearings. He tried to fight off censure instead of welcoming it and fighting back. Why? It was partly, as I have said, because he had never organized his followers and had never given them anything which might have led them to organize themselves. But this in itself demands explanation. Why had he failed to offer more? The answer, in my opinion, is that he himself never believed in anything. He was the purest of cynics,[6] and pure cynics are a very rare breed. McCarthy never seemed to believe in himself or in anything he had said. He knew that Communists were not in charge of American foreign policy. He knew that they weren't running the United States Army. He knew that he had spent five years looking for Communists in the Government and that—although some must certainly have been there, since Communists had turned up in practically every other major Government in the world—he hadn't come up with even one.

[25] His basic weakness, and it is one for which the Republic may be properly grateful, was a lack of seriousness. His only discernible end was mischief. When he had exhausted the possibilities for mischief in any given investigation, he lost interest. He announced that there were Communists "with a razor poised over the jugular vein" in radar laboratories and defense plants. This got big headlines for a while, but when the type grew smaller he moved on to something else, with the razor still poised, the vein still vulnerable. He said that the "worst situation" of all existed in the Central Intelligence Agency, where by his count there were more than "100 Communists." The Eisenhower Administration was at that time giving him a free hand almost everywhere. But as he advanced upon the C.I.A., the Administration grew nervous. To head McCarthy off, the President appointed a commission under General Mark Clark to look into the C.I.A. The Clark investigation turned up nothing. McCarthy, seeing that the situation might get a bit sticky if he pushed for his own investigation, did nothing. "I guess I'll skip it," he said, letting the "worst situation" prevail and the 100 Communists remain. . . .

[26] How much further could he have gone if he had been really serious about it? We Americans have very little experience on which to base any judgment. There were demagogues before McCarthy but they were regional figures for the most part or religious sectarians. . . . McCarthy was our first

---

[6]a person who believes that only selfishness motivates human actions and who disbelieves in or minimizes selfless acts

national demagogue. He was the first, and thus far the only one, to find a national audience and to seize upon a truly national issue, foreign policy. He surfaced in a period when national and international issues were becoming the dominant ones in American politics and when advances in communications were making it possible for a man to reach a national audience in a relatively short period of time.

[27] He could certainly, I think, have stayed around longer and made more trouble than he did. Five years is a very short time in which to see the beginning and the ending of a gifted politician's career. My general feeling has always been that while he could have stayed on and kept on stirring up confusion, he had already done about all the damage he could do to the system itself. For the system at last turned against him, as it simply had to. Eisenhower had very much wanted to avoid a showdown, but after only a year this proved impossible. McCarthy, a chronic oppositionist, had to turn against his own party and his own Administration, and once he did the Administration had to fight back. It did not cover itself with glory in its resistance, but it did resist. The Senate, too, feared a confrontation, but the day came when he gave it no choice. Some historians say that American institutions showed up rather badly in meeting the challenge he offered. Some assuredly did. The mass media often truckled to him. The big wheels in Hollywood and on Madison Avenue were scared stiff of him. Manufacturers fearing boycotts from his supporters were careful to give no cause for offense.

[28] For the most part, though, the institutions that allowed themselves to be bullied by him had never been noted for stiffness of spine. Many of them were in the pandering business and survived by seeking to satisfy every taste and give no customer cause for resentment. But other institutions came off quite well. Even while he stormed on Capitol Hill and trampled on the rights of witnesses, the Supreme Court was strengthening individual rights and arming his victims for their own resistance. Most of those newspapers and magazines that were anything more than extensions of the mass entertainment industry exposed and opposed him at every turn. In the academic and intellectual communities, it would have taken more courage to defend him than to attack him. The churches in the main threw their weight against him, and so, with certain exceptions, did the trade unions. None of this, of course, was much consolation to those in the Government whose careers he had ruined or those outside the Government whose reputations he had sought to blacken. But the best of American institutions held firm, and the threat was at last turned back.

[29] It would be harder to turn back an equally gifted and more determined man in a more desperate time. Since his day no one of comparable talents has appeared. But a more desperate time may one day be upon us and offer similar opportunities for demagogy, and there will be demagogues, perhaps even more gifted, who will try to seize them.

EXERCISES

Questions

1. Rovere's title states his theme. What evidence does he present which reveals the talents of McCarthy? How was he a successful demagogue?
2. In paragraph 8, Rovere defines demagogue. How did McCarthy differ from the "classic model"? What was his chief technique? What were his chief targets and interests? In what ways was he an atypical demagogue even in the modern sense?
3. What, according to Rovere, was McCarthy's motive for his campaign? What were *not* motivating factors? Is there any relation between his motive and his cynicism?
4. What is the "Multiple Untruth"? Give an example of it. How does it differ from the Big Lie? Are there any evidences of use of the Multiple Untruth today?
5. How was McCarthy's technique a form of parody on scholarship? Explain the psychological impact on the person to whom the "research" was delivered. What was the "genuis in this" technique as Rovere called it?
6. Discuss the various reasons Rovere gives for McCarthy's defeat: the weaknesses of the man himself; the strengths of the national system; the opposition of institutions.
7. There is an implied warning in Rovere's last paragraph. Is it valid? Are there any potential demagogues in view today? What makes them (him) so?
8. Did Rovere provide sufficient proof for his theme? Did you find any places where he did not supply sufficient proof?
9. What is Rovere's attitude toward McCarthy? Cite specific examples which reveal it.
10. Consider paragraph 22; how many loaded terms can you find?
11. Study paragraph 3 for expository technique. What is the theme sentence? How is it developed? What is the theme of paragraph 17? How is it developed? What is the theme of paragraphs 8 and 9? How are they developed?

Vocabulary

discernible
expatriates
exploitation
marathon
pandering
promulgation

prudent
refutation
soporific
spurious
truckled

For Discussion and Writing

1. Residual McCarthyism
2. The Congressional committee: Its function and its limitations
3. The Big Lie in political campaigning
4. The limits of free speech in the Senate
5. George Wallace: Contemporary demagogue?

CROSS REFERENCES

LAMPELL: "I Think I Ought to Mention I Was Blacklisted"
SOLOMON: "Free Speech at Ohio State"

RECOMMENDED READING

WARREN, ROBERT PENN: *All the King's Men* (Modern Library: 1953)

GERTRUDE SAMUELS

"A STATISTIC NAMED MARY"

INTRODUCTION

Gertrude Samuels has been a staff writer for *The New York Times* since 1943. Her articles have covered a wide range of social problems, such as: divorce, juvenile delinquency, drug addiction, and women's prisons. Miss Samuels also served as a war correspondent in Korea in 1952. Her stories on the Little Rock integration crisis won her a Front Page Award from the American Newspaper Guild. Widely anthologized, she has also written one novel, *The People Vs. Baby* (1967) on juvenile delinquency.

TO THE READER

The tone of any article indicates its writer's attitude. Miss Samuels shows her attitude toward Mary not by what she says about her, but by how she writes about her.

Harlem Youth Unlimited—
Training & Rehabilitation Center
For Young & Unwed Mothers

The sign on the door, which was illustrated with a mother-and-baby drawing, listed a number of study projects offered to the new registrants at the Drew Hamilton Community Center in Central Harlem: homemaking, counseling, prenatal care, postnatal care, heritage-appreciation. I entered a large room, where Mary and a dozen other girls were waiting for me.

[2]   A tall, attractive teen-ager with smooth, shining black hair, Mary looked like any schoolgirl in her sweater and skirt, knee-high white stockings and brown loafers—except for her obvious pregnancy. Aside from the four Youth Leaders, all of the girls sitting around the long table, or registering for the first time like Mary, were in early or advanced stages of pregnancy. The Youth Leaders themselves had gone through Haryou's program for unwed mothers last year, and had already given birth; they were now helping with the orientation of "new girls." All were in their teens—Mary being 15.

[3]   Mary had filled out a registration form which gave some essential details: she was living with her mother, had dropped out of high school four months before "because of morning sickness"; didn't know what "career" she was interested in, but she liked to type; the family wasn't on welfare—her father was in construction work overseas; no, she wasn't married; her "fiancé" was in the South with his family.

[4]   Another girl registering was having a second baby out of wedlock. Yes, she said to a Youth Leader, it was the same 20-year-old father. Yes, she expected to marry him . . . maybe . . . in 1968 "when he was furloughed." She loves him, but he had told her that he felt that he wasn't ready for marriage.

[5]   "He's ready to produce babies, but not ready to marry?" the Youth Leader asked.

[6]   The girl nodded dumbly.

[7]   The Youth Leader scribbled furiously, head down, mumbling, "Lots of them like that."

[8]   This was Mary's first day at Haryou Unlimited, and my first meeting with her. But in a way I had met Mary before—as a statistic.

[9]   A constantly startling fact of modern American life is that girls under 17 years of age account for about 50,000 annual out-of-wedlock births. Illegitimacy in the U.S. has been increasing steadily, from 3.8 per cent of all live births in 1940 to 6.9 per cent in 1961—from an estimated 89,500 to 240,000. Despite more interest in birth-control information in the last few years, the figures keep going up: some 275,700 illicit births in 1964. Among nonwhites, illicit births are highest: 25 per cent of all nonwhite babies, compared with 3.4 per cent of white babies.

[10] In New York City in 1965, of a total of 158,815 live births, 20,980 were out of wedlock. More than 3,000 of these so-called O.W.'s were to girls 17 years of age and younger. Most depressing was the Department of Health report that in 1965, 46.5 per cent of all births in Central Harlem, where Mary lives, were out of wedlock, in contrast with 13.2 per cent for the whole city.

[11] Thus when the statistic that is Mary comes to life at Haryou Unlimited —a social work group that is struggling to teach and train some of these young unwed mothers-to-be—the visitor tries to learn why the tragedy occurred, especially so early in life.

[12] As soon as one steps from subway to street in Central Harlem, one "sees" Mary in the context of her surroundings. For I clearly wasn't about to interview a girl from a sheltered white culture with its middle-class morality and code of behavior. Going into Central Harlem is like going to another country. To be sure, the main streets are modern enough, with their generally attractive shops. But many of the side streets on which the people live, in deteriorated brownstones and apartment buildings, are dreary and sinister-looking, some of them haunts of policy runners and drug addicts; here a white face draws more curiosity than hostility.

[13] Many sidewalks were heaped with rubbish. Basement alleyways overflowed with trash. One long fence, shutting off a filthy lot between buildings, was decorated, mockingly it seemed, with ashcan covers hung as if they were gladiators' shields on display.

[14] The community center stood like a beacon—bright, inviting.

[15] I met Mary and the other girls through Mrs. Charlotte Jefferson, a social worker who created the Haryou program two years ago. A graduate of Stillman College in Alabama, Mrs. Jefferson is a young mother, married to a brokerage assistant. She carefully explained the purpose of my visit to the girls, assuring them that none needed to talk except voluntarily; but that I sought one girl who would articulate her feelings and would be candid and honest—to help me and others understand her story. Mary volunteered.

[16] She was four months pregnant when we began the interviews. Besides Haryou, she was occasionally attending a prenatal clinic at Harlem Hospital, which admits many girls having O.W. babies from the area. Their babies are eventually born there.

[17] What follows is the substance of several interviews I had with Mary:

> How do you feel about motherhood, Mary?
> It's all right. I don't hate the idea.
> Well, do you think it's going to hurt your child not to have a father?
> No. Because we could get married when I finish school, which may be two years from now.
> Mary, the law says that people should be married to protect the babies and give them a good start in life. How do you feel about that?
> It is a sin, I feel, to have babies before you're married. But (defensively) it's not no crime. Because it's nature.
> What do you mean—nature?
> Having babies is nature.
> Who told you that?
> A lot of people told me that having babies is nature, ain't no sin.
> But, Mary, you said that it is a sin.

Well, it is a sin by the Bible and by law. But I don't feel that it's a sin to *myself*. I'm kinda happy that I'm pregnant 'cause this is my first child.
What did your boy friend say when you told him you were pregnant?
I wrote him. He's down South. He said he would get a job and take care of the baby.
Well, did he seem happy with the news?
He was happy.
How old is he?
He's 17.
How long has be been down South?
For several months. He's with his family.
Has your boy friend finished school?
No. He wants to get a job.
Mary, would you say what you and your boy friend decided, about the baby?
Well, I was supposed to go South and get married.
Why didn't you go?
Because . . . I didn't want to get married. I . . . wouldn't have been able to finish school.
But you left school. Is that the only reason, Mary? Was his family against it?
No. His mother called my mother long-distance.
Why did you think you couldn't finish school if you got married?
(Hesitant, confused) Because I . . . guess I didn't think about that.
In other words, you haven't really thought the situation through?
No . . . that's true.
Are you telling me, Mary, that you're uncertain about what you really feel for your boy friend?
Yes. Because I really don't know if I'm . . . in love.
Well, how long were you and Robert dating?
About 10 months.
Where did you go on dates?
We didn't go no place. We went to the movies sometimes. We went to his house.
Is that where you had sex relations?
Yes.
Mary, were you a virgin before you met Robert?
Yes, no relations before him.
Well, how did you learn about sexual intercourse?
My mother told me, a long time ago. She said I could get pregnant by having intercourse with a boy. And she said that she hoped that I wouldn't get pregnant and let her down. She didn't tell me not to do it, and she didn't tell me to do it. She just said not to let her down.
Why did you have sex relations?
I don't exactly know why. He didn't force himself on me. I wanted it . . . because if it would please him, then I wanted to have the relationship with him.
Was it love then, Mary?
Yes, I think so. That's what I thought it was . . . then.
Did you tell your mother?

No.

Why not?

Because I thought she would get mad at me.

When did your mother learn about your pregnancy?

Well, she found a letter from my boy friend that he'd written in reply to mine, saying he was going to 'take care of the baby' and get a job.

What did your mother do, Mary, when you said you were pregnant?

She cried and fussed, and said what was I going to do. But then she said there's a first mistake for everybody. She said she was proud of being a grandmother.

What did your father say?

My father was overseas when my mother wrote that I was pregnant. And at first he was so angry he wrote back that he wanted to put me away — in an unwed mother's home or something. He told my mother that either she puts me away or he wasn't going to come home. But then my mother wrote letters to him, begging, and he sent a telegram saying he changed his mind and I could stay home.

Who's going to pay for your medical care, Mary, and for the baby's clothes and food and all the other things that babies need?

Well, my mother and my father and the baby's father.

Do you have sisters?

Yes, an older sister. She asked me, did I want to get rid of the baby, so I said no. So she said, I'd better tell my mother. Then about a week after I told my sister, my mother found the letter.

Is your sister ashamed of you?

No, she's not ashamed. She keeps telling me that she's proud to be an aunt.

And how do you feel? Are you ashamed, Mary?

(Surprised) No. Because I'm not the first one in my block that had a baby that's my age. 'Cause one of my friends had a baby when she was 14. Her mother sent her away to a home for unwed mothers in Queens. There's a lot of girls on my block who had babies when they were young.

[18] As an inducement to attend the Haryou program, the girls are paid $1.50 an hour for a six-hour day. The program is basically an attempt to reorient the girls in their behavior and thinking, and also to train them for the responsibilities of motherhood. One "must" is that they go on with some regular schooling — despite the fact that the Board of Education has not established a full-time program for these dropouts. Harlem Hospital has instituted a two-hour-a-day academic program in a nearby center, to which the school board has assigned an accredited teacher. One morning soon after Mary had entered the Haryou program I went with her to her first "day" at the "school."

[19] In a well-lighted room with a small library, a spinet piano and a bulletin board hung with art and music notices, half a dozen pregnant girls sat at two tables which had been pushed together, facing the blackboard. The white teacher, very blonde and earnest, was attempting to teach several subjects practically at the same time.

[20] Mary and one or two other girls pored over books on biology and science, in particular a chapter headed "Your Cells and Their Needs," which seemed not untimely. The teacher moved first to this group, then to that, working with girls at various stages of stenography, math, Spanish, science. (On the blackboard the "Words to Learn" included "foe, oath, showed.")

[21] "What do the chromosomes contain, Mary?" she asked.

[22] Mary hesitated, made a stab at it, guided by her book. "Genes?"

[23] "Genes, good."

[24] The teacher briskly described the place of the "nucleus" in the scheme of life, the "genes that we inherit from our ancestors," and how everything "starts from the cell."

[25] Mary yawned and looked tired. She read quietly to herself, her lips moving.

[26] "Mary, that's slowing up comprehension," the teacher called. "Lips closed, please." Mary nodded and closed her lips.

[27] After the two hours the girls put their books away and said good-by. Mary and I then walked together to Harlem Hospital, where she wanted to make an appointment with a social worker connected with the prenatal clinic. She greeted a girl—pregnant like herself.

[28] "She's coming to Haryou this afternoon," Mary confided. "I told her about the program, and she wants to be in it. I like it better than just seeing a social worker [at the hospital] a couple of times a month."

[29] Why was she so tired, yawning in class?

[30] "Yeah, well, I'm not used to getting up so early. I been sleeping late since I dropped out of school, and I still have morning sickness. The hospital give me some yellow pills to take."

[31] What I learned later was that Mary was going out with her friends several nights a week to a neighborhood candy store and staying there until 1 or 2 o'clock in the morning, dancing to the jukebox. That information came from her worried mother, who sought Mrs. Jefferson's help in getting Mary to stay home evenings.

[32] Now at Harlem Hospital, Mary guided me expertly through a labyrinth of corridors to the elevators. On the crowded third floor, she made an appointment with her social worker. Mary had been born here, and her baby would be born here.

[33] We went out to lunch, and I pointed to a luncheonette that seemed satisfactory from the outside, but Mary shuddered.

[34] "Oh, no, not that one. It's full of dope addicts and number men. I stay far away from them," she said.

[35] Back at the Drew Hamilton Center where the Haryou girls were waiting for an afternoon session, other activities were in full swing: preschool children were playing in the nursery; older children were coming in for their after-school games; old people had gathered to play bingo.

[36] Mary and a score of new registrants sat together in their own room for orientation from the Youth Leaders. (More formal counseling from adults, like Charlotte Jefferson, has since begun.) The 1966 program from which these Youth Leaders had emerged had been made up of 40 girls aged 16 to 21 years. Most were high-school dropouts; some were motivated by Haryou to get jobs, as telephone operators, waitresses, clerks, nurse's aides. Three of the 40 had had a previous pregnancy out of wedlock. Seven of the 40 were now married, and a number were "engaged."

[37] Now Helen, the most vocal of the Youth Leaders, who married her boy friend, told the others earnestly: "We feel that you shouldn't be here just for the money, but for the training that you're going to get—on home life and family planning and education. The experts are trying to make sure that we're getting off on the right foot—even after we've made a mistake."

[38] Mary leaned into the table. "Do you have mother's care?"

[39] Helen started to describe the prenatal instruction that would be provided, and suddenly the girls were talking all at once, eager to unload their feelings:

[40] "I didn't even know what was happenin' inside . . ."

[41] "My baby bothers me so much, it stops me from sleepin' . . ."

[42] "My baby kicks me at my back . . ."

[43] "You have to have that suitcase ready, you know, two weeks ahead of time, with your hair rollers an' robe an' slippers . . ."

[44] Nina, the prettiest and most volatile girl at the meeting—she had just had her baby—turned the discussion to love and marriage, and now said contemptuously: "There's nothing wrong in not getting married just because you're pregnant. I feel that if my fiancé don't want me, I can live without marriage . . . unless I can find another fella."

[45] "Well, I don't agree," Helen argued. "It's not really all right. You're not supposed to go out on the street and have a baby with someone you think you happen to love."

[46] "That's like saying, get married with someone you don't even love no more," Nina scoffed, "just because you're having his baby." She added that the father of her child was in Vietnam, and she could have married him when he came home on furlough, but she found that he had been writing to her girl friend.

[47] "But I wasn't positive I wanted to marry him anyway," she added, tossing her head. "Be sure, I say!" she told the girls. "Be positive! I have a feeling I want to be free. Now I'm loco. I don't know if I want to get married or if I want to stay single."

[48] Some of the girls nodded with understanding. Helen looked glum.

[49] Did they feel they should give up their babies, for adoption or foster-home care?

[50] Mary spoke up sharply. "I don't want to give my baby up for no adop-

tion. It's mine, my child, I'll bear the pain to have it. I don't think it's fair to give your child away."

[51] "Why?"

[52] "Because it's not their right mother and father, and that's cruel."*

[53] Helen added fervently: "He didn't ask to come in the world in the first place. I don't think I should give him to anyone else. I would be afraid I mightn't ever see him again and that would bother me most of all. With me, if I had it to do all over again," she told the girls sadly, "I would have waited and not got pregnant. I would have taken pills or something. But I saw other girls were worse off than me. Some girls, their mothers threw them out. Some girls went to homes. But my mother stood by me. She helped me."

[54] All the girls listened quietly to Helen. Mary nodded. She, too, was being helped by her mother. Her mother had come to talk to the social worker, Charlotte Jefferson. She was a tall, neatly dressed woman with easy, weary smiles who worked, she said, as a clean-up woman, earning about $44 a week.

[55] "Who's going to take care of the baby when Mary goes back to school?"

[56] "Me. I'm going to give up my job and stay home when the baby comes," the mother said. She wanted Mary to go back to school. She was "thankful" that Mary was in the Haryou program—"better than her laying around at home, in bed all the time."

[57] Did she think that Mary should get married?

[58] The mother smiled her tired smile. "No, no, no. He's too young, only 17. They'll only have more children for me to take care of."

[59] What would the new baby do to the income of the home if she quit her job and took on the whole responsibility? Her husband would send enough, they would manage. But, she told Mrs. Jefferson heavily, she had a real problem—and she spoke of Mary's going to the candy store and dancing half the night. When Mary got home, the mother said, and she was warned that she was ruining her health and the baby's, Mary replied: "I've gotta have fun."

[60] Would Mrs. Jefferson talk to Mary and tell her that it was hurting her health?

[61] Mrs. Jefferson would.

[62] "I did my best," the mother said, her eyes filling.

[63] "This isn't something that happened just to *you*," Mrs. Jefferson told her firmly. "Keep your chin up. It happens to rich and poor. Mary is lucky to have a mother who is taking on her problem and has chosen to let her have her baby and stay in the home. That's an awful lot."

[64] After the mother had gone, Mrs. Jefferson talked to Mary in a no-nonsense tone: "Don't you feel you're being unfair to your mother? You've

*Studies show that few white unmarried mothers keep their O.W.'s; that more than two-thirds of the girls and women bearing O.W.'s and keeping them are nonwhite.

got to stop thinking of yourself and more about the baby. Now you will be getting assignments to work on at home when you leave here each day, and you must go home to rest. Are any of your friends that you go dancing with pregnant?"

[65] Mary hesitated.

[66] "Yeah, one of them is."

[67] "Okay, she's not in the program, so try to interest her in coming in, too," Mrs. Jefferson said briskly.

[68] The scope of the O.W. problem has so alarmed New York officials that the State Board of Social Welfare has revised its regulations to allow local welfare boards to give birth-control information to its clients—even when the clients do not ask for it. And now the 1967 Yellow Pages of the New York City telephone directory contain a new addition—a complete listing of "Birth Control Information Centers."

[69] At a home-making session at the Drew Hamilton Center (the girls had prepared a sample breakfast of waffles and syrup), I asked Mary if she knew about birth control and contraceptives.

[70] "Yeah, I knew about them. I heard that if you had sex you could take quinine pills and a bottle of gin—you have to boil the gin—to bring on your period."

[71] "Did you do that, Mary?"

[72] "No. One of my girl friends did it but it didn't help her. She got pregnant just the same. That's why I didn't trust it."

[73] "But didn't you know about birth-control pills or other ways to protect yourself?"

[74] "Yeah, I heard about them, but I didn't use them because every time after I had sex, I had my period. So I felt lucky, until I got caught." She grimaced. "Now I'm getting a coil at the hospital, after I have my baby." (She referred to the Margolies coil, named for its developer, one of a number of I.U.C.D.'s, or intrauterine contraceptive devices, that must be installed by physicians.)

[75] "Who suggested that to you, Mary?"

[76] "My girl friend who had her baby. You can't get pregnant with that. It stays in you until you *want* to have another baby. Then you take it out."

[77] A few days later Mary went with the girls of her group to the Y on West 135th Street, where Haryou had arranged for a lecture on family planning. Seated on chairs before a blackboard, the girls—who were joined by a second Haryou group, over half of whom had had their babies—were told by Mrs. Jefferson: "This is Mrs. Relva Harris, a registered nurse in the field of education who has taught at Tuskegee Institute School of Nursing and at Montefiore Hospital, and she is going to talk to you about the reproductive system of the female—how you get pregnant and how not to get pregnant."

[78] Mrs. Harris, a vibrant, informal young woman in a red knit suit,

established a quick rapport with the girls. "Now this is the uterus and the womb," she said briskly, making sketches on the board under the heading, "Human Reproduction." Briefly she lectured them on the menstrual cycle. Then: "How does pregnancy take place?"

[79] Dead silence. Mary leaned forward intensely, but remained as silent as the others. At last one girl ventured: "Don't the ovaries move?"

[80] "No, the ovaries don't move. Mary?"

[81] "No, I don't know."

[82] A show of hands revealed that none of the pregnant girls knew how pregnancy actually happens.

[83] "If intercourse takes place, how many sperms are ejaculated?" asked Mrs. Harris.

[84] "One . . . ?"

[85] "About a . . . million?"

[86] "About 250 million," Mrs. Harris said slowly and firmly, "at one time, in just a little bit of male semen, and they are deposited in the vaginal canal. Most of those, of course, don't go up here," pointing to her drawing, as she explained, in technical and nontechnical terms, how human life is created.

[87] The lecture turned to birth control—the pill and other contraceptives. "The most common and easiest to use is the pill," Mrs. Harris said. "I don't care if you get those sperms by the hour"—self-conscious laughter from the girls—"the pill, if taken regularly, will stop the ovulation."

[88] "So what happens to the sperms?"

[89] "They die."

[90] Mrs. Harris described the alternative contraceptives: the diaphragm (Don't borrow anyone else's, because it won't work; it must be measured for you alone and fitted by a doctor—you have to wear it like your underwear"), and the coil, sometimes called the loop. "So you have a choice, the pill, the diaphragm, and the coil—and if you use one or the other, you will not get pregnant."

[91] Earlier Mrs. Jefferson had asked the girls: "What about your boy friends? All they have to do is go to the drugstore and buy what they need to protect you." Several girls had laughed derisively: "They wouldn't!"

[92] After this meeting, Mrs. Jefferson asked Mary, "Do you think it would have helped you if you had been given this sort of lesson in school before you got pregnant, Mary?"

[93] The girl nodded.

[94] "I'm interested now in . . . birth control," she said.

[95] One evening Mary took me to visit her mother at home. Home was a railroad flat in a rundown apartment house. Sparsely furnished, with peeling walls and torn linoleum, it was nevertheless clean. In the kitchen, the mother, wearing a bright yellow, starched apron, was cooking a chicken-giblet stew for herself and her four children.

[96] One bedroom contained, besides a large bed, a dozen family pictures and a portable TV. A nondescript dog and a cage of canaries were
part of the scene in the small living room.

[97] With Mary listening, her mother said with her sad smile: "Yes, I felt
hurt when she told me she was pregnant. But after I got over it, and my
husband got over it . . ." She shrugged, as though listening to her thoughts.
Mary nodded.

[98] "Now you're going to have work from that Mrs. Jefferson," the mother
told Mary, "so you'll stay in, darling, and have your rest. A pregnant girl
needs her rest."

[99] Mary nodded again.

[100] "Everyone in my family—everyone—had kids before they was married," the mother said suddenly. "So it's sort of in the family—what can
you do?" She seemed to be struggling with her feelings. "I made a mistake
myself before I got married, with my first one. So who am I to put my daughter away?"

[101] There was a silence. Mary, sunk deep in the overstuffed chair, stroked
the dog and looked at her mother.

[102] "We'll work it out," the mother said calmly.

EXERCISES

Questions

1. The theme of this piece is not expressed. It is what Gertrude Samuels
    learned when she speculated on "why the tragedy occurred" (para-
    graph 11). Why did this tragedy occur? Is there one simple reason?
2. What is the purpose of the title?
3. In the long question-and-answer session between the author and Mary
    (paragraph 17), what attitudes are revealed about Mary's pregnancy,
    for example, her reaction? her family's reaction? Were her answers
    any different from what you expected? In what way?
4. What are the prospects for Mary's baby? Why does Mary's mother
    oppose Mary's marrying the father of the child? Do you agree?
5. What are the attitudes of the various girls toward marriage and toward
    giving their babies away? Discuss the morality of their answers.
6. Is it of any significance that none of the girls knew how pregnancy took
    place? And that Mary originally knew nothing of contraception?
7. Discuss the usual public attitude toward unwed mothers. What in-
    formation is introduced into the article about Mary and her family to
    break and to support the stereotypes about unwed mothers?
8. What is Miss Samuels' attitude toward Mary and the other girls? How is
    her attitude reflected in the article's tone?
9. What is the effect of having the Youth Leader speak (paragraphs 5–7,
    for example)?

10.   Note how the author weaves in the statistical and factual data about O. W.'s and Haryou. What is the effect of this technique?

11.   Notice the supporting material Miss Samuels uses, in paragraphs 9–10, for example. How many different kinds of supporting material can you find?

Vocabulary

articulate
volatile

For Discussion and Writing

1.   The morality of birth control devices
2.   The immorality of birth control devices
3.   Sex before marriage
4.   Abortion: Is it ever justifiable?
5.   Sex education: Its effect on promiscuity

CROSS REFERENCES

HUDSON: "Children of the Harvest"
RUSSELL: Prologue to the *Autobiography of Bertrand Russell*
STEINBECK: "America and Americans"

HARRY MARK PETRAKIS

"LOVE LETTER
TO AN ERA THAT'S PAST"

INTRODUCTION

Harry Mark Petrakis (1923–   ) was born and raised in Chicago but now lives in California. He writes both short stories and novels. He has won several awards, including the Atlantic First Award for the short story, a sure recognition of merit. His first novel, in 1959, was titled *Lion At My Heart*. Subsequent works reveal the author's Greek heritage: *The Odyssey of Kostas Volakis* (1963), a novel; and *Pericles on 31st Street* (1965), a collection of short stories.

TO THE READER

The author does more than evoke a picture of the past. Near the end of the essay, he introduces a second theme concerning the writer's function.

The tone of the essay gives it distinction. Note how the writer controls sentiment and keeps the reminiscence from being maudlin or gushy.

O̲n the South Side of Chicago, between Michigan Av. and Cottage Grove, 61st St. runs like a frontier between the neon glitter of 63rd St. and the expanse of Washington Park. Studs Lonigan[1] roamed its pavements and idled under the arabesque of the elevated tracks.

Reprinted from the *Chicago Sun-Times,* September 19, 1965, p. 16. By permission of Toni Strassman, 130 East 18th St., Apt. 7–D, New York, N.Y. 10003, agent.

[2]   This was my street during my childhood and in my adolescence, for we lived close to it in a succession of dark flats with long narrow halls and tiers of tangled back porches. This was also the street which marked the boundaries of my father's life. He was the priest of the Greek Orthodox church at 61st and Michigan for almost 25 years and he died in the Wood-lawn Hospital at 61st and Drexel.

[3]   When I was a boy, no more than 10 or 11, he woke me early on Sun-day morning and I would dress quickly and we would walk together down the streets of the sleeping city. The windows of the shops were shadowed and still, our steps sharp upon the silent streets. Only a prowling tomcat marked our passage with baleful eyes. When we entered the church it would be sodden with the dampness of the night. The janitor came and began to light the numerous candles before the icons of the white bearded saints. I would help my father into his vestments, binding the layers of cord and cloth.

[4]   When he was ready the church would be bursting with the flame of the candles, the parishioners filled the benches, the white-collared and black-gowned girls of the choir watched the extended fingers of the choir-master. The pillar of the *iconostasis* would be pushed aside and my father would emerge, the light glistening on his brocaded vestments and the flame of an Old Testament prophet across his cheeks. The haunting beauty of the ancient Byzantine hymns would roll and sweep with a kind of majesty across my heart.

[5]   In the afternoon, on Sundays, we returned home for the main meal of that day. Visiting priests, theological students, young Talmudists, commer-cial travelers—all set their feet with anticipation under my mother's table. I very early understood the miracle of the loaves and fishes because my mother was accomplished at such feats. Whether 10 or 15 or even 20 visi-tors gathered in our house for that meal, my mother fed them all with savor and skill and a rampant guile.

[6]   There were only one or sometimes two chickens, but many large pans of *pilaf,* that succulent steaming rice that provides the belly such a feeling of abundance. We ate great plates of *pilaf* covered by the spiced and redolent tomato sauce, and among the kernels small slivers of chicken glittered, sug-gesting there had been meat on the menu as well.

[7]   After the meal there were small cups of sweet, heavy coffee and tiny glasses of cognac and trays of honey-nut sweets. The cigars were lit and the discussion and debate began.

[8]   My brother and sister were students at the University of Chicago then, ardent with their faith in the tenets of reason and believers in scientific truth. My father, smiling in his chair at the head of the table, would finally

[1]main character in a trilogy by James Farrell

let them loose. The words and arguments flew up like feathers plucked from startled chickens. After a while a harried priest might turn to my father to ask how he condoned this agnosticism[2] in his house. My father's answer was always the same.

[9]   "Democracy," he would say softly and shrug wryly, "Democracy."

[10] On Monday mornings my younger sister and I walked on either side of my father down 61st to the parish school. The storekeepers opening their shops, sweeping their walks, would greet his dark tall figure with affection and respect, bowing with an old country courtliness that seemed to overlap across my own erect shoulders as well. In the afternoons when school was over I sometimes returned to these same stores with my mother.

[11] There was Belson's grocery, a neat clean store, the fruits and vegetables in crated rows. Max Belson, himself, came to wait on my mother, the wife of the Greek priest.

[12] "How much for this lettuce, Mr. Belson?" my mother would ask. This would be accompanied by her holding the lettuce gingerly in her hand, involving it precariously on the scale of her decision. Max Belson would look at her with the suffering visage of a man who had seen and heard too many such questions too many times.

[13] Whatever the daily price he quoted my mother, her response was always the same. With the fervor of a tragic chorus she would emit a low, muted moan and drop the lettuce back on the pile where it seemed to shrivel in shame. Max Belson calmly smoothed the ruffled leaf.

[14] "Your price, Mrs. Petrakis, you tell me. You tell Belson what you think it's worth."

[15] But my mother would not be drawn into that artful game and had already swept on to the tomatoes, to do battle over still another patch of ground, until the fortifications were breached by a dozen ladders and the defender so distracted he could not be sure where the final assault would come.

[16] Further along the street was a narrow candy store, no more inside than a glass counter of jelly beans and spice drops and a popcorn and caramel corn machine. The owner, a gentle man who spent as much time on a nickel sale as he did on a dollar purchase, drew almost all his trade from the small neighborhood show next door.

[17] During the depression the show was sold to a pair of enterprising men, strangers from the North Side, and they quickly installed a candy counter and popcorn machine of their own. It was not long afterwards that the candy store closed its door for good. For a long while, each time I passed I mourned the abandoned Coke placard in the window that faded in the sun and darkened with dust.

[18] But that violation did not prevent me passing out prevue handbills for

[2]a doctrine that affirms the uncertainty of all claims to ultimate knowledge, that is, the existence of God

the new theater owners. About 15 other 10-year-olds and myself spent an hour after school each day, putting the handbills into mailboxes, pursued by a half-dozen older boys hired to make sure we did not dump our handbills into the first convenient garbage can.

[19] Our payment came in the form of one free admission for the week's work. On Saturday afternoon, pursuers and pursued were grouped together in a roped off area to the side of the lobby while the children who paid for their admissions walked briskly in. Only after the picture, a Western or a Laurel and Hardy comedy, had started and had run about 10 minutes were we allowed to file quietly to our assigned rows. Those 10 minutes that we waited after the picture began and we could hear the laughter from inside were among the most agonizing moments of my childhood.

[20] There was a delicatessen I can only remember in a pungent, breathless scent, a shop of kosher and melodies, trays of glistening corned beef and great dill pickles dripping in brine.

[21] There was a magazine store filled with long rows of racked pulp magazines (before the days of the pocketbook and TV) and the tall, thin owner who never varied in his dialog with me. I was developing my adolescent character and extending my literary insight with a regular purchase of Spicy Western stories. (That was the real West.)

[22] "Does your father know you are buying magazines like this?"

[23] "They're for my older brothers," I said.

[24] That was not true and I think he knew it. But the regular question and answer satisfied the proprieties.

[25] We lived on Michigan Av. and on 60th St. across from Washington Park and on Vernon, and then for the longest span of time on Eberhart Av. On this street of clustered three-flat buildings and a few huge courts I made some good, close friends. The Salants next door; Marvin, the youngest son who became my closest friend, and his sister, lovely Selma, who encouraged me to sing to her on their back porch while a crowd of cynics groaned and howled in the alley below.

[26] There was Danny Neimer and Seymour Corenson and in a two-flat about the middle of the block the Asher girls, Berniece and Florence. Those names will forever connote for me those dark-eyed and black-haired beauties, sisters who graced our block with a kind of basaltic and tawny elegance, reminiscent of a novel by Sir Walter Scott.

[27] Our neighborhood was a city within the city, a city that lived within the walls of our streets. We knew there was a downtown area, made infrequent trips there with one of our parents, saw the great boulevards that ran along the lake. We knew there was a North Side and a West Side, but for all the relevance this had for us they might have been sections of cities in Europe.

[28] When the first Negro families crossed South Park moving east, a group of frightened neighbors brought my father a petition to sign, asking owners to

band together to resist the invasion. They explained how much luster my father's name would add to their petition. My father listened and told them if they obtained his boss's signature he would be permitted to sign.

[29] "Your bishop?" they asked.

[30] "The Big Boss," my father said. "Jesus Christ."

[31] From Michigan Av., where his church stood, to the Woodlawn Hospital on Drexel is a span of 13 city blocks. It took my father 25 years to make that journey. He died in this hospital after an illness of many months. In the last weeks of his life my mother stayed with him through the day and most of the night, often sleeping in a chair beside his bed. My sisters and brothers and I sat with him and marveled at the endless stream of nurses and doctors who struggled to save him. I was older by then, out of my teens, married a year. And yet in that small, white-walled room my father taught me the last — perhaps the most significant — lesson of my life to that time.

[32] He enjoyed sitting for a short while by the window, looking down upon the street, across the roofs of buildings toward the barely visible spire and bell tower of his church. Since he no longer had the strength to walk, I lifted him from his bed and carried him to his chair. He had been a big man, but the months of illness had wasted him.

[33] One day, alone with him in the room, as I carried him the few feet from bed to chair, he placed his cheek against my own and in a voice of incredible gentleness, said, "As I once carried you in my arms, now you carry me."

[34] In that searing moment I knew the cycle had come full circle, and that my father was going to die. I was torn by a dreadful sense of loss and yet at the same time I noted the way his veins looked huge and purple at his wrists, how transparently his flesh spread across his long, slender fingers, the pulse that wriggled like a small, dark worm in his forehead.

[35] I saw his eyes glazed as if reflecting the landscape of some terrain visible only to those about to die. And I understood then the dichotomies[3] between life and death and love, and I understood then what it meant to want to write. That in those anguished moments when we were torn by love and loss, a part of us still had to remain aware of each word and each detail and the recesses of the emotion so they might be recalled and used in our books and stories.

[36] Where are they now, the lovely girls and boys I laughed with and sang to and roamed beside? Where is Belson, who suffered with patience and fortitude the daily assaults of a hundred determined women? Where are the cruel men (invaders from the far North Side) who made us wait those frenzied 10 minutes on Saturday afternoons? Where are all the storekeepers who greeted my father and my sister and myself each morning as we walked proudly beside him on our way to school?

[3]a division into two mutually exclusive and exhaustive groups

[37] Of my father, I know. He is dead now and lies straight and still beneath a flowered patch of cemetery sod. Many of the storekeepers must be dead, too, and their sons and daughters scattered across the world, raising children of their own.

[38] Perhaps I fool myself, but I feel as long as I am able to remember and to record the memories, as long as I am able to put words about them on paper, they will remain alive, bouncing with a kind of zest and vigor. And if I could say to them: This is the way it was on that morning in the spring, that afternoon in winter, that twilight in the summer, with the sweep of fans hissing from the dark porches and the voices of hidden children calling plaintively to one another in the shadows.

[39] This is what I remember. And I have written it down for you.

EXERCISES

Questions

1. Paragraphs 35 and 38 imply the theme. What is the function of a writer? How does a creative person use memory differently from an ordinary person? Compare Mr. Petrakis' view with that of Harry Schwartz.

2. The relationship between Harry Petrakis and his father is a central concern of this essay. Describe the relationship. What does it reveal about each man?

3. In paragraph 27, Petrakis says his neighborhood was a city within a city. How does he illustrate this? What images are used to evoke the neighborhood? What personalities are suggested to delineate the picture?

4. What does Petrakis do to fuse the old world and the new? What example can you cite to show the blending of European beliefs and customs with American beliefs and customs?

5. In how many ways and places does Petrakis invoke religion? How is it integrated into the life of the family?

6. What were the chief characteristics of the "Era That's Past"? Was it an era, or a place, or a part of his life—or some of all of these—that he remembered? Is it possible for an "era" like this to exist today? Why or why not?

7. The organization is clear and combines the techniques of fiction and nonfiction. What do the first two paragraphs do?

8. The body of the essay has four distinct sections: Sunday; the neighborhood; neighbors and friends; and the death of the father. Where does each section begin and end? How is the character of the father used to supply a unifying force?

9. Some incidents in this essay achieve their impact primarily through diction. Reread the incident involving the first Negro family in the area. (Paragraphs 28–30.) Why does referring to God as the "Big Boss" create the impact of this incident?

10.   Mr. Petrakis controls his tone via his use of language. Where and how is humor employed? Instead of adjectives, he uses hyperbole (deliberate exaggeration) in paragraphs 4 and 13 and metaphor in paragraphs 8 and 15. Identify these and find other examples. In the death scene, effusive, weepy adjectives are avoided. What words are used instead to evoke the great poignancy of the scene?

11.   Notice how Petrakis ties his paragraphs together by repeating key words or ideas. Paragraph 6, for example, discusses a meal; paragraph 7 begins with "after the meal"; paragraph 7 ends with "(the) debate began"; paragraph 8 describes the debate. How many other transitions like this can you find?

Vocabulary

arabesque
baleful
basaltic
Byzantine
icons
redolent
Talmudists
tawny

For Discussion and Writing

1.   The immigrant in my family
2.   My grandfather's youth
3.   American rootlessness — a source of instability
4.   My "old" neighborhood
5.   The neighborhood in the big city
6.   The disappearance of immigrant neighborhoods

CROSS REFERENCES

HUDSON: "Children of the Harvest"
SCHWARTZ: "Why Write a Book?"
WHITE: "The Meaning of Democracy"

RECOMMENDED READING

DAY, CLARENCE: *Life with Father*
TURGENEV, IVAN: *Fathers and Sons*

LOIS PHILLIPS HUDSON

"CHILDREN OF THE HARVEST"

INTRODUCTION

Lois Phillips Hudson (1927–   ), the daughter of a farmer, became a mi-grant as she describes below. Most of what we know and imagine about the migrants has been influenced by John Steinbeck's *The Grapes of Wrath,* and we have come to believe that there is an almost hopeless trap built in to the migrant's way of life. It is good to see someone who has broken free. Mrs. Hudson, who holds both a bachelors and masters degree, has been both a teacher and a writer. She has written one full-length book, *The Bones of Plenty* (1962), and has contributed several articles to *The Reporter* and *The New Yorker* magazines.

TO THE READER

The child in this narrative does considerable growing up. The contrasts be-tween innocent expectancy and mature reality are pointed up by several sig-nificant incidents.

The title of this essay is ambiguous; see how many meanings you can derive from it.

On a suffocating summer day in 1937, the thirteenth year of drought and the seventh year of depression, with our mouths, nostrils, and eyes full of the dust blowing from our bare fields, my family sold to our neighbors at auction most of the accoutrements of our existence. Then we loaded what was left into a trailer my father had made and drove West to find water and survival on the Washington coast.

[2]   During the auction the two classmates with whom I had just finished the fourth grade hung about the desultory bidders giving me looks of respect and undisguised envy. They envied me not so much for the things they could imagine as for the things they couldn't—the unimaginable distance I was going and the unimaginable things along it and at the end of it.

[3]   How could any of us have imagined an end to the prairie's limitless sky and the giddy encroachments rising higher and higher against that sky that were the Rocky Mountains? How could we have imagined how in burning summer the forested profiles of the Cascades could echo everywhere the shouts of white falls above us and green rivers below? Who could have imagined, once confronted with their gray expanse, that the waters of Puget Sound were not actually the Pacific, but only a minute stray squiggle of it? Who, finally, could have imagined that there were so many people in the world or that the world could offer them so hospitable a habitation?

[4]   There were so many things I could scarcely believe even when I was doing them or looking at them or eating them. We lived in a cabin on an island for a few weeks after we arrived, and it always seemed impossible to me that we could be surrounded by so much water. I spent every moment of the hour-long ferry trip from the mainland hanging over the rail gazing down at the exhilarating wake of my first boat ride. The island was exactly what any island should be—lavish green acres covered with woods and orchards and fields of berries, ringed by glistening sandy beaches richly stocked with driftwood. Once in North Dakota my aunt had brought a very small basket of black cherries to my grandfather's house, and I had made the four or five that were my share last all afternoon. I would take tiny bites of each cherry, then suck the pit and roll it around with my tongue to get the faint remaining taste, till it came out as clean and smooth as a brook-bottom pebble. But on the island I would climb into the trees with my five-year-old sister and have contests with her, seeing which of us could get the most cherries in our mouths at once. Then we would shoot the wet pits, no longer hungrily scoured of their slipperiness, at each other and at the robins who perched above us. Sometimes I would go into the fields with my mother and father and spend an hour helping pick raspberries or blackberries or loganberries or any of the other things they worked in, but there were really only two important things to do—play on the beaches and eat fruit.

[5]   It didn't occur to me that things would ever be different again, but one day early in August the last berry was picked and we took the ferry into Seattle,

where we bought a big brown tent and a gas stove. We added them to our trailer load and drove back over the green-and-white Cascades, beneath the glacial sunrise face of Mount Rainier, and down into the sweaty outdoor factory that is the Yakima Valley. There the Yakima River is bled for trans-fusions to the millions of rows of roots, its depleted currents finally dragging themselves muddily to their relieved merger with the undiminishable Co-lumbia. One can follow the Yakima for miles and miles and see nothing but irrigated fields and orchards—and the gaunt camps of transient laborers.

[6]   The workers come like a horde of salvaging locusts, stripping a field, moving to the next, filling their boxes or crates or sacks, weighing in, col-lecting the bonuses offered to entice them to stay till the end of the season, and disappearing again. They spend their repetitive days in rows of things to be picked and their sweltering nights in rows of tents and trailers. We pitched our tent beside the others, far from our pleasant island where the owners of the fields were neighbors who invited my sister and me among their cherry trees. Here the sauntering owners and their bristling foremen never smiled at those children who ran throught the fields playing games and only occa-sionally at those who worked beside their parents.

[7]   In North Dakota I had worked on our farm—trampling hay, driving a team of horses, fetching cows, feeding calves and chickens—but of course that had all been only my duty as a member of the family, not a way to earn money. Now I was surrounded by grown-ups who wanted to pay me for working, and by children my own age who were stepping up to the pay window every night with weighing tags in their hands and collecting money. I saw that the time had come for me to assume a place of adult independence in the world.

[8]   I made up my mind I was going to earn a dollar all in one day. We were picking hops then, and of all the rows I have toiled my way up and down, I remember hop rows the most vividly. Trained up on their wires fif-teen feet overhead, the giant vines resemble monster grape arbors hung with bunches of weird unripe fruit. A man who does not pick things for a living comes and cuts them down with a knife tied to a ten-foot pole so the people below can strip them off into sacks. Hops don't really look like any other growing thing but instead like something artificially constructed—pine cones, perhaps, with segments cleverly cut from the soft, limp, clinging leaves that lie next to the kernels of an ear of corn. A hop in your hand is like a feather, and it will almost float on a puff of air. Hops are good only for making yeast, so you can't even get healthily sick of them by eating them all day long, the way you can berries or peas.

[9]   Pickers are paid by the pound, and picking is a messy business. Some-times you run into a whole cluster that is gummy with the honeydew of hop aphids, and gray and musty with the mildew growing on the sticky stuff. Tiny red spiders rush from the green petals and flow up your arms, like more of the spots the heat makes you see.

[10] The professionals could earn up to six dollars a day. One toothless grandmother discouraged us all by making as much as anybody in the row and at the same time never getting out of her rocking chair except to drag it behind her from vine to vine. My father and mother each made over three dollars a day, but though I tried to work almost as long hours as they did, my pay at the end of the day would usually be somewhere between eighty and ninety cents.

[11] Then one day in the second week of picking, when the hops were good and I stayed grimly sweating over my long grey sack hung on a child-sized frame, I knew that this was going to be the day. As the afternoon waned and I added the figures on my weight tags over and over again in my head, I could feel the excitement begin making spasms in my stomach. That night the man at the pay window handed me a silver dollar and three pennies. He must have seen that this was a day not for paper but for silver. The big coin, so neatly and brightly stamped, was coolly distant from the blurred mélange of piled vines and melting heat that had put it into my hand. Only its solid heaviness connected it in a businesslike way with the work it represented. For the first time in my life I truly comprehended the relationship between toil and media of exchange, and I saw how exacting and yet how satisfying were the terms of the world. Perhaps because of this insight, I did not want the significance of my dollar dimmed by the common touch of copper pettiness. I gave the vulgar pennies to my little sister, who was amazed but grateful. Then I felt even more grown-up than before, because not everybody my age was in a position to give pennies to kids.

[12] That night I hardly slept, lying uncovered beside my sister on our mattress on the ground, sticking my hand out under the bottom of the tent to lay it on the cooling earth between the clumps of dry grass. Tired as I was, I had written post cards to three people in North Dakota before going to bed. I had told my grandmother, my aunt, and my friend Doris that I had earned a dollar in one day. Then, because I did not want to sound impolitely proud of myself, and to fill up the card, I added on each one, "I'm fine and I plan to pick again tomorrow. How are you?"

[13] I couldn't wait to get to the field the next day and earn another dollar. Back home none of my friends would have dreamed of being able to earn so much in one day. The only thing to do back there for money was to trap gophers for the bounty; and even the big kids, who ran a fairly long trap line and had the nerve to cut the longest tails in half, couldn't make more than twenty cents on a good day, with tails at two cents apiece. I earned a dollar and forty cents the next day and the day after that, and at least a dollar every day for another week until we moved to another place of picking—a pear orchard.

[14] By that time it was September, and most of us children from the rows of tents stood out at the gateway of the camp and waited each day for the long yellow school bus. I had never seen a school bus before, and my sister and I

were shy about how to act in such a grand vehicle. We sat together, holding our lunch buckets on our knees, looking out at the trees beside the roads, trying to catch a glimpse of our mother and father on the ladders.

[15] The school had about three times as many pupils in it as there were people in the town back in North Dakota where we used to buy coal and groceries. The pupils who were planning to attend this school all year were separated from those who, like me, did not know how many days or weeks we would be in that one spot. In our special classes we did a great deal of drawing and saw a number of movies. School was so luxurious in comparison with the hard work I had done in North Dakota the previous year that I wrote another post card to Doris, telling her that we never had to do fractions and that we got colored construction paper to play with almost every day. I copied a picture of a donkey with such accuracy that my teacher thought I had traced it until she held the two to the window and saw that the lines were indisputably my own. After that I got extra drawing periods and became very good at copying, which always elicited more praise than my few original compositions.

[16] I was understandably sad when we left that school after two weeks and went to Wenatchee. For the first time, we were not in a regular camp. The previous year my father, recognizing that the crops had not brought in enough to get us through the winter, had taken the train to Wenatchee after the sparse harvest was in and picked apples for a man named Jim Baumann. Baumann wanted him back, so he let us pitch our tent on his land not far from his house. We made camp, and after supper Baumann came down to talk about the next day's arrangements. The school was not so large as the other one, and there was no school bus for us because we were only a half mile away from it. Baumann was shorthanded in the packing shed and needed my mother early in the morning. Besides, there was no reason why she should have to take us to school, because he had a daughter who was in my grade who could walk with us and take us to our respective rooms.

[17] "Why, isn't that lovely!" my mother exclaimed with unwonted enthusiasm. "Now you'll have a nice little girl to play with right here and to be your friend at school."

[18] Her excitement was rather remarkable, considering the dubious reaction she had to everybody else I had played with since we started camping. It hadn't seemed to me that she had liked even the boy who made me a pair of stilts and taught me to walk them. Now here she was favorably predisposed toward somebody I didn't even know. I agreed that it would be nice to have a nice little girl to play with.

[19] The next morning my sister and I sat on the steps of the Baumanns' front porch, where Barbara's mother had told us to make ourselves at home, waiting for her to finish her breakfast. We had already been up so long that it seemed to me we must surely be late for school; I began picturing the humiliating tardy entrance into a roomful of strange faces.

[20] Two of Barbara's friends came down the driveway to wait for her. They both wore the kind of plaid skirts I had been wondering if I could ask my mother about buying — after all, she *had* said all my dresses were too short this fall because of all the inches I'd grown in the summer. The two girls looked at us for a moment, then uncoiled shiny-handled jump ropes and commenced loudly shouting two different rhymes to accompany their jumping.

[21] Barbara came out on the porch, greeted her friends with a disconcerting assurance, jumped down the steps past us, insinuated herself between them, and clasped their hands. "I have to show these kids where the school is," she told them. Turning her head slightly she called, "Well, come if you're coming. We're going to be late." Swinging their arms together, they began to skip down the driveway.

[22] A couple of times on the way to school they stopped and waited until we got near them; I yanked irritably on my little sister's arm and thought about how her shorter legs had been holding me back ever since she was born. I always seemed to be the one who had to drag a little kid along.

[23] The teacher kept me standing at her desk while she called the roll and started the class on a reading assignment. When she looked up at me, I got the irrational impression that I had already managed to do something wrong. She asked where I had come from and I said "North Dakota," thinking it would be simpler than trying to tell all the places I had been in the last three months. She gave me the last seat in a row behind a boy in dirty clothes. As she passed by him she made the faintest sound of exhalation, as though she was ridding her nostrils of a disagreeable smell.

[24] At recess a boy in a bright shirt and new cream-colored corduroy pants yelled "North Dakota, North Dakota!" in a funny way as he ran past me to the ball field. The boy who sat ahead of me came up and said confidentially, "We been out all around here for two years. We come from Oklahoma. We're Okies. That's what you are too, even if you didn't come from Oklahoma." I knew I could never be anything that sounded so crummy as "Okie," and I said so. "Oh, yeah!" he rejoined stiffly. I walked away before he could argue any more and went to find my sister, but the primary grades had recess at a different time, so I went and stood by the door until the period was over. That afternoon I stayed in my seat reading a history book, but the teacher, who seemed to want to go outdoors herself, said "It's better for the room if everybody goes outside for recess." So I went out and stood around the fringes of two or three games and wondered what was funny about North Dakota. Somehow I had the feeling that it would hurt my mother if I asked her.

[25] The last part of the day was given to a discussion period, when each of us who wanted to was given a chance to tell about an important day in his live. The important days of my classmates, all about having a part in a play or learning to ride a bike, seemed so pathetically juvenile that I was impelled

to speak. I stood at my seat and told about how I had earned a dollar all in one day in the hop fields.

[26] From two sides of the room Barbara's friends turned to send her looks which I intercepted but found inscrutable. I had been looking at her too, watching for her reaction. A boy near me poked another and whispered in mocking awe, "A whole dollar!"

[27] The boy ahead of me jumped suddenly to his feet, banging his leg against the desk so hard that the entire row shook. "Heck," he cried, "we just come from there, too, and I made more'n a buck and a half *every* day." He gave me a triumphant smile and sat down. Then I knew I hated that boy. That night I told my mother about how there was a mean boy just like those other mean boys at the camps and how the teacher *would* have to put me right behind him. "Well," she sighed, "just try not to pay any attention to him."

[28] By the time I had found my sister after school, Barbara and her friends had gone. The next morning when we went up to the big house she was gone, too.

[29] After that, my sister and I walked together. Sometimes we would be close enough to hear Barbara's friends who were always with her laugh and call her "Bobby." I had never known any Barbaras before, and the name seemed full of unapproachable prestige and sophistication—the name that only a girl with as many dresses as Barbara Baumann would have. "Bobby" was yet more awesome, as if she were as consequential as a boy. At school, if I recited in class, she acted queerly self-conscious, as though she were responsible for me—the way I often felt around my sister when she said something stupid to kids my age.

[30] For various reasons I had that same embarrassed feeling of an enforced distasteful relationship with the boy who sat ahead of me. Once in a while somebody in the class would tease me about him or would say something about "the hop pickers." I was bitterly determined to dissociate myself from the boy, and whenever he turned around to talk to me I would pretend he was trying to copy my paper. I would put my hand over it while I kept my eyes glued to the desk and felt my face grow hot.

[31] There were some things about the school I liked very much. We were allowed to use the library a great deal, and for the first time in my life I had access to numbers of books I hadn't already read. By reading at noon and recess I could finish a book at school every two days. I would also have a book at home that I would read in a couple of nights. One of the nice things about living in a tent was that there were hardly any household chores to do and I could read as much as I wanted.

[32] Frosty mornings came with October, and my sister and I would try to dress under the quilts before we got up to eat our oatmeal. Leaves began to blow across the road, apples grew redder with each cold night, pickers hurried from tree to tree, filling the orchards with the soft thunder of hard

round fruit rolling out of picking sacks into boxes, and packers worked faster and faster, trying to get the apples twisted up in fancy tissue and into boxes before they jammed up too thickly on the perpetually moving belts. After school my sister and I would go to the box shed behind the big house where Harry, Barbara's big brother, would be nailing boxes together for a nickel apiece. He was always glad to have company, and would let us stand at a respectful distance and watch him pound in nail after nail with two strokes, a tap to set it, then a mighty clout to send it in, three to an end, six to a side.

[33] One afternoon, with the chill blue sky brilliant behind the orange and black Halloween cutouts on the windows, I was sitting at my desk dreamily drawing a witch in a moon when the teacher called my name. She told me that she wanted me to take all my books out of my desk and take them to the front of the room. Then she told everybody in my row to pack up his books and move one seat back. My heart banged alarmingly up in my throat and I nearly gagged from the sudden acute sensations in my viscera. In North Dakota such drastic action was taken only when an offender, after repeated warnings, had proved too incorrigible to sit anywhere except right in front of the teacher's desk. The fact that I had no idea of why I was now classified as such an incorrigible only augmented my anguish. While books banged and papers and pencils fell to the floor and boys jostled each other in the aisle, I managed to sidle numbly up to the front. I sat down in my new seat, trying not to notice how shamefully close it was to the big desk facing it, and I was careful not to raise my eyes higher than the vase of zinnias standing on the corner nearest me.

[34] When school was out I hurried to find my sister and get out of the schoolyard before seeing anybody in my class. But Barbara and her friends had beaten us to the playground entrance and they seemed to be waiting for us. We started to walk around them but they fell into step with us. Barbara said, "So now you're in the 'A' class. You went straight from the 'C' class to the 'A' class." She sounded impressed.

[35] "What's the 'A' class?" I asked.

[36] Everybody made superior yet faintly envious giggling sounds. "Well, why did you think the teacher moved you to the front of the room, dopey? Didn't you know you were in the 'C' class before, 'way in the back of the room?"

[37] Of course I hadn't known. The Wenatchee fifth grade was bigger than my whole school had been in North Dakota, and the idea of subdivisions within a grade had never occurred to me. The subdividing for the first marking period had been done before I came to the school, and I had never, in the six weeks I'd been there, talked to anyone long enough to find out about the "A," "B," and "C" classes.

[38] I still could not understand why that had made such a difference to Barbara and her friends. I didn't yet know that it was disgraceful and dirty to be a transient laborer and ridiculous to be from North Dakota. I thought

living in a tent was more fun than living in a house. I didn't know that we were gypsies, really (how that thought would have thrilled me then!) and that we were regarded with the suspicion felt by those who plant toward those who do not plant. It didn't occur to me that we were all looked upon as one more of the untrustworthy natural phenomena, drifting here and there like mists or winds, that farmers of certain crops are resentfully forced to rely on. I didn't know that I was the only child who had camped on the Baumanns' land ever to get out of the "C" class. I did not know that school administrators and civic leaders held conferences to talk about how to handle the problem of transient laborers.

[39] I only knew that for two happy days I walked to school with Barbara and her friends, played hopscotch and jump rope with them at recess, and was even invited into the house for some ginger ale — an exotic drink I had never tasted before.

[40] Then we took down our tent and packed it in the trailer with our mattresses and stove and drove on, because the last apples were picked and sorted and boxed and shipped to the people all over the world, whoever they were, who could afford to buy them in 1937. My teacher wrote a letter for me to take to my next school. In it, she told me, she had informed my next teacher that I should be put in the "A" class immediately. But there wasn't any "A" class in my room, the new teacher explained.

[41] By then I was traveled enough to realize that it was another special class for transients. The teacher showed us movies almost every day.

EXERCISES

Questions

1. Paragraph 38 implies the theme via a number of illustrations. State the theme in your own words. Describe the education of the migrant. Restate in your own words her evaluation of it. Also, study paragraph 38 to see how the techniques of narrative and of comparison and contrast are used here. Note how comparison and contrast is used in the rest of the article.

2. Paragraph 1 has a great deal of information packed into it. What do you learn from it?

3. Paragraphs 8–14 relate the experience of picking hops. What insights do we gain about migrant life from this narrative?

4. What are the several significances you can find to the earning of the first dollar?

5. In paragraph 15, Mrs. Hudson describes her first classroom experience. Contrast this with the last paragraph of the essay. What difference is there in tone? in the perceptive powers of the child of the narrative?

6. What is revealed about the nature of prejudice in paragraphs 23–24 and 38? How does the education she describes contribute to this?

7. Find the various instances of prejudice evidenced against Mrs. Hudson on her first day of school at Wenatchee. In what ways was her behavior toward the farm boy similar to the way in which she was treated by the other children? What does this reveal about human nature?

8. What significance is there to her misinterpretation of her "promotion"? How does this relate to other interpretations she gave other occurrences in her life? How does the last sentence of the essay reveal the author's emerging maturity?

9. Notice the change in tone from paragraph 4 to 5 as the author prepares the reader for the change in experience. What other contrasts can you find between unaware childhood and the realities of the difficult migrant experience?

10. Paragraph 6 describes the difficult life of the migrant. Pick out the phrases which convey the images.

11. Examine paragraphs 8 and 9 closely. What words make hop picking sound pleasant? What words make the reader reevaluate the experience? What is the effect of the use of the verbs "rush" and "flow" to describe the spiders?

Vocabulary

accoutrement	inscrutable
desultory	sidle
encroachment	transient
gaunt	unwonted
incorrigible	viscera

For Discussion and Writing

1. Migrant farm labor in my state
2. Education and the migrant child
3. Minimum wage and hour law for migrants
4. Unions for migrants
5. Reflection on a disillusioning experience
6. Retrospect: A childhood experience

CROSS REFERENCES

PETRAKIS: "Love Letters to an Era That's Past
SAMUELS: "A Statistic Named Mary"

RECOMMENDED READING

STEINBECK, JOHN: *The Grapes of Wrath*

MILLARD LAMPELL

"I THINK I OUGHT TO MENTION I WAS BLACKLISTED"

INTRODUCTION

Millard Lampell (1919–   ) tells much of his own background in the essay that follows. A successful screen writer with a long string of credits, suddenly he found himself without assignment. Established once again, Lampell has added to his credits on film and on television. He has written for the Hallmark Hall of Fame, has won a Peabody Award and an Emmy, as well as the Sidney Hillman and Anti-Defamation League awards for a script for the television series, "East Side, West Side," entitled, "No Hiding Place." In addition to songs, screenplays, and television specials, he has written documentaries for the screen, notably "A Walk in the Sun."

TO THE READER

At one point, Lampell refers to Franz Kafka, an Austrian writer, whose books had a nightmarish quality. Notice how the nightmare of unknown accusers and unknown punishers plays into Lampell's life.

From *The New York Times,* August 21, 1966. © 1956–1966 by The New York Times Company. Reprinted by permission of The New York Times Company and the author.

What makes this account so frightening is that it happened in the U.S.A., not in a dictatorship.

In 1950, I began to keep a journal with a title borrowed from Dostoevsky: "Notes From Underground." In it I recorded the ironic, sometimes bizarre, sometimes ludicrous experience of living in the twilight world of the blacklist. The last entry is dated 1964.

[2]   I am not by nature an injustice collector. I think martydom is for the saints and self-pity is a bore. So, at the Television Academy Award ceremonies, when I went up to accept an Emmy for my Hallmark drama, "Eagle in a Cage," it was with some surprise that I heard myself saying, "I think I ought to mention that I was blacklisted for ten years."

[3]   At the press conference afterward, a reporter asked why I had said it. I had to stop and consider, and a line of the philosopher Santayana's swam into my mind, "Those who cannot remember the past are condemned to repeat it."

[4]   The Emmy broadcast brought a flood of letters, including a number that asked in puzzlement, "What was this blacklist?"

[5]   Well, brothers and sisters, it was like this:

[6]   By 1950, I had been a professional writer for eight years, including the time spent as a sergeant in the Air Force that produced my first book, "The Long Way Home." I had published poems, songs and short stories, written a novel and adapted it as a motion picture, authored a respectable number of films, radio plays and television dramas, collected various awards, and seen my Lincoln cantata, "The Lonesome Train," premiered on a major network, issued as a record album, and produced in nine foreign countries.

[7]   Then, quietly, mysteriously and almost overnight, the job offers stopped coming.

[8]   Free-lance writing is a fiercely competitive arena, and when work bypasses you and goes to others, the logical conclusion is that they have more talent. At the same time, however, there was another disturbing note. I began to have increasing difficulty in getting telephone calls through to producers I had known for years.

[9]   It was about three months before my agent called me in, locked her door, and announced in a tragic whisper, "You're on the list."

[10] It seemed that there was a list of writers, actors, directors, set designers, and even trapeze artists, choreographers and clowns who were suspected of Communist leanings and marked by all the film studios, networks and advertising agencies as unemployable. No, my agent had never actually laid eyes on this list. She had not even been officially informed that I was a pariah.[1] It was all hints, innuendos and enigmatic murmurs. "I understand he's in a little trouble."

[1]an outcast

[11] What made it all so cryptic was the lack of accusations or charges. Fearing legal suits, the film companies and networks flatly denied that any blacklist existed. There was no way of getting proof that I was actually on a list, no way to learn the damning details. My income simply dropped from a comfortable five figures to $2,000 a year.

[12] Finally I ran into an old friend, a producer who had downed a few too many martinis, and he leveled with me. "Pal, you're dead. I submitted your name for a show and they told me I couldn't touch you with a barge pole." He shrugged unhappily. "It's a rotten thing, I hate it, but what can I do?" And with a pat on my cheek: "Don't quote me, pal, because I'll deny I said it."

[13] Through the next several years, bit by bit, the shadowy workings of the blacklist came into sharp focus. There were, to begin with, numerous lists. Their common chief origin was the Attorney General's unofficial and highly arbitrary index of "subversive organizations," and the published reports of the sessions of the House Committee on Un-American Activities — testimony from self-styled experts on Communism, a steamy mixture of fact, fancy and hearsay. Among those who had been named as subversives before the committee were the 16th-century playwright Christopher Marlowe and Shirley Temple, characterized in 1938 as an unwitting Communist dupe. But also named at one session or another were hundreds of working professionals in the communications and entertainment fields. Then somebody got the profitable idea of publishing "Red Channels," a handy, paperback compendium of the names of the suspected. Every time a name listed in this pamphlet appeared among the credits of a film or a broadcast, it was greeted with complaints written under the letterheads of various obscure patriotic organizations. It took only a handful of these letters to stir panic in the executive corridors.

[14] By 1951, standard equipment for every Madison Avenue and Hollywood producer's desk included, along with the onyx ash tray and penholder and the gold cigarette lighter, a copy of "Red Channels" in the bottom drawer.

[15] Perhaps one has to begin by calling up the atmosphere of those days, the confusing, stalemate fighting in Korea, the flareup of belligerent patriotism, the growing government impatience with any dissent from official policy. It was a time of security checks, loyalty oaths, FBI investigations, tapped phones, secret dossiers, spy scandals, library book-burnings, and Senator Joseph McCarthy of Wisconsin waving a briefcase at the television cameras and rasping that it contained the names of a battalion of Reds in the State Department. A time of suspicion, anonymous accusation, and nameless anxiety. Friends I had known for years passed me by on the street with no sign of recognition but a furtive nod. Invitations ebbed away. I tried to be philosophical about it, but it was subtly unnerving, like being confronted on every side by advertisements insinuating dandruff, tooth decay, and underarm odor, leaving me with a nagging sense of social failure.

[16] Years later, my memories of those days were to serve me well when I sat down to write a play based on John Hersey's "The Wall," and had to create the atmosphere of the early days of the Warsaw Ghetto.

[17] I sold my car, moved my wife and children to a cramped apartment in a cheap neighborhood and, when my savings ran out, lived on small loans from friends and what I could earn from a thin trickle of odd, ill-paid assignments. Using a pseudonym, I wrote a few radio broadcasts for the Government of Israel, an educational film for the Government of Puerto Rico, a few scripts for benefits given by charitable organizations.

[18] Then, in the spring of 1952, a wispy, harrassed man in an ill-fitting suit appeared at my door, flipped through a bulging folder, and handed me a subpoena from the Senate Committee on Internal Security. It was in Washington, at a closed session of the committee, that for the first time I got some clues to the nature of the charges against me.

[19] In 1940, I had come up from West Virginia and, with Pete Seeger, Woody Guthrie, and Lee Hays, formed a folk-singing group called the Almanacs. Now, when every third college student seems to be toting a guitar, when used car lots advertise "Hootenanny Sale," and willowy girls drive around in Alfa-Romeos bought with the royalties from their albums of chain-gang blues and piney woods laments, it seems unbelievable that when I first came to New York The Almanacs were, to my knowledge, the only folk-singing group north of the Cumberland Gap.

[20] Leadbelly[2] was around, newly arrived and living in obscurity. Josh White and Burl Ives were managing to scrape out a meager living. There wasn't exactly a clamor for folk-singers, and we were grateful for any paid bookings we could get. Mostly we found ourselves performing at union meetings and left-wing benefits for Spanish refugees, striking Kentucky coal miners, and starving Alabama sharecroppers.

[21] We were all children of the Depression, who had seen bone-aching poverty, bummed freights across country, shared gunny-sack blankets with the dispossessed and disinherited. We had learned our songs from gaunt, unemployed Carolina cotton weavers and evicted Dust Bowl drifters. Such as they were, our politics were a crude, hand-me-down cross between Eugene Debs[3] and the old Wobblies.[4] A primitive, folk version of what Franklin D. Roosevelt was saying in his fireside chats. We were against hunger, war and silicosis, against bankers, landlords, politicians, and Dixie deputy sheriffs. We were for the working stiff, the underdog, and the outcast, and those were the passions we poured into our songs. We were all raw off the road, and to New York's left-wing intellectuals we must have seemed the authentic voice of the working class. Singing at their benefits kept us in soup and guitar-string money.

---

[2]one of the first great American folk singers
[3](1855–1926) U.S. labor leader: Socialist candidate for president 1900–1920
[4]members of the Industrial Workers of the World

[22] Then came the army, and the week after I was discharged I appeared on Town Hall of the Air teamed with Bill Mauldin, debating two generals on the subject, "What The GI Wants." It was a natural set-up for audience sympathy, enlisted men against the brass. I got almost two thousand fan letters, and overnight found myself a kind of celebrity, in demand as a public speaker. I spoke anywhere that the subject was peace or prejudice, and never thought to give a damn who the sponsoring organization was. Nobody ever tried to tell me what to say.

[23] Years later, before the Senate Committee, I found that period haphazardly reported and presented as evidence that I had taken part in a subversive plot to bring riot and ruin to my native land. I was ordered to account for my life and to give the names of everyone I could ever remember having seen at those bygone benefits. Considering privacy of belief to be a constitutional right of all Americans, I refused.

[24] Even though I appeared at a closed session of the committee, it didn't take very long for the news to get around. The blacklist slammed doors completely shut.

[25] In the late summer of 1952, I gave myself a deadline of three months, resolving that if I couldn't earn a living as a writer, I would pack up my family, return to the city where I was born, and go back to work in a dye factory.

[26] Excerpt from my journal:

> This morning, nine days before the deadline, the director V. calls to offer me a job writing a documentary film about an oil boom town in North Dakota. He is aware that I am blacklisted, but is willing to take a chance. Apologizes for not being able to give me name credit. Disgusted by the blacklist, he will, as a protest, not ask me to use a pseudonym. The credits will not mention any writer.

[27] If the predominant tenor[5] of the era was fear, there was also moving evidence of courage and compassion:

> [28] In today's mail, a letter from the prominent actor, C. Some time ago he starred in a radio play of mine, but I really do not know him very well. He is a rockribbed conservative, but in the envelope I find a $500 check and a brief note. "I have a feeling that life is going to get pretty rough in the days ahead. This is a gift, to use when you need to catch your breath and get back your perspective." I return the check with thanks and a dignity which I probably cannot afford.

[29] Leafing through the journal, I come upon an entry that is pure Gogol[6] farce:

> [30] The television writer L. stops me on the street with a nightmare tale. A year ago, having no political activity in his past, but fearing he might become a victim of some reckless accuser, he sought out a professional in-

[5]the predominant course of thought which marks the period
[6]a Russian writer

vestigator who does a brisk trade with the advertising agencies, checking out talent at $5 a head. L. paid to have himself investigated, asking only that, after being proved innocent, he be given a written certificate of clearance, [31] In due time, L. was found to be free of taint, and given his document, only to discover that he was no longer able to get work. It appears that in the course of probing him, the investigator questioned a number of network executives. He assured them that it was only a routine check and L. was not under suspicion. Their reaction was skeptical. "Where there's smoke, there's fire." L. haunts the waiting room of the networks, a gaunt ghost desperately brandishing his certificate. He has not worked in eight months.

[32] In those first years, the two major sources of work were other writers suffering from a creative block and desperate producers with deadline and budget trouble. I spent four months filling the assignments of a well-known writer who found himself unable to face his typewriter. It was a lucky and profitable arrangement that ended when he appeared one midnight and haggardly told me that his analyst had advised him that signing his name to my work was giving him an even deeper psychological problem. "He says I'm losing my identity."

[33] By taking everything that came our way, a few dozen of us on the East Coast and in Hollywood were working sporadically and managing to survive. For every blacklisted writer who anonymously kept at his trade, ten fell by the wayside. If you could turn out a feature film in a couple of weeks or an hour television play in five days for a twenty-fifth of your former price, you had a chance.

[34] It was a lot tougher for the directors and the actors. They couldn't work without being present in person. One brilliant clown who has since become the toast of Broadway and Time magazine used to go around roaring, "I'm Z., the man of a thousand faces, all of them blacklisted!"

> [35]   The doorbell rings, and I find myself confronted by the well-known character actor, S. In the last decade he has appeared in more than fifty Western movies. Blacklisted now, he is peddling Christmas cards house-to-house. He displays his wares, and I regretfully explain that I can't afford to send cards this year. He settles for a cup of coffee, and reminisces about Gary Cooper and Gene Autry.

[36] By the mid 1950's, the situation had eased a bit. A sympathetic fledgling producer, employing the talents of blacklisted writers, came up with two extremely successful network children's adventure series. And the word was getting around that such-and-such a Hollywood box-office smash, though signed by Y., was actually written by X. There even began to grow a certain mystique about the spectacular feats of the twilight writers. It was not uncommon for me to get calls from acquaintances who would chortle, "I just saw your play on television. Okay, okay, you can't say anything. But you can't kid me, I'd recognize your style anywhere." Sometimes it actually was my work, sold under another name. Sometimes it was not,

my protests were of little avail, and I wasn't sure whether to feel amused or embarrassed.

> [37]   The producer T. tells me that the head of a major Hollywood studio threw the fourth draft of a script back at him, yelling, "It stinks. Do me a favor, stop wasting money, go find yourself a blacklisted writer."

[38]   It was a scramble, and I found myself writing all sorts of things I'd never tried before, industrial training films, travel shorts, doctoring Broadway plays. I wouldn't choose to go through it again, but in many ways it sharpened my skills and expanded my sense of invention.

> [39]   The actor C. invites me to lunch and proposes that I write the pilot script for a series that one of the networks has asked him and his wife to do. I explain that I am blacklisted, and while I would very much like the job, I will have to use a pseudonym. He insists that my name will be on it, brushing aside my warnings that it may cause trouble, telling me that he considers the blacklist morally repugnant.
> [40]   I write the pilot, and the star is delighted with it. He delivers it personally to the network's vice president in charge of production who glances at my name and hands it back. "It's lousy." C. protests that he hasn't even read it, only to be informed, "Look, even if it was Tolstoy, it would be lousy."
> [41]   Sobered but stubborn, C. offers me the job anyhow. I can sign my work with another name. Only it will have to be the name of an actual writer who can appear at script conferences and rehearsals. After some searching, I find a gifted young writer who is willing to collaborate, and whose name and face will represent us both.

[42]   In the end, I was writing under four different pseudonyms, including a Swedish name I used for sensitive art-house films. And there were two or three cleared writers willing to sign my work when the network or agency demanded a name with experience and a list of reputable credits.
[43]   I had read Kafka, but nothing prepared me for the emotions of living in the strange world of the nameless. A script of mine won a major award, and I remember the queer feeling of being a nonperson when another writer went up to claim it. At that, I think it was even worse for him. He tried to give me the trophy, miserably telling me that he felt like a fraud. We ended up tossing it in a trash can, and then went out and got drunk together.
[44]   Of course, there was a way to avoid all the difficulties. One could always appear before the committee and purge oneself. There were two lawyers who specialized in arranging this, one in New York and one in Hollywood. The established fee was $5,000, for which one got expert advice in composing a statement of *mea culpa*,[7] avowing that, being an

---

[7](Latin) my fault

artist, one was naïve about the devious ways of politics and had been the dupe of diabolical forces. One was also required to offer the names of former friends and acquaintances who were the real subversives. If one knew no such names, the lawyer would obligingly supply some, in one case arguing away the qualms of a famous choreographer who was anxious to clear himself but reluctant to become an informer with the reassuring thought, "Hell, they've all been named already, so you're not really doing them any harm. They can't be killed twice."

[45] I find a whole section of my journal devoted to those who sought to purge themselves, pathetic case histories of the anatomy of panic:

> [46] K. has known the playwright O. since the thirties, a close and senti-
> mental friendship. One of O.'s plays is currently playing in a revival, and he
> has insisted that K. be hired as stage manager.
> [47] After being blacklisted for a number of years, O. arranged to go before
> the Committee and clear himself. At two in the morning, K.'s doorbell rings.
> It is O., looking ill and exhausted. He points at K. and says in a terrible whis-
> per, "I named you." Then he turns and shuffles back toward the elevator.
> From others, I gather he spent the whole night making the rounds of the friends
> he turned in to the Committee.

[48] Who can ever fully understand what fear can do to a man? There were things that happened which, even now, I find myself unable to explain:

> [49] Opening night party at the house of the film and stage director, K.
> He draws me into a corner and tells me that, on the road in New Haven, he
> was visited by an investigator from the Un-American Activities Committee.
> "I told him to drop dead." K. goes on for twenty minutes, describing his
> indignation and defiance, reviling the blacklist. The next day, I learn from
> his friend T. that when all this took place, K. had already appeared before the
> Committee and named names.

[50] During those years, I reread the entire works of Dostoevsky, and Lord, how much better I understood them. For by then, I had had my first painful experiences with self-abasement and the need for absolution.

> [51] Walking down Broadway, someone catches my elbow from behind.
> It is R., whom I have known for fifteen years, and who recently appeared as
> a "cooperative witness" before the Committee. He asks plaintively why I
> passed him without saying hello, and I explain that I didn't see him. He
> shakes his head, "No, no, you stared right at me." He grimaces. "I don't
> blame you. I'm disgusting. Do you think I'm disgusting?" I am not particularly
> proud of the fact that I nodded yes and walked away. Who appointed me his
> judge? He's as much a victim as the rest of us.

[52] In 1960, what seemed to be a wide crack appeared in the wall of the blacklist. I was offered the job of writing a film in London, working with a

renowned Hollywood director who had fled a committee subpoena. It was a suspense film of, I think, considerable artistic quality, and despite the fact that our names were on it, American distribution rights were purchased by a major Hollywood company. When the first publicity came out, a few weeks before it was to open on Broadway, a Long Island post of the American Legion threatened to picket the theater. The film corporation hastily abandoned plans for the premiere. But they had half a million dollars at stake, and their lawyers met with Legion representatives to work out a deal to protect their investment. The film would have no official opening. A few months would be allowed to pass, to let things cool off. Then the picture would be quietly sneaked into the neighborhood theaters as part of a double bill with a Cary Grant comedy.

[53] And so it went. Truce came to Korea, and McCarthy, after being outmaneuvered at one of his own hearings by Department of the Army lawyer Joseph Welch, was squashed by his colleagues in the Senate, and eventually died. Dalton Trumbo won an Oscar under the name of Robert Rich, and emerged from underground to write "Exodus" in his own name for Otto Preminger. John Henry Faulk sued several of the self-appointed patriots who had put pressure on the networks, and won a whopping award for character damage. The blacklist began to crumble and producers assured me that in their hearts they had always opposed it. Along Madison Avenue and Sunset Boulevard, people wondered exactly how it had ever happened in the first place.

[54] Actually, blacklisting lasted longest in broadcasting. By 1961, my cantata "The Lonesome Train" was beginning to be performed again in schools and colleges. In 1962, I got my first name credit on a film for a Hollywood major studio, without picket lines or protest. But it was not until 1964 that David Susskind and Dan Melnick's Talent Associates approached me to write a script for their CBS series, "East Side West Side." I said I wouldn't consider doing it without credit, and they answered unhesitatingly, "Of course." The play I wrote was called "No Hiding Place." It was about a Negro family moving into a white suburb. The first time my name had appeared on the home screen in more than a decade, my script won half a dozen awards, and the network scheduled a special repeat broadcast.

[55] George Schaefer, director of Hallmark's Hall of Fame, happened to see it, and had his assistant look up my name in the telephone book. He asked if I would accept a commission to write an original drama for the program. The result was "Eagle in a Cage," with Trevor Howard playing Napoleon in exile on St. Helena.

[56] Meanwhile, I had started writing for the theater. My first play opened on Broadway, and my second was premiered at Washington D. C.'s Arena Stage. A long scene from that second play, "Hard Travelin'," was presented last spring at the White House Festival of the Arts, and I was invited to be

there for the occasion. Then came the Emmy award, and it seemed that I had at last come in from the cold.

[57] Or had I?

[58] Once again we are involved in a confusing, bloody, stalemate conflict in a far-off place. Once again there is a flare-up of belligerent patriotism, signs of official impatience with dissent.

[59] I remember arguing until dawn, some years ago, with Antek, one of the handful of surviving fighters from the Warsaw Ghetto. He insisted that terror was not a matter of geography, and that the fear and savagery that exploded in Warsaw might happen anywhere. And I avowed that it could never happen here. Not in a nation with the tradition of Jefferson and Lincoln.

[60] Assuming that we remember that heritage, and our lapses from it. Assuming that Carl Sandburg was wrong the day I heard him say, grinning crookedly in that way of his, "Man has a quick forgettery."

EXERCISES

Questions

1. This memoir has a two-fold thesis which is never specifically stated: the first has to do with the shortness of men's memories; the second, and more basic theme, is the question of integrity. How does the first theme make the second more meaningful? What, other than his blacklisting, does he not want us to forget?

2. In paragraphs 7 to 9, Lampell says he got the first clues to the reason for the boycott of his services. What impacts were felt in his standard of living? How is this treatment similar or dissimilar to the usual due process procedures in the U.S.?

3. How does blacklisting work? What fallacy of reasoning is involved? How did Lampell get on the "list?" How did he get off it? How could he have protected himself from it?

4. Paragraphs 23 and 24, about his appearance before a Congressional committee, are vital in this essay. What fallacy of reasoning was exhibited by the Senate committee? What do these paragraphs reveal about the problems and relationships concerning the individual: his private life, his livelihood, government interference, the business community?

5. Lampell implies that the treatment he was given was in some ways like the treatment the Nazis gave the Jews (paragraph 16). In what ways is such an implication valid? invalid? shocking?

6. Discuss the irony of Lampell's ghost writing. What does this tell us about the effectiveness of blacklisting? What does it reveal about censorship?

7. Paragraphs 33–35 indicate many other writers, directors and actors who were in the same predicament. Assuming some of these people (if not all) were innocent, did their being blacklisted help America in its fight against subversives?

8. How did the blacklist serve not only to harm Lampell but to destroy the integrity of others? the integrity of our government?

9. What implications does Lampell feel lie in his experience that are relevant today?

10. How does the theme of memory act as a unit of organization for the essay?

11. In paragraph 13, what supporting evidence does Lampell present? Evaluate it. On the other hand, evaluate the evidence presented in paragraphs 52 to the end. Which is better? Why?

12. Reread the rather telegraphic journal entries (paragraphs 26–34). Why did Lampell include them in that form? What is their total impact? Discuss whichever one is the most revealing to you.

Vocabulary

compendium
cryptic
mystique

For Discussion and Writing

1. When the right of the government to protect itself infringes on the right of the individual

2. The Legion of Decency and movie censorship.

3. Book banning

4. Public opinion as an influence on justice

CROSS REFERENCES

McDONALD: "The Habit of Lying"
ROVERE: "The Most Gifted and Successful Demagogue This Country Has Ever Known"
WHITE: "The Meaning of Democracy"

RECOMMENDED READING

KAFKA, FRANZ: *The Trial*
MILLER, ARTHUR: *The Crucible*

iii

Controlling
the Earth
from the Earth

THE WORKINGS
OF THE MIND

ISAAC ASIMOV

"MATTER OVER MIND"

INTRODUCTION

Isaac Asimov (1920–   ), a biochemist with his Ph.D. from Columbia, is so prolific that a list of his books fills more than one full column in *Publisher's Guide* which has print as small as the phone book. He started writing at the age of thirty, and seventeen years later had over eighty titles to his credit with subject matter ranging from science texts to science fiction. One sample year, 1962, reveals such diverse titles as *Life and Energy, Words in Genesis, Fact and Fancy*. The·following year he published five books. *Is Anyone There?* appeared in 1967; this essay is the first chapter of the book.

TO THE READER

Dr. Asimov views the brain as a chemical complex, and he details some hopeful predictions about treating some mental illnesses. With definition and illustration to clarify all terms and points, he makes a complex subject clear and understandable.

> *What is mind? No matter!*
> *What is matter? Never mind!*

This ancient witticism testifies to man's firm conviction through the ages that the human mind transcends the material, that it is not bound by the ordinary rules that govern gross matter.

[2]   The physical structure of the living organism is accepted as a thing of atoms and molecules, governed by the same laws that govern the rocks underfoot and the stars overhead. That is as true for Man the Proud as for Worm the Lowly. But man's mind? Can one analyze the creative genius that gives rise to a masterpiece? Can one weigh, count, and measure emotion and imagination, love and hate, passion, thought, and a sense of good and evil?

[3]   There has always been a strong impulse to place mind over matter and to apply different and more subtle rules to the former. It seems natural, then, that doctor's medicine should prove unable to work on the mind. Shakespeare has Macbeth ask cynically of the doctor treating his nightmare-ridden wife:

> Canst thou not minister to a mind diseased,
> Pluck from the memory a rooted sorrow,
> Raze out the written troubles of the brain,
> And with some sweet oblivious antidote
> Cleanse the stuffed bosom of that perilous stuff
> Which weighs upon the heart?

[4]   To which the doctor can only reply humbly:

> Therein the patient
> Must minister to himself.

[5]   Three centuries after Shakespeare, when doctors began to "minister to a mind diseased," they did it without any "sweet oblivious antidote," without any potion, nostrum, or material device. To reach the mind the laws of matter were insufficient; the mind itself had to be the tool. Doctors began to talk to patients and, more important, to listen while patients talked. In place of the physician's stethoscope and the clinician's test tube we had the psychiatrist's couch.

[6]   Physical scientists have been strongly tempted to leave it at that and to make no move toward the mentally disturbed person upon the psychiatrist's couch. To approach the vast complexities of the mind with the cold, material instruments of science required a kind of heroism. There was a grim promise of inevitable failure about the fire-breathing dragon of mind-chemistry that tended to daunt the would-be St. George of the microscope and the slide rule.

[7]   And yet the brain is made up of atoms and molecules — as is the rest of the body. The molecules in the cells of the body, and in those of the brain in particular, are so many and so various and so versatile that they interact and change in a dazzling pattern that we do not, as yet, understand well. But the very dazzle of this chemical complexity is hopeful, for it is, quite conceivably, complex enough to account for all the nearly infinite subtlety of what we call the mind.

[8]   This complexity is now being tackled by new techniques that are making top news out of advances in brain chemistry and physiology. Computers are being used to analyze brain-wave data with a completeness never before possible. Greater understanding of nucleic acids in connection with the machinery of heredity is producing exciting hints concerning the mechanics of memory.

[9]   Most of all, new drugs are being used that affect the workings of the brain, sometimes drastically, and by that very fact are giving us possible insights into these workings. It is this last technique that has been creating the most stir, for it involves, among other things, the compound called LSD, which offers mankind a new dimension in drug use and drug consequence.

[10]   The new advances, striking as they do at the most subtle manifestations of the brain—memory, perception, reason—do not come from nowhere. There is a century of advance in connection with the less complex aspects of brain action. Although the nervous system is an intricately interlaced whole on almost every level of its activity, it shows, in some respects, a sort of gradually increasing complexity of function from the bottom upward. This has helped scientists move onward by easy stages until now they can reasonably try to cope with the mental machinery that knits together all levels of the nervous system.

[11]   Below the brain is the spinal cord, a narrow 18-inch-long mass of nerve tissue that runs down the center of the bones making up the spinal column. The spinal cord is a switching center for many of our common reflexes. Touch something hot and the sensation sparks its way to the cord and is converted into an outward-surging nerve impulse calling for a quick withdrawal. Your finger moves away even before your conscious mind has a chance to say, "It's hot."

[12]   (Mind you, this is not to say that this is *all* the spinal cord does. It is knit by nerve tracts to the various centers of the brain and it forms part of a unified whole. However, it is this reflex action that was first understood, and I am deliberately over-simplifying to get across the historical perspective.)

[13]   At its upper end the spinal cord widens into the medulla oblongata, or "brain stem," upon which the brain itself sits like a swollen piece of wrinkled fruit. The brain stem handles matters that are more complicated than the simple reflexes. It is an important center for the control of the manner in which we stand, for instance.

[14]   In standing, we are actively using muscles to keep our back and legs stiff against the pull of gravity. To do this efficiently, there must be a constant, delicately adjusted interplay. No one set of muscles is allowed to overbalance us to one side or another without a countering set being quickly thrown in to readjust the balance accurately. We are not ordinarily aware of this activity, but if we have been standing a long time, weariness makes itself unpleasantly evident, and if we lose consciousness while standing, the muscles relax and we crumple to the ground at once.

[15] If it were our conscious mind that were continually concerned with the muscles involved in standing, we would have little time for anything else. It is the brain stem that is in charge, however, with scarcely any conscious interference. We remain standing, balancing ourselves accurately, no matter how distracted we are, no matter how lost in thought, provided only that we are not actually asleep or unconscious.

[16] Above the brain stem are two swollen bodies with wrinkled surfaces, each divided nearly in half. The larger is the cerebrum (the Latin word for brain); the smaller, in the rear, is the cerebellum (little brain).

[17] The cerebellum goes one step beyond the brain stem. It does more than keep us balanced while motionless; it keeps us balanced in motion. While we walk, we lift one leg, throw ourselves off balance temporarily and then move the leg forward and bring it to a halt upon the ground in just the manner calculated to retrieve that balance. If we move our hand toward a pencil, that hand must begin to slow before it reaches the pencil and must come to a halt just as it reaches it.

[18] There must be "feedback." We must see (or otherwise sense) the motion of a portion of our body, estimate its distance from its goal and adjust its speed and direction constantly on the basis of the changing situation. It is the cerebellum that is in charge of this. It takes care of the matter automatically, so that if we reach for a pencil we seize it with perfect efficiency, without any awareness of the delicacy of the task. But watch someone with cerebral palsy who cannot manage this feedback. He is unable to perform the slightest task without a pathetic overshooting and undershooting of the mark.

[19] In accomplishing all this, incoming sensations must produce chemical changes in the brain cells which, in turn, give rise to nerve impulses that produce specific muscle responses. What the details of these chemical changes might be we don't know.

[20] As we come to the cerebrum we find ourselves more directly involved with chemistry. At the bottom of the cerebrum, for instance, is a section called the hypothalamus, one of the functions of which is to act as a thermostat. The body's heat is produced through a constant gentle vibration of the muscles at a rate of from seven to thirteen times per second, a fact reported in 1962. The hypothalamus senses the temperature of the blood passing through it. If that temperature is too low, it sparks an increase in the vibration rate, producing additional heat. If the temperature is too high, the vibration rate is lowered. This is one way in which body heat is maintained at almost constant level despite changes in outside temperature.

[21] The hypothalamus also detects the water concentration in the blood and acts through a nearby gland, the pituitary, to adjust the workings of the kidney accordingly. More water is eliminated if the blood is getting too thin; less water, if it is too thick. The hypothalamus is also constantly measuring the sugar concentration in the blood. When that concentration falls too low, the hypothalamus acts to set up hunger sensations.

[22] Here we have clearer examples of actual chemical involvement. Small

(as yet harmless) chemical changes in the blood call forth alterations in the body's mechanism to prevent any further (and increasingly harmful) changes in that direction. The body's chemistry is thus kept in accurate balance.

[23] The details must be extraordinarily complex, however. The body's mechanism is intricately interconnected, and the hypothalamus must bring about desiable changes in one part of that supercomplicated network without bringing about undesirable changes elsewhere. The difficulty here is exemplified by the manner in which almost every man-applied drug, despite the most careful use, has always the possibility of bringing on unpleasant "side effects." The hypothalamus must work with the kind of incredible sure-footedness that avoids side effects.

[24] But what about the upper parts of the cerebrum — the parts particularly concerned with conscious motion and sensations, with thought and reason, memory and imagination? If we are stumped by the chemistry of such things as reflexes and water balance, surely we must be completely, hopelessly, and helplessly at sea in connection with the chemistry of memory, for instance?

[25] In fact, we are not. We are actually making progress, or seem to be, in the understanding of memory, and the most exciting prospects may be looming on the far horizon.

[26] And it is not only the reasonably healthy mind that is in question. What we call mental disorders may simply be shifts in the chemical workings of brain. If mental disease is a material malfunction, then through the study of brain chemistry we may well find the cures that have steadily eluded the psychiatrists.

[27] Consider schizophrenia, for instance — the most common of the serious mental illnesses. The name was coined in 1911 by a Swiss psychiatrist, Paul E. Bleuler, from the Greek words meaning "split mind" because it was frequently noted that persons suffering from this disease seemed to be dominated by one set of ideas (or "complex") to the exclusion of others, as though the mind's harmonious workings had been disrupted and split, with one portion of that split mind seizing control of the rest. An older name for the disease was dementia praecox ("early ripening madness"), a term intended to differentiate it from senile dementia, mental illness affecting the old through the deterioration of the brain with age. Schizophrenia shows itself at a comparatively early age, generally between 18 and 28.

[28] Schizophrenia may exist in several varieties, depending on which complex predominates. It may be hebephrenic ("childish mind"), where one prominent symptom is childish or silly behavior. It may be catatonic ("toning down"), in which behavior is indeed toned down and the patient seems to withdraw from participation in the objective world, becoming mute and rigid. It may also be paranoid ("madness"), characterized by extreme hostility and suspicion, with feelings of persecution.

[29] At least half of all patients in mental hospitals are schizophrenics of

these or other types, and it is estimated that one percent of mankind is affected. This means that there are at least 30 million schizophrenics in the world, a figure equal to the total population of a nation like Spain.

[30] Can this most common variety of the mind diseased be treated by "some sweet oblivious antidote"?

[31] There are precedents that give us ground for hope. Some mental illnesses have already been cured, and the mind has shown itself amenable to physical treatment — in certain cases at least.

[32] One example is pellagra, a disease once very common in Mediterranean lands and in our own South. It was characterized by what were called the three D's: diarrhea, dermatitis, and dementia. As it turned out, pellagra was caused by a vitamin deficiency, the lack of niacin in the diet. Once niacin was supplied to patients in the necessary quantities the disease cleared up. Not only did the diarrhea stop, not only was the red, inflamed, roughened skin restored to normal, but the mental disorders ceased. The same chemical that healed the body healed the mind. In this instance, at least, it was a case of matter over mind.

[33] Pellagra is caused by a failure of supplies from outside. But what about malfunctions caused by inadequacies in the body's own chemical machinery? Every chemical reaction in the body is controlled by complex substances known as enzymes; each reaction has its own particular enzyme. What, then, if a person is born without the ability to manufacture some particular enzyme?

[34] This is the situation in cases of a disease called phenylpyruvic oligophrenia, which is characterized by serious mental deficiency. This disease (not common, fortunately) is present at birth. A child is born without the ability to make a certain enzyme that brings about the conversion of a substance called phenylalanine into another called tyrosine. The phenylalanine, unable to follow its normal course, changes into other, abnormal substances. These abnormal substances accumulate and interfere with brain chemistry.

[35] Here, unfortunately, the situation cannot be corrected as simply as in the case of pellagra. Although it is easy to supply a missing vitamin, it is as yet impossible to supply a missing enzyme. However, some improvement in mental condition has been reported among patients with the disease who have been kept on a diet low in phenylalanine.

[36] Is it possible, then, that schizophrenia is also the result of a chemical failure, either from without or within? Dr. A. Hoffer at the University Hospital in Saskatoon, Canada, has been treating schizophrenia for years by the administration of large doses of niacin and has been reporting considerable success. Apparently at least some forms of schizophrenia are a vitamin-deficiency disease rather like a more serious pellagra.

[37] It takes more niacin to handle schizophrenia than pellagra, and Hoffer suggests a reason for this. Niacin is converted in the body into a more complex substance called NAD, which is what really does the work. The normal

body can form NAD out of niacin easily and quickly if the latter is present in the diet. (Hence pellagra is cured as soon as small quantities of niacin are added to the otherwise deficient diet.) But the schizophrenic may have a disordered chemistry, characterized in part by the inability to form NAD easily. Therefore, a great deal of niacin must be supplied as a means of seeing to it that the inefficient chemical machinery produces at least a little NAD.

[38] Hoffer reports that in the first half of 1966 he tried administration of NAD, ready-made, with very hopeful results. Smaller doses produced more rapid improvement. (As is usual in the case of experimental treatments on the border of the known, there have also been reports from other laboratories that NAD treatment has proven disappointing.)

[39] The chemical failure in the case of the schizophrenic (whether it is the inability to make NAD out of niacin, or something else altogether) is apparently something that is inherited; for certainly the tendency to develop the disease is inherited. The chance of a particular individual in the general population developing schizophrenia is about 1 in 100. If, however, a person has a brother or sister who is schizophrenic, he has a one in seven chance of becoming schizophrenic himself. If he has an identical twin who is schizophrenic, his own chances rise to three in four.

[40] People aren't usually born with schizophrenic symptoms to be sure; it is not inborn in the sense that phenylpyruvic oligophrenia is. We might put it this way: The schizophrenic is born not with a part of his chemical machinery missing but rather with a part that is fragile and wears out relatively early in life. It is the fragility of the part that is inherited.

[41] But what is it that NAD (if it is NAD) does that keeps the body normal? What goes wrong in the body if NAD is missing?

[42] Suspicion has fallen upon a portion of the chemical scheme that begins with a substance called adrenalin. In very tiny quantities, adrenalin stimulates certain nerves controlling the heart beat, blood pressure, breathing rate and so on. The adrenal gland (a small bit of tissue over each kidney) has, as one of its functions, the secretion of adrenalin into the blood stream in times of stress. When we are angry or afraid, adrenalin is produced at once so that our blood pressure rises, our heart beats faster, our lungs pump more rapidly. We are placed on an emergency footing that fits us to fight or run.

[43] Naturally, it is important that, once the emergency is over, the body be returned to normal. For that reason the body has chemical devices for the rapid destruction of adrenalin. This destruction is supervised by an enzyme called amine oxidase, which combines with adrenalin and holds it still, so to speak, while it is altered into harmlessness.

[44] But suppose the enzyme is occupied in some other direction? Ordinarily, enzymes are quite specific; that is, they will deal only with certain molecules possessing one particular shape and will not work with any others. This is the "lock-and-key" view of enzyme-workings. A particular key will open a particular lock, and other keys will not do.

[45] Enzyme specificity is not perfect, however. An enzyme may combine with a molecule that is nearly but not quite the shape of the right one. The wrong molecule then competes with the right one for union with the enzyme, and if the enzyme is busy with the wrong molecule it cannot work with the right one, so that its action is inhibited. This phenomenon is called "competitive inhibition" and it can be serious indeed.

[46] When the enzyme unites with the right molecule, it performs a task upon it and lets go; but when it unites with the wrong one it may find itself more or less permanently stuck, like a wrong key jammed into a lock and broken off there. When that happens, even a tiny quantity of a wrong molecule can bring about a long-continued chemical disorder that may do permanent damage or even bring about death. Poisons generally work in this way.

[47] Perhaps, then, some enzyme, amine oxidase or some other, is subjected to competitive inhibition by something that is formed in the absence of NAD but not in its presence.

[48] The possibility that competitive inhibition is indeed involved is pointed up dramatically by the case of a cactus, native to the American Southwest, that contains the compound called mescaline. The mescaline molecule bears a general resemblance to adrenalin — apparently close enough to allow mescaline to interfere with amine oxidase. This kind of interference, even with a single enzyme, can have a widespread effect upon brain function. The chemical workings of the brain can be likened to a vast three-dimensional lacework, intricately interconnected. A jab or yank at any one portion is going to move and shift every other portion to one extent or another. Consequently, when the portions of the cactus containing mescaline are chewed, the adrenalin-destroying enzyme is occupied with the mescaline and the adrenalin accumulates, producing all sorts of effects. A person experiences sense perceptions that have no objective existence. Ordinary objects take on strange and bizarre overtones. In short, the mescaline produces hallucinations and is therefore a "hallucinogen."

[49] Furthermore, the reactions of the mescaline eater are inappropriate to the real universe. They depend on his distorted sense perceptions — and sometimes don't even match those. His behavior becomes peculiar and unpredictable. The Indians of the Southwest, experiencing all this when they ate the cactus, made the rather natural assumption that they were opening a door into a world beyond the common one of the ordinary senses. They made use of mescaline, therefore, in religious rites.

[50] Mescaline-induced behavior resembles that of schizophrenics, and it is natural to wonder if perhaps a chemical may be formed within the body which produces effects similar to those of mescaline. Perhaps the chemical is formed more easily in the case of NAD deficiency, so that people born with a tendency to develop inefficiencies in the NAD-manufacturing reactions will therefore be subjected to the effect of these chemicals.

[51] In the test tube, adrenalin can be easily altered to a slightly changed compound called adrenochrome. Adrenochrome, if injected into the blood stream, will also produce temporary bouts of schizophrenic-like behavior. To be sure, adrenochrome isn't formed in the normal body, but it might be in the schizophrenic.

[52] It became a matter of interest, then, to study and analyze in detail those portions of the schizophrenic body which could be easily obtained and tested—the blood, for instance, or the urine. Any substance that could be found in all schizophrenics and was not found in all, or almost all, non-schizophrenics would be instantly suspect.

[53] One way of testing body fluids is to use a technique called paper chromatography. Different kinds of molecules in the fluids are made to spread out and occupy separate spots on pieces of porous paper. These spots can then be made visible by allowing the molecules occupying them to undergo a chemical reaction that produces a colored material.

[54] In 1962, Arnold J. Friedhoff of New York University found that with a certain course of treatment a pink spot could be obtained from the urine of 15 out of 19 schizophrenics, but from not one of 14 nonschizophrenics.

[55] Similar tests have since been conducted on larger numbers of people. In one series of experiments, conducted by C. A. Clarke at the University of Liverpool, not one pink spot was found in tests on 265 healthy people—or on 126 people who were sick with diseases other than schizophrenia. Pink spots *were* found, however, with 46 out of 84 schizophrenics. Most of the schizophrenics who did not show the pink spot were of the paranoid variety. Among the nonparanoids, four out of every five showed it.

[56] And what was the pink spot? It turned out to be a chemical called dimethoxyphenylethylamine (DMPE), and its structure lies somewhere between adrenalin and mescaline!

[57] In other words, certain schizophrenics (whether for lack of NAD or some other cause) *form their own hallucinogens* and are, in effect, on a permanent mescaline kick.

[58] This is only a bare beginning in the physical-chemical attack on schizophrenia, but it is a hopeful beginning. The pink spot (and any other chemical giveaways that may turn up) can help doctors spot the oncoming of schizophrenia earlier than might otherwise be possible and at a time when therapy might be easier. By studying the chemical processes that give rise to the pink spot, the abnormal section of the chemical mechanism in a schizophrenic may be detected and treatment might then be sharpened.

[59] But adrenalin is not the only chemical that seems to be intimately concerned with the workings of the brain. There is also a substance called serotonin.

[60] Serotonin's importance was brought out most dramatically in connection with lysergic acid diethylamide, the now-famous LSD. LSD has a structure somewhat more complicated than serotonin, but chemists can easily

trace out a serotonin "backbone" in the LSD molecule. It is not surprising, then, that LSD may compete with serotonin for a particular enzyme as DMPE competes with adrenalin—and with the same results. In other words, the ingestion of LSD may lead to the accumulation of serotonin in the brain and the appearance of schizophrenic-like symptoms.

[61] This fact was discovered accidentally in 1943, when a chemist, Dr. Albert Hofmann, was working on LSD with some perfectly ordinary chemical purpose in mind. He must have gotten a few crystals on his fingertips and transferred them to his lips, for he fell into a dreamlike state that left him unable to work. He returned home and experienced a kind of drunken fantasy of hallucination. He suspected it was the LSD and the next day (with remarkable courage) he swallowed about a hundred-thousandth of an ounce of it, risking only what he thought was a small test dose. It was actually a large dose, as it happened, for a tenth that quantity would have been sufficient. The fantasies and hallucinations returned and the rest is history.

[62] Hofmann was completely normal after 24 hours, and he did no harm to himself or to others while he was under its influence. Unfortunately, this is not something we can rely on as a general rule. Each individual has a chemical machinery of his own, so that the effect of LSD will vary from one person to another. One will experience a mild case of fantasy, others a severe one; some will recover quickly, others much more slowly.

[63] The chemical machinery is, in some individuals, more fragile at particular key points than in others in the sense that it may be more prone to snap at those points. If the point in question is one which would produce schizophrenia if broken, taking LSD is certainly not an advisable experiment.

[64] Ordinarily, the fragile point in the chemical scheme might hold up quite well through a long lifetime of ordinary stress so that a person might be schizophrenia-prone, without ever developing schizophrenia. Yet under the powerful jab of LSD, the point gives, and what might be merely an unusual and temporary experience for someone else becomes a permanent and serious change in the man in question.

[65] Since none of us know just how firm some crucial part of our chemical fabric might be, using LSD without the greatest of professional care is a kind of mental Russian roulette. It is an invitation to temporary insanity for all—and possibly permanent insanity for some.

[66] LSD is an important tool for research into mental illness. It is by studying the causes of illness that we may work out the cure. We can see that from the medical researchers who, a century ago, were led to study dangerous bacteria in order to work out a cure for infectious disease. By and large they succeeded and it is to be hoped that the second half of the 20th century will be to mental disease what the second half of the 19th century was to infectious disease.

[67] But there is one important difference. College students in the late 19th century didn't think it was exciting fun to inject themselves with cholera bacilli.

EXERCISES

Questions

1. This essay was originally called "That Odd Chemical Complex, the Human Mind." Which is the better title? Why?
2. Asimov's theme is compactly expressed in paragraphs 7, 8, 9, and 66. Express the connection in your own words.
3. Halfway through the article, Dr. Asimov shifts from an analysis of parts of the nervous system to an analysis of schizophrenia and related chemical disorders in the brain. Is the unity of the article broken? In what ways is the shift in keeping with the article's basic theme?
4. To support his thesis, Asimov describes the spinal cord, the medulla oblongata, and the cerebellum. What characteristics do all three have in common?
5. What does knowledge of the cause and treatment of pellagra and phenylpyruvic oligophrenia contribute to our understanding of schizophrenia? Has research supported this suggested connection? Why should Asimov be so concerned about schizophrenia?
6. Use your dictionary to check Asimov's definition of schizophrenia and each of its various manifestations. How close is each definition to its derivation?
7. Make a list of the new facts you have learned about schizophrenia's causes, treatment and its incidence.
8. What is an hallucinogen? What makes mescaline work as an hallucinogen? What is the relationship between mescaline-induced behavior and schizophrenia?
9. How does LSD produce its hallucinogenic effect?
10. In what ways is taking LSD like Russian Roulette? Why is taking any drug hazardous in relation to the chemical machinery of the brain?
11. How does Asimov use illustration to make the function of the cerebellum clear? Find another example of the use of illustration as a clarifier.
12. One of the reasons this essay is easy to read is that Asimov does an excellent job of leading the reader from one idea to the next. What different methods of relating ideas does he use? Paragraph 26 serves as a transitional paragraph. What several elements does it connect? What does it introduce?
13. In paragraphs 13 and 14, Asimov explains the medulla oblongata. What techniques does he use to make this analysis clear? How does Asimov support the conclusion expressed in paragraph 57?
14. In paragraph 57, he forms a conclusion tying together evidence first begun in paragraph 27 with the introduction of the subject of schizophrenia, then reinforced in paragraph 36 with the discussion of mescaline's impact on the brain. Create an outline of paragraphs 27–58 to analyze the sturcture of the material presented.

Vocabulary

amenable   nostrum   transcends

For Discussion and Writing

1. The LSD kick of 1967
2. Mescaline, mushroom, and banana highs
3. Pep pills and tranquilizers: The polite drugs
4. After drugs, what? The search for kicks
5. Hallucinogens as used by primitives
6. Attitudes toward the mentally retarded
7. Treatment of the mentally ill in your state

CROSS REFERENCES

PLUMB: "A Drug Is a Drink Is a Smoke"
WECHSLER: "The I.Q. Is an Intelligent Test"

RECOMMENDED READING

HERSEY, JOHN: *Too Far to Walk* (Knopf: 1966)

DAVID WECHSLER

"THE I.Q. IS AN INTELLIGENT TEST"

INTRODUCTION

David Wechsler (1896–   ) is, very possibly, to the intelligence test what Sigmund Freud was to psychoanalysis: a great pioneer and a man of inestimable significance. He has been associated with Bellevue Hospital since 1952, and one of the world's foremost intelligence tests bears their name jointly: the Wechsler-Bellevue Intelligence Scale for Adult Measurement. For over 25 years, Dr. Wechsler has also been on the faculty of the New York University College of Medicine. In 1949, he devised the Wechsler Intelligence Scale for Children.

TO THE READER

After discounting the various attacks on I.Q. tests, Wechsler defines intelligence and explains the purpose of testing.

It is now two years since the New York City school system eliminated the I.Q. from pupils' records. Banned under the pressure of groups that claimed the I.Q. was unfair to the culturally deprived, it has been replaced by achievement tests. Meanwhile, a great deal of effort is being put into developing new, nonverbal scales to measure schoolchildren's abilities while eliminating the troublesome factor of language.

[2] Neither of these substitutes is an adequate replacement for the I.Q. In my opinion, the ban was misdirected in the first place and we should restore the I.Q. to its former position as a diagnostic tool as soon as possible. The substitutes simply do not test enough of the abilities that go to make up individual intelligence.

[3] To understand what I.Q. tests do, and why they are valuable, we must first be clear about what intelligence is. This is a surprisingly thorny issue. Too much depends upon how one defines intelligence. In this respect psychologists are in no better agreement than the lay public. Divergency of view stems largely from differences in emphasis on the particular abilities thought to be central to the definition one envisages. Thus, an educator may define intelligence primarily as the ability to learn, a biologist in terms of ability to adapt, a psychologist as the ability to reason abstractly and the practical layman as just common sense.

[4] One difficulty is similar to what a physicist encounters when asked to state what he means by energy, or a biologist what he means by life. The fact is that energy and life are not tangible entities; you cannot touch them or see them under a microscope even though you are able to describe them. We know them by their effects or properties.

[5] The same is true of general intelligence. For example, we must assume that there is something common to learning to count, avoiding danger and playing chess which makes it possible for us to say that they are evidence of intelligent behavior, as against learning to walk, being accident prone and playing bingo, which seemingly have little if anything to do with it.

[6] Intelligence, operationally defined, is the aggregate[1] capacity of the individual to act purposefully, to think rationally and to deal effectively with his environment. Although it is not a mere sum of intellectual abilities, the only way we can evaluate it quantitatively is by the measurement of various aspects of these abilities.

[7] Any test is primarily a device for eliciting and evaluating a fragment of behavior. An intelligence test is one by which an examiner seeks to appraise this bit of behavior insofar as it may be called intelligent. Various abilities can be used for this purpose because manifestations of ability are the means by which a subject can communicate and demonstrate his competences. To this end it is not so much the particular ability that is tested which is important, as the degree to which it correlates with posited[2] criteria. A test is considered a good measure of intelligence if it correlates, for example, with learning ability, ability to comprehend, evidence of ca-

[1]total; combined
[2]postulated: assumed without proof

pacity to adjust and so on. If it does so to a satisfactory degree it is said to be valid. But, even when a test has been established as valid, there still remains a question: For what class of subjects is it valid? The answer will depend in a large measure upon the population on which the test was standardized — for example, middle-class white children, Southern Negro children or recently arrived Puerto Ricans.

[8]   Thus I.Q. tests are attacked on the ground that they are overweighted with items depending on verbal ability and academic information. Individuals with limited educational backgrounds are obviously penalized, and non-English-speaking subjects are admittedly incapable of taking the tests at all. This is an important stricture[3] and test makers, contrary to some opinion, are fully aware of it. One way of "solving" the problem would be to provide separate normal or average scores for different populations, but apart from the practical difficulty of obtaining such norms, there is always the stricture that they bypass rather than meet the central issue. A compromise approach is practiced in some school systems, where intelligence tests continue to be used — under the more acceptable name of "aptitude tests."

[9]   Almost from the start, psychologists have sought to cope with the problem of literacy and language disability by devising nonverbal tests of intelligence. Thus, soon after the Binet tests were introduced more than a half-century ago, two American psychologists, Pintner and Paterson, developed the Non-Language Individual Performance Scale for non-English-speaking subjects. Similarly, when the Army Alpha (the main verbal test of World War I) was devised for the military services, a companion non-verbal test (the Army Beta) was prepared along with it.

[10] The Pintner-Paterson scale required the subject to give evidence of his capacities by filling in appropriate missing parts on familiar pictures, putting together form boards, learning to associate signs with symbols, etc. The Army Beta consisted of such tasks as following mazes, reproducing picture designs, counting cubes, etc. — with directions presented to the subject by gesture or mime

[11] Many similar tests — the so-called "culture-free" or "culture-fair" tests — have followed. The most recent one reported is the Johns Hopkins Perceptual Test devised by Dr. Leon Rosenberg and associates at the Johns Hopkins School of Medicine. This test was initially developed for children who did not speak or who were handicapped by certain functional or organic disorders; it has also been recommended as a more effective intelligence test for the very young and for culturally deprived children.

[12] The Johns Hopkins Perceptual Test consists of a series of designs from which a child is asked to choose appropriate patterns to match others shown to him. Its primary merit is that it eliminates the factor of language. It is also claimed to be less dependent than verbal tests upon acquired skills,

[3]a remark or comment, especially an adverse criticism

which, of course, depend to some extent upon a child's environmental experience. But this test, like other performance tests, does not measure a sufficient number of the abilities that go to make up the total picture of intelligent behavior.

[13] Contrary to claims, the results of performance tests have been generally disappointing. The findings indicate that while they may be useful in certain situations, and for certain diagnostic groups, they prove quite unsatisfactory as alternates for verbal scales. They correlate poorly with verbal aptitudes and are poor prognosticators[4] of over-all learning ability as well as school achievement. Above all, they have turned out to be neither culture-free nor culture-fair.

[14] Culture-free tests fail to attain their end because, in the first place, the items usually employed are themselves subject to particular environmental experiences. A circle in one place may be associated with the sun, in another with a copper coin, in still another with a wheel. In some places a dog is a pet, in others a detested animal. Pictures, in the long run, are just symbols and these may be as difficult to understand and recognize as words; they have to be interpreted, as anyone who has attempted to learn sign language knows. Putting together blocks may be a challenge or a threat, working fast a sign of carelessness or an incentive to competition. Nonverbal, even more than verbal tests, need to be related to particular environments and, from a practical point of view, are both limited in range and difficult to contrive.

[15] Finally, many performance items when increased in difficulty tend to become measures of special abilities rather than having any significant correlation with over-all measures of intelligence. Thus, while tests of visual motor coordination may be useful items on intelligence tests for young children they are no longer effective at later ages. Copying a diamond is a good test at the 7-year level, but whether a child of 12 can reproduce a complicated design has little to do with his general intelligence and represents at most a special ability.

[16] The effect of culture on test performance is a subject that demands serious concern, but here one deals with the problem of what one understands by the word "culture." In the United States there is a strong trend among contemporary writers to identify the term with socio-economic levels. This is in contrast to the historic and broader meaning of the term, which covers all human as well as environmental influences that serve to characterize the intellectual and moral status of a civilization.

[17] Not all the poor are culturally deprived. Although standards may differ widely, "culturally different" does not mean "culturally deprived." The Jews and Italians who lived on the Lower East Side had their culture, and so have the Negroes in the slums of Harlem. They differ widely in re-

---

[4]predictors

spect to almost any variable one might employ, and culture is no exception. What this implies is that "culture" no more than color of skin should be a basis for assessing individuals.

[18] The comments relating to the question of cultural impact apply with equal force to the problem of racial and national differences. One may start with the hypothesis that such differences exist and not necessarily be overwhelmed by their importance. This, in the writer's opinion, is a reasonable position.

[19] This opinion is based on studies done in the field and, in particular, on data from World War I and World War II United States Armed Forces testing programs. The data from World War I included not only tables for the over-all draft population but for a great many subgroupings. Among these were separate test-score summaries according to national origin of the draftees, and a particularly detailed one comparing Negroes and whites. As might have been expected, differences between groups compared were found, and as might also have been expected invidious comparisons were immediately made and exploited. Particularly emphasized were the lower scores made by Negroes as compared with those made by white soldiers. Neglected, on the other hand, were the differences found between occupational levels and the more general ones between urban and rural populations.

[20] It was not too difficult to correct the erroneous inferences made by the racists.[5] But, in disposing of the racial claims, some authors went much beyond what the data warranted. Eventually, statements were made that other test findings revealed no significant differences between any national or racial groups—a fact which is equally questionable, and in any event still needs to be demonstrated. In the author's opinion, national and racial differences do exist—probably of both genetic and environmental origins, in varying degree. But the fact is that these differences are not large or relevant in the individual case.

[21] We now come to the biggest bugaboo of intelligence testing—the I.Q. itself. The scientific literature on it is as large as its assailants are numerous. It has been attacked by educators, parents, writers of popular articles and politicians. During the Korean War it was investigated by Congress. Now that we are once more having trouble with draft quotas, the I.Q. will most likely be investigated again. It is doubtful whether the I.Q. can be brought into good grace at this time, but perhaps much of the fire sparked by the I.Q. can be quenched by an objective explanation of what it really is.

[22] An I. Q. is just a measure of relative brightness. It merely asserts that, compared with persons of his own age group, an individual has attained a certain rank on a particular intelligence test. For example, a 10-year-old

[5]those who believe that human races have distinctive characteristics that determine their respective cultures, usually involving the idea that one's own race is superior and has the right to rule others.

takes the Stanford-Binet test and attains a certain score, which happens to be that for the statistically average 8-year-old. We then divide the child's mental age (8) by his chronological age (10) and obtain a quotient, which we multiply by 100 simply to remove the inconvenience of decimal points. The result is called the Intelligence Quotient (or I.Q.)—in this case, 80. This particular figure tells us that, as compared with others in his age group, the child has performed below normal (which would be 100).

[23] When this procedure of comparative grading is applied to a geography or bookkeeping test—when a teacher apportions class grades on a bell curve or a sliding scale—nobody gets excited. But when it is used with a mental test the reaction is quite different.

[24] Opposition is generally focused not on the way that I.Q.'s are computed, but, more pointedly, on the way they are interpreted and utilized. One interpretation that has caused understandable concern is the notion that a person is "born with" an I.Q. which remains immutable.[6] This is an allegation proclaimed by those who are opposed to the I.Q. rather than a view maintained by psychologists. What is asserted by psychologists, and supported by test-retest findings, is that I.Q.'s once accurately established are not likely to vary to any considerable degree. This does not mean that an I.Q. never changes, or that the conditions under which it was obtained may not have affected its validity.

[25] The so-called constancy of the I.Q. is relative, but compared with other commonly used indexes, it is surprisingly stable. It is much more stable, for instance, than an individual's electrocardiogram or his basal metabolism level, which are accepted without question.

[26] There are always exceptional cases which cannot be overlooked or bypassed. But one does not throw out the baby with the bath water. When for any reason a subject's I.Q. is suspect, the sensible thing to do is to have him retested. I.Q.'s, unlike the laws of the Medes and the Persians, are not irrevocable, but they should be respected.

[27] While retest studies show that I.Q.'s are relatively stable, they also reveal that in individual cases large changes may occur—as much as 20 points or more. Thus, conceivably, an individual could move from the "dull normal" group to "average," or vice versa.

[28] Much depends upon the age at which the original test was administered and the interval between testings. In general, I.Q.'s obtained before the age of 4 or 5 are more likely to show discrepancies between test and retest; those in the middle years least. Discrepancies are also likely to be larger as the intervals between retests increase. All this evidence points to reasons for not making a definitive intelligence classification on the basis of a single test, and more especially on one administered at an early age. This precaution is necessary not because the tests are unreliable but

[6]unchangeable, unalterable

because rates of mental maturity are often factors that have to be taken into account. Such variations tend not only to penalize slow developers but also to overrate early bloomers.

[29] Various skills are required for effective test performance at different age levels. The fact that they are not present at a particular age level does not indicate that a child who lacks them is necessarily stunted. It may only be that these skills have not as yet emerged. Early training has a bearing on test readiness, but it is not true that if a child has not had this training at one age, he will not develop the skills required at a later age. On the other hand, deliberately teaching a child skills in order to have him "pass" an intelligence test, as now seems to be the vogue, is not the answer to acquiring a high I.Q.

[30] An important conclusion to be drawn from the above is that more, rather than less, testing is needed. Unfortunately, when this is suggested, one encounters the objection that extended testing programs in public schools would be too costly. The expensiveness of school testing has been greatly exaggerated, especially when considered in relation to the over-all cost of keeping a child in school (an average of $600 to $700 per child per year in most parts of the country).

[31] Particularly neglected is the individual intelligence examination, which at present is administered in most public schools only to "problem cases." In the author's opinion, an individual intelligence examination ought to be given to all children as they enter school. Most private schools require such an examination, and there is good reason why the public schools should also provide it.

[32] Allowing $50 per examination administered once over a four-year period, the cost would be a minuscule addition to the school's budget. In return, a systematic individual examination could serve as a means of evaluating a child's assets and liabilities before he was subjected to the hazards of arbitrary placement. Finally, it must be borne in mind that intelligence tests are intended as a means not merely for detecting the intellectually retarded, but also for discovering the intellectually gifted.

[33] In discussions of the merits and limitations of intelligence tests, one important aspect, frequently overlooked, is their basic aim. This objective is most effectively summed up in the late Prof. Irving Lorge's definition of what intelligence tests aim to measure — namely, "the ability to learn and to solve the tasks required by a particular environment."

[34] This definition implies a multiple approach to the concept of intelligence and intelligence testing. In the latter process, one is of necessity engaged in evaluating an individual's particular abilities. Of course, in doing so, one obtains information regarding a subject's liabilities and handicaps. This information is both useful and important, but is really only an incidental aspect of what one wishes to discover from an intelligence test.

[35] When it is asserted that intelligence tests are unfair to the disadvan-

taged and minorities, one must be mindful of the fact that they are simply recording the unfairness of life. They show also, for example, that our mental abilities, whoever we may be, decline with advancing age. (Of course, this decline is in many cases counterbalanced by increased experience.)

[36] Intelligence tests were not devised for the handicapped alone but for everybody. What then can be the reason for believing they may not be suitable for the major segments of our population—or for prohibiting their administration to the majority of children in a school system? The current New York City I.Q. ban is a case in point, and especially discouraging when one sees what is being used instead.

[37] The tests that have been substituted are a series of achievement tests—in particular, reading tests. Of all the possible choices, one can hardly imagine a worse alternative. For all areas in which the disadvantaged child is handicapped, reading heads the list. The main difference between an intelligence (or aptitude) test and an achievement test is that the former is less tied to curriculum content. If it is true that a low score on an intelligence test presents a misleading picture of a pupil's learning capacity, how much more unfair would be an even lower score on an achievement test. It is possible that the I.Q. was banned in New York because those who supported the ban wished primarily to combat what they believed to be a widespread view that the I.Q. is "somehow a fixed, static and genetic measure of learning ability." One may wonder, however, whether political pressures may not have played some role in the decision—and one may hope that the ban will soon be retracted.

[38] The I.Q. has had a long life and will probably withstand the latest assaults on it. The most discouraging thing about them is not that they are without merit, but that they are directed against the wrong target. It is true that the results of intelligence tests, and of others, too, are unfair to the disadvantaged, deprived and various minority groups but it is not the I.Q. that has made them so. The culprits are poor housing, broken homes, a lack of basic opportunities, etc., etc. If the various pressure groups succeed in eliminating these problems, the I.Q.'s of the disadvantaged will take care of themselves.

EXERCISES

Questions

1. In what way does Dr. Wechsler's title serve as his thesis? Does the article support the title?
2. Why is intelligence so hard to define? How is this difficulty related to recent criticism regarding the verbal nature of I.Q. tests?

3. What is a nonverbal test? a culture-free test? What is the basic failure of the culture-free test? What is the chief drawback of the performance test?

4. What is the chief failure in the use of the word "culture," especially as it relates to the cliché "culturally deprived"? What term does Dr. Wechsler use that is more accurate? Why?

5. What is the I.Q.? How is it attained? What is its relevance?

6. What is the I.Q. test? What is the aim of an I.Q. test?

7. Dr. Wechsler refutes, in several ways, the idea that an I.Q. is fixed from birth. What are his refutations? What exceptions does he indicate? What conclusions does he draw from this?

8. What are the values of giving every school child an individual I.Q. test? What is the chief drawback of substituting achievement tests, especially reading tests, for the I.Q.?

9. This essay relies on definition. In paragraph 6, intelligence is defined. Does the definition take into account the separate factors indicated in paragraph 3? Reread paragraphs 6, 7, and 22. What devices of definition are used to promote clarity?

Vocabulary

allegation
assessing
envisages
invidious
miniscule

For Discussion and Writing

1. Taking tests when emotionally upset
2. The environment of poverty and the I.Q.
3. The Hot Lunch Program in the schools
4. Cultural loading of I.Q. tests
5. High school dropouts: Who are they?

CROSS REFERENCES

ASIMOV: "Matter over Mind"
COUSINS: "The Environment of Language"
FRIED: "A Four-Letter Word That Hurts"

JAMES HARVEY ROBINSON

"ON VARIOUS KINDS
OF THINKING"

INTRODUCTION

James Harvey Robinson (1863–1936), dead now more than three decades, had the kind of mind that is perpetually modern. He held his doctorate in history and was Professor of History for twenty-seven years. He was also one of the organizers and lecturers of the New School for Social Research, a college that is still considered avant-garde in its course offerings. Among his books were: *The Humanizing of Knowledge* (1923); the two volume *History of Modern Europe* (1924, 1926); and his last book, with its prophetic title, *The Ordeal of Civilization* (1926). The following article, in a somewhat abridged form, was taken from a chapter in his most important book, *The Mind in the Making* (1921).

TO THE READER

Robinson presents four kinds of thinking arranged in order of the amount of conscious effort they require; all are different, but none entirely separate from the others.

The truest and most profound observations on Intelligence have in the past been made by the poets and, in recent times, by story-writers. They have been keen observers and recorders and reckoned freely with the emotions and sentiments. Most philosophers, on the other hand, . . . thought of mind as having to do exclusively with conscious thought. It was that within man which perceived, remembered, judged, reasoned, understood, believed, willed. But of late it has been shown that we are unaware of a great part of what we perceive, remember, will, and infer[1]; and that a great part of the thinking of which we are aware is determined by that of which we are not conscious. . . .

[2]   The insufficient elimination of the foul and decaying products of digestion may plunge us into deep melancholy, whereas a few whiffs of nitrous monoxide may exalt us to the seventh heaven of supernal knowledge and godlike complacency. And *vice versa*, a sudden word or thought may cause our heart to jump, check our breathing, or make our knees as water. There is a whole new literature growing up which studies the effects of our bodily secretions and our muscular tensions and their relation to our emotions and our thinking.

[3]   Then there are hidden impulses and desires and secret longings of which we can only with the greatest difficulty take account. They influence our conscious thought in the most bewildering fashion. Many of these unconscious influences appear to originate in our very early years. The older philosophers seem to have forgotten that even they were infants and children at their most impressionable age and never could by any possibility get over it.

[4]   The term "unconscious," now so familiar to all readers of modern works on psychology, gives offense to some adherents of the past. There should, however, be no special mystery about it. It is . . . simply a collective word to include all the physiological changes which escape our notice, all the forgotten experiences and impressions of the past which continue to influence our desires and reflections and conduct, even if we cannot remember them. What we can remember at any time is indeed an infinitesimal part of what has happened to us. We could not remember anything unless we forgot almost everything. As Bergson says, the brain is the organ of forgetfulness as well as of memory. Moreover, we tend, of course, to become oblivious to things to which we are thoroughly accustomed, for habit blinds us to their existence. So the forgotten and the habitual make up a great part of the so-called "unconscious."

[5]   We do not think enough about thinking, and much of our confusion is the result of current illusions in regard to it. Let us forget for the moment any impressions we may have derived from the philosophers, and see what seems to happen in ourselves. The first thing that we notice is that our

[1]derive by reasoning

thought moves with such incredible rapidity that it is almost impossible to arrest any specimen of it long enough to have a look at it. When we are offered a penny for our thoughts we always find that we have recently had so many things in mind that we can easily make a selection which will not compromise us too nakedly. On inspection we shall find that even if we are not downright ashamed of a great part of our spontaneous thinking it is far too intimate, personal, ignoble or trivial to permit us to reveal more than a small part of it. I believe this must be true of everyone. We do not, of course, know what goes on in other people's heads. They tell us very little and we tell them very little. . . . We find it hard to believe that other people's thoughts are as silly as our own, but they probably are.

[6]   We all appear to ourselves to be thinking all the time during our waking hours, and most of us are aware that we go on thinking while we are asleep, even more foolishly than when awake. When uninterrupted by some practical issue we are engaged in what is now known as a *reverie*. This is our spontaneous and favorite kind of thinking. We allow our ideas to take their own course and this course is determined by our hopes and fears, our spontaneous desires, their fulfillment or frustration; by our likes and dislikes, our loves and hates and resentments. There is nothing else anything like so interesting to ourselves as ourselves. All thought that is not more or less laboriously controlled and directed will inevitably circle about the beloved Ego. It is amusing and pathetic to observe this tendency in ourselves and in others. We learn politely and generously to overlook this truth, but if we dare to think of it, it blazes forth like the noontide sun.

[7]   The reverie or "free association of ideas" has of late become the subject of scientific research. While investigators are not yet agreed on the results, or at least on the proper interpretation to be given to them, there can be no doubt that our reveries form the chief index to our fundamental character. They are a reflection of our nature as modified by often hidden and forgotten experiences. We need not go into the matter further here, for it is only necessary to observe that the reverie is at all times a potent and in many cases an omnipotent rival to every other kind of thinking. It doubtless influences all our speculations in its persistent tendency to self-magnification and self-justification, which are its chief preoccupations, but it is the last thing to make directly or indirectly for honest increase of knowledge.*

---

*The poet-clergyman, John Donne, who lived in the time of James I, has given a beautifully honest picture of the doings of a saint's mind: "I throw myself down in my chamber and call in and invite God and His angels thither, and when they are there I neglect God and His angels for the noise of a fly, for the rattling of a coach, for the whining of a door. I talk on in the same posture of praying, eyes lifted up, knees bowed down, as though I prayed to God, and if God or His angels should ask me when I thought last of God in that prayer I cannot tell. Sometimes I find that I had forgot what I was about, but when I began to forget it I cannot tell. A memory of yesterday's pleasures, a fear of to-morrow's dangers, a straw under my knee, a noise in mine ear, a light in mine eye, an anything, a nothing, a fancy, a chimera in my brain troubles me in my prayer." — Quoted by ROBERT LYND, *The Art of Letters*, pp. 46–47.

[8]   The reverie, as any of us can see for himself, is frequently broken and interrupted by the necessity of a second kind of thinking. We have to make practical decisions. Shall we write a letter or no? Shall we take the subway or a bus? Shall we have dinner at seven or half past? Shall we buy U.S. Rubber or a Liberty Bond? Decisions are easily distinguishable from the free flow of the reverie. Sometimes they demand a good deal of careful pondering and the recollection of pertinent facts; often, however, they are made impulsively. They are a more difficult and laborious thing than the reverie, and we resent having to "make up our mind" when we are tired, or absorbed in a congenial reverie. Weighing a decision, it should be noted, does not necessarily add anything to our knowledge, although we may, of course, seek further information before making it.

Rationalizing

[9]   A third kind of thinking is stimulated when anyone questions our belief and opinions. We sometimes find ourselves changing our minds without any resistance or heavy emotion, but if we are told that we are wrong we resent the imputation[2] and harden our hearts. We are incredibly heedless in the formation of our beliefs, but find ourselves filled with an illicit passion for them when anyone proposes to rob us of their companionship. It is obviously not the ideas themselves that are dear to us, but our self-esteem, which is threatened. We are by nature stubbornly pledged to defend our own from attack, whether it be our person, our family, our property, or our opinion. A United States Senator once remarked to a friend of mine that God Almighty could not make him change his mind on our Latin-America policy. We may surrender, but rarely confess ourselves vanquished. In the intellectual world at least peace is without victory.

[10]   Few of us take the pains to study the origin of our cherished convictions; indeed, we have a natural repugnance to so doing. We like to continue to believe what we have been accustomed to accept as true, and the resentment aroused when doubt is cast upon any of our assumptions leads us to seek every manner of excuse for clinging to them. *The result is that most of our so-called reasoning consists in finding arguments for going on believing as we already do.*

[11]   I remember years ago attending a public dinner to which the Governor of the state was bidden. The chairman explained that His Excellency could not be present for certain "good" reasons; what the "real" reasons were the presiding officer said he would leave us to conjecture. This distinction between "good" and "real" reasons is one of the most clarifying and essential in the whole realm of thought. We can readily give what seem

[2]accusation

to us "good" reasons for being a Catholic or a Mason, a Republican or a Democrat, an adherent or opponent of the League of Nations. But the "real" reasons are usually on quite a different plane. Of course the importance of this distinction is popularly, if somewhat obscurely, recognized. The Baptist missionary is ready enough to see that the Buddhist is such . . .because he happened to be born in a Buddhist family in Tokio. But it would be treason to his faith to acknowledge that his own partiality for certain doctrines is due to the fact that his mother was a member of the First Baptist church of Oak Ridge. A savage can give all sorts of reasons for his belief that it is dangerous to step on a man's shadow, and a newspaper editor can advance plenty of arguments against the Bolsheviki. But neither of them may realize why he happens to be defending his particular opinion.

[12] The "real" reasons for our beliefs are concealed from ourselves as well as from others. As we grow up we simply adopt the ideas presented to us in regard to such matters as religion, family relations, property, business, our country, and the state. We unconsciously absorb them from our environment. They are persistently whispered in our ear by the group in which we happen to live. Moreover, as Mr. Trotter has pointed out, these judgments, being the product of suggestion and not of reasoning, have the quality of perfect obviousness, so that to question them

> . . . is to the believer to carry skepticism to an insane degree, and will be met by contempt, disapproval, or condemnation, according to the nature of the belief in question. When, therefore, we find ourselves entertaining an opinion about the basis of which there is a quality of feeling which tells us that to inquire into it would be absurd, obviously unnecessary, unprofitable, undesirable, bad form, or wicked, we may know that that opinion is a nonrational one, and probably, therefore, founded upon inadequate evidence.*

[13] Opinions, on the other hand, which are the result of experience or of honest reasoning do not have this quality of "primary certitude."[3] I remember when as a youth I heard a group of business men discussing the question of the immortality of the soul, I was outraged by the sentiment of doubt expressed by one of the party. As I look back now I see that I had at the time no interest in the matter, and certainly no least argument to urge in favor of the belief in which I had been reared. But neither my personal indifference to the issue, nor the fact that I had previously given it no attention, served to prevent an angry resentment when I heard *my* ideas questioned.

[14] This spontaneous and loyal support of our preconceptions—this process of finding "good" reasons to justify our routine beliefs—is known to modern psychologists as "rationalizing"—clearly only a new name for

---

*Instincts of the Herd, p. 44.
[3]freedom from doubt; certainty; confidence

a very ancient thing. Our "good" reasons ordinarily have no value in promoting honest enlightenment, because, no matter how solemnly they may be marshaled, they are at bottom the result of personal preference or prejudice, and not of an honest desire to seek or accept new knowledge.

[15] In our reveries we are frequently engaged in self-justification, for we cannot bear to think ourselves wrong, and yet have constant illustrations of our weaknesses and mistakes. So we spend much time finding fault with circumstances and the conduct of others, and shifting on to them with great ingenuity the onus[4] of our own failures and disappointments. *Rationalizing is the self-exculpation[5] which occurs when we feel ourselves, or our group, accused of misapprehension or error.*

[16] The little word *my* is the most important one in all human affairs, and properly to reckon with it is the beginning of wisdom. It has the same force whether it is *my* dinner, *my* dog, and *my* house, or *my* faith, *my* country, and *my* God. We not only resent the imputation that our watch is wrong, or our car shabby, but that our conception of the canals of Mars, of the pronunciation of "Epictetus," of the medicinal value of salicine, or the date of Sargon I, are subject to revision.

[17] Philosophers, scholars, and men of science exhibit a common sensitiveness in all decisions in which their *amour propre*[6] is involved. Thousands of argumentative works have been written to vent a grudge. However stately their reasoning, it may be nothing but rationalizing, stimulated by the most commonplace of all motives. A history of philosophy and theology could be written in terms of grouches, wounded pride, and aversions, and it would be far more instructive than the usual treatments of these themes. Sometimes, under Providence, the lowly impulse of resentment leads to great achievements. Milton wrote his treatise on divorce as a result of his troubles with his seventeen-year-old wife, and when he was accused of being the leading spirit in a new sect, the Divorcers, he wrote his noble *Areopagitica* to prove his right to say what he thought fit, and incidentally to establish the advantage of a free press in the promotion of Truth.

[18] All mankind, high and low, thinks in all the ways which have been described. The reverie goes on all the time not only in the mind of the mill hand and the Broadway flapper, but equally in weighty judges and godly bishops. It has gone on in all the philosophers, scientists, poets, and theologians that have ever lived. Aristotle's most abstruse speculations were doubtless tempered by highly irrelevant reflections. He is reported to have had very thin legs and small eyes, for which he doubtless had to find excuses, and he was wont to indulge in very conspicuous dress and rings and was accustomed to arrange his hair carefully.* Diogenes the Cynic exhibited

---

[4]burden
[5]clearing one's self from the charge of guilt
[6]self-esteem, self-respect, literally self-love
*Diogenes Laertius, book v.

the impudence of a touchy soul. His tub was his distinction. Tennyson in beginning his "Maud" could not forget his chagrin over losing his partimony years before as the result of an unhappy investment in the Patent Decorative Carving Company. These facts are not recalled here as a gratuitous disparagement[7] of the truly great, but to insure a full realization of the tremendous competition which all really exacting thought has to face, even in the minds of the most highly endowed mortals.

[19] And now the astonishing and perturbing suspicion emerges that perhaps almost all that had passed for social science, political economy, politics, and ethics in the past may be brushed aside by future generations as mainly rationalizing. John Dewey has already reached this conclusion in regard to philosophy* Veblen† and other writers have revealed the various unperceived presuppositions of the traditional political economy, and now comes an Italian sociologist, Vilfredo Pareto, who, in his huge treatise on general sociology, devotes hundreds of pages to substantiating a similar thesis affecting all the social sciences. This conclusion may be ranked by students of a hundred years hence as one of the several great discoveries of our age. It is by no means fully worked out, and it is so opposed to nature that it will be very slowly accepted by the great mass of those who consider themselves thoughtful. As a historical student I am personally fully reconciled to this newer view. Indeed, it seems to me inevitable that just as the various sciences of nature were, before the opening of the seventeenth century, largely masses of rationalizations to suit the religious sentiments of the period, so the social sciences have continued even to our own day to be rationalizations of uncritically accepted beliefs and customs.

[20] *It will become apparent as we proceed that the fact that an idea is ancient and that it has been widely received is no argument in its favor, but should immediately suggest the necessity of carefully testing it as a probable instance of rationalization.*

How Creative Thought Transforms the World

[21] This brings us to another kind of thought which can fairly easily be distinguished from the three kinds described above. It has not the usual qualities of the reverie, for it does not hover about our personal complacencies and humiliations. It is not made up of the homely decisions forced upon us by everyday needs, when we review our little stock of existing information, consult our conventional preferences and obligations, and make a choice of action. It is not the defense of our own cherished beliefs and prejudices just because they are our own — mere plausible excuses

---

[7]something that causes loss of dignity or reputation
Reconstruction in Philosophy.
†*The Place of Science in Modern Civilization.* [Thorstein Veblen (1857–1929): U.S. economist and sociologist]

for remaining of the same mind. On the contrary, it is that peculiar species of thought which leads us to *change* our mind.

[22] It is this kind of thought that has raised man from his pristine, sub-savage ignorance and squalor to the degree of knowledge and comfort which he now possesses. On his capacity to continue and greatly extend this kind of thinking depends his chance of groping his way out of the plight in which the most highly civilized peoples of the world now find themselves. In the past this type of thinking has been called Reason. But so many mis-apprehensions have grown up around the word that some of us have be-come very suspicious of it. I suggest, therefore, that we substitute a recent name and speak of "creative thought" rather than of Reason. *For this kind of meditation begets knowledge, and knowledge is really creative inasmuch as it makes things look different from what they seemed before and may indeed work for their reconstruction.*

[23] In certain moods some of us realize that we are observing things or making reflections with a seeming disregard of our personal preoccupa-tions. We are not preening or defending ourselves; we are not faced by the necessity of any practical decision, nor are we apologizing for believing this or that. We are just wondering and looking and mayhap seeing what we never perceived before.

[24] Curiosity is as clear and definite as any of our urges. We wonder what is in a sealed telegram or in a letter in which some one else is absorbed, or what is being said in the telephone booth or in low conversation. This inquisitiveness is vastly stimulated by jealousy, suspicion, or any hint that we ourselves are directly or indirectly involved. But there appears to be a fair amount of personal interest in other people's affairs even when they do not concern us except as a mystery to be unraveled or a tale to be told. The reports of a divorce suit will have "news value" for many weeks. They constitute a story, like a novel or play or moving picture. This is not an example of pure curiosity, however, since we readily identify ourselves with others, and their joys and despair then become our own.

[25] We also take note of, or "observe," as Sherlock Holmes says, things which have nothing to do with our personal interests and make no personal appeal either direct or by way of sympathy. This is what Veblen so well calls "idle curiosity." And it is usually idle enough. Some of us when we face the line of people opposite us in a subway train impulsively consider them in detail and engage in rapid inferences and form theories in regard to them. On entering a room there are those who will perceive at a glance the degree of preciousness of the rugs, the character of the pictures, and the personality revealed by the books. But there are many, it would seem, who are so absorbed in their personal reverie or in some definite purpose that they have no bright-eyed energy for idle curiosity. . . .

[26] Veblen, however, uses the term "idle curiosity" somewhat ironically, as is his wont. It is idle only to those who fail to realize that it may be a very rare and indispensable thing from which almost all distinguished hu-

man achievement proceeds. Since it may lead to systematic examination and seeking for things hitherto undiscovered. For research is but diligent search which enjoys the high flavor of primitive hunting. Occasionally and fitfully idle curiosity thus leads to creative thought, which alters and broadens our own views and aspirations and may in turn, under highly favorable circumstances, affect the views and lives of others, even for generations to follow. An example or two will make this unique human process clear.

[27] Galileo was a thoughtful youth and doubtless carried on a rich and varied reverie. He had artistic ability and might have turned out to be a musician or painter. When he had dwelt among the monks at Valambrosa he had been tempted to lead the life of a religious. As a boy he busied himself with toy machines and he inherited a fondness for mathematics. All these facts are of record. We may safely assume also that, along with many other subjects of contemplation, the Pisan maidens found a vivid place in his thoughts.

[28] One day when seventeen years old he wandered into the cathedral of his native town. In the midst of his reverie he looked up at the lamps hanging by long chains from the high ceiling of the church. Then something very difficult to explain occurred. He found himself no longer thinking of the building, worshipers, or the services; of his artistic or religious interests; of his reluctance to become a physician as his father wished. He forgot the question of a career and even the *graziosissime donne*. As he watched the swinging lamps he was suddenly wondering if mayhap their oscillations, whether long or short, did not occupy the same time. Then he tested this hypothesis by counting his pulse, for that was the only timepiece he had with him.

[29] This observation, however remarkable in itself, was not enough to produce a really creative thought. Others may have noticed the same thing and yet nothing came of it. Most of our observations have no assignable results. Galileo may have seen that the warts on a peasant's face formed a perfect isosceles triangle, or he may have noticed with boyish glee that just as the officiating priest was uttering the solemn words, *ecce agnus Dei*, a fly lit on the end of his nose. To be really creative, ideas have to be worked up and then "put over," so that they become a part of man's social heritage. The highly accurate pendulum clock was one of the later results of Galileo's discovery. He himself was led to reconsider and successfully to refute the old notions of falling bodies. It remained for Newton to prove that the moon was falling, and presumably all the heavenly bodies. This quite upset all the consecrated views of the heavens as managed by angelic engineers. The universality of the laws of gravitation stimulated the attempt to seek other and equally important natural laws and cast grave doubts on the miracles in which mankind had hitherto believed. In short, those who dared to include in their thought the discoveries of Galileo and his successors found themselves in a new earth surrounded by new heavens.

[30] On the 28th of October, 1831, three hundred and fifty years after Galileo had noticed the isochronous[8] vibrations of the lamps, creative thought and its currency had so far increased that Faraday was wondering what would happen if he mounted a disk of copper between the poles of a horseshoe magnet. As the disk revolved an electric current was produced. This would doubtless have seemed the idlest kind of an experiment to the stanch business men of the time, who, it happened, were just then denouncing the child-labor bills in their anxiety to avail themselves to the full of the results of earlier idle curiosity. But should the dynamos and motors which have come into being as the outcome of Faraday's experiment be stopped this evening, the business man of to-day, agitated over labor troubles, might, as he trudged home past lines of "dead" cars, through dark streets to an unlighted house, engage in a little creative thought of his own and perceive that he and his laborers would have no modern factories and mines to quarrel about had it not been for the strange practical effects of the idle curiosity of scientists, inventors, and engineers.

[31] The examples of creative intelligence given above belong to the realm of modern scientific achievement, which furnishes the most striking instances of the effects of scrupulous, objective thinking. But there are, of course, other great realms in which the recording and embodiment of acute observation and insight have wrought themselves into the higher life of man. The great poets and dramatists and our modern story-tellers have found themselves engaged in productive reveries, noting and artistically presenting their discoveries for the delight and instruction of those who have the ability to appreciate them.

[32] The process by which a fresh and original poem or drama comes into being is doubtless analogous[9] to that which originates and elaborates so-called scientific discoveries; but there is clearly a temperamental difference. The genesis and advance of painting, sculpture, and music offer still other problems. We really as yet know shockingly little about these matters, and indeed very few people have the least curiosity about them.* Nevertheless, creative intelligence in its various forms and activities is what makes man. Were it not for its slow, painful, and constantly discouraged operations through the ages man would be no more than a species of primate living on seeds, fruit, roots, and uncooked flesh, and wandering naked through the woods and over the plains like a chimpanzee.

    •   •   •   •   •   •

[33] We have now examined the various classes of thinking which we

---

[8]equal or uniform in time; characterized by motions or vibrations of equal duration
[9]corresponding in some particulars
*Recently a re-examination of creative thought has begun as a result of new knowledge which discredits many of the notions formerly held about "reason." See, for example, *Creative Intelligence,* by a group of American philosophic thinkers; John Dewey, *Essays in Experimental Logic* (both pretty hard books); and Veblen, *The Place of Science in Modern Civilization.* Easier than these and very stimulating are Dewey, *Reconstruction in Philosophy,* and Woodworth, *Dynamic Psychology.*

can readily observe in ourselves and which we have plenty of reasons to believe go on, and always have been going on, in our fellow-men. We can sometimes get quite pure and sparkling examples of all four kinds, but commonly they are so confused and intermingled in our reverie as not to be readily distinguishable. The reverie is a reflection of our longings, exultations, and complacencies, our fears, suspicions, and disappointments. We are chiefly engaged in struggling to maintain our self-respect and in asserting that supremacy which we all crave and which seems to us our natural prerogative. It is not strange, but rather quite inevitable, that our beliefs about what is true and false, good and bad, right and wrong, should be mixed up with the reverie and be influenced by the same considerations which determine its character and course. We resent criticisms of our views exactly as we do of anything else connected with ourselves. Our notions of life and its ideals seem to us to be *our own* and as such necessarily true and right, to be defended at all costs.

[34] *We very rarely consider, however, the process by which we gained our convictions.* If we did so, we could hardly fail to see that there was usually little ground for our confidence in them. Here and there, in this department of knowledge or that, some one of us might make a fair claim to have taken some trouble to get correct ideas of, let us say, the situation in Russia, the sources of our food supply, the origin of the Constitution, the revision of the tariff, the policy of the Holy Roman Apostolic Church, modern business organization, trade unions, birth control, socialism, the League of Nations, the excess-profits tax, preparedness, advertising in its social bearings; but only a very exceptional person would be entitled to opinions on all of even these few matters. And yet most of us have opinions on all these, and on many other questions of equal importance, of which we may know even less. . . .

[35] It is clear, in any case, that our convictions on important matters are not the result of knowledge or critical thought, nor, it may be added, are they often dictated by supposed self-interest. Most of them are *pure prejudices* in the proper sense of that word. We do not form them ourselves. They are the whisperings of "the voice of the herd." We have in the last analysis no responsibility for them and need assume none. They are not really our own ideas, but those of others no more well informed or inspired than ourselves, who have got them in the same careless and humiliating manner as we. It should be our pride to revise our ideas and not to adhere to what passes for respectable opinion, for such opinion can frequently be shown to be not respectable at all. We should, in vew of the considerations that have been mentioned, resent our supine credulity. As an English writer has remarked:

[36] "If we feared the entertaining of an unverifiable opinion with the warmth with which we fear using the wrong implement at the dinner table, if the thought of holding a prejudice disgusted us as does a foul disease,

then the dangers of man's suggestibility would be turned into advantages."*
[37] The purpose of this essay is to set forth briefly the way in which the notions of the herd have been accumulated. . . .

[38] I do not flatter myself that this general show-up of man's thought through the ages will cure myself or others of carelessness in adopting ideas, or of unseemly heat in defending them just because we have adopted them. But if the considerations which I propose to recall are really incorporated into our thinking and are permitted to establish our general outlook on human affairs, they will do much to relieve the imaginary obligation we feel in regard to traditional sentiments and ideals. Few of us are capable of engaging in creative thought, but some of us can at least come to distinguish it from other and inferior kinds of thought and accord to it the esteem that it merits as the greatest treasure of the past and the only hope of the future.

EXERCISES

Questions

1. Robinson's title serves as his thesis, and he presents a capsule account of the four kinds of thinking in paragraphs 21 and 22. As briefly as possible, define each.
2. What is the "unconscious"? Why is it important to a discussion of thinking? Discuss the paradox that the brain is the organ of forgetfulness.
3. What are the chief characteristics of the reverie? What is its chief danger? Can you trace the direction of your last thought that had nothing to do with this assignment? Are you sure it was your last thought?
4. How is decision making different from reverie? How is it similar? What is its relationship to knowledge? Speculate on why Robinson gives the least amount of space to this form of thinking. Is there any comment to be inferred insofar as we think of ourselves as a nation of doers and practical men?
5. What is rationalizing? How is it different from ordinary decision making? What is the difference between rationalizing and reasoning?
6. What is the difference between "good" and "real" reasons for our beliefs? Why are the "real" reasons for beliefs difficult to pinpoint? How does the discussion of the "real" reasons in paragraph 12 tie in with the introduction to the essay?
7. What is the significance of the word "my"? What is its relationship to rationalizing? Why is the "quality of primary certitude" usually a sign of shakily formed opinion? Discuss the validity of the statement: "My country right or wrong."
8. What does Robinson mean when he says "A history of philosophy could be written in terms of grouches, wounded pride, and aversions"? What are the implications of this statement?

*Trotter, *op. cit.*, p. 45. The first part of this little volume is excellent.

9. Why do you think paragraph 20 is italicized? Consider its content in the light of popular democratic belief in the will of the majority. What questions may we raise concerning customs and beliefs?

10. Paragraph 21 summarizes and serves as transition into the fourth form of thought. How does creative thought compare to the other three kinds Robinson discusses? Why is "creative thought" used as a term preferable to reason?

11. What is the function of curiosity to creative thought? What are the varieties of curiosity? What is the irony of "idle curiosity"? What is the chief difference between observation and real creativity?

12. How is the creation of a poem like the creation of an electric motor? Of which do we know more?

13. How important is creative thought?

14. Which form of thinking can exist completely independently?

15. What is the relationship of conviction to prejudice? Why should changing our ideas be our chief pride as against adhering to them?

16. Reread paragraph 8. What method does Robinson use to make his paragraph theme clear? Reread paragraph 12. What method does he use there? Find other examples of these techniques.

Vocabulary

abstruse	pristine
ignoble	supernal
infinitesimal	supine
oscillations	

For Discussion and Writing

1. Examining Convictions:
   Why I hate communism—real reasons and good reasons
   Why I am a Democrat or Republican—real reasons and good reasons
   Why I fear _____ —trace its origin
   My strongest allegiance—trace its origin
2. Poetry as truth
3. Rationalizing in history

CROSS REFERENCES

FRIED: "A Four-Letter Word That Hurts"
HONWANA: "The Hands of the Blacks"
SCHWARTZ: "Why Write a Book?"
WHITE: "The Second Tree from the Corner"

RECOMMENDED READING

SHIRLEY JACKSON, *The Lottery; Or, the Adventures of James Harris* (Farrar, Straus and Giroux: 1949)

E. B. WHITE

"THE SECOND TREE
FROM THE CORNER"

INTRODUCTION

E. B. White has already been introduced to you as the author of "The Meaning of Democracy." In addition to his essays and nonfiction prose, he has also written fiction including two children's tales, *Charlotte's Web* (1952) and *Stuart Little* (1945), both of which have become classics. Mr. White's narrative skill is apparent in "The Second Tree from the Corner."

TO THE READER

White uses Trexler's visits to a psychiatrist to explore men's aspirations. He indicates that what men say they want is not always what they really want and what they really want they can't or won't speak about.

"Ever had any bizarre thoughts?" asked the doctor.

[2]   Mr. Trexler failed to catch the word. "What kind?" he said.

[3]   "Bizarre," repeated the doctor, his voice steady. He watched his pa-

tient for any slight change of expression, any wince. It seemed to Trexler that the doctor was not only watching him closely but was creeping slowly toward him, like a lizard toward a bug. Trexler shoved his chair back an inch and gathered himself for a reply. He was about to say "Yes" when he realized that if he said yes the next question would be unanswerable. Bizarre thoughts, bizarre thoughts? Ever have any bizarre thoughts? What kind of thoughts *except* bizarre had he had since the age of two?

[4]   Trexler felt the time passing, the necessity for an answer. These psychiatrists were busy men, overloaded, not to be kept waiting. The next patient was probably already perched out there in the waiting room, lonely, worried, shifting around on the sofa, his mind stuffed with bizarre thoughts and amorphous fears. Poor bastard, thought Trexler. Out there all alone in that misshapen antechamber, staring at the filing cabinet and wondering whether to tell the doctor about that day on the Madison Avenue bus.

[5]   Let's see, bizarre thoughts. Trexler dodged back along the dreadful corridor of the years to see what he could find. He felt the doctor's eyes upon him and knew that time was running out. Don't be so conscientious, he said to himself. If a bizarre thought is indicated here, just reach into the bag and pick anything at all. A man as well supplied with bizarre thoughts as you are should have no difficulty producing one for the record. Trexler darted into the bag, hung for a moment before one of his thoughts, as a hummingbird pauses in the delphinium. No, he said, not that one. He darted to another (the one about the rhesus monkey), paused, considered. No, he said, not that.

[6]   Trexler knew he must hurry. He had already used up pretty nearly four seconds since the question had been put. But it was an impossible situation —just one more lousy, impossible situation such as he was always getting himself into. When, he asked himself, are you going to quit maneuvering yourself into a pocket? He made one more effort. This time he stopped at the asylum, only the bars were lucite—fluted, retractable. Not here, he said. Not this one.

[7]   He looked straight at the doctor. "No," he said quietly. "I never have any bizarre thoughts."

[8]   The doctor sucked in on his pipe, blew a plume of smoke toward the rows of medical books. Trexler's gaze followed the smoke. He managed to make out one of the titles, "The Genito-Urinary System." A bright wave of fear swept cleanly over him, and he winced under the first pain of kidney stones. He remembered when he was a child, the first time he ever entered a doctor's office, sneaking a look at the titles of the books—and the flush of fear, the shirt wet under the arms, the book on t.b., the sudden knowledge that he was in the advanced stages of consumption, the quick vision of the hemorrhage. Trexler sighed wearily. Forty years, he thought, and I still get thrown by the title of a medical book. Forty years and I still can't stay on life's little bucky horse. No wonder I'm sitting here in this dreary joint at the

end of this woebegone afternoon, lying about my bizarre thoughts to a doctor who looks, come to think of it, rather tired.

[9]   The session dragged on. After about twenty minutes, the doctor rose and knocked his pipe out. Trexler got up, knocked the ashes out of his brain, and waited. The doctor smiled warmly and stuck out his hand. "There's nothing the matter with you — you're just scared. Want to know how I know you're scared?"

[10] "How?" asked Trexler.

[11] "Look at the chair you've been sitting in! See how it has moved back away from my desk? You kept inching away from me while I asked you questions. That means you're scared."

[12] "Does it?" said Trexler, faking a grin. "Yeah, I suppose it does."

[13] They finished shaking hands. Trexler turned and walked out uncertainly along the passage, then into the waiting room and out past the next patient, a ruddy pin-striped man who was seated on the sofa twirling his hat nervously and staring straight ahead at the files. Poor, frightened guy, thought Trexler, he's probably read in the *Times* that one American male out of every two is going to die of heart disease by twelve o'clock next Thursday. It says that in the paper almost every morning. And he's also probably thinking about that day on the Madison Avenue bus.

[14] A week later, Trexler was back in the patient's chair. And for several weeks thereafter he continued to visit the doctor, always toward the end of the afternoon, when the vapors hung thick about the pool of the mind and darkened the whole region of the East Seventies. He felt no better as time went on, and he found it impossible to work. He discovered that the visits were becoming routine and that although the routine was one to which he certainly did not look forward, at least he could accept it with cool resignation, as once, years ago, he had accepted a long spell with a dentist who had settled down to a steady fooling with a couple of dead teeth. The visits, moreover, were now assuming a pattern recognizable to the patient.

[15] Each session would begin with a résumé of symptoms — the dizziness in the streets, the constricting pain in the back of the neck, the apprehensions, the tightness of the scalp, the inability to concentrate, the despondency and the melancholy times, the feeling of pressure and tension, the anger at not being able to work, the anxiety over work not done, the gas on the stomach. Dullest set of neurotic symptoms in the world, Trexler would think, as he obediently trudged back over them for the doctor's benefit. And then, having listened attentively to the recital, the doctor would spring his question: "Have you ever found anything that gives you relief?" And Trexler would answer, "Yes. A drink." and the doctor would nod his head knowingly.

[16] As he became familiar with the pattern Trexler found that he increasingly tended to identify himself with the doctor, transferring himself into the doctor's seat — probably (he thought) some rather slick form of escapism.

At any rate, it was nothing new for Trexler to identify himself with other people. Whenever he got into a cab, he instantly became the driver, saw everything from the hackman's angle (and the reaching over with the right hand, the nudging of the flag, the pushing it down, all the way down along the side of the meter), saw everything — traffic, fare, everything — through the eyes of Anthony Rocco, or Isidore Freedman, or Matthew Scott. In a barbershop, Trexler was the barber, his fingers curled around the comb, his hand on the tonic. Perfectly natural, then, that Trexler should soon be occupying the doctor's chair, asking the questions, waiting for the answers. He got quite interested in the doctor, in this way. He liked him, and he found him a not too difficult patient.

[17] It was on the fifth visit, about halfway through, that the doctor turned to Trexler and said, suddenly, "What do you want?" He gave the word "want" special emphasis.

[18] "I d'know," replied Trexler uneasily. "I guess nobody knows the answer to that one."

[19] "Sure they do," replied the doctor.

[20] "Do you know what you want?" asked Trexler narrowly.

[21] "Certainly," said the doctor. Trexler noticed that at this point the doctor's chair slid slightly backward, away from him. Trexler stifled a small, internal smile. Scared as a rabbit, he said to himself. Look at him scoot!

[22] "What *do* you want?" continued Trexler, pressing his advantage, pressing it hard.

[23] The doctor glided back another inch away from his inquisitor. "I want a wing on the small house I own in Westport. I want more money, and more leisure to do the things I want to do."

[24] Trexler was just about to say, "And what are those things you want to do, Doctor?" when he caught himself. Better not go too far, he mused. Better not lose possession of the ball. And besides, he thought, what the hell goes on here, anyway — me paying fifteen bucks a throw for these séances and then doing the work myself, asking the questions, weighing the answers. So he wants a new wing! There's a fine piece of theatrical gauze for you! A new wing.

[25] Trexler settled down again and resumed the role of patient for the rest of the visit. It ended on a kindly, friendly note. The doctor reassured him that his fears were the cause of his sickness, and that his fears were unsubstantial. They shook hands, smiling.

[26] Trexler walked dizzily through the empty waiting room and the doctor followed along to let him out. It was late; the secretary had shut up shop and gone home. Another day over the dam. "Goodbye," said Trexler. He stepped into the street, turned west toward Madison, and thought of the doctor all alone there, after hours, in that desolate hole — a man who worked longer hours than his secretary. Poor, scared, overworked bastard, thought Trexler. And that new wing!

[27] It was an evening of clearing weather, the Park showing green and desirable in the distance, the last daylight applying a high lacquer to the brick and brownstone walls and giving the street scene a luminous and intoxicating splendor. Trexler meditated, as he walked, on what he wanted. "What do you want?" he heard again. Trexler knew what he wanted, and what, in general, all men wanted; and he was glad, in a way, that it was both inexpressible and unattainable, and that it wasn't a wing. He was satisfied to remember that it was deep, formless, enduring, and impossible of fulfillment, and that it made men sick, and that when you sauntered along Third Avenue and looked through the doorways into the dim saloons, you could sometimes pick out from the unregenerate ranks the ones who had not forgotten, gazing steadily into the bottoms of the glasses on the long chance that they could get another little peek at it. Trexler found himself renewed by the remembrance that what he wanted was at once great and microscopic, and that although it borrowed from the nature of large deeds and of youthful love and of old songs and early intimations, it was not any one of these things, and that it had not been isolated or pinned down, and that a man who attempted to define it in the privacy of a doctor's office would fall flat on his face.

[28] Trexler felt invigorated. Suddenly his sickness seemed health, his dizziness stability. A small tree, rising between him and the light, stood there saturated with the evening, each gilt-edged leaf perfectly drunk with excellence and delicacy. Trexler's spine registered an ever so slight tremor as it picked up this natural disturbance in the lovely scene. "I want the second tree from the corner, just as it stands," he said, answering an imaginary question from an imaginary physician. And he felt a slow pride in realizing that what he wanted none could bestow, and that what he had none could take away. He felt content to be sick, unembarrassed at being afraid; and in the jungle of his fear he glimpsed (as he had so often glimpsed them before) the flashy tail feathers of the bird courage.

[29] Then he thought once again of the doctor, and of his being left there all alone, tired, frightened. (The poor, scared guy, thought Trexler.) Trexler began humming "Moonshine Lullaby," his spirit reacting instantly to the hypodermic of Merman's healthy voice. He crossed Madison, boarded a downtown bus, and rode all the way to Fifty-second Street before he had a thought that could rightly have been called bizarre.

EXERCISES

Questions

1. White states his theme in paragraph 27. What is it that all men want? Why is Trexler glad that what he wants is inexpressible and unattain-

able? Explore the contradiction of wanting something "at once great and microscopic."

2. Why are we told that Trexler identifies with cab drivers and barbers?

3. The relationship between Trexler and the psychiatrist is one of the keys to this essay. Describe their relationship during their first meeting. How do you know? When does it change? What is their relationship like at the end of the fifth visit?

4. If he is going to him for help, why would Trexler want to conceal information or to lie to the psychiatrist?

5. On what key issue does the balance of power between the two men shift? Why is this such an important issue? Is there anything wrong with the psychiatrist's response that he wants a "new wing" on his house?

6. Is it a bizarre thought to want the second tree from the corner? Why does Trexler than want "the second tree from the corner, just as it stands"? Why is that last clause so important?

7. Remembering his visits to the psychiatrist, and especially their last conversation, comment on Trexler's reflections (in paragraph 28) that "his sickness seemed health, his dizziness stability" and "he felt content to be sick, unembarrassed at being afraid, and in the junble of his fear he glimpsed . . . the flashy tail feathers of the bird courage." Why is the use of paradox appropriate?

8. What does White apparently think of psychiatry? Did the psychiatrist help Trexler?

9. White uses very forceful verbs. Notice "creeping" (paragraph 3), "perched" (paragraph 4), "darted . . . and hung" (paragraph 5). Can you find any others?

10. Note White's metaphors: "knocked the ashes out of his brain" (paragraph 9), "a fine piece of theatrical gauze" (paragraph 24), and "flashy tail feathers of the bird courage" (paragraph 28). Find others. Discuss their effectiveness.

11. White's sentences are interesting because he consistently particularizes. Whenever possible, he mentions a specific person, place or thing. Reread paragraph 16, for example. How many specific words can you pick out? Find other examples.

Vocabulary

amorphous	retractable
despondency	seance
fluted	unregenerate
neurotic	

For Discussion and Writing

1. Your "second tree from the corner, just as it stands"

2. "*Ah*, but a man's reach should exceed his grasp, or what's a heaven for?"
   —"Andrea del Sarto" Robert Browning

3. Poetry: expression of the inexpressible

CROSS REFERENCES

KING: "I Have a Dream"
ROBINSON: "On Various Kinds of Thinking"
RUSSELL: Prologue to the *Autobiography of Bertrand Russell*

DAVID SPITZ

"THE TIMKEN EDITION OF LENIN"

INTRODUCTION

David Spitz (1916–   ) is a professor of political science at Ohio State University, but he has spent his summers teaching at other major educational centers in this country and abroad. Dr. Spitz's interest in the democratic process is reflected in the titles of his four books: *Patterns of Anti-Democratic Thought* (1949; revised in 1965); *Democracy and the Challenge of Power* (1958); *The Liberal Idea of Freedom* (1964); and *Political Theory and Social Change* (1967). The following essay first appeared in *Harper's Magazine*.

TO THE READER

Dr. Spitz's search for truth starts because of ignorance but ends when he discovers fraud that is promoted and supported by business and the press.

It is commonplace that professors are peculiar people. They think, among other things, that truth is important; whereas most practical men seem to go on the assumption that belief and not truth is what counts.

[2]   The distinction is not a frivolus one; for belief, like patent medicines, can be manufactured, attractively packaged, and sold. Truth, on the other hand, has to be discovered rather than made, and is generally hard to come by; when found, it is often inconvenient or displeasing, and in appearance sometimes uncouth. As a result, it can almost always be expected to generate sales resistance.

[3]   These lugubrious reflections are occasioned by a recent exchange of views—if one may call it that—between this professor and some hard-headed and realistic men. If I seem in this account to have played a pathetically naive role, it is in part because I have always been reluctant to surrender the admittedly feeble hope that even materialistically-minded men, when faced with an obvious truth, would submit to it. Not, of course, because they believe that this or any other truth might make them free; but because, as practical men, they would understand that the revelation that they were marketing something dubious might prove embarrassing and destructive of their own purposes.

[4]   My little tale begins on February 22, 1960. On that day the Timken Roller Bearing Company—an Ohio concern dedicated to the preservation of what it fondly believes is the free enterprise system—published a political advertisement in the *Columbus Dispatch*. This is an influential journal which labels itself "Ohio's Greatest Home Newspaper" and wages daily war against political sin and intellectual heresy. By these the *Dispatch* means any doctrine or practice inconsistent with the views of Ohio's late President Harding or former Senator Bricker, or, quadrennially, any sentiments differing from those of the Republican Presidential candidate.

[5]   The Timken Company's advertisement, spread over more than half an eight-column page, featured the enigmatic countenance of Lenin and immediately below this, in large type, the following legend: "We shall force the United States to spend itself to destruction."

[6]   To one who has been under a professional obligation to read the writings of Lenin and other professed Marxists, this quotation came as something of a surprise. I had not been aware that Lenin, in the midst of fomenting a revolution and establishing a Communist regime in Russia, was at the same time engaged in seeking to undermine the United States by devious financial policies often associated—at least in the editorials of the *Columbus Dispatch*—with the spending policies of the Roosevelt and Truman Administrations. However, I was prepared to learn; so the next day I wrote to the Columbus office of the Timken Company requesting the volume and page citation where this quotation could be found.

[7]   Almost by return mail, in a letter dated February 25, I received from the Superintendent of Labor Relations of the Timken Company a direct and unambiguous reply. After referring to my letter of inquiry, the Superintendent said: "I am told by our Public Relations Department in Canton that this is

a literal translation of a speech by Lenin, made before the Soviet Presidium in 1919. It can be found in Volume 21, of Lenin's collected works."

[8]   Somewhat abashed by this exposure of my ignorance, I hurried to my university library and secured the designated volume. Unfortunately, the quotation was not there. This may be explained by the fact that in the English edition of Lenin's *Collected Works,* Volume 21 deals only with the year 1917; while in the Russian edition Volume 21 treats of the 1914–1915 period. However, a careful examination of later volumes in both editions dealing with the year 1919 did not turn up the quoted sentence either.

[9]   So on February 29 I wrote again to the Timken Company, reporting my inability to locate the relevant passage and asking, this time, for "(1) the specific date of Lenin's speech, (2) the correct volume and the page on which the sentence appears, and (3) the sentence in the Russian language of which the English quotation is the literal rendering."

[10] Two weeks passed, but there was no reply. Tortured by this abysmal gap in my information, and annoyed—I must confess it—by the weird thought that perhaps Lenin had not in fact made such a statement, I wrote once again to the Timken Company. To help stimulate a response, I even asked whether I was to construe the Company's silence as an admission of the fact that Lenin had not actually made this statement.

[11] This elicited a reply from the Manager of Public Relations of the main (Canton, Ohio) office of the firm. After apologizing for the delay, he wrote (in a letter dated March 23):

[12]   Our investigations into the subject show that while Lenin may not have said verbatim,[1] "We shall force the United States to spend itself to destruction," the substance of what Lenin writes in Volumes 21 and 22 of his *Collected Works* amounts to substantially the same thing.

[13]   Thank you very much for your interest and concern in the Timken Company's institutional advertising.

[14] I do not now clearly recall the whole of my reaction to this preposterous admission. I know that I felt great relief at discovering that I had not heretofore been guilty, even through inadvertence, of keeping from my students an essential bit of Lenin's teaching. I know, too, that I sat for a time in numbed amazement staring at this unapologetic statement. And I remember wondering why corporation executives send their sons and daughters to our colleges, and recruit their future top personnel from those colleges, when they so amiably intend to disregard the primary value inculcated, or at least professed by the colleges: a simple respect for and observance of truth.

[15] But with this correspondence in hand, the next step was obvious. I wrote (on March 29) to the Managing Editor of the *Columbus Dispatch,* enclosing copies of the full correspondence and requesting that editor's "as-

[1] in exactly the same words; word for word

surance that in the interests of truthful journalism the *Columbus Dispatch* will refuse in the future to accept and publish this misleading advertisement."

[16] Apart from acknowledging receipt of my letter, the Managing Editor wrote only to say that it had been turned over to the Director of Advertising for his consideration. But the weeks, and now the months, have gone by, and the ensuing silence has approximated the glacial response of a bank president asked to lend money without interest.

[17] I attempted twice more to elicit a reply: in a letter of April 14 to the Director of Advertising, and again in a letter of May 4 to the Managing Editor. I even asked in my last letter whether I was to infer from this silence that "it is the policy of the *Columbus Dispatch* to ignore the content of its advertising." But my efforts were futile. The editors of the newspaper were clearly not going to repeat the blunder of the Timken Company. Nor, it would seem, did they mean to go on record as condemning or abandoning the Timken Roller Bearing Company's political advertisements.

[18] So, in these practices of a free industrial enterprise and a free press, we are brought once again to the ancient questions: whether it is truth, or falsehood, that will make men free; and whether it profiteth a man to make money if in the process he loses his soul. But this, of course, is to assume that corporation executives and newspaper editors have, or concern themselves with souls. And this may well be the largest question of all.

EXERCISES

Questions

1. The theme is stated immediately in the first two paragraphs. What is the difference between truth and belief? How does Spitz's narrative point up this difference? Can you find examples from your own experience to validate the statement? Can you challenge it?

2. What evidence has Spitz accumulated which permits him to conclude that the advertisement is misleading? What is the chief weakness of the final answer from the Timken Company?

3. Was the investigation of the advertisement's statement sufficiently thorough? Is his evaluation of the Timken people and the *Dispatch* fair? Is his generalized conclusion about business and truth valid?

4. Why was Dr. Spitz so shocked by the Public Relations Manager's letter? Were you? Why or why not?

5. Why didn't the *Columbus Dispatch* take action on the professor's letters? What does this imply about a "free press"? Were you surprised at the newspaper's reaction? Why or why not?

6. What reactions in the reader did the Timken Company hope to exploit by their advertisement? Why should a company want to use such an advertising campaign?

7. Does the tone of the essay reflect its content? Why do you suppose Spitz took this somewhat cynical approach? What words in the first three paragraphs reveal the attitude?
8. What words in paragraph 4 suggest that the author is highly critical of both the Timken Company and the *Columbus Dispatch*?
9. Professor Spitz often uses parallel structure in balanced sentences. Consider, for example, the second sentence of paragraph 1. Look for other examples.

Vocabulary

abashed	inadvertence
abysmal	inculcated
enigmatic	lugubrious
elicited	quadrennially
heresy	

For Discussion and Writing

1. How free is our free press?
2. Freedom of the press: has it a limit?
3. Truth in advertising
4. The business ethic — is it ethical?
5. The responsibility of a college press
6. The responsibility of the reader
7. Truth or belief: which is more important?

CROSS REFERENCES

McDONALD: "The Habit of Lying"
PLATO: "Apology"
ROVERE: "The Most Gifted and Successful Demagogue This Country Has Ever Known"
SOLOMON: "Free Speech at Ohio State"

RECOMMENDED READING

THURBER, JAMES and ELLIOTT NUGENT: "The Male Animal" (Random House: 1940)

STRINGFELLOW BARR

"THE CIVILIZATION
OF THE DIALOGUE"

INTRODUCTION

Stringfellow Barr (1897–   ) is best known as the man who inaugurated the
Great Books Curriculum at St. Johns University where he was president from
1937 to 1946. This program is an intensive study of the classics to prepare man
for modern life. After his service as an administrator, Professor Barr returned
to the classroom and, since 1955, has been a Professor of Humanities at
Rutgers. In 1961, he won the Lindback Award for distinguished teaching.
Among his books are *The Pilgrimage of Western Man* (1949), revised in
1962; *The Will of Zeus* (1961); *Mask of Jove* (1966); and a novel, *Purely
Academic* (1958). The following brief excerpt was taken from *The Three
Worlds of Man.*

TO THE READER

The chapter from which this excerpt was taken is called "Wisdom." The
new title for the excerpt further identifies the content.

W hat is the nature of the dialectic that Socrates prescribed as the
final preparation of his Guardians if they would rule wisely and that he

himself practiced while offering his prescription? It is fundamentally a kind of argument between two persons, but it is a kind rarely heard in Athens in his day and perhaps even more rarely in twentieth-century America. Most arguments then and now tend to be what Socrates called eristic. Now, the word eristic is derived from *eris,* the Greek word for strife. In eristic both sides are trying to win. In dialectic, both sides argue hard but not to win. They have a common goal: to find the true answer to the problem. For both sides may start off with a false or incomplete opinion. We may look to a sport like tennis to see the difference. Two men may play a tennis match in which each contestant is even more anxious to win than to play good tennis. Two other men may play, with each man trying to put up the best game possible, regardless of who wins. There is a quality of sportsmanship in this second way of playing. There is a quality of professionalism in the first way, whether money changes hands or not. In the first match only one player can achieve his purpose — a victorious score. In the second match both sides can achieve their common purpose — tennis playing of high quality. The first match has the quality of eristic but it has no common purpose. The second has the quality of Socratic dialectic and has a very high common purpose — good play.

[2]   The analogy between ways of arguing and ways of playing tennis is not yet exhausted. It takes at least two persons to play either game. Moreover, both kinds of tennis and both kinds of argument must be rigorously, not sloppily, scored. Again, if either side plays or argues eristically, defeat is likely to be bitter, since the defeated player gains nothing that he wants. Again, an eristic player is likely to assume that his opponent's goal, like his own, is the eristic goal, even if in actual fact his opponent is playing dialectically. Similarly, if the true dialectician seems to enough of his opponents to have won eristic victories from them he may find the silver cup he wins brimful of hemlock;[1] he may, like Socrates, be ordered to drink it. When Socrates drank hemlock in his prison cell, no doubt many of those he had appeared to triumph over felt that at last they had triumphed over Socrates. Had he not met the greatest defeat of all — death? But Plato's *Crito* and *Phaedo* show Socrates still playing his game of dialectic in his prison cell with whatever friends came to call. His goal remained unchanged: the joint pursuit of truth through the dialectical destruction of those false and inadequately examined and deeply cherished opinions which men hold as truth itself. And when he won the cup of hemlock, he willingly drained it, hoping to gain entrance to some place where he could play his game of dialectic with great players who had lived in Hellas[2] long before and had preceded him to that other place.

[3]   If we read Plato's *Dialogues* and listen to Socrates himself practice dialectic, we observe that his preferred method is to ask short questions

[1]poison
[2]ancient name for Athens

and to encourage short answers. This cross-examination tests his opponent's opinion somewhat as a laboratory scientist tests his own or another's hypothesis. But over and over again in the *Dialogues* the person questioned grows violent, raises his voice, and substitutes for the short answer the long, vague, rhetorical[3] speech. As signs multiply that his opinion is about to be refuted,[4] and out of his own mouth at that, he fears personal disgrace. This confusion between refutation and disgrace is perhaps reflected by the Greek word *elenchos,* which, depending on its gender, means either refutation or disgrace. The basic trouble, of course, is that Socrates' sparring partner views the encounter in terms of eristic and fears defeat. But for Socrates the testing of the opinion is the goal, and it is not important who happens to be the opinion's advocate.[5] If the opinion fails, it will be logic, not Socrates, which condemns it.

EXERCISES

Questions

1. Though Barr devotes most of this piece to distinguishing between two kinds of dialogue, the key to the essay lies in his title. What is he apparently making a plea for? What does it mean to civilize a dialogue? What application do you see for this?
2. What is eristic argument? What are its shortcomings? What is dialectic argument? What are its advantages? Its shortcomings? Give examples of eristic and dialectic arguments.
3. What is the relationship between refutation and disgrace? What is the defeat in dialectic argument? In eristic argument? Which would Socrates or Barr consider the more serious defeat? Which does the average man consider the more serious defeat?
4. What was Socrates' goal? Why was he the victor even though condemned to death?
5. Does the illustration of the tennis players clarify the definition? How? Where else does Barr use illustration to clarify?
6. Analyze the construction of paragraph 1, noting how each sentence takes the reader one step further into the discussion. Can any sentence be omitted? Are his second and third paragraphs as tightly constructed?

For Discussion and Writing

1. Labor disputes: eristic or dialectic?
2. Political campaigns: eristic or dialectic?
3. Editorials: eristic or dialectic?

[3]insincere or overly elaborate
[4]overthrown by evidence or proof
[5]one who pleads a cause, especially before a court

4. Family arguments: eristic or dialectic?
5. Scientific research as dialectical logic
6. Dialectical logic and international treaties, for example, neutralizing space
7. Foreign policy and eristic logic
8. The United Nations and dialectic logic

CROSS REFERENCES

PLATO: "Apology"
ROBINSON: "On Various Kinds of Thinking"

RECOMMENDED READING

PLATO: *The Death of Socrates*

HARRY SCHWARTZ

"WHY WRITE A BOOK?"

INTRODUCTION

Harry Schwartz (1919–   ) is a member of the Editorial Board of *The New York Times* and is a specialist on Soviet affairs. He holds a doctorate in economics from Columbia University (1943). During World War II, he served in the Army and also as an expert on Soviet economic intelligence for the Office of Strategic Services. Dr. Schwartz has taught at several universities and for several years was Professor of Economics at Syracuse University. He has written extensively on communism. Among his titles are: *The Red Phoenix* (1961); *Russia's Soviet Economy* (1954) (1961); *The Soviet Economy Since Stalin* (1965); and, *Tsars, Mandarins and Commissars,* on Chinese-Russian relations (1964).

TO THE READER

Ask yourself why you think writers write; then discover Dr. Schwartz's unexpected reason for writing.

"Why do you waste your time writing books?"

[2]   The question was my accountant's. He asked it during the latest of

Reprinted from *Saturday Review,* August 14, 1965, with the permission of Saturday Review, Inc., and the author.

those annual moments of truth that come early each April. His accusing tone seemed to imply near treason to my major and silent partner, Uncle Sam. It carried a hint that I might more profitably have spent my time baby sitting or mowing lawns for the neighbors.

[3]   "So he's joined them too," I groaned inwardly while trying to keep a poker face.

[4]   By "them" I had in mind the normal phalanx[1] of opponents that a person who has a regular job and tries to write books in his spare time encounters daily. "Them" includes the wife and children, who cannot understand that evenings, weekends, and vacations exist for gathering material and pounding a typewriter rather than for going away, seeing a movie, or visiting friends. "Them" includes the doctor, who keeps on muttering about the alleged virtues of regular outdoor exercise and the supposed advantages of regular periods of relaxation. And I have fellow book-writing addicts who report that "them" includes their bosses, suspicious churls who apparently wonder whether a man can give his all to his 9-to-5 job if he spends all the rest of his waking hours working on some magnum opus.[2] There are, of course, bosses who have the same monkey on their backs. They tend to be more understanding—sometimes.

[5]   The accountant left finally, adding as a final shot, "Why don't you write magazine articles or give lectures? They pay pretty well I understand. Anyway, they can't pay less per hour than the books you write."

[6]   I tried to ignore this philistine,[3] but his words had set me thinking. Why did I write books? Why, for that matter, did anyone write books—the 20,000 or so titles that come off the presses each year? With a shock I realized that I had been writing books by instinct for decades, yet this was a serious matter deserving careful analysis. I began to draw up categories.

[7]   There are obviously people who write books because they make lots and lots of beautiful money. I drooled with envy as I thought of the artists of the word who can get a million-dollar advance for the paperback rights alone on a novel they haven't even begun. Wouldn't it be lovely to be one of those wizards whose publishers expect as a matter of course that every one of their volumes will be a Book-of-the-Month-Club selection? I know one of them, and he reports that the single time the Club's rulers fumbled his ball for some reason they wrote him a long and contrite letter of apology. Life can be beautiful.

[8]   Very few people are in this elite group, but surely many others must write books in the hope that they, too, will hit the jackpot. Was I one of their number? Did I harbor—hidden away deep in my subconscious, far beyond the probing reach of my favorite analyst—fantasies about my typewriter really being a gold mine? At this point cold reason reasserted itself. People

[1] a body of heavily armed infantry formed in close ranks
[2] a great work, usually the greatest achievement of an artist
[3] a crass, priggish individual guided by material rather than intellectual or artistic values

like me — who write about such matters as Russia's relations with China in the eighteenth century and the latest developments in Muscovite econometrics — simply cannot have such unrealistic expectations. Not for us the jackpot. That's clear.

[9]   Then, of course, there are all the professors who write books because they have to as part of the expected obeisance before the Great God Research. An academic friend of mine once explained the arithmetic of "Publish or Perish" to me. "It's simple," I recall him saying, "just publish an article every two years and a book every five or six years. Nobody reads them, of course, but they look awfully good in your bibliography and they assure you'll be a full professor by the time you're thirty-five, or forty. Your department chairman thinks you're pulling your weight, and you can join him in tut-tutting about the 'lack of productivity' of that young whippersnapper who never writes anything but comes out first when the school newspaper rates the members of your department." Then, as a final thought, he added, "Besides you can always get a foundation grant or some government money to write a book."

[10]   That last remark hit me hard. Like every other literate person I have had my Walter Mitty moments dreaming of somebody (for some reason I always think of him as wearing a homburg and striped pants) from Ford or Carnegie or Rockefeller accosting me with offers of oodles of money to write the definitive treatise on the economic geology of Yakutia. Perhaps I write books as a means of wigwagging that Barkus is willin'? But then again pitiless reason intervened. With all the practice, Ford, Carnegie, Rockefeller et al. have had over the years ignoring my wigwagging — if that's what I've been doing — they're hardly likely ever to kick that particular habit. I dismissed the hypothesis.

[11]   What about the people who write books because they have a message for humanity? I thought of Marx slaving over *Das Kapital* in the British Museum, of Lenin expounding *What Is To Be Done* before he went out and did it, of Darwin reluctantly and slowly applying pen to paper to break the bad news about man's unsavory origins. Even now, I know — they all seem able to get past the receptionist and pester me — there are hordes of people convinced they have a priceless message for humanity, all of them willing at any provocation — or none at all — to expound it for 100,000 or 200,000 words if somebody will only put up the money to pay the printer and the bookbinder.

[12]   But I don't fall into this category either. For some reason — a defect, no doubt, in the nucleotide structure of the double helix of my deoxyribonucleic acid (DNA to those in the know) — I don't seem to have any very important message for humanity. I don't know how to end the Vietnam War or the Dominican mess. I have no sure-fire formula for perpetual prosperity or even for perpetual motion. If they're looking for someone to fulfil Einstein's unrealized dream of uniting relativity theory with quantum mech-

anics, they'll have to look elsewhere. I'm not up to it, and don't even understand either subject if the humiliating truth be told. I just like to write books, even if they don't carry some message that will cause endless turmoil, like those of Marx and Lenin, or give the theologians sleepless nights, like those of Darwin.

[13] It was at this point in my ruminations that the underlying cause of my idiosyncrasy finally came to the surface: I like to write books because I learn so much in the process, because only by doing the galley-slave labor that is research for a book can I learn how many unfacts I carry around in my mind as facts.

[14] The process of book conception is always the same. By now I think of it as a highly stylized ritual on a par with the old Chinese Opera before they did away with the emperors, princesses, and Robin Hood types and substituted heroic workers and rotten American imperialists, or at least their corrupt agents.

[15] It always begins with a phone call. "This is Mr. Brown" (or White or Black or Blue — publishers seem to have a penchant for colorful names, though I must admit I'm still waiting for Mr. Fuchsia), "I'd like to talk to you about a book," he says. Adhering to the strictest ritual, I reply, "Well, it won't hurt to talk about it. Let's have lunch." His reply, equally stylized, is "Fine, what about the Century Club (or it may be the Harvard Club. I've come to realize that I don't rate the Four Seasons) next Friday."

[16] The second act — at the Century Club or its equivalent — also follows the classical rules. "We'd like you to do a book on the role of the Bashkirs in the Russian Revolution. Our market-research people have discovered that a lot of Bashkirs came to this country in 1912 and settled in Texas sagebrush that turned out to hide oil wells. Their affluent sons and grandsons will want the book, and most of them can read by now. Besides our college salesmen tell us the trend in Russian history courses these days is to treat the revolution in depth — no more superficial stuff like Chamberlin's two volumes or Carr's three volumes. They want real fundamental works that pinpoint what happened at the grassroots, in key areas like Bashkiria. I know you can toss it off in no time at all. Why the first time I heard of the Bashkirs was in an article you wrote for the *Times* a couple of months ago. (Checking always reveals the article appeared ten years ago and was by a colleague of mine.) And just to show we're serious, we're willing to offer an advance."

[17] At this portentous and decisive moment, he names a figure and brings out his checkbook. In the by now heated and alcohol-enlivened atmosphere, the figure seems huge. I hastily divide it by the monthly mortgage payment and there's something left over. I forget to do what my accountant tells me to do, allow for income tax at the highest rate I can think of. I have been hooked.

[18] I go home, my brain whirling with ideas. The Bashkirs in the Russian Revolution! I once read a book that mentioned the subject. Oh yes, Lenin

called them Russia's Hottentots in 1919, didn't he? They fought the Reds almost to a draw under the colorful Mustafa Riyazev. Clearly this will be an exciting story, full of exotic detail and deeds of bold derring-do. Maybe Orville Prescott[4] will review the book. Miracles do happen after all.

[19] My wife recognizes the symptoms. She protests loudly, threatens divorce. My children throw themselves imploringly at my feet; one of them bites me in the leg. But I remain firm. I bolt supper and rush off to the library.

[20] That first night at the library is always a discouraging experience. In all those thousands of books it turns out there's only one that mentions the Bashkirs in the Russian Revolution. And it claims that Mustafa Riyazev was not the colorful leader of the Bashkir anti-Communists. It mentions that he was the first Bashkir to join the Bolsheviks — presumably under the influence of alcohol, the author adds in a footnote. The leader of the Bashkirs was one Abdullah Illyuyayev, this source maintains, and he was so incompetent that the feeble Bashkir revolt petered out after two days and one skirmish in which there was only one casualty — Abdullah, whose rifle exploded (it was the first time he had ever fired one).

[21] I go home depressed. But there's no way out. The contract has been signed, and most of the advance was spent on the way home to buy a little glamorous something for the wife in the effort (predictably vain) to win her assent this time.

[22] The next day is Saturday. It is a fine day — the sun is shining; all the neighbors are off to the golf course or sailing on Long Island Sound. I go to the Slavic Room of the New York Public Library. Maybe this project can be rescued yet.

[23] Here there's material! My memory was right. I find the book I remember having read. There it is in black and white, Mustafa was the leader of the Bashkir anti-Communists. The author has a footnote that the "legend of Mustafa Riyazev joining the Communist party was a typical Stalinist falsification spread in the 1930s to reconcile the Bashkirs to Communist slavery." Abdullah Illyuyayev, this book notes, "was a Communist agent who tried to worm his way into the Bashkir ranks, but who was exposed as a Russian, not a Bashkir, when he inadvertently revealed his ignorance of the sacred Bashkir fertility rite."

[24] At this point I know all is well. Once again the sources contradict each other. Once again no two authors on the same subject agree on what happened to whom where and when. A long and pleasant task — much more fun than the double-crostic, I think, but my wife disagrees — is ahead of me: trying to figure out what really did take place. And at the end of the road I know will be my own book, a major additional contribution to the general confusion.

[25] But what will my accountant say next April?

---

[4]book critic for *The New York Times*

EXERCISES

Questions

1.   The title, first, and sixth paragraphs all say the same thing. Justify the use of repetition. Schwartz's theme appears midway in paragraphs 13 and 24; what does the second half (paragraphs 14–23) contribute in content and attitude? What does he mean by "unfacts [carried] around in my mind as facts"?
2.   Which sentence would it have been better to end the article with: the last one, or the next to the last one? Why?
3.   The article is part classification, part process analysis. Where does the one end and the other begin? At what point are the two drawn together? What basic problems of serious research does Schwartz reveal, despite his kidding?
4.   According to Schwartz, for what other reasons do people write books? How does he feel about them? How do you feel about them?
5.   Why do some people object to those who write in their spare time? Has Schwartz omitted any reasons?
6.   Does it matter whether Mustafa was pro- or anti-Communist?
7.   What is the tone of the essay? In what ways does it contribute to its success? What are the sources of Schwartz's humor?
8.   Reread paragraph 4. What words reveal Schwartz's attitude? Describe this attitude.
9.   Schwartz is interesting because he uses concrete and specific words. Reread paragraph 11. How many specific words are there? Find another paragraph so developed.

Vocabulary

churls	portentous
idiosyncrasy	ruminations
obeisance	

For Discussion and Writing

1.   Why painters paint
2.   Why do homework?
3.   Research—handling contradictions
4.   Best sellers—this year, last year, ten years ago

CROSS REFERENCES

ROBINSON: "On Various Kinds of Thinking"
SPITZ: "The Timken Edition of Lenin"

SOME THOUGHTS ON WORDS

S. I. HAYAKAWA

"HOW WORDS CHANGE
OUR LIVES"

INTRODUCTION

S. I. Hayakawa (1906–   ) was born in British Columbia and crossed the border to the United States in 1929 to complete his education by earning his doctorate at the University of Wisconsin in 1935. As one of the country's leading semanticists, he is primarily concerned with words, but his interests range from psychology and anthropology to consumer research and jazz, and he has held memberships (even directorships) in national organizations concerned with each of these. He has also written several books, mostly on semantics, including *Language in Action* (1941); *Our Language and Our World* (1959); and his most recent, *Symbol, Status and Personality* (1965).

TO THE READER

Dr. Hayakawa indicates that we must examine some of our responses to words: where the responses came from originally, why they have remained fixed, and how we can go about changing attitudes by changing word responses.

The end product of education, yours and mine and everybody's, is the total pattern of reactions and possible reactions we have inside ourselves. If you did not have within you at this moment the pattern of reactions which we call "the ability to read English," you would see here only meaningless black marks on paper. Because of the trained patterns of response, you are (or are not) stirred to patriotism by martial music, your feelings of reverence are aroused by the symbols of your religion, you listen more respectfully to the health advice of someone who has "M.D." after his name than to that of someone who hasn't. What I call here a "pattern of reactions," then, is the sum total of the ways we act in response to events, to words and to symbols.

[2]   Our reaction patterns—our semantic habits, as we may call them—are the internal and most important residue of whatever years of education or miseducation we may have received from our parents' conduct toward us in childhood as well as their teachings, from the formal education we may have had, from all the sermons and lectures we have listened to, from the radio programs and the movies and television shows we have experienced, from all the books and newspapers and comic strips we have read, from the conversations we have had with friends and associates, and from all our experiences. If, as the result of all these influences that make us what we are, our semantic habits are reasonably similar to those of most people around us, we are regarded as "well-adjusted," or "normal," and perhaps "dull." If our semantic habits are noticeably different from those of others, we are regarded as "individualistic" or "original," or, if the differences are disapproved of or viewed with alarm, as "screwball" or "crazy."

[3]   Semantics is sometimes defined in dictionaries as "the science of the meaning of words"—which would not be a bad definition if people didn't assume that the search for the meanings of words begins and ends with looking them up in a dictionary.

[4]   If one stops to think for a moment, it is clear that to define a word, as a dictionary does, is simply to explain the word with more words. To be thorough about defining, we should next have to define the words used in the definition, then define the words used in defining the words used in the definition . . . and so on. Defining words with more words, in short, gets us at once into what mathematicians call an "infinite regress." Alternatively, it can get us into the kind of run-around we sometimes encounter when we look up "impertinence" and find it defined as "impudence," so we look up "impudence" and find it defined as "impertinence." Yet—and here we come to another common reaction pattern—people often act as if words can be explained fully with more words. To a person who asked for a definition of jazz, Louis Armstrong is said to have replied, "Man, when you got to ask what it is, you'll never get to know," proving himself to be an intuitive semanticist as well as a great trumpet player.

What Semantics Is About

[5]   Semantics, then, does not deal with the "meaning of words" as that expression is commonly understood. P. W. Bridgman, the Nobel-prize winner and physicist, once wrote, "The true meaning of a term is to be found by observing what a man does with it, not by what he says about it." He made an enormous contribution to science by showing that the meaning of a scientific term lies in the operations, the things done, that establish its validity, rather than in verbal definitions.

[6]   Here is a simple, everyday kind of example of "operational" criticism. If you say, "This table measures six feet in length," you could prove it by taking a foot rule, performing the operation of laying it end to end while counting, "One . . . two . . . three . . . four . . ." But if you say — and revolutionists have started uprisings with just this statement — "Man is born free, but everywhere he is in chains!" — what operations could you perform to demonstrate its accuracy or inaccuracy?

[7]   But let us carry this suggestion of "operationalism" outside the physical sciences where Bridgman applied it, and observe what "operations" people perform as the result of both the language they use and the language other people use in communicating to them. Here is a personnel manager studying an application blank. He comes to the words "Education: Harvard University," and drops the application blank in the wastebasket (that's the "operation") because, as he would say if you asked him, "I don't like Harvard men." This is an instance of "meaning" at work — but it is not a meaning that can be found in dictionaries.

[8]   If I seem to be taking a long time to explain what semantics is about, it is because I am trying, in the course of explanation, to introduce the reader to a certain way of looking at human behavior. Semantics — especially the general semantics of Alfred Korzybski (1879–1950), Polish-American scientist and educator — pays particular attention not to words in themselves, but to semantic reactions — that is, human responses to symbols, signs and symbol-systems, including language.

[9]   I say *human* responses because, so far as we know, human beings are the only creatures that have, over and above that biological equipment which we have in common with other creatures, the additional capacity for manufacturing symbols and systems of symbols. When we react to a flag, we are not reacting simply to a piece of cloth, but to the meaning with which it has been symbolically endowed. When we react to a word, we are not reacting to a set of sounds, but to the meaning with which that set of sounds has been symbolically endowed.

[10] A basic idea in general semantics, therefore, is that the meaning of words (or other symbols) is not the words, but in our own semantic reactions. If I were to tell a shockingly obscene story in Arabic or Hindustani

or Swahili before an audience that understood only English, no one would blush or be angry; the story would be neither shocking nor obscene — indeed, it would not even be a story. Likewise, the value of a dollar bill is not in the bill, but in our social agreement to accept it as a symbol of value. If that agreement were to break down through the collapse of our Government, the dollar bill would become only a scrap of paper. We do not understand a dollar bill by staring at it long and hard. We understand it by observing how people act with respect to it. We understand it by understanding the social mechanisms and the loyalties that keep it meaningful. Semantics is therefore a social study, basic to all other social studies.

[11] It is often remarked that words are tricky — and that we are all prone to be deceived by "fast talkers," such as high-pressure salesmen, skillful propagandists, politicians or lawyers. Since few of us are aware of the degree to which we use words to deceive ourselves, the sin of "using words in a tricky way" is one that is always attributed to the other fellow. When the Russians use the word "democracy" to mean something quite different from what we mean by it, we at once accuse them of "propaganda," of "corrupting the meanings of words." But when we use the word "democracy" in the United States to mean something quite different from what the Russians mean by it, they are equally quick to accuse us of "hypocrisy." We all tend to believe that the way we use words is the correct way, and that people who use the same words in other ways are either ignorant or dishonest.

Words Evoke Different Responses

[12] Leaving aside for a moment such abstract and difficult terms as "democracy," let us examine a common, everyday word like "frog." Surely there is no problem about what "frog" means! Here are some sample sentences:

[13] "If we're going fishing, we'll have to catch some frogs first." (This is easy.)

[14] "I have a frog in my throat." (You can hear it croaking.)

[15] "She wore a loose, silk jacket fastened with braided frogs."

[16] "The blacksmith pared down the frog and the hoof before shoeing the horse."

[17] "In Hamilton, Ohio, there is a firm by the name of American Frog and Switch Company." In addition to these "frogs," there is the frog in which a sword is carried, the frog at the bottom of a bowl or vase that is used in flower arrangement, and the frog which is part of a violin bow. The reader can no doubt think of other "frogs."

[18] Or take another common word such as "order." There is the *order* that the salesman tries to get, which is quite different from the *order* which

a captain gives to his crew. Some people enter holy *orders*. There is the *order* in the house when mother has finished tidying up; there is the batting *order* of the home team; there is an *order* of ham and eggs. It is surprising that with so many meanings to the word, people don't misunderstand one another oftener than they do.

[19] The foregoing are only striking examples of a principle to which we are all so well accustomed that we rarely think of it; namely, that most words have more meanings than dictionaries can keep track of. And when we consider further that each of us has different experiences, different memories, different likes and dislikes, it is clear that all words evoke different responses in all of us. We may agree as to what the term "Mississippi River" stands for, but you and I recall different parts of the river; you and I have had different experiences with it; one of us has read more about it than the other; one of us may have happy memories of it, while the other may recall chiefly tragic events connected with it. Hence your "Mississippi River" can never be identical with my "Mississippi River." The fact that we can communicate with each other about the "Mississippi River" often conceals the fact that we are talking about two different sets of memories and experiences.

Fixed Reactions to Certain Words

[20] Words being as varied in their meanings as they are, no one can tell us what the correct interpretation of a word should be in advance of our next encounter with that word. The reader may have been taught always to revere the word "mother." But what is he going to do the next time he encounters this word, when it occurs in the sentence "Mother began to form in the bottle"? If it is impossible to determine what a single word will mean on next encounter, is it possible to say in advance what is the correct evaluation of such events as these: (1) next summer, an individual who calls himself a socialist will announce his candidacy for the office of register of deeds in your city; (2) next autumn, there will be a strike at one of your local department stores; (3) next week, your wife will announce that she is going to change her style of hairdo; (4) tomorrow, your little boy will come home with a bleeding nose?

[21] A reasonably sane individual will react to each of these events in his own way, according to time, place and the entire surrounding set of circumstances; and included among those circumstances will be his own stock of experiences, wishes, hopes and fears. But there are people whose pattern of reactions is such that some of them can be completely predicted in advance. Mr. A will never vote for anyone called "socialist," no matter how incompetent or crooked the alternative candidates may be. Mr. B–1 always disapproves of strikes and strikers, without bothering to inquire whether or not this strike has its justifications; Mr. B–2 always sympathizes

with the strikers because he hates all bosses. Mr. C belongs to the "stay sweet as you are" school of thought, so that his wife hasn't been able to change her hairdo since she left high school. Mr. D always faints at the sight of blood.

[22] Such fixed and unalterable patterns of reaction—in their more obvious forms we call them prejudices—are almost inevitably organized around words. Mr. E distrusts and fears all people to whom the term "Catholic" is applicable, while Mr. F, who is Catholic, distrusts and fears all non-Catholics. Mr. G is so rabid a Republican that he reacts with equal dislike to all Democrats, all Democratic proposals, all opposite proposals if they are also made by Democrats. Back in the days when Franklin D. Roosevelt was President, Mr. G disliked not only the Democratic President but also his wife, children and dog. His office was on Roosevelt Road in Chicago (it had been named after Theodore Roosevelt), but he had his address changed to his back door on 11th Street, so that he would not have to print the hated name on his stationery. Mr. H, on the other hand, is an equally rabid Democrat, who hates himself for continuing to play golf, since golf is Mr. Eisenhower's favorite game. People suffering from such prejudices seem to have in their brains an uninsulated spot which, when touched by such words as "capitalist," "boss," "striker," "scab," "Democrat," "Republican," "socialized medicine," and other such loaded terms, results in an immediate short circuit, often with a blowing of fuses.

[23] Alfred Korzybski, the founder of general semantics, called such short-circuited responses "identification reactions." He used the word "identification" in a special sense; he meant that persons given to such fixed patterns of response identify (that is, treat as identical) all occurrences of a given word or symbol; they identify all the different cases that fall under the same name. Thus, if one has hostile identification reactions to "women drivers," then all women who drive cars are "identical" in their incompetence.

[24] Korzybski believed that the term "identification reaction" could be generally used to describe the majority of cases of semantic malfunctioning. Identification is something that goes on in the human nervous system. "Out there" there are no absolute identities. No two Harvard men, no two Ford cars, no two mothers-in-law, no two politicians, no two leaves from the same tree, are identical with each other in all respects. If, however, we treat all cases that fall under the same class label as one at times when the differences are important, then there is something wrong with our semantic habits.

Another Definition of General Semantics

[25] We are now ready, then, for another definition of general semantics. It is a comparative study of the kinds of responses people make to the sym-

bols and signs around them; we may compare the semantic habits common among the prejudiced, the foolish and the mentally ill with those found among people who are able to solve their problems successfully, so that, if we care to, we may revise our own semantic habits for the better. In other words, general semantics is, if we wish to make it so, the study of how not to be a damn fool.

[26] Identification reactions run all the way through nature. The capacity for seeing similarities is necessary to the survival of all animals. The pickerel, I suppose, identifies all shiny, fluttery things going through the water as minnows, and goes after them all in pretty much the same way. Under natural conditions, life is made possible for the pickerel by this capacity. Once in a while, however, the shiny, fluttery thing in the water may happen to be not a minnow but an artificial lure on the end of a line. In such a case, one would say that the identification response, so useful for survival, under somewhat more complex conditions that require differentiation between two sorts of shiny and fluttery objects, proves to be fatal.

[27] To go back to our discussion of human behavior, we see at once that the problem of adequate differentiation is immeasurably more complex for men than it is for pickerel. The signs we respond to, and the symbols we create and train ourselves to respond to, are infinitely greater in number and immeasurably more abstract than the signs in a pickerel's environment. Lower animals have to deal only with certain brute facts in their physical environment. But think, only for a moment, of what constitutes a human environment. Think of the items that call for adequate responses that no animal ever has to think about: our days are named and numbered, so that we have birthdays, anniversaries, holidays, centennials, and so on, all calling for specifically human responses; we have history, which no animal has to worry about; we have verbally codified patterns of behavior which we call law, religion and ethics. We have to respond not only to events in our immediate environment, but to reported events in Washington, Paris, Tokyo, Moscow, Beirut. We have literature, comic strips, confession magazines, market quotations, detective stories, journals of abnormal psychology, bookkeeping systems to interpret. We have money, credit, banking, stocks, bonds, checks, bills. We have the complex symbolisms of moving pictures, paintings, drama, music, architecture and dress. In short, we live in a vast human dimension of which the lower animals have no inkling, and we have to have a capacity for differentiation adequate to the complexity of our extra environment.

Why Do People React as They Do?

[28] The next question, then, is why human beings do not always have an adequate capacity for differentiation. Why are we not constantly on the lookout for differences as well as similarities instead of feeling, as so

many do, that the Chinese (or Mexicans, or ballplayers, or women drivers) are "all alike"? Why do some people react to words as if they were the things they stand for? Why do certain patterns of reaction, both in individuals and in larger groups such as nations, persist long after the usefulness has expired?

[29] Part of our identification reactions are simply protective mechanisms inherited from the necessities of survival under earlier and more primitive conditions of life. I was once beaten up and robbed by two men on a dark street. Months later, I was again on a dark street with two men, good friends of mine, but involuntarily I found myself in a panic and insisted on our hurrying to a well-lighted drugstore to have a soda so that I would stop being jittery. In other words, my whole body reacted with an identification reaction of fear of these two men, in spite of the fact that "I knew" that I was in no danger. Fortunately, with the passage of time, this reaction has died away. But the hurtful experiences of early childhood do not fade so readily. There is no doubt that many identification reactions are traceable to childhood traumas,[1] as psychiatrists have shown.

[30] Further identification reactions are caused by communal patterns of behavior which were necessary or thought necessary at one stage or another in the development of a tribe or nation. General directives such as "Kill all snakes," "Never kill cows, which are sacred animals," "Shoot all strangers on sight," "Fall down flat on your face before all members of the aristocracy," or, to come to more modern instances, "Never vote for a Republican," "Oppose all government regulation of business," "Never associate with Negroes on terms of equality," are an enormous factor in the creation of identification reactions.

[31] Some human beings—possibly in their private feelings a majority— can accept these directives in a *human* way: that is, it will not be impossible for them under a sufficiently changed set of circumstances to kill a cow, or not to bow down before an aristocrat, to vote for a Republican, or to accept a Negro as a classmate. Others, however, get these directives so deeply ground into their nervous systems that they become incapable of changing their responses no matter how greatly the circumstances may have changed. Still others, although capable of changing their responses, dare not do so for fear of public opinion. Social progress usually requires the breaking up of these absolute identifications, which often make necessary changes impossible. Society must obviously have patterns of behavior; human beings must obviously have habits. But when those patterns become inflexible, so that a tribe has only one way to meet a famine, namely, to throw more infants as sacrifices to the crocodiles, or a nation has only one way to meet a threat to its security, namely, to increase its armaments, then such a tribe or such a nation is headed for trouble. There is insufficient capacity for differentiated behavior.

[1]a startling experience which has a lasting effect on mental life; a shock

[32] Furthermore — and here one must touch upon the role of newspapers, radio and television — if agencies of mass communication hammer away incessantly at the production of, let us say, a hostile set of reactions at such words as "Communists," "bureaucrats," "Wall Street," "international bankers," "labor leaders," and so on, no matter how useful an immediate job they may perform in correcting a given abuse at a given time and place, they can in the long run produce in thousands of readers and listeners identification reactions to the words — reactions that will make intelligent public discussion impossible. Modern means of mass communication and propaganda certainly have an important part to play in the creation of identification reactions.

[33] In addition to the foregoing, there is still another source of identification reactions; namely, the language we use in our daily thought and speech. Unlike the languages of the sciences, which are carefully constructed, tailor-made, special-purpose languages, the language of everyday life is one directly inherited and haphazardly developed from those of our prescientific ancestors: Anglo-Saxons, primitive Germanic tribes, primitive Indo-Europeans. With their scant knowledge of the world, they formulated descriptions of the world before them in statements such as "The sun rises." We do not today believe that the sun "rises." Nevertheless, we still continue to use the expression, without believing what we say.

Erroneous Implications in Everyday Language

[34] But there are other expressions, quite as primitive as the idea of "sunrise," which we use uncritically, fully believing in the implications of our terms. Having observed (or heard) that *some* Negroes are lazy, an individual may say, making a huge jump beyond the known facts, "Negroes are lazy." Without arguing for the moment the truth or falsity of this statement, let us examine the implications of the statement as it is ordinarily constructed: "Negroes are lazy." The statement implies, as common sense or any textbook on traditional logic will tell us, that "laziness" is a "quality" that is "inherent" in Negroes.

[35] What are the facts? Under conditions of slavery, under which Negroes were not paid for working, there wasn't any point in being an industrious and responsible worker. The distinguished French abstract artist Jean Hélion once told the story of his life as a prisoner of war in a German camp, where, during the Second World War, he was compelled to do forced labor. He told how he loafed on the job, how he thought of device after device for avoiding work and producing as little as possible — and, since his prison camp was a farm, how he stole chickens at every opportunity. He also described how he put on an expression of good-natured imbecility whenever approached by his Nazi overseers. Without intending to do so, in describing his own actions, he gave an almost perfect picture of the liter-

ary type of the Southern Negro of slavery days. Jean Hélion, confronted with the fact of forced labor, reacted as intelligently as Southern Negro slaves, and the slaves reacted as intelligently as Jean Hélion. "Laziness," then, is not an "inherent quality" of Negroes or of any other group of people. It is a *response* to a work situation in which there are no rewards for working, and in which one hates his taskmasters.

[36] Statements implying inherent qualities, such as "Negroes are lazy" or "There's something terribly wrong with young people today," are therefore the crudest kind of unscientific observation, based on an out-of-date way of saying things, like "The sun rises." The tragedy is not simply the fact that people make such statements; the graver fact is that they believe themselves.

[37] Some individuals are admired for their "realism" because, as the saying goes, they "call a spade a spade." Suppose we were to raise the question "Why should anyone call it a spade?" The reply would obviously be, "Because that's what it is!" This reply appeals so strongly to the common sense of most people that they feel that at this point discussion can be closed. I should like to ask the reader, however, to consider a point which may appear at first to him a mere quibble.

[38] Here, let us say, is an implement for digging made of steel, with a wooden handle. Here, on the other hand, is a succession of sounds made with the tongue, lips and vocal cords: "spade." If you want a digging implement of the kind we are talking about, you would ask for it by making the succession of sounds "spade" if you are addressing an English-speaking person. But suppose you were addressing a speaker of Dutch, French, Hungarian, Chinese, Tagalog? Would you not have to make completely different sounds? It is apparent, then, that the common-sense opinion of most people, "We call a spade a spade because that's what it is," is completely and utterly wrong. We call it a "spade" because we are English-speaking people, conforming, in this instance, to majority usage in naming this particular object. The steel-and-iron digging implement is simply an object standing there against the garage door; "spade" is what we *call* it—"spade" is a *name*.

[39] And here we come to another source of identification reactions— an unconscious assumption about language epitomized in the expression "a spade is a spade," or even more elegantly in the famous remark "Pigs are called pigs because they are such dirty animals." The assumption is that everything has a "right name" and that the "right name" names the "essence" of that which is named.

[40] If this assumption is at work in our reaction patterns, we are likely to be given to premature and often extremely inappropriate responses. We are likely to react to names as if they gave complete insight into the persons, things or situations named. If we are told that a given individual is a "Jew," some of us are likely to respond, "That's all I need to know." For, if names

give the essence of that which is named, obviously, every "Jew" has the essential attribute of "Jewishness." Or, to put it the other way around, it is because he possesses "Jewishness" that we call him a "Jew"! A further example of the operation of this assumption is that, in spite of the fact that my entire education has been in Canada and the United States and I am unable to read and write Japanese, I am sometimes credited, or accused, of having an "Oriental mind." Now, since Buddha, Confucius, General Tojo, Mao Tse-tung, Syngman Rhee, Pandit Nehru and the proprietor of the Golden Pheasant Chop Suey House all have "Oriental minds," it is hard to imagine what is meant. The "Oriental mind," like the attribute of "Jewishness," is purely and simply a fiction. Nevertheless, I used to note with alarm that newspaper columnists got paid for articles that purported to account for Stalin's behavior by pointing out that since he came from Georgia, which is next to Turkey and Azerbaijan and therefore "more a part of Asia than of Europe," he too had an "Oriental mind."

Improving Your Semantic Habits

[41] Our everyday habits of speech and our unconscious assumptions about the relations between words and things lead, then, to an identification reaction in which it is felt that all things that have the same name are entitled to the same response. From this point of view, all "insurance men," or "college boys," or "politicians," or "lawyers," or "Texans" are alike. Once we recognize the absurdity of these identification reactions based on identities of name, we can begin to think more clearly and more adequately. No "Texan" is exactly like any other "Texan." No "college boy" is exactly like any other "college boy." Most of the time "Texans" or "college boys" may be what you think they are: but often they are not. To realize fully the difference between words and what they stand for is to be ready for differences as well as similarities in the world. This readiness is mandatory to scientific thinking, as well as to sane thinking.

[42] Korzybski's simple but powerful suggestion to those wishing to improve their semantic habits is to add "index numbers" to all terms, according to the formula: A_1 is not A_2. Translated into everyday language we can state the formula in such terms as these: Cow_1 is not cow_2; cow_2 is not cow_3; $Texan_1$ is not $Texan_2$; $politician_1$ is not $politician_2$; ham and eggs (Plaza Hotel) are not ham and eggs (Smitty's Café); socialism (Russia) is not socialism (England); private enterprise (Joe's Shoe Repair Shop) is not private enterprise (A.T.&T.). The formula means that instead of simply thinking about "cows" or "politicians" or "private enterprise," we should think as factually as possible about the differences between one cow and another, one politician and another, one privately owned enterprise and another.

[43] This device of "indexing" will not automatically make us wiser and better, but it's a start When we talk or write, the habit of indexing our general terms will reduce our tendency to wild and woolly generalization. It will compel us to think before we speak—think in terms of concrete objects and events and situations, rather than in terms of verbal associations. When we read or listen, the habit of indexing will help us visualize more concretely, and therefore understand better, what is being said. And if nothing is being said except deceptive windbaggery, the habit of indexing may—at least part of the time—save us from snapping, like the pickerel, at phony minnows. Another way of summing up is to remember, as Wendell Johnson said, that "To a mouse, cheese is cheese—that's why mousetraps work."

EXERCISES

Questions

1. Do words "change" our lives, or do they "make" our lives? Or are we "made" by words and thus in need of being "changed"?
2. What does Hayakawa mean by a "pattern of reaction"? What forms our reaction patterns to semantic habits? What determines whether they are normal? What is your semantic pattern of reaction? Can you trace the origin of any part of it?
3. Hayakawa defines semantics five different ways. Find them. What is his final definition?
4. Paragraphs 3–19 present three sources of confusion regarding definitions of words. What is the inadequacy of mere dictionary definitions? How does Bridgman's contribution work? What is the problem of multiple meanings? What is the influence of personal responses to words? How can its interference with communication be controlled?
5. Why are words tricky? In what ways is the trickiness based on the words themselves, our feelings toward others, or our feelings toward ourselves?
6. Paragraphs 20–22 show certain stock or fixed reactions to questions. What is the relationship of stock or "identification reactions" to generalizations and prejudice? Why is this a particularly critical weakness for humans?
7. What is the difference between identification and differentiation?
8. What are some of the roadblocks to differentiation and how did they originate? Outline them and find examples other than those presented by Hayakawa.
9. How is "a spade is a spade" related to the logical fallacy called circular reasoning?
10. Why did it take Hayakawa so much longer to explain *how* we use language than to explain *why* we use it so?

11. What two suggestions does Hayakawa present for avoiding semantic pitfalls?
12. The readability of this essay is partly the result of his use of example. Notice especially paragraphs 12–19. How many other examples of illustration can you find used to clarify a semantic point?
13. Paragraphs 20–24 are tied together by the repetition, in different forms, of the four illustrations concluding paragraph 20. How are these ideas repeated and used in the rest of the section?

Vocabulary

intuitive
rabid

For Discussion and Writing

Examine these loaded terms:
    fuzzy-minded liberal, "liberal," and ultraliberal;
    peacenik, dove, and draft dodger;
    militant, hawk, super-patriot;
    free love, the Pill, sexual revolution
What do they reveal about attitudes? Can they be ranked?
    Examine your reactions to the following words and note which you respond to positively and which negatively. Line up the + words separately from the − words. Do they reveal anything to you about your attitudes?

liberal	integration	nun	capitalist
Catholic	conservative	atheist	individualism
radical	Jew	labor	Negro
pacifist	intermarriage	Protestant	agnostic
conscience	premarital sex	agitator	police

CROSS REFERENCES

COUSINS: "The Environment of Language"
FRIED: "A Four-Letter Word That Hurts"
McDONALD: "The Habit of Lying"
ROBINSON: "On Various Kinds of Thinking"
WHITE: "The Meaning of Democracy"

RECOMMENDED READING

CHASE, STUART: *The Power of Words* (Harcourt, Brace & World: 1954)

NORMAN COUSINS

"THE ENVIRONMENT OF LANGUAGE"

INTRODUCTION

Norman Cousins (1912–   ) has been editor of the *Saturday Review* since 1942, when it was still called the *Saturday Review of Literature*. The change in the title reflects Mr. Cousins' direction of the magazine: formerly chiefly a critical literary review, it became a critical review of all aspects of national and international life. In his private life, too, Mr. Cousins maintains many interests; he has been on the boards of such different organizations or publications as Freedom House, the *Encyclopaedia Britannica,* the World Federalists, and the Educational Television and Radio Center. Included in his several books are these provocative titles, *Modern Man Is Obsolete* (1945); *Who Speaks for Man?* (1952); and *In Place of Folly* (1961). His most recent book is *Present Tense—An American Editor's Odyssey* (1967).

TO THE READER

Our thinking is shaped by the word associations of our environment, making reactions to language almost an unconscious reflex.

Reprinted from *Saturday Review,* April 8, 1967, with the permission of Saturday Review, Inc., and the author.

The words men use, Julian Huxley once said, not only express but shape their ideas. Language is an instrument; it is even more an environment. It has as much to do with the philosophical and political conditioning of a society as geography or climate. The role of language in contributing to men's problems and their prospects is the subject of an imaginative and valuable study now getting under way at Pro Deo University in Rome, which is winning recognition in world university circles for putting advanced scholarship to work for the concept of a world community.

[2]   One aspect of the Pro Deo study, as might be expected, has to do with the art of conveying precise meaning from one language to another. Stuart Chase, one of America's leading semanticists, has pointed out that when an English speaker at the United Nations uses the expression "I assume," the French interpreter may say "I deduce" and the Russian interpreter may say "I consider." When Pope Paul VI sent a cable to Prime Minister Alexei Kosygin and Party Chairman Leonid Brezhnev on their accession to office, he expressed the hope that the historic aspirations of the Russian people for a fuller life would be advanced under the new leadership. As translated into Russian by the Vatican's own interpreter, the Pope's expression of hope came out in a way that made it appear that the Pope was making known his endorsement of the new regime. The eventual clarification was inevitably awkward for all concerned.

[3]   The Pro Deo study, however, will not be confined to problems of precise translation. The major emphasis has to do with something even more fundamental: the dangerous misconceptions and prejudices that take root in language and that undermine human values. The color of a man's skin, for example, is tied to plus-or-minus words that inevitably condition human attitudes. The words "black" and "white," as defined in Western culture, are heavily loaded. "Black" has all sorts of unfavorable connotations; "white" is almost all favorable. One of the more interesting papers being studied by the Pro Deo scholars is by Ossie Davis, the author and actor. Mr. Davis, a Negro, concluded on the basis of a detailed study of dictionaries and *Roget's Thesaurus* that the English language was his enemy. In *Roget's,* he counted 120 synonyms for "blackness," most of them with unpleasant connotations: blot, blotch, blight, smut, smudge, sully, begrime, soot, becloud, obscure, dingy, murky, threatening, frowning, foreboding, forbidden, sinister, baneful, dismal, evil, wicked, malignant, deadly, secretive, unclean, unwashed, foul, blacklist, black book, black-hearted, etc. Incorporated in the same listing were words such as Negro, nigger, and darky.

[4]   In the same *Roget's,* Mr. Davis found 134 synonyms for the word "white," almost all of them with favorable connotations: purity, cleanness, bright, shining, fair, blonde, stainless, chaste, unblemished, unsullied, innocent, honorable, upright, just, straightforward, genuine, trustworthy,

honesty, etc. "White" as a racial designation was, of course, included in this tally of desirable terms.

[5]   No less invidious[1] than black are some of the words associated with the color yellow: coward, conniver, baseness, fear, effeminacy, funk, soft, spiritless, poltroonery, pusillanimity, timidity, milksop, recreant, sneak, lilylivered, etc. Oriental peoples are included in the listing.

[6]   As a matter of factual accuracy, white, black, and yellow as colors are not descriptive of races. The coloration range of so-called white people may run from pale olive to mottled pink. So-called colored people run from light beige to mahogany. Absolute color designations — white, black, red, yellow — are not merely inaccurate; they have become symbolic rather than descriptive. It will be argued, of course, that definitions of color and the connotations that go with them are independent of sociological implications. There is no getting around the fact, it will be said, that whiteness means cleanliness and blackness means dirtiness. Are we to doctor the dictionary in order to achieve a social good? What this line of argument misses is that people in Western cultures do not realize the extent to which their racial attitudes have been conditioned since early childhood by the power of words to ennoble or condemn, augment or detract, glorify or demean. Negative language infects the subconscious of most Western people from the time they first learn to speak. Prejudice is not merely imparted or superimposed. It is metabolized in the bloodstream of society. What is needed is not so much a change in language as an awareness of the power of words to condition attitudes. If we can at least recognize the underpinnings of prejudice, we may be in a position to deal with the effects.

[7]   To be sure, Western languages have no monopoly on words with connotations that affect judgment. In Chinese, whiteness means cleanliness, but it can also mean bloodlessness, coldness, frigidity, absence of feeling, weakness, insensitivity. Also in Chinese, yellowness is associated with sunshine, openness, beauty, flowering, etc. Similarly, the word black in many African tongues has connotations of strength, certainty, recognizability, integrity, while white is associated with paleness, anemia, unnaturalness, deviousness, untrustworthiness.

[8]   The purpose of Pro Deo University in undertaking this study is not just to demonstrate that most cultures tend to be self-serving in their language. The purpose is to give educational substance to the belief that it will take all the adroitness and sensitivity of which the human species is capable if it is to be sustained. Earth-dwellers now have the choice of making their world into a neighborhood or a crematorium. Language is one of the factors in that option. The right words may not automatically produce the right actions but they are an essential part of the process.

[1]offensively or unfairly discriminating; harmful; injurious

EXERCISES

Questions

1. Cousins' theme is expressed in his last paragraph. What is the purpose of the Pro Deo University study? Why is it especially important today?
2. In what areas do words serve as our environment? What problems of translation are revealed?
3. How do prejudices take root in language? How does this serve to undermine human values?
4. What negative meanings does Cousins show for black? What positive associations? Are there others of either kind you can supply?
5. What positive meanings are given for white? What negative associations? What others can you supply?
6. What positive and negative meanings are given for yellow?
7. In what ways are cultures self-serving in word choice? Why is this such a massive problem?
8. Since we cannot change the language, what can we do to control or offset the effort of prejudiced language?
9. Notice that Cousins usually begins his paragraphs with the theme sentences. For a quick reading of the essay, reread just the first two sentences of each paragraph.
10. How has Cousins used comparison and contrast to strengthen his thesis?
11. How do continuous references to the Pro Deo University serve to strengthen the article?

Vocabulary

adroitness
augment
demean
metabolized
pusillanimity
recreant

For Discussion and Writing

1. Red — positive and negative responses
2. Martin Luther King's campaign: "Black is Beautiful"
3. Blackness and fear: origin and irrationality
4. Woman: positive and negative responses
5. Man: positive and negative responses
6. The diplomatic languages, French and English: Are they really representative?

CROSS REFERENCES

FRIED: "A Four-Letter Word That Hurts"
HAYAKAWA: "How Words Change Our Lives"
HONWANA: "The Hands of the Blacks"
ROBINSON: "On Various Kinds of Thinking"
THURBER: "The Trouble with Man Is Man"

RECOMMENDED READING

MELVILLE, HERMAN: *Moby Dick,* chapter 42, "The Whiteness of the Whale"

DONALD McDONALD

"THE HABIT OF LYING"

INTRODUCTION

Donald McDonald (1920–   ) is a former dean of the College of Journalism at Marquette Univeristy. Since 1965, he has been a staff member of the Center for the Study of Democratic Institutions which publishes the *Center Diary* from which this article was taken. Mr. McDonald is also a syndicated columnist, having written for Catholic weekly newspapers since 1952. He was an editor of *Religion and Freedom* in 1958, and author of *Catholics in Conversation* (1960).

TO THE READER

McDonald presents the dangers of abstract thinking: lying is not only a matter of morality; it is a demonstration of selective thinking.

Gabriel Marcel, the French Catholic philosopher, provides an illuminating insight into the question of how man can rationalize[1] something as irrational as war.

Reprinted from *Center Dairy: 14*, with the permission of the Center for the Study of Democratic Institutions, 1966, and the author.
    [1]to invent plausible explanations for acts, opinions, and so forth, that are actually based on other causes

212

[2]   In his book, *Man Against the Masses,* Marcel devotes a chapter to "the spirit of abstraction² as a factor making for war." Earlier, in his preface, he recalls that from the time of his first philosophical researches, in 1910 and 1911, he had developed a dislike and a distrust of the "spirit of abstraction."

[3]   Now, a half century later, he is more than ever convinced that this spirit is both an intellectual and a moral disease, that another word for it is *lying,* and that there is an inseparable connection between it and the making of war.

[4]   Marcel makes clear he is not condemning abstractions as such, a necessary mental operation by which one, for the sake of pursuing a determinate purpose, methodically omits certain aspects which, though they may be important in themselves, are for the moment irrelevant to that purpose.

[5]   It is important, he maintains, that in performing this mental operation of abstraction the person "retain a precise and distinct awareness of those methodical omissions."

[6]   Once one loses this awareness, he falls into the "spirit of abstraction," mistakes what is only an expedient method (abstraction) for truth itself, and develops a "contempt" for the concrete conditions on which all mental operations must be based.

[7]   Once immersed in this "spirit of abstraction," man is no longer really performing an "intellectual operation"; he is substituting the abstraction for reality itself. In a word, he is lying. One of the forms of this lying is the isolation of a single category, assigning to it an arbitrary primacy, and then proceeding to "interpret the whole pattern of human reality" on the basis of that category.

[8]   The spirit of abstraction, lying, permits one to justify the waging of war because it ignores the concrete realities of war — killing, maiming, burning — and the concrete consequences of it.

[9]   "In the actual world we are living in," says Marcel, "it is impossible not to recognize that making war is linked to lying . . . lying to others and lying to oneself. . . .

[10]   "A person who is not lying to himself can hardly fail to observe that in its modern forms war is a disaster from which no counterbalancing advantage can be reaped. . . .

[11]   "It is only through organized lying that we can hope to make war acceptable to those who must wage or suffer it. . . . As soon as people (*people,* that is to say, the State or a political party or a faction or a religious sect, or whatever it may be) claim of me that I commit myself to a warlike action against other human beings whom I must, as a consequence of my commitment, be ready to destroy, it is very necessary from the point of view of those who are influencing me that I lose all awareness of the individual reality of the being whom I may be led to destroy.

²the act of considering something as a general quality or characteristic, apart from concrete realities, specific objects, or actual instances

[12] "In order to transform him into a mere impersonal target, it is absolutely necessary to convert him into an abstraction: *the* Communist, *the* anti-Fascist, *the* Fascist, and so on."

[13] (It might be noted here how often we read in the dispatches from Vietnam that today "our side" killed so-and-so-many "Communists," never men; and one can assume that the dispatches from "their side" report so-and-so-many "imperialists" killed, never American men. Brutality is noble, so long as it is a "Communist" or an "imperialist" who is killed or crippled.)

[14] Marcel has much more to say about lying and the spirit of abstraction. He believes it is closely linked with the lack of reflection and of the contemplative spirit (which enables man to see his fellow-man in his full concreteness), and that the lack of reflection in modern man can be laid, in great part, at the doorstep of the "popular press," which "by its nature has a bias against reflection, against reflection of every type."

EXERCISES

Questions

1. What is abstract reasoning? What is meant by an "awareness of omissions" of abstract thinking?
2. Differentiate between "abstraction" and the "spirit of abstraction." What makes one acceptable and the other a lie?
3. According to Marcel, how important are the concrete realities of a situation? How important are they today?
4. What is the reality that warfare ignores? How is war then made acceptable?
5. What do men do to dehumanize the enemy? How does this dehumanize themselves?
6. What are "reflection" and "contemplation"? How are they related to abstraction? How are they the solution to the habit of lying?
7. The first half (paragraphs 1–8) of this essay is definition. What purpose does the second half serve?
8. What is the value of the frequent reference to Gabriel Marcel?

Vocabulary

expedient
primacy

For Discussion and Writing

1. Lying and the credibility gap
2. States' rights—a lying term
3. The big lie versus the small one

4.   Is a white lie white?
5.   Depersonalization of the "other side" in newspaper reports
6.   Dehumanization and computerization of educational processes

CROSS REFERENCES

ROBINSON: "On Various Kinds of Thinking"
SPITZ: "The Timken Edition of Lenin"

RECOMMENDED READING

HELLER, JOSEPH: *Catch 22* (Simon & Schuster, 1961)
REMARQUE, ERICH MARIA: *All Quiet on the Western Front* (Little, Brown
   & Co.: 1929)

GRANVILLE HICKS

"RIGHT WORD, WRONG SPELLING"

INTRODUCTION

Granville Hicks (1901–   ), a contributing editor to the *Saturday Review*, is probably one of the most influential book reviewers in the country. Earlier in his career, Mr. Hicks worked as a literary consultant to the *New Leader* magazine and on the faculties of several of the nation's leading colleges and universities. He has written quite extensively, and his works include fiction, biography, and criticism. Among his titles are *The Great Tradition: An Interpretation of American Literature since the Civil War*, his first book written in 1933 and revised in 1935; *Part of the Truth* (an autobiography written in 1965); and his most recent book, written in 1968, *John Reed: The Making of a Revolutionary*.

TO THE READER

This one time, don't go to the dictionary; enjoy Hicks' gradual revelation of the meaning of borborygmus.

Abridged from an article in *Saturday Review*, June 25, 1966. Reprinted with the permission of *Saturday Review* and the author.

My column of May 7, "The Wrong Word for It," has so far produced 166 communications, most of them intended to set me straight on "boryborygmus." As I pointed out in the letter that appeared in *SR* May 28, I had miscopied the word, introducing an extra "y." A correspondent in France, addressing me as "Drear Sire," stated: "Your heave an probulem. Toot marny sletters. Tinny trypo addled top obscurcity. Warong world." Most of the writers assumed, correctly, that I meant "borborygmus," and gently and often amusingly contributed to my education. Several arrived at the English word by way of its French equivalent, "*borborygme.*"

[2]   What surprises me is that "borborygmus" seems not to be a particularly unusual word. A dozen persons thought of it in connection with Humphrey Bogart's "digestive tintinnabulation" in *The African Queen.* Some thought *Time* applied the word to Bogart's performance, and perhaps it did; but Jim Hines of Fullerton High School, Fullerton, California, cites an article in *Life* for March 31, 1952: "an unshaven borborygmic bum."

[3]   Next to Bogart, the person most often mentioned was Aldous Huxley, who, according to my correspondents, used the word in *Crome Yellow* or maybe *Antic Hay* or maybe *Point Counter Point* or maybe *After Many a Summer Dies the Swan.* Whatever the source, the passage seems to have been "the stertorous[1] borborygmus of the dyspeptic Carlyle," or something to that general effect.

[4]   Two readers encountered the word in Richard Haydn's *The Journal of Edwin Carp,* a book that I don't know but probably should. Two others mention a story by Graham Greene about a man whose borborygmi were likely to imitate anything from a Brahms symphony to an air raid warning. (I once knew an elderly man who, when embarrassed by borborygmus, would say, "Listen to the sleigh bells.") Others recall an editorial in the *New York World,* saying that G. K. Chesterton, who was visiting this country at the time, often "mistook his borborygmus for the rumblings of the universe." Conrad Aiken, I am reminded, entitled a poem "King Borborigmi," and someone quotes from Ogden Nash:

> Once my internal rumblings at parties
>   caused me to wish I could shrink to
>   nothing, or at least to a pigmy,
> But now I proudly inquire, Can every-
>   body hear my borborygmi?

[5]   As is not surprising, doctors are more familiar with the word than

---

[1]breathing in a heavy, snoring manner

most people and make more use of it. One doctor says that a friend of his used to write a column called "Borborygmi." Another reports that there is "an LP record on sale entitled 'Borborygmi,' being a group of original songs sung by a group of, no doubt, original M.D.'s." Still another speaks of a play with the title *Borborygmi*, staged by dental students at the University of Pittsburgh. And the Student Medical Conference of the University of California sporadically publishes a periodical named *Borborygmi*, in one issue of which, sent me as a sample, I found a calm, informative discussion of LSD.

[6]   The word, obviously, is capable of figurative use. Two correspondents have had experience with borborygmic radiators, one in literature and one in life. And a good friend of mine, who says she had never heard of the word until she read my column, promptly encountered it in *The Diary of George Templeton Strong*: on March 17, 1874, Strong recorded that there were rumors of volcanic action in North Carolina. The next day he wrote, "Rumors continue of subterraneous singults and borborygmi in North Carolina . . ." ("Singult" is defined by Webster as "a sob.")

[7]   As for the limerick in question, I have known it for years in a form somewhat different from that immortalized by Bennett Cerf:

> I sat by the duchess at tea
> It was just as I knew it would be
>   Her rumblings abdominal
>   Were simply abominable
> And everyone blamed them on me.

[8]   Although this has a nice onomatopoeic ring, the bad rhyme has always bothered me; Cerf's "abdominal/ phenomenal," also to be found in a number of versions supplied by correspondents, is better, though perhaps tamer. One correspondent offers as third and fourth lines: "For her organs internal/Made noises infernal," but that seems namby-pamby. Then there was a French version sent me, with the lines, *"Mais ses forts borborygmes/ Etaient des paradigmes."*

•   •   •   •   •   •

[9]   I have no quarrel with the use of uncommon words; I think they're fun. Perhaps a writer of fiction runs a risk if he breaks his own spell to send a reader to the dictionary, but that is his business. I am grateful to Mrs. Martin Hulquist for telling me about a charming word, "merrythought," which means "wishbone"; and I think Professor George S. Welsh of the University of North Carolina, who suggests that readers might be interested in discovering the difference between a zax and a zarf.

EXERCISES

Questions

1. Hicks' theme appears in paragraph 9. Does the piece support his theme?
2. What sets the tone of the article and reinforces Hicks' declaration: "I think they're fun"?
3. When did you begin to catch on to what the word meant? When you understood, did you go back and reread the earlier uses to get their humor? If you didn't, go back now.
4. What different devices of definition does Hicks use?
5. What is the denotation of borborygmus? What are the connotations?
6. What is the difference between zax and zarf?

Vocabulary

dyspeptic
onomatopoeia
sporadically
tintinnabulation

For Discussion and Writing

Find the wackiest word you can in the dictionary.

CROSS REFERENCES

COUSINS: "The Environment of Language"
HAYAKAWA: "How Words Change Our Lives"

RECOMMENDED READING

IONESCO, EUGENE: *The Bald Soprano* (Grove Press: 1965)
THURBER, JAMES: *Fables for Our Time* (Harper & Row: 1952)

ARTHUR SCHLESINGER, JR.

"A NOTE ON LANGUAGE"

INTRODUCTION

Arthur Schlesinger, Jr. (1917–   ), a historian and teacher, served as an adviser and speech writer to President John Kennedy from 1960 to 1963. Mr. Schlesinger has won many honors and awards, including the Pulitzer Prize for History, and a Guggenheim Fellowship. An authority on Franklin D. Roosevelt and Andrew Jackson, he wrote *The Age of Jackson* (1945) and *The Coming of the New Deal* (1958). With Richard Rovere, in 1951, he wrote *The General and the President*. He is best known, however, for his personal history of the Kennedy administration, *A Thousand Days*, from which this brief excerpt is taken.

TO THE READER

Policy makers in the State Department are subject to the same errors and criticisms in their use of words as freshmen students.

The intellectual exhaustion of the Foreign Service expressed itself in the poverty of the official rhetoric. In meetings the men from State would

Reprinted from *A Thousand Days*, by Arthur Schlesinger, Jr., with the permission of Houghton Mifflin Co., the publishers, and the author.

talk in a bureaucratic patois[1] borrowed in large part from the Department of Defense. We would be exhorted to "zero in" on "the purpose of the drill" (or of the "exercise" or "operation"), to "crank in" this and "phase out" that and "gin up" something else, to "pinpoint" a "viable" policy and, behind it, a "fall-back position," to ignore the "flak" from competing government bureaus or from the communists, to refrain from "nit-picking" and never to be "counterproductive." Once we were "seized of the problem," preferably in as "hard-nosed" a manner as possible, we would review "options," discuss "over-all" objectives, seek "breakthroughs," consider "crash programs," "staff out" policies—doing all these things preferably "meaningfully" and "in depth" until we were ready to "finalize" our deliberations, "sign on to" or "sign off on" a conclusion (I never could discover the distinction, if any, between these two locutions[2]) and "implement" a decision. This was not just shorthand; part of the conference-table vocabulary involved a studied multiplication of words. Thus one never talked about a "paper" but always a "piece of paper," never said "at this point" but always "at this point in time."

[2]   Graceless as this patois was, it did have a certain, if sometimes spurious,[3] air of briskness and efficiency. The result was far worse when the Department stopped talking and started writing. Whether drafting memoranda, cables or even letters or statements for the President, the Department fell into full, ripe, dreariness of utterance with hideous ease. The recipe was evidently to take a handful of clichés (saying something in a fresh way might create unforeseen troubles), repeat at five-minute intervals (lest the argument become clear or interesting), stir in the dough of the passive voice (the active voice assigns responsibility and was therefore hazardous) and garnish with self-serving rhetoric (Congress would be unhappy unless we constantly proclaimed the rectitude[4] of American motives).

[3]   After the Bay of Pigs, the State Department sent over a document entitled "The Communist Totalitarian Government of Cuba as a Source of International Tension in the Americas," which it had approved for distribution to NATO, CENTO, SEATO, the OAS and the free governments of Latin America and eventually for public release. In addition to the usual defects of Foggy Bottom[5] prose, the paper was filled with bad spelling and grammar. Moreover, the narrative, which mysteriously stopped at the beginning of April 1961, contained a self-righteous condemnation of Castro's interventionist activities in the Caribbean that an unfriendly critic, alas! could have applied, without changing a word, to more recent actions by the United States. I responded on behalf of the White House:

[1]an ungrammatical mixture of two or more languages
[2]a style of speech or verbal expression
[3]not genuine, authentic, or true; counterfeit
[4]rightness of principles or practice; moral virtue
[5]the derisive name commonly given the State Department

It is our feeling here that the paper should not be disseminated in its present form. . . .

Presumably the document is designed to impress, not an audience which is already passionately anti-Castro, but an audience which has not yet finally made up its mind on the gravity of the problem. Such an audience is going to be persuaded, not by rhetoric, but by evidence. Every effort to heighten the evidence by rhetoric only impairs the persuasive power of the document. Observe the title: "The Communist Totalitarian Government of Cuba . . . " This title presupposes the conclusion which the paper seeks to establish. Why not call it "The Castro Regime in Cuba" and let the reader draw his own conclusions from the evidence? And why call it both "Communist" and "totalitarian"? All Communist governments are totalitarian. The paper, in our view, should be understated rather than overstated; it should eschew[6] cold war jargon; the argument should be carried by facts, not exhortations. The writing is below the level we would hope for in papers for dissemination to other countries. The writing of lucid and forceful English is not too arcane[7] an art.

[4]   The President himself, with his sensitive ear for style, led the fight for literacy in the Department; and he had the vigorous support of some State Department officials, notably George Ball, Harriman and William R. Tyler. But the effort to liberate the State Department from automatic writing had little success. As late as 1963, the Department could submit as a draft of a presidential message on the National Academy of Foreign Affairs a text which provoked this resigned White House comment:

This is only the latest and worst of a long number of drafts sent here for Presidential signature. Most of the time it does not matter, I suppose, if the prose is tired, the thought banal and the syntax bureaucratic; and, occasionally when it does matter, State's drafts are very good. But sometimes, as in this case, they are not.

A message to Congress is a fairly important form of Presidential communication. The President does not send so many — nor of those he does send, does State draft so many — that each one cannot receive due care and attention. My own old-fashioned belief is that every Presidential message should be a model of grace, lucidity and taste in expression. At the very least, each message should be (a) in English, (b) clear and trenchant[8] in its style, (c) logical in its structure and (d) devoid of gobbledygook. The State Department draft on the

[6]shun; avoid
[7]mysterious; secret; obscure
[8]incisive; vigorous; effective

Academy failed each one of these tests (including, in my view, the first).

Would it not be possible for someone in the Department with at least minimal sensibility to take a look at pieces of paper designed for Presidential signature before they are sent to the White House?

It was a vain fight; the plague of gobbledygook was hard to shake off. I note words like "minimal" (at least not "optimal") and "pieces of paper" in my own lament. I can only testify with what interest and relief the President and the White House read cables from ambassadors who could write — Galbraith from New Delhi with his suave irony, David Bruce from London with his sharp wit, Kennan from Belgrade with his historical perspective and somber eloquence, John Bartlow Martin from Santo Domingo and William Attwood from Guinea with their vivid journalistic touch.

[5]   Theodore H. White summed it all up in a letter he sent me from the Far East in the summer of 1961 — a dispatch the President read with great interest. "The State Department and its competitive instruments," White wrote, "have in the years since I worked with them become so tangled as to be almost unfit for any policy-making purpose or decision. . . . Somewhere there exists in the State Department a zone, or a climate, or inertia, which prevents it from thinking in terms of a new kind of politics, new departures in technique, an inertia which binds it rigidly to the fossil routine of conferences, negotiations, frozen positions. What must be changed must be changed first in Washington, at the center."

EXERCISES

Questions

1.   Schlesinger presents his theme in his first sentence. How was this "official rhetoric" poverty stricken? What is the reciprocal relationship between language and thinking that Schlesinger is demonstrating?
2.   How many overused metaphors does he illustrate in paragraph 1? How many of these are still in use? Can you add some? How many redundancies are there in paragraph 1?
3.   What is the apparent significance of the reliance on military language by the State Department?
4.   Discuss the effectiveness of the cooking metaphor in paragraph 2.
5.   Read the two memos carefully. What errors in writing is the author pointing out? What does he say good writing should be?
6.   Discuss the significance of Theodore White's memo.

Vocabulary

exhortation

For Discussion and Writing

Examine any recent press statement from the State Department for the errors Schlesinger wrote about in 1965.

CROSS REFERENCES

FULBRIGHT: "The Cold War in American Life"
HAYAKAWA: "How Words Change Our Lives"
SCHOENSTEIN: "This Is Our Goodest Hour"
SPITZ: "The Timken Edition of Lenin"
THURBER: "The Trouble with Man Is Man"

RALPH SCHOENSTEIN

"THIS IS OUR GOODEST HOUR"

INTRODUCTION

Ralph Schoenstein (1933–   ) has been writing humor for one media or another for most of his professional life. He has written a humor column for various newspapers, contributed to magazines like *McCall's, The Saturday Evening Post,* and *Saturday Review,* has been included in anthologies, and has broadcast on television for both CBS and NBC. In 1962, he won the Grantland Rice Memorial Award for a nonfiction sports story, "A Giant Fan's Lament." In 1960, he published *The Block* and in 1965, *Time Lurches On,* from which this essay was taken. It originally appeared in a somewhat different form in *Saturday Review.*

TO THE READER

The sarcasm evident in the title is the key to this essay. If you have ever rebelled against the language of advertising or been bewildered by government directives, you should like this.

Reprinted from *Saturday Review,* October 14, 1961, with the permission of Saturday Review, Inc., and the author. The author has updated the article for this book.

The Army may have recalled me this morning, but I can't be sure. I received a six-page directive from the headquarters of the Army Security Agency. The first sentence says: "Dissemination of the contents of this directive will be restricted to key personnel who are directly concerned with the implementation thereof." Now a friend of mine who knows a little English says this sentence means that the directive applies only to the people it applies to; but I think his translation misses the full meaning. For example, what about "the implementation thereof?" I think the directive applies only to men with shovels.

[2]   Fortunately, the next paragraph clarifies everything. It explains: "Policies and procedures prescribed herein are sufficiently flexible to permit latitude in implementation. Detailed guidance is provided only when uniformity is required." So it turns out that the men with shovels can dig wherever they want, while the non-shovelers will be told what to do only when the Army wants them all to do it the same way. Otherwise, improvised chaos is permissible.

[3]   Of course, the directive has its definitions. One section says: "Significant terms used herein are defined as follows: (a) AS-USAR Personnel — Includes both male and female; (b) Spouse — A husband or wife." By making it clear that the directive applies only to the Army's men and women, the Security Agency has freed all active reserve dogs, commissioned children, and National Guard cows to operate on their own. Moreover, note the splendid camouflage in the definition of spouse. This is to mislead the Russians, who'll never suspect that a spouse is really a bourbon-powered rocket carrying a very mellow mouse.

[4]   All this khaki prose made Judy and me start reminiscing about the English language. You remember the English language. You can still contact it in documentaries about Winston Churchill; and you can even find it taught at a few little colleges that aren't implementing the mass production of scientists. Judy and I were wondering exactly when English became a dead language — and thus the perfect vehicle for my moribund career. She felt that it took a mortal wound on the day a man picked up his crayon to write "tastes good like a cigarette should." This inspired conjunction opened the floodgates: it made English suspect. During the peak of its popularity, I was reckless enough to tell a friend, "This hair tonic tastes good as a hair tonic should." He looked at me as if I'd just kicked my mother — sorry, *like* I'd just kicked my mother.

[5]   "You pedants[1] think I don't know that like isn't a conjunction," he said. "Well, my wisdom goes far beyond archaic grammar. A language must be a living, growing thing. In colloquial speech, what's correct often sounds stilted. Like I know I really should say 'tastes good *insomuch as a*

---

[1]people who make an excessive or inappropriate show of learning

cigarette should.' But like *sounds* better. Of course, there are certain times when it doesn't. Take the man who said, 'Don't know what to call her, but she's mighty like a rose.' Imagine the *strength* this line would have gained had he been colloquially wise enough to say, 'Don't know what to call her, but she's mighty as a rose.' His beloved not only would've had beauty but stamina, too."

[6]   My friend had sounded the battle cry for the Colloquial Revolution. Soon, ads were telling me about a stocking with "a marvelously young heel," not to be confused with a stocking that had a senile heel, or even one wearily middle-aged. No longer was a marvelously young heel an old rat who'd taken hormones. Usagewise, from Madison Avenue to the Pentagon, English was getting spoke better like *The Scarlet Letter*. It was a fun time for all.

[7]   Not to be outdone by the Pentagon, the Treasury Department helped the revolution by describing a new system for the purchase of foreign money. "This action," said the Treasury, "in a limited degree may help to illustrate some of the potentialities of this possible line of development." All over the world, T-men sprung into effectuation.

[8]   The revolution won a major victory when a certain soft drink started making people as young as their socks. The drink was suddenly advertised "for those who think young." Unfortunately, I had to stop taking it, for something that made you think young would surely be poison for a reminiscing fool like me who spent most of his time thinking old and blue.

[9]   Soon, one could reach nirvana merely by sipping this drink in a room heated by the gas that advertised "Think clean." All over America, people made childish by the drink began taking the gas for a chaser; for what good was it to be young and *dirty?* Booksellers pushing Henry Miller wanted to fight back by saying "Think purple;" but they knew that since cleanliness was next to godliness, to fight against minds purified by the gas would be to fight on the side of Satan.

[10] This living, growing language, this drive to effectuate something better than English, received a federal blessing when Pentagon officials military secretwise finalized a quite unique problem of implementing the release of photographic-type pictures to press and air media by saying, "Not classified but not publishable." Local officials quickly joined the crusade. Throughout New York, I began seeing posters about a government pamphlet that told "the true facts about inflation." These were not to be confused with the *false* facts about inflation, which were in a different and much grimmer pamphlet. As part of the city's safety campaign, other posters showed a cat that said, "I've got nine lives. Do you?" Do *I've* got nine lives? Of course I've don't.

[11] The true facts about inflation are part of a trend toward reinforced language that was started by Hollywood, where only a naked noun is indecent, where one artist is now dreaming about a story "even greater than *The Greatest Story Ever Told*." "She's very dead," says the private eye in a

movie that's "Strictly for Adults Only." (Movies that are merely "For Adults Only" admit children who shave.) "Tough break," says his secretary. "She was slightly pregnant." Soon, very dead won't be strong enough: our deadest people will have to be very much dead, or perhaps colossally dead. Then being merely dead will be a state of health. I wonder if the teen-ager who's slightly pregnant has an easier time breaking the news to mother than one who's pregnant without modification. Of course, the girl who's very pregnant has already taken gas. Let's hope it was the brand that took her out thinking clean.

[12] The colloquial crusade has been so successful that I just heard a jingle in which a little girl sings that a certain cereal "is gooder than all the rest." Finding such an eloquent child to do this jingle wasn't easy: she had to be stolen from a soft drink that she'd been calling "the deliciousest." Then she had to be trained to correct a speech defect, for she kept saying that the cereal was "the best." For a long time, the best — sorry, the goodest — she could do was to call the cereal "the most good," which was hardly goodest enough for a sponsor spending that kind of money.

[13] In addition to training a backward child, this sponsor also spent thousands of dollars to find the goodest slogan to make people eat his cereal. He hired top motivational research men who spent months probing the psychology of non-Asiatic-oriented consumer group response to visual inducements evidenced as video stimuli. After definitizing extenso-intensive study of the purchase-type sales of consumered products, these experts concluded that most people are morons, brainwise. This surely was useful knowledge for the sponsor, but he had to know more. Were these morons also *hungry?*

[14] He and his advertising agency then considered the most poetic slogans: 1) Crummies is gooder than all the rest; 2) Crummies has deliciousness; 3) Crummies is the eatingest cereal; and a few slangy ones. Number two was quickly eliminated because it was too close to English; one account executive swore it *was* English. Some of the men liked number three, but it was similar to the slogan of a toothpaste that called itself "the cleaningest." One man wanted "Crummies nutritions you up." His colleagues said that this was pure Keats, but people weren't ready for it. Ironically, the next day a tea manufacturer advertised that his bag "psyches you up." Now the Crummies people realized that they'd underrated the intelligence of their consumers. "We've got to stop writing down to the morons," said a media man.

[15] "Well, that's water over the flagpole," said another. "What about 'Crummies libidos[2] you up'?"

[16] "It swings good," said the account executive, "but it's a bad image to orientate the kids with, sexwise. 'Crummies libidos you *down*' would be more wider accepted, parentwise."

[2]usually a noun referring to the sex drive

[17] "I'm frankly afraid of libido up *or* down," said the sponsor. "I'd rather not use foreign words. Let's skip the Italian and finalize this with simple English: 'Crummies is gooder.'"

[18] In his next ad, the tea manufacturer said that his tea not only psyches you up but is also "the most cheerful stuff in the world" (and therefore even more euphoric[3] than the soft drink with "laughing bubbles"). I was delighted to read this because I hate sullen tea, though I don't mind if my coffee is a bit depressed. Of course, coffee no longer has to be blue now that a certain instant is advertising "a wake-up flavor." This brand isn't to be confused with "the coffee-er coffee," which doesn't have to wake you up because it doesn't let you sleep in the first place.

[19] My favoritest coffee is the one made from "aged Colombians." Some of my friends are upset by the barbaric way this brew must be made; but I feel that most of those old folks were ready to go anyway, so why not put them into a tasty national product. We must be careful about imposing democracy on countries not ready for it; perhaps the Colombians laugh at Social Security. Moreover, there's absolutely nothing senile-tasting about this coffee. In fact, it actually youngers-up the pancakes on which I put the syrup that's "richer pouring," a syrup made from only the finest old debentures.[4]

[20] If English is dying, what's replacing it? A new language I call dung-tongue, which is often so close to English that nine out of ten independent doctors can't tell the difference. "Have a *real* cigarette!" cries the man who's telling you that his brand actually contains tobacco and not sawdust or chow mein like a cigarette shouldn't. He wants you to try a cigarette that's too virile to "air-soften every puff" or "travel and gentle the smoke," one that may not be "friendly to your taste" but at least is ruggedly cordial. His will be the best cigarette until the fear of lung cancer triggers the birth of an even better one, a cigarette whose pitchmen will be telling us, "Smoke benign."[5]

[21] Yes, our health does concern the bards of dung-tongue. Yesterday while riding a bus, depressed by tired blood, old heels, and dirty thoughts, I suddenly saw an ad that said, "Stops useless coughing!" How heartened I was by this news! How exhilarated I felt to know that at least one medicine on this sick planet lets you do only *useful* coughing. Lord knows there's little enough of it.

[22] This is the dung-tongue of the present; but at the New York World's Fair, one can see the dung-tongue of the future: one can see an authentic "refreshment complex." What is a refreshment complex? Some scholars say it's a hot dog stand for wealthy tourists; others say it's a fear of taking showers. But no matter what it may be, it's the American language of the future.

---

[3]exaggerated and unreal sense of well-being
[4]a certificate of indebtedness
[5]healthful, pleasant, or beneficial; not malignant

Also pointing towards this future are dung-tongue ads that now urge us to drink beer from a "new glass can." This may be a dramatic breakthrough in the invention of the bottle.

[23] If useful coughing is here and the bottle is on the way, we may be at the dawn of our goodest hour. Perhaps there's still hope for a people fighting air pollution by smoking "twice as refreshed," a people growing softer each day from "spongeability," which I'd always thought meant a talent for free-loading. Perhaps the time is near when we'll also have the pill that will stop useless hemorrhage. When that time comes, will *I* start using dung-tongue? Of course not. Us English-speakers would rather *fight* than switch!

EXERCISES

Questions

1. Schoenstein states his theme in paragraph 20. How is this related to his title? Why is English dead? Or is it only wounded?
2. What does the Army directive say? Why does Schoenstein refer to shovels? Why call the letter a "directive"? What is the effect of "a little English" and "the full meaning"?
3. Any living language changes. Is Schoenstein opposed to this change? Reread any two or three of his examples. What specifically does he object to?
4. Reread paragraph 4. Is English "suspect"? Why? How is this related to the three sources of "dung-tongue" he cites? What do you think of his decision to "fight rather than switch"?
5. Is "like" a conjunction? If it isn't, what is it?
6. There are three enemies responsible for the death of English — the government, the advertising industry, and Hollywood. What are the attacks on language illustrated by each?
7. Paragraph 6 contains two puns, two grammatical errors, and two word misuses. Find them.
8. Read sentence 1 in paragraph 10. What are the errors in it? How does the horrible style relate to the essay's content? What are the other errors in the paragraph? Explain what is wrong.
9. Paragraph 13 kids the language of social scientists. What jargon terms can you find? Translate.

Vocabulary

effectuation
moribund

For Discussion and Writing

1. Dung-tongue in current advertisements
2. Dung-tongue in insurance policies

CROSS REFERENCE

SCHLESINGER: "A Note on Language"

THE USES OF LEISURE

NELSON A. ROCKEFELLER

"THE GOVERNOR LECTURES ON ART"

INTRODUCTION

Nelson A. Rockefeller (1908–   ) is known to virtually all Americans as a member of one of the nation's wealthiest families and as the governor of New York. Fewer people know him as an avid art collector and as a patron of modern art. Early in his administration, Governor Rockefeller sponsored the New York State Council on the Arts, the purpose of which was to make great works of art, music, and drama more available to the people of the state. He also used the Executive Mansion as a showcase for modern art. After his term of office expires, Governor Rockefeller plans to leave some of the paintings and sculptures in the Executive Mansion as gifts to the state and its citizens.

TO THE READER

This lecture was delivered in March 1967 at the New School for Social Research in New York City.

Mr. Rockefeller believes that art need not be "understood"; it must be felt. He encourages freedom in both the expression and acceptance of art.

From *The New York Times Magazine*, April 9, 1967. © 1967/1966 by The New York Times Company. Reprinted by permission of The New York Times Company and the author.

I had a grandfather—don't jump to any conclusion; he was my mother's father—and he was a collector of art. He also happened to be a politician, which is a rather unusual combination, frankly.

[2]   He was a United States Senator from Rhode Island and he usually accompanied my mother and her sister abroad in the summers. He was a collector of European art and art of various early Mediterranean civilizations.

[3]   My grandfather was concerned in those days—around the turn of the century—with the lack in this country of evidences of great culture from the past. And as someone whose life blended politics and art, he sponsored a bill, which passed the Congress, to exempt antiques and art more than 100 years old from the U.S. import duty.

[4]   I might add that politically he was a figure of the Old Guard for 17 years in the Senate and finally was ousted by Teddy Roosevelt. But why get into politics? He was a collector, which is the point I wanted to make.

[5]   I think the matter of heredity and environment is tremendously important in shaping the taste of an art collector—generally and in my own case. The major influence in my life as a collector was the influence of my mother. She, in turn, got this interest from her father, and she spent her life assembling a collection that evolved with her taste. I think she would have been classified as one of the avant-garde collectors in her day.

[6]   She started with Japanese prints—as many in Europe did—which were an important influence on the impressionist[1] painters. She collected primitive art, which was one of the important influences on the postimpressionist painters. She was a collector of Far Eastern sculpture. She then became tremendously interested in American primitive art and assembled a very interesting collection, which was really built around the collection made by Elie Nadelman, the sculptor. He was a marvelous person, and though he came from abroad, from central Europe, he was one of the first to discover the excitement of American folk art made during the early days of this country.

[7]   I knew Nadelman quite well and one of the things that fascinated me about him was this: having collected many of the items of early Americana found in antique shops—chickens and things like that—he also tried to develop papier-mâché classical sculpture. One of his great objectives was to develop a form of papier-mâché popular art that could sell for a few pennies and bring good sculpture to the people of this country. He never succeeded in the papier-mâché field. He did succeed in the sculpture field, as any of you can tell if you've been in the State Theater at Lincoln Center and have seen those two large sculptures of two ladies.

[8]   Well, getting back to my mother, she also collected American contemporary art and then the whole modern European period, from the post-

---

[1]one who paints in a style developed in the late nineteenth century, a style marked by short brush strokes and bright colors

Courtesy of Lincoln Center for the Performing Arts, Inc.—Photograph by Bob Serating

"Two Female Nudes" Elie Nadelman Lincoln Center for the Performing Arts

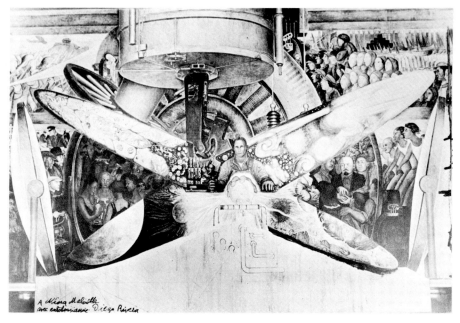

Diego Rivera's controversial mural (originally in Rockefeller Center; now destroyed) The photograph shows the work in progress.

"Red Horses"   Franz Marc   Folkwang Museum, Essen, Germany

Two gilt-bronze papier-mâché figurines   Elie
Nadelman   Collection: Nelson A. Rockefeller

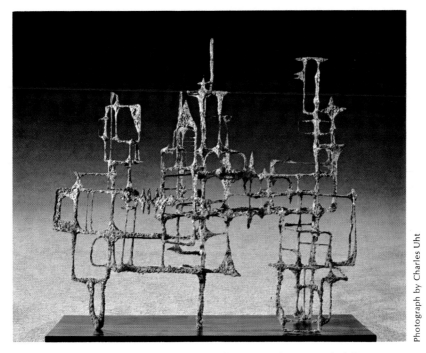

"Galaxy of Andromeda"   Ibram Lassaw   Collection: Nelson A. Rockefeller

"The Angelus"   Jean François Millet   The Louvre, Paris

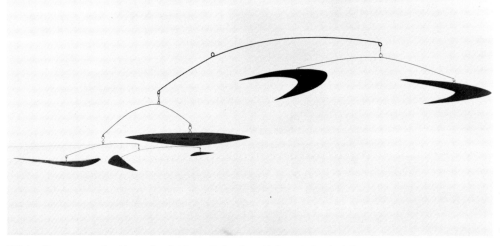

"Flying Boomerangs"   Alexander Calder   Collection: Nelson A. Rockefeller

(untitled)   Lee Bontecou   Collection: Nelson A. Rockefeller

"The Farm"   Emil Weiss (after Van Gogh)   Collection: Nelson A. Rockefeller

"Green Globe"   Barbara Hepworth   Collection: Nelson A. Rockefeller

"Plumbob"   Yasuhide Kobashi   Collection: Nelson A. Rockefeller

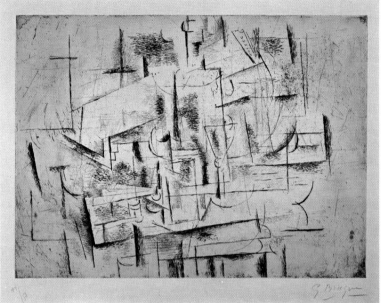

"Composition"   Georges Braque   Collection: Nelson A. Rockefeller

"The Bathers"   Paul Cézanne   Collection: Nelson A. Rockefeller

(untitled)   Pablo Picasso   Collection: Nelson A. Rockefeller

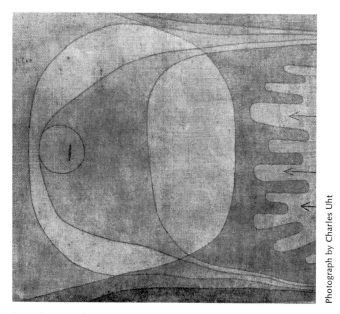

"Fear"   Paul Klee   Collection: Nelson A. Rockefeller

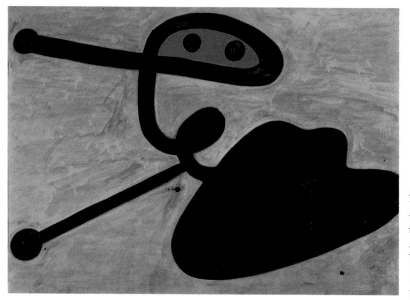

(untitled)   Joan Miró   Collection: Nelson A. Rockefeller

impressionists on. She had a gallery in the house and was always changing "shows." So I grew up in this atmosphere, and it was very exciting as well as influential. I remember, for example, that during my senior year at college I was fortunate enough to get a fellowship and didn't have to take any courses. Since I could do what I wanted, I stopped majoring in economics and spent that last year studying art, architecture and landscape architecture. So even then those hereditary and environmental forces were operative.

[9] In this connection I should mention another factor I think is interesting. My mother was a founder of the Museum of Modern Art. Back in the nineteen-twenties a group of eight or ten collectors in New York decided that they wanted to try to reduce the time between creation of a work of art and its appreciation by the public, so that a Van Gogh, say, didn't have to die in poverty before his paintings were recognized. Concurrent recognition would bridge the time gap, help the artist avoid poverty and lure potential artistic ingenuity into new forms of creativity.

[10] This recognition was urgent. Symptomatic of the need, for example, was the attitude of the Metropolitan Museum of Art, whose board of trustees I joined in 1930. The Metropolitan would not show any so-called modern art. They would not collect it and they would not show it, and one of the reasons the Museum of Modern Art was established was that this otherwise great institution was not ready to move into the field.

[11] Well, because the people in charge of the Museum of Modern Art were excellent—Alfred H. Barr, Jr., was its first director and is still the director of collections—it has been really one of the tremendously significant factors in developing standards in the whole field of contemporary forms of expression, both in Europe and here. Artistic recognition has become a reality and the museum has been a very exciting influence in our community.

[12] Part of the excitement, of course, arises from the impact of new cultural experiences on eyes that are open and on minds that are responsive. We are all subject to experiences, cultural experiences, particularly those of us who are fortunate enough to be in big metropolitan centers where there is so much that is exciting going on and so many great museums have art from all periods available.

[13] Many people, of course, don't feel this way. Their eyes are not open, their minds are not responsive to new cultural experiences. Maybe they are afraid of them; maybe they don't notice them. This is why preparation in the schools or the home is so important in orienting people to something that is different and getting them to appreciate even shades of difference.

[14] In my own case, I would like to mention a few of those experiences which had a major impact on me over the years.

[15] I spent a year traveling around the world in 1930, which was a great opportunity to start collecting. At that point I was interested in primitive art, particularly Far Eastern primitive art, and I began to buy very simple things—not important objects.

[16] I will never forget being in Sumatra, which was then part of the Dutch

East Indies. I had gone out to some of the villages, purchased a few delightful, simple carvings and brought them back with some pride to the local Dutch functionary. "Don't bother," he said, "don't bother. All the good things are gone, and what isn't gone was burned by the missionaries. Everything you find now is made in Germany and shipped here for the tourists."
[17] This was 1930. It was rather a disillusioning experience, but rather a good one to have early.
[18] Three years later I had the opportunity of spending a month or so in Mexico, primarily touring the country and studying the vast range of its cultural life, past and present. Well, by 1939, just to show how things happen, I was president of the Museum of Modern Art and one of the first shows that we presented when I became president was "20 Centuries of Mexican Art." I went to see the President of Mexico and got him to put up some funds. It was the first major exhibition of Mexican culture to show all the great periods in one spot.
[19] I had another interesting experience in Peru. I ran across a man named Dr. Tello, an archeologist who made the mistake of getting elected a Senator. Then the politics changed and another party came into office.
[20] Now it just happened that he had about 60 bundles of Indian mummies that he had brought in from the Peruvian desert. But, with the new Government, there was no interest in what they considered Indian art—they were Spanish colonials, you might say, in their point of view. So I went to see the President of Peru and he let me take one bundle back to the United States. I had the idea that maybe I could get the Metropolitan Museum and the Museum of Natural History interested in starting a program in the Americas, and we could carry on digs and joint operations the way the British did in Egypt and other areas.
[21] But the director of the Metropolitan then was an Egyptologist and since he viewed this whole pre-Columbian field as a major threat to his program in Egypt, he was able to snuff it out before it got started.
[22] Just as the Museum of Modern Art was created because of a lack of interest in contemporary forms of expression, later—maybe 15 years later—by which time I had collected enough in the primitive art field from around the world, I set up the Museum of Primitive Art, which is an exciting, small museum and fulfills a function that is not yet fulfilled by the Metropolitan, although the Brooklyn Museum does a great deal in this field.
[23] Let me relate another incident that grew out of a partly cultural, partly commercial experience. My mother and I tried to help my father in the decoration of Rockefeller Center. We engaged Diego Rivera and he undertook a major mural. Well, Frieda, his wife, was very attractive, but her political involvements were even stronger than his and she got him to incorporate the most unbelievable subjects into this mural.
[24] Although I know that birth control now has become more acceptable, in those days it wasn't. And, of course, we were right across from St. Patrick's, as you know. Then he had Stalin—or was it Lenin? I've forgotten—

featured in the center of the mural. He also included some social commentaries on American life, such as a lady with a syphilitic ulcer on her face playing cards. I finally said, "Look, Diego, we just can't have this. Art is free in its expression, but this is not something that you are doing for yourself, nor for us as private collectors. This is a commercial undertaking. Therefore, we have to have something that is not going to offend our customers but that is going to give them pleasure and joy. Instead, you've included just about every sensitive political and religious subject in your mural."

[25] I had pretty well threshed this out, I thought, and I periodically peeked in the door to keep check on developments. But it turned out that whenever I went out, Frieda came in.

[26] Well, we made two installments on the payment and Rivera worked 24 hours without stopping to get the mural finished. Then we gave him his final check and thanked him, and just took the mural down. It was a little rough for a while.

[27] Then I had a very amusing idea. I thought if we could take the mural off the wall and put it in the Museum of Modern Art—I was treasurer of the museum—and charge $1 admission, we could finance the museum for quite a while. The idea was never tried, though.

[28] By this time my father has lost interest in contemporary forms of expression. He was a collector of Chinese porcelains.

[29] Though my mother and I lost ground on the Rivera mural, we soon had another little experience. The W.P.A. was just getting under way with mural paintings and, though I should have known better by then, the Junior Advisory Committee of the Museum of Modern Art, of which I happened to be the chairman, invited several American painters to join in doing a sketch for a mural. They were not all mural painters, but we thought we would get them into this field and the request would be timely and exciting.

[30] It was—unfortunately. One of the painters, William Gropper, saw fit to do a mural of Mr. J. P. Morgan that also included a chorus girl with a glass of champagne and a man clutching a bulging money bag.

[31] Well, Mr. Morgan was the president of the Metropolitan Museum of Art and I was also on the Metropolitan board at that time so we had a problem: what would we do with it? We decided if we didn't hang it, the news would be on the front page of every paper. By this time the trustees of the Museum of Modern Art were less than a little enthusiastic about their Junior Advisory Committee.

[32] Anyhow, I decided I would go and see Mr. Morgan before the show opened and explain what had happened. It was one of the great experiences of my life. He understood completely. "Of course, you've got to hang it," he said. "Don't give it another thought."

[33] I mention these things because the impact of new cultural experiences on the lives of individuals can be tremendous, if—as I've said—their eyes are open and their minds are sensitized.

[34] I have always liked forms of art in which I could feel—feel the artist, feel the material. Sculpture appeals to me particularly. Perhaps that is why I feel so strongly about primitive art—because you feel the individual directly.

[35] I never will forget a course I took in my senior year in college that was known as Universe I because it was pretty general. I remember that one day the professor showed two pictures, "Red Horses" by the German painter Franz Marc and the sunset scene and the church towers of "The Angelus" by the French painter Millet. Then the professor asked the class, "Which picture do you prefer?"

[36] Well, let's face it, some of the other members of the class hadn't been exposed, perhaps, as I had been, so they all liked the scene of Millet's, and I said I liked "Red Horses."

[37] Well, the teacher agreed with me, and explained why. He said, "If you had these two paintings in your house, you would rapidly associate the Millet with all the emotional and spiritual religious values in which you believe. The thought in this painting is very powerful, and pretty soon you would forget the painting. You've got the impact without looking at it."

[38] On the other hand, "Red Horses"—one of them is red, one of them is mauve—is not a subject portrayed as if you had taken a photograph of three fine-looking horses. This is a subject in which the composition, the color, the motion, the strength, constantly keep hitting you. If you are in a different mood than when you previously saw it, you are going to see a different painting, different portions, with their fine points of variation in color, size and relationship, contrasted against the entire perspective, together with varying shades and volume of light, as viewed through the slightly tinted glasses of a different mood or attitude of the day, all yielding different emphases and changes in meaning and interpretation. Talking now not of this particular painting alone but in general, this always makes such artistry exciting.

[39] Frankly, that is why cubist painting appealed to me very much—with its strength and vitality—and the various forms of expression that have come since, such as abstract painting. I find if I get mixed up with the subject matter, I lose the ability to enjoy the esthetic values in the painting. And if you get the subject, you stop looking at the painting.

[40] So I think this is one of the reasons why, in this civilization in which we live, with photography having been developed to the point it has—and I was very interested in photography—realism is something you find in life. But what we really are looking for is something that takes us out of ourselves and gives us the kind of excitement, the kind of esthetic satisfaction and challenge, that is unending, and from which you can constantly get new satisfaction and rewards.

[41] I must say I think that art takes its inspiration from the broad currents of its time. And the interesting fact, of course, is that art now is universal, and therefore the forms of expression are very difficult. It's very difficult

to identify them with a region or a nation because the forces and the influence are worldwide.

[42] This leads me to another aspect of art: the relationship between art and politicians. It's a little like oil in water, frankly. They don't mix. For some reason politicians have a feeling that culture is a very dangerous subject and they should avoid it. This is really true, more than I realized.

[43] When I was fortunate enough to be elected Governor, I decided I would share my enjoyment of some of the objects I had collected with my fellow politicians in Albany.

[44] Well, let's face it. It was a new experience for Albany. And for those legislators. They had never seen anything like it. You know: "My son, who's 3 years old, could have done better." I got the standard reaction. It was delightful.

[45] But the exciting and the interesting development was to come. Just as I was fortunate enough to grow up with an art gallery in the house, these people came to the Mansion, with their wives, and we had big parties. Little by little they got used to the art and they would come to see if there was anything new in the house. We had a list printed that they could take home containing the names of the artists and pertinent data.

[46] There was a lot of art education to be done, however. When the problem of Lincoln Center came up I suggested that the state ought to recognize the importance of New York's contribution to culture by building a State Theater at Lincoln Center—$15 million was the contribution. If I told you the exchange that took place on the floor of the Legislature—well, I couldn't in this company. But it was very interesting.

[47] Finally they said, "Well, as a personal courtesy to you, out of friendship for you, we'll go along." At this time my party controlled both houses. The bill didn't even have to be bipartisan.

[48] Now I would like to show you a few slides of this collection from the Executive Mansion which really—if you will excuse me—did have an impact on our legislators. It helped make it possible to get elected officials to support another program, the State Council on the Arts.

[49] Here is a sculpture, a piece by Ibram Lassaw, the "Galaxy of Andromeda," which created a tremendous stir in Albany when it got there. The first group couldn't understand it. They thought it looked like a building after a fire. We went through all kinds of speculation.

[50] Next, two little Nadelman figurines, part of the series I was talking to you about, when he was trying to develop the papier-mâché technique. These are on the wall in the dining room.

[51] Of course, no collection would be complete without a Sandy Calder. This one is called "Flying Boomerangs" and is on the ceiling of the gallery upstairs. All ages can enjoy this, believe me. Calder is easily understood.

[52] Now a Lee Bontecou, untitled—one of the early ones. This creates quite a degree of excitement because its's three-dimensional, and they all want to know what the hole is for. The only thing I tell them is, "If you try

to understand, you are lost. Just don't think. Just look and feel and register, and then go away and come back. That's the best way."

[53] Next, a Barbara Hepworth—"Green Globe"—small but lovely if you get completely away from any possibility of reality. Legislators can take sculpture better than they can take painting, I find—at least those who are uninhibited.

[54] This is also a delightful work, "Plumbob" by Yasuhide Kobashi. You can pull the balls up and down, two of them on each string, so you can make your own composition. Not only for the legislators but also for our son, this is a great source of satisfaction. It lets you participate, and participating in life is a very important part of life's enjoyment.

[55] Those are a few of the pieces of sculpture, and I think we are preparing our legislators for larger pieces of sculpture in the future, to be owned by the state in public buildings. I haven't made any commitment yet publicly on that subject, but I think we are ready for it.

[56] Next, I would like to go to some lithographs. This one is "The Farm" by Emil Weiss after Van Gogh. Of course, the legislators feel very much at home with it. It is reassuring when they come across a piece of this kind.

[57] Next, Cézanne—"The Bathers." They get concerned here with nudity, but it is something they have to get used to.

[58] Here, a Braque, "Composition." That's the kind that makes them say, "Well, my son did better in school."

[59] This is a Picasso lithograph. I was going to give it to my brother Winthrop in Arkansas, but I got to like it myself and so I didn't send it to him.

[60] Those are just a few of the lithographs and the prints. Now let's go to one or two of the paintings.

[61] Here's a Miró, which is the only painting that they recognize. They all think it's Fiorello La Guardia's hat. It's nostalgic for the New York delegation and evokes a lot of enthusiasm.

[62] It's a little hard for them to grasp this one, by Paul Klee. It's called "Fear," and when you explain the title they start getting aboard.

[63] I will never forget the late Harry Luce, who was one of the great people of this country and one of the great patrons of the arts, and a trustee of the Museum of Modern Art. Just after World War II he said that they were very concerned about modern art. He had a new editor who had just come out of Yale to *Life* magazine, and Luce said he was beginning to feel that maybe modern art was one of the most dangerous factors threatening the strength of democracy, and that he and his editors were considering whether they should expose and denounce it as a destructive force in America.

[64] I was then president of the museum. I said, "Harry, we all better sit down and talk this over before you take a stand." Bill Paley was a trustee, too, and Jock Whitney and Alfred Barr and René d'Harnoncourt. First, we had dinner and then we went on to the museum to talk some more—a sort of illustrated conversation. Alfred Barr was the principal philosopher

of the evening. He said to Luce, "You're a missionary's son and I'm a missionary's son. I understand your concern and your point of view."

[65] The fascinating thing about this experience is that we ended up the evening with Harry being convinced that modern forms of artistic expression were the only area left in democracy where there was true freedom, where you had absolute freedom, and there were no holds barred. He went from a deep concern that modern art was a destructive force, to the conclusion it was one of the great areas of freedom, one of the bastions of freedom and strength in our lives.

[66] Well, I don't know where we're going to go as a great civilization, or where art is going to go. But I am sure of one thing—it's going to be exciting.

EXERCISES

Questions

1. Rockefeller's theme is partially expressed in paragraph 33. What does the article suggest regarding the source and nature of these cultural experiences?
2. What is the importance of one's environment in developing one's taste in art? What was the Governor's personal experience?
3. Why was the Museum of Modern Art organized? Why was the Museum of Primitive Art formed? How does this reflect on the acceptance of innovation in art?
4. What factors other than personal interest often influence taste in art?
5. Consider the various illustrations of the relationship between business and the arts. What is revealed? In what way was Morgan's reaction unusual?
6. Rockefeller indicates that art and politics are frequently in conflict. Concerning political subject matter, what is revealed in the conflict between Rivera, the artist, and Rockefeller? What does this show about the artist-patron relationship? Concerning the politicans in Albany, what is revealed about their acceptance of new expressions in art?
7. What kind of stimulation does modern art offer the modern mind that conventional or realistic art does not? What is the esthetic satisfaction that art brings?
8. In paragraph 52, the Governor says, "If you try to understand, you are lost. Just don't think. Just look and register, and then go away and come back." What is implied here about the "meaning" of art?
9. Some modern art invites participation, for example, "Plumbob". Why does this enhance enjoyment of art? What other art forms invite participation?

10. In the conclusion, art is described as a great bastion of freedom. Why?
11. The organization of this talk is loose yet the total effect is not incoherent. What unifying elements can you find? What devices were used to maintain interest? What evidence can you find that reveal this as a spoken composition, not one formally drafted?

For Discussion and Writing

1. The fallacy that "any kid can do it"
2. Abstract art: its validity
3. The universality that primitive art reveals
4. Politics and art
5. My favorite work of art

CROSS REFERENCES

MacLEISH: "Thoughts on an Age That Gave Us Hiroshima"
RICH: "Ringo, Paul, Lenny, George, Elvira, Dave, Wolfgang and John"

RECOMMENDED READING

BARR, ALFRED: *What Is Modern Painting?* (Museum of Modern Art: 1958)

ARTHUR KNIGHT

"THE EUCALYPTIC DREAM"

INTRODUCTION

Arthur Knight enhanced his interest in films during the several years he spent as assistant curator of the Film Library at the Museum of Modern Art in New York City. He has worked as a film consultant and has also lectured on the film at such colleges as City College of New York and the New School for Social Research. He has a regular film column in the *Saturday Review,* where this article originally appeared, and he has also written for such other magazines as *Harper's Bazaar* and *Esquire.* In 1957, Mr. Knight published *The Liveliest Art: A Panoramic History of the Movies.*

TO THE READER

Hollywood's preoccupation with profit and Hollywood's dream version of American life has made the industry schizophrenic — at times concerned with public morality and at times reflecting private morality. Hollywood's estimate of reality is about as solid as the title of this article.

Hollywood, it has often been said, is not really a place, but a state of mind; and for those who now work in the movie business, this has become

Reprinted from *Saturday Review,* September 23, 1967, with the permission of Saturday Review, Inc. and the author.

particularly true. It is a state of mind that has spread west of Hollywood's original boundaries — west of Doheny and into the hills of Beverly and Bel-Air, and thence on to Malibu and the sea. It has spread north of the Hollywood Hills into the San Fernando Valley, where such communities as Studio City, Encino, and Tarzana provide the industry's upper brackets with ultra-modern tract housing flanked by kidney-shaped pools and two-car garages. Indeed, geographically, Beverly Hills has supplanted the old Hollywood as the industry's heartland. Not only do its broad, curving streets hold the highest concentration of filmland's talent (their houses cheek-by-jowl in the weirdest agglomeration of architectural styles assembled anywhere outside of a World's Fair), but physically it affords easy access to any studio in at most a twenty-minute run in the inevitable Porsche, Jaguar, or MG.

[2]   Despite this gain in square mileage, however, Hollywood remains a terrifyingly insular[1] place. It is perhaps understandably difficult for men who work at make-believe to make believe that any world exists beyond their own. Or, if they are aware, intellectually, that not everyone dwells in a split-level, ranch-style home under eternally sunny skies (give a little, take a little smog now and then), and that some may even ride the bus or subway to work instead of tooling along in a sports convertible, this information is filtered through their own rose-colored sunglasses. Not too atypical is the story — alas, not apocryphal[2] — of a top producer in a major studio who protested to his costume designer about the elegance of his heroine's garment. "Remember, she's a school teacher," he admonished. "What can she make — maybe three or four hundred a week!"

[3]   The surface gloss that is the distinctive mark of the Hollywood film is not an additive, not an extra purchasable for a few dollars more. It is bound into the fabric of each production as inextricably as the stars themselves. It is part of the philosophy of film-making as an entertainment, part of Hollywood's state of mind. Nobody must go away mad, or even slightly riled up, because, after all, movies are made for fun — and for profit. Symptomatically, at the finale of one of this year's most somber and realistic dramas, a chain-gang story called *Cool Hand Luke,* Paul Newman as an escaped convict is savagely butchered in cold blood. But does the film end there? It does not. To mitigate this harsh conclusion, there follows a quick montage of still photos of Mr. Newman smiling his boyish, toothpaste grin. Mustn't send the customers home unhappy!

[4]   And is not this production philosophy precisely what gave the American film its economic, if not artistic, pre-eminence throughout the world? Audiences — particularly the vast, inarticulate, middle-class audiences that are the primary targets and supporters of the movie industry — have always shown a marked preference for, as a TV producer once phrased it to Herbert

[1]detached; standing alone; isolated
[2]of doubtful authorship or authenticity

Gold, "happy stories about happy people with happy problems." This is something that Hollywood, by inclination as well as by orientation, has traditionally been turning out.

[5]   Originally New York-based, the American industry at first supplied moralistic little melodramas (interspersed with vaudeville-turn comedies and brief educational reels) to its preponderantly working-class audiences in slum nickelodeons. As early as 1909, however, film companies began to move into the Los Angeles area, attracted jointly by its unparalleled possibilities for year-round outdoor picture-making and its superb scenic variety. Almost simultaneously—although it would perhaps be unfair to suggest cause and effect—the pictures themselves began to change. They grew longer and more complex, borrowing their themes now from popular novels, theatrical successes, even grand opera (despite the fact that movies were still silent), thus deliberately switching their appeal to the middle-classes that had hitherto shunned the medium. They grew increasingly opulent in settings and costumes, affecting the tastes and styles of women all over the country. And, perhaps most far-reaching of all, American films introduced the glamour of the star system, and with it a whole firmament of archetypical[3] figures to be emulated and adored. By the end of World War I, such stars as Charlie Chaplin, Douglas Fairbanks, William S. Hart, and Mary Pickford had become household gods not only in the United States but, quite literally, throughout most of the civilized world.

[6]   Paradoxically, it was the stern reality of World War I that established Hollywood as the center of make-believe, the movie capital of the world. Coal and power shortages shuttered most of the small studios that dotted New York City, or that had sprung up in Fort Lee just across the Hudson. Their owners, after briefly casting eyes toward Miami and Chicago, hastened westward to join the pioneers, such as Cecil B. De Mille, D. W. Griffith, and Mack Sennett, who had already staked their claims in Los Angeles's enchanting environs. More important, the same shortages—plus the fact that celluloid, the film base, and high explosives both shared the same strategic chemicals—closed down completely most of the European studios. But people caught up in the throes of war desperately craved entertainment; and Hollywood rushed in to fill the vacuum. The American film at that crucial time gained a hold on the screens of the world that it has never since relinquished.

[7]   With money pouring in from Europe, and unchallenged in the rich domestic market, the Hollywood studios were enabled to enter upon a period of unparalleled expansion. In less than a decade, men like William Fox, Samuel Goldwyn, and Adolph Zukor had leaped from a marginal existence in a new and precarious field to positions of power in multimillion-dollar enterprises. Unlettered themselves, they were soon shaping the creative ef-

[3]based on an original pattern or model

forts of writers, directors, designers, and performers. Inevitably, the sybaritic[4] luxury that their wealth permitted them to enjoy found its way onto the the screen in the form of drunken orgies, petting parties, and overly acquiescent females. It should not be forgotten, however, that immediately after World War I, America itself was in transition from the stern Victorian morality that Griffith so primly depicted to the hedonistic pleasures heralded by Cecil B. De Mille and Elinor Glyn. De Mille swathed his ladies in satins and silks of the highest *couture,* dunked them in perfumed bathtubs, and beset them with problems of marital infidelity, incompatibility, and divorce; Mme Glyn gave her esteemed approval to the frenzied escapades of the emerging flapper generation—and the word "It" to describe the flapper's special allure.

[8]   No sooner did these manifestations of the new morality appear on the screen than American housewives began to change not only their bathtubs, but their husbands as well; while their dancing daughters mastered the intricacies of the Charleston, bobbed their hair, and drank bathtub gin from the boyfriend's hip-pocket flask. And no sooner did *this* happen than the voice of the reformer was heard throughout the land, claiming that Hollywood was single-handedly paving the way to a twentieth-century Sodom and Gomorrah. Hollywood was, for the first time, caught up in a dilemma that has plagued it ever since. To be sure, the studios could amass ample evidence to demonstrate that everything they put into their pictures—and more—had its real-life counterpart, that their movies were merely reflecting the times. What they could *not* demonstrate—what perhaps defies definitive demonstration—was the extent to which their glamorized, fictionalized versions of life, plus the empathic presence of their star personalities, gave the seal of approval to such behavior, and a green light to the Twenties' go-go generation.

[9]   Faced with the threat of a national censorship, the industry reluctantly backed down, agreeing, somewhat hypocritically, to a code for on-screen morality that has remained in effect, with strikingly few changes, right up until this past year. It was a morality created not to appeal, but to appease —an ad hoc morality, a codification of specific or hypothetical objections by state and municipal censors all over the country. This code gained its teeth when, in 1934, the Catholic Legion of Decency was formed to apply economic sanctions against any picture it found objectionable. For the next three decades, the industry's Production Code Administration worked hand-in-glove with the Legion to avert such a catastrophe. New fears beset the industry when, in 1948, the House Un-American Activities Committee began its investigations to ferret out subversives on the studios' payrolls. Again, the studios responded in characteristic fashion, withdrawing from production any script that smacked of progressive thinking, and forming an un-

[4]loving luxury or sensuous pleasure

official blacklist that everyone firmly denied, but knew existed.

[10] Thus, Hollywood has had a long history of schizophrenia—a private face and a public face, a private morality and a public morality. And this dichotomy is evident in all of its films. Small wonder that the standard reaction to European pictures is that they seem "more honest" than the domestic product. They are so simply because their production is rarely surrounded by the special codes and compromises that guide the executives of Hollywood's major studios. And they are so because their budgets are rarely so astronomical that they have to be made wholly palatable to millions upon millions of people. It is safe to say that no film has ever gone before the cameras in Hollywood that has not been flawed by one or both of these considerations.

[11] Despite these flaws, however, Hollywood's movies capture to an extraordinary degree the look of America, the feel of America. Behind Doris Day, that supermarket may be the one you went to this morning. Over Rock Hudson's shoulder, that service station might be the one on the next corner. Europeans who arrive here for the first time are rarely surprised by what anything looks like; they have seen it all before in the movies. In this area, at least, nobody tries to alter the truth—and probably couldn't, even if they wanted to. As critic Otis Ferguson once observed, "The men and women, from both sides of the camera, were in so many instances a part of common life just yesterday that they haven't had time to forget it, dress it up, and bury it." Indeed, the studios properly pride themselves on the verisimilitude of their back-lot New York streets, Western streets, and rural American towns —and studio executives audibly grumble when an independent producer today exercises his option to take his cameras off to an authentic locale.

[12] But if an independent goes on location merely for the look of a place, he is wasting both his time and his studio's money. What needs to be found on location is the authenticity that exists outside of Hollywood's state of mind—the kind of authenticity, for example, that Arthur Penn was recently able to instill into his *Bonnie and Clyde*. It is less a matter of place than a manner of thinking, a scraping away at the barnacles that have gathered over the last half century upon the hulk of the Hollywood industry. Francis Ford Coppola managed it nicely recently in *You're a Big Boy Now;* Arthur Hiller tried it again, not quite so successfully, in his upcoming version of Murray Schisgal's *The Tiger,* retitled *The Tiger Makes Out.* Neither adheres to studio standards of morality, nor to conventional studio attitudes toward Mom and Dad, or husband and wife. As a result, whatever other deficiencies these films may have, they offer a freshness and originality that stamps them as almost anti-Hollywood.

[13] Indeed, it might be stated almost categorically that any break in the conventions must come from outside of Hollywood itself, completely away from the inhibiting influence of the studio mentality. Stanley Kubrick is a good example of an American director who, while still working for Holly-

wood companies, found that he could function best 6,000 miles away from them, in England—with films like *Lolita* and *Dr. Strangelove* to prove his point. The studios themselves seem to undergo some kind of sea change once they leave Los Angeles; MGM could never have made *Blow-up*—perhaps the most genuinely innovational film of the past decade—on its Culver City lot, any more than Universal would have approved the searing *Privilege* for production at its Universal City facility. These are not what used to be called "runaway productions." Although produced for Hollywood majors, both represent breakthroughs that Hollywood can neither countenance nor comprehend. Meanwhile, the home lots are being used increasingly as the base for TV's endless round of situation comedies and spy melodramas, and these represent no change whatsoever from the routine B and C pictures that studded the studios' production schedules in Hollywood's more halcyon[5] days.

[14] For Hollywood has learned to live quite comfortably within its limitations. It has mastered a form of doublethink that enables it to grind out, week after week, for theaters and for television, a glossy, highly commercial entertainment that is without counterpart anywhere else in the world, a kind of picture that is known and readily recognized as the Hollywood film. Unfortunately, the great majority of Hollywood's most successful film-makers, who are neither rogues nor clowns, are successful precisely because they have acquired its values as their values—and see nothing wrong with the process.

[15] "I like to make beautiful pictures about beautiful people," producer Ross Hunter once said. "If audiences want to see realism, let them look at home movies." Not all movie people are quite so drastic, but it is part of Hollywood's self-imposed insularity that the home movies these beautiful people choose to look at themselves are all too often their own. In the warm glow of Southern California's golden sun, harsh truths tend to dissolve into fantasies of goodwill (*In the Heat of the Night*), and deep-rooted social problems can still supposedly be solved by individual acts of heroism (*Up the Down Staircase*). If there is a war on poverty currently in progress, or a war in Vietnam, they have yet to appear in any of Hollywood's pictures—mainly because these cannot be "licked" by any of the studios' conventional formulae. Poverty and Vietnam just aren't commercial.

[16] Hollywood, whatever its geographic boundaries, remains a state of mind whose principal export is a somewhat outmoded version of the American dream. Shaded from reality by eucalyptus and palm, caught up in a long tradition of compromised art and profitable fantasy, it has become a backward pocket in the swift current of the cultural revolution now sweeping through Southern California. One can only hope that, as the revolution is consolidated, Hollywood and its beautiful people will also be engulfed.

[5]happy, joyful, carefree

EXERCISES

Questions

1. Knight presents his theme in his last paragraph. What briefly, is his indictment of Hollywood?
2. What is the "state of mind" that Knight believes characterizes Hollywood? What effect has this had on the movies it produces?
3. What two developments around the period of World War I aided in the development of Hollywood as the center of the movie industry?
4. When accused of fostering immorality, film-makers responded that they were only reflecting American behavior. Who was right?
5. What was the Production Code Administration? The Legion of Decency? Why did Hollywood give in? What other pressures have forced compromise?
6. What has been the cumulative effect of outside pressures on moviemakers and movies?
7. What kind of authentic life does Hollywood succeed in producing? What kind does it fail at?
8. What is the difference between the comment to Herbert Gold in paragraph 4 and Ross Hunter's comment in paragraph 15? What is both good and bad about their attitudes?
9. In what ways does the last paragraph serve as a summary? What are the main supporting points Knight has made?
10. What is Knight's attitude toward Hollywood's compromise with itself? What evidence is scattered throughout the essay?
11. Knight makes effective use of transitional devices to tie his paragraphs together. Reread the first few words of paragraphs 2, 4, 8–14 and mark the transitional devices.

Vocabulary

acquiescent
agglomeration
dichotomy
empathic
environs
ferret
hedonistic
montage
verisimilitude

For Discussion and Writing

1. The Production Code versus public censorship
2. The movies and public taste: leader or follower
3. Why go to movies?

4.   Super spectacular — art or waste
5.   The Legion of Decency
6.   The influence of the movie star

CROSS REFERENCE

LAMPELL: "I Think I Ought to Mention I Was Blacklisted"

RECOMMENDED READING

SCHULBERG, BUDD: *What Makes Sammy Run?* (Modern Library: 1941)

GILBERT HIGHET

"WHAT USE IS POETRY?"

INTRODUCTION

Gilbert Highet (1906–   ) was born in Scotland and educated at Glasgow University and Oxford, earning a Master of Arts degree from both, before he came to the United States where he has since become a citizen. A professor at Columbia since 1938, he also gained recognition for a radio program, "People, Places and Books," with which he was associated from 1952 to 1959. Mr. Highet is chairman of the editorial board of *Horizon* and has, for many years, been a judge of the Book-of-the-Month Club. In addition, he has written several books including *People, Places and Books* (1953); his most recent book, *The Anatomy of Satire;* and *A Clerk of Oxenford* (1954), from which this essay was taken.

TO THE READER

Working from children's almost instinctive love of music and song, Highet develops five adult "uses" for poetry.

Children ask lots and lots of questions, about religion, about sex, about the stars. But there are some questions which they never ask: they leave grown-ups to ask them and to answer them. Often this means that the questions are silly: that they are questions about nonexistent problems, or questions to which the answer is obvious. Sometimes it means that the questions *should* be asked, but that the answer is difficult or multiplex.

[2]   So, children never ask what is the good of music. They just like singing and dancing, and even drumming on a low note of the piano. In the same way, they never ask what is the use of poetry. They all enjoy poems and songs, and very often come to like them before they can even talk properly; but it never occurs to them that they ought to find reasons for their enjoyment. But grown-ups do inquire about the justification of poetry: they ask what is the point of putting words in a special order and extracting special sound effects from them, instead of speaking plainly and directly. And often—because they get no adequate answer, either from the poets or from the professors—they conclude that poetry is only a set of tricks like conjuring, or a complicated game like chess; and they turn away from it in discouragement . . . until, perhaps, a poetic film like *Henry V* shocks them into realizing something of its power; or, as they grow older, they find that a poem learned in childhood sticks in their mind and becomes clearer and more beautiful with age.

[3]   What is the use of poetry?

[4]   There must be a number of different answers to the question. Just as a picture can be meant to give pleasure, or to carry a puzzle, or to convey information, so poems are meant for many different things. We can begin to get some of the answers if we look at the poetry that children themselves naturally enjoy, and then see how it is connected with the most famous grown-up poems.

[5]   The first pleasure of poetry is the simplest. It is the same pleasure that we have in music—the pleasure of following a pattern of sound. Everyone loves talking, and most people like what might be called doodling in sound. So, if you look through the *Oxford Dictionary of Nursery Rhymes,* you will find several tongue-twisters, like this:

> Peter Piper picked a peck of pickled pepper;
> A peck of pickled pepper Peter Piper picked;
> If Peter Piper picked a peck of pickled pepper,
> Where's the peck of pickled pepper Peter Piper picked?

On a grown-up level, many a famous poem is little more than a pattern of sound: for instance, Shakespeare's love song:

> It was a lover and his lass,
>   With a hey and a ho and a hey nonino,
> That o'er the green cornfield did pass,
>   In the spring time, the only pretty ring time,
>   When birds do sing, hey ding a ding ding;
>   Sweet lovers love the spring.

Much of the best poetry of Swinburne is pattern-making in sound, with a very light core of meaning. Here are four exquisite lines which really mean very little more than the sound of spring showers;

> When the hounds of spring are on winter's traces,
>   The mother of months in meadow or plain
> Fills the shadows and windy places
>   With lisp of leaves and ripple of rain.

Small meaning, but lovely rhythm and melody.

[6]   Now, there is a second pleasure in poetry. This is that it is sometimes better than prose for telling a story. It even gives authority to a story which is illogical or incredible, or even gruesome. That is one reason children love the poem that tells of the tragic fate of Jack and Jill. There is an interesting variant of it: the cumulative story, in which one detail is piled up on another until the whole story has been set forth with the simple exactitude of a primitive painting: for instance, 'The House That Jack Built,' and the funeral elegy, 'Who Killed Cock Robin?' and the famous old Jewish rhyme, 'Had Gadyo,' about the kid bought for two pieces of money—which is said to symbolize a vast stretch of the history of the Jewish people. Another variant is the limerick, which is simply a funny story in verse. Many a man who would protest that he knew no poetry, and cared nothing for it, could still recite eight or ten limericks in the right company.

[7]   In serious adult poetry there are many superb stories, including the two oldest books in Western literature, the *Iliad* and the *Odyssey*. Every good collection of poems will include some of the most dramatic tales ever told, the English and Scottish ballads, which are still occasionally sung in our own southern states. One of the strangest things about the stories told as ballads is their terrible abruptness and directness. They leave out a great deal. They give only a few details, a name or two; they draw the outlines, harsh and black or blood-red, and they concentrate on the actions and the passions. Such is the ballad about an ambush in which a knight was killed by his own wife's brother. It is called 'The Dowie Houms of Yarrow' (that means the sad fields beside the river Yarrow, in the Scottish borders), and it opens immediately with the quarrel, almost with the clash of swords:

> Late at een, drinkin' the wine,
>   And ere they paid the lawin',
> They set a combat them between,
>   To fight it in the dawin'.

Within only a few verses, the knight has been surrounded, and treacherously murdered, fighting against heavy odds; and when his widow goes out to find his body, her anguish is described in one of the most terrible stanzas in all poetry:

> She kissed his cheek, she kamed his hair,
>   As oft she did before, O;
> She drank the red blood frae him ran,
>   On the dowie houms o'Yarrow.

That story in poetry and a few others like 'Edward, Edward' — in which a mother persuades her son to kill his own father, and drives him mad — are absolutely unforgettable.

[8]   But besides storytelling, poetry has another use, known all over the world. This is mnemonic. Put words into a pattern, and they are easier to remember. I should never have known the lengths of the months if I had not learned:

> Thirty days hath September,
> April, June, and November;
> All the rest have thirty-one,
> Excepting February alone,
> And that has twenty-eight days clear
> And twenty-nine in each leap year.

This is certainly four hundred years old, for it occurs in an English manuscript dated about 1555, and there is a French poem, with the same rhyme scheme, written three hundred years earlier. (It might be easier to change the calendar, but mankind is by nature conservative.) On a simpler level there are many nursery rhymes in every language which are designed to teach children the very simplest things; for instance, counting and performing easy actions:

> One, two,
> Buckle my shoe,
> Three, four,
> Shut the door.

And even earlier, before the child can speak, he is lucky if his mother can recite the poem that goes over his five toes or fingers, one after another:

> This little pig went to market,
> This little pig stayed at home,

up to the comical climax when the child is meant to squeak too, and to enjoy staying at home.

[9]   Adults also remember facts better if they are put into verse. Nearly every morning I repeat to myself:

> Early to bed and early to rise
> Makes a man healthy and wealthy and wise.

And nearly every evening I change it to Thurber's parody:

> Early to rise and early to bed
> Makes a male healthy and wealthy and dead;

or occasionally to George Ade's variant:

> Early to bed and early to rise
> Will make you miss all the regular guys.

This is the source of what they call didactic poetry, poetry meant to teach. The best-known example of it is the Book of Proverbs in the Bible, which ought to be translated into rhythmical prose, or even verse. The third oldest book in Greek literature, not much younger than Homer, is a farmer's handbook all set out in poetry, so that it could be learned off by heart and remembered: it is the *Works and Days* by Hesiod. To teach has long been one of the highest functions of the poet: great poetry can be written in order to carry a message of philosophical or practical truth—or sometimes an ironical counsel, as in this strange poem by Sir Walter Scott:

> Look not thou on beauty's charming;
> Sit thou still when kings are arming;
> Taste not when the winecup glistens;
> Speak not when the people listens;
> Stop thine ear against the singer;
> From the red gold keep thy finger;
> Vacant heart and hand and eye,
> Easy live and quiet die.

[10] There is one peculiar variation on the poem that conveys information. This is the riddle poem, which tells you something—but only if you are smart enough to see through its disguise. There are some such riddles in the Bible: Samson created a good one, about the dead lion with a hive of wild bees inside it. Legend has it that Homer died of chagrin because he could not solve a rather sordid poetic puzzle. The nursery rhyme 'Humpty Dumpty' was really a riddle to begin with (before Lewis Carroll and his illustrator gave it away). We are supposed to guess what was the mysterious person or thing which fell down, and then could not possibly be put together again, not even by all the king's horses and all the king's men, and nowadays by all the republic's scientific experts: the answer is an egg. There is a beautiful folk song made up of three such riddles: the cherry without a stone, the chicken without a bone, and the baby that does not cry. It is at least five hundred years old, and yet for four hundred years it was passed on from one singer to another, without ever being printed.

[11] Again, there are some famous and splendid poems that deal with mystical experience in riddling terms, phrases which have two meanings,

or three, or one concealed: these are also didactic, informative, and yet riddles. One such poem, by an American poet, deals with the paradox of God — the complete God, who includes all the appearances of the universe, both the appearance of good and the appearance of evil. This is Emerson's 'Brahma.'

> If the red slayer think he slays,
>   Or if the slain think he is slain,
> They know not well the subtle ways
>   I keep, and pass, and turn again.
>
> Far or forgot to me is near;
>   Shadow and sunlight are the same;
> The vanished gods to me appear;
>   And one to me are shame and fame.
>
> They reckon ill who leave me out;
>   When me they fly, I am the wings;
> I am the doubter and the doubt,
>   And I the hymn the Brahmin sings.
>
> The strong gods pine for my abode,
>   And pine in vain the sacred Seven;
> But thou, meek lover of the good!
>   Find me, and turn thy back on heaven.

This is a riddle which is meant not for children but for adults. There are similar riddles in the Bible, sometimes equally beautiful. Such is the meditation on old age at the end of that mysterious and rather unorthodox book called *Koheleth*, or *Ecclesiastes*:

> Remember now thy Creator in the days of thy youth,
>   while the evil days come not,
>   nor the years draw nigh, when thou shalt say, I have
>   no pleasure in them;
>
> while the sun or the light or the moon or the stars be
>   not darkened, nor the clouds return after the rain;
>
> in the day when the keepers of the house shall tremble,
>   and the strong men shall bow themselves,
>   and the grinders cease because they are few,
>   and those that look out of the windows be darkened,
> and the doors shall be shut in the streets,
>   when the sound of the grinding is low,
>   and he shall rise up at the voice of the bird,
>   and all the daughters of music shall be brought low,
> also when they shall be afraid of that which is high,

and fears shall be in the way,
and the almond tree shall flourish,
and the grasshopper shall be a burden,
and desire shall fail:
    because man goeth to his long home
    and the mourners go about the streets;

or ever the silver cord be loosed,
    or the golden bowl be broken,
    or the pitcher be broken at the fountain
    or the wheel broken at the cistern.

Then shall the dust return to the earth as it was;
    and the spirit shall return unto God who gave it.

All these enigmatic and memorable phrases are descriptions of the symptoms of the last and almost the bitterest fact in life, old age. They show that it is pathetic, and yet they make it beautiful.

[12] Such poetry is unusual. Or rather, its manner is unusual and its subject is a fact of common experience. It is possible for poets to speak plainly and frankly about everyday life; and that is one more of the uses of poetry—one of the best known. Poetry can express general experience: can say what many men and women have thought and felt. The benefit of this is that it actually helps ordinary people, by giving them words. Most of us are not eloquent. Most of us—especially in times of intense emotion—cannot say what we feel; often we hardly know what we feel. There, in our heart, there is the turmoil, be it love or protest or exultation or despair: it stirs us, but all our gestures and words are inadequate. As the emotion departs, we know that an opportunity was somehow missed, an opportunity of realizing a great moment to the full. It is in this field that poetry comes close to religion. Religion is one of the experiences which the ordinary man finds most difficult to compass in words. Therefore he nearly always falls back on phrases which have been composed for him by someone more gifted. Many, many thousands of times, in battles and concentration camps and hospitals, beside death beds, and even on death beds, men and women have repeated a very ancient poem only six verses long, and have found comfort in it, such as no words of their own would have brought them. It begins, 'The Lord is my shepherd; I shall not want.
[13] If we look at poetry or any of the arts from this point of view, we shall gain a much greater respect for them. They are not amusements or decorations; they are aids to life. Ordinary men and women find living rather difficult. One of their chief difficulties is to apprehend their own thoughts and feelings, and to respond to them by doing the right things and saying the right sentences. It is the poets who supply the words and sentences. They too have felt as we do, but they have been able to speak, while we are dumb.

[14] Not only that. By expressing common emotions clearly and eloquently, the poets help us to understand them in other people. It is difficult to under-stand—for any grown-up it is difficult to understand—what goes on in the mind of a boy or girl. Parents are often so anxious and serious that they have forgotten what it was like to be young, and vague, and romantic. It is a huge effort, rather an unpleasantly arduous effort, to think oneself back into boy-hood. Yet there are several poems which will allow us to understand it, and even to enjoy the experience. One of them is a fine lyric by Longfellow, called 'My Lost Youth':

> I remember the gleams and glooms that dart
>   Across the schoolboy's brain;
> The song and the silence in the heart,
> That in part are prophecies, and in part
>   Are longings wild and vain.
>   And the voice of that fitful song
>   Sings on, and is never still:
>   'A boy's will is the wind's will,
> And the thoughts of youth are long, long thoughts.'
>
> There are things of which I may not speak;
>   There are dreams that cannot die;
> There are thoughts that make the strong heart weak,
> And bring a pallor into the cheek,
>   And a mist before the eye.
>   And the words of that fatal song
>   Come over me like a chill:
>   'A boy's will is the wind's will,
> And the thoughts of youth are long, long thoughts.'

If you have a young son who seems to be woolgathering half the time, and who sometimes does not even answer when he is spoken to, you should read and reflect on that poem of Longfellow.

[15] This function of poetry is not the only one, but it is one of the most vital: to give adequate expression to important general experiences. In 1897, when Queen Victoria celebrated her Diamond Jubilee, the Poet Laureate was that completely inadequate little fellow, Alfred Austin; but the man who wrote the poem summing up the emotions most deeply felt during the Jubilee was Rudyard Kipling. It is call 'Recessional.' It is a splendid poem, almost a hymn—Biblical in its phrasing and deeply prophetic in its thought:

> The tumult and the shouting dies—
>   The captains and the kings depart—
> Still stands Thine ancient sacrifice,
>   An humble and a contrite heart.
> Lord God of Hosts, be with us yet,
> Lest we forget, lest we forget!

[16] However, as you think over the poems you know, you will realize that many of them seem to be quite different from this. They are not even trying to do the same thing. They do not express important general experiences in universally acceptable words. On the contrary, they express strange and individual experiences in abstruse[1] and sometimes unintelligible words. We enjoy them not because they say what we have often thought but because they say what we should never have dreamed of thinking. If a poem like Kipling's 'Recessional' or Longfellow's 'Lost Youth' is close to religion, then this other kind of poetry is close to magic: its words sound like spells; its subjects are often dreams, visions, and myths.

[17] Such are the two most famous poems by Coleridge: 'The Ancient Mariner' and 'Kubla Khan.' They are scarcely understandable. They are unbelievable. Beautiful, yes, and haunting, yes, but utterly illogical; crazy. Coleridge himself scarcely knew their sources, deep in his memory and his subconscious—sources on which a modern scholar has written a superb book. Both of them end with a mystical experience that none of us has ever had: 'The Ancient Mariner' telling how, like the Wandering Jew, he must travel forever from country to country, telling his story with 'strange power of speech'; and 'Kubla Khan' with the poet himself creating a magical palace:

> I would build that dome in air,
> That sunny dome! those caves of ice!
> And all who heard should see them there,
> And all should cry, Beware! Beware!
> His flashing eyes, his floating hair!
> Weave a circle round him thrice,
>   And close your eyes with holy dread,
>   For he on honey-dew hath fed,
> And drunk the milk of Paradise.

[18] Not long after those fantastic verses were written, young Keats was composing a lyric, almost equally weird, which is now considered one of the finest odes in the English language. It ends with the famous words which we all know, and which few of us believe:

> Beauty is truth, truth beauty,—that is all
>   Ye know on earth, and all ye need to know.

It is the 'Ode on a Grecian Urn'; but how many of us have ever stood, like Keats, meditating on the paintings that surround a Greek vase? and, even if we have, how many of us have thought that

> Heard melodies are sweet, but those unheard
>   Are sweeter?

[1]hard to understand

[19] It is a paradox. The entire ode is a paradox: not an expression of ordinary life, but an extreme extension of it, almost a direct contradiction of usual experience.

[20] Most modern poetry is like this. It tells of things almost unknown to ordinary men and women, even to children. If it has power over them at all, it is because it enchants them by its strangeness. Such is the poetry of Verlaine, and Mallarmé, and Rimbaud; of the difficult and sensitive Austrian poet Rilke; in our own language, such is most of Auden's poetry, and Ezra Pound's; and what could be more unusual than most of T. S. Eliot—although he is the most famous poet writing today? Suppose we test this. Let us take something simple. Spring. What have the poets said about the first month of spring, about April? Most of them say it is charming and frail:

> April, April,
> Laugh thy girlish laughter;
> Then, the moment after,
> Weep thy girlish tears!

That is Sir William Watson: turn back, and see Shakespeare talking of

> The uncertain glory of an April day;

turn forward, and hear Browning cry

> O to be in England
> Now that April's there!

and then hundreds of years earlier, see Chaucer beginning his *Canterbury Tales* with a handshake of welcome to 'Aprille, with his shoures soote.' Indeed, that is what most of us feel about April: it is sweet and delicate and youthful and hopeful. But T. S. Eliot begins *The Waste Land* with a grim statement which is far outside ordinary feelings:

> April is the cruellest month, breeding
> Lilacs out of the dead land, mixing
> Memory and desire, stirring
> Dull roots with spring rain.

And the entire poem, the best known of our generation, is a description of several agonizing experiences which most of us not only have never had but have not even conceived as possible. Yet there is no doubt that it is good poetry, and that it has taken a permanent place in our literature, together with other eccentric and individual visions.

[21] But some of us do not admit it to be poetry—or rather claim that, if it is so extreme and unusual, poetry is useless. This is a mistake. The universe is so vast, the universe is so various, that we owe it to ourselves to try to

understand every kind of experience — both the usual and the remote, both the intelligible and the mystical. Logic is not enough, Not all the truth about the world, or about our own lives, can be set down in straightforward prose, or even in straightforward poetry. Some important truths are too subtle even to be uttered in words. A Japanese, by arranging a few flowers in a vase, or Rembrandt, by drawing a dark room with an old man sitting in it, can convey meanings which no one could ever utter in speech. So also, however extravagant a romantic poem may seem, it can tell us something about our world which we ought to know.

[22] It is easier for us to appreciate this nowadays than it would have been for our grandfathers in the nineteenth century, or for their great-grandfathers in the eighteenth century. Our lives are far less predictable; and it is far less possible to use logic alone in organizing and understanding them. Therefore there are justifications, and good ones, for reading and memorizing not only what we might call universal poetry but also strange and visionary poetry. We ourselves, at some time within the mysterious future, may well have to endure and to try to understand some experience absolutely outside our present scope: suffering of some unforeseen kind, a magnificent and somber duty, a splendid triumph, the development of some new power within us. We shall be better able to do so if we know what the poets (yes, and the musicians) have said about such enhancements and extensions of life. Many a man has lived happily until something came upon him which made him, for the first time, think of committing suicide. Such a man will be better able to understand himself and to rise above the thought if he knows the music that Rachmaninoff wrote when he, too, had such thoughts and conquered them, or if he reads the play of *Hamlet*, or if he travels through Dante's *Comedy*, which begins in utter despair and ends in the vision of

love, that moves the sun and the other stars.

[23] And even if we ourselves are not called upon to endure such extremes, there may be those around us, perhaps very close to us, who are faced with situations the ordinary mind cannot assimilate: sudden wealth, the temptations of great beauty, the gift of creation, profound sorrow, unmerited guilt. The knowledge of what the poets have said about experiences beyond the frontiers of logic will help us at least to sympathize with them in these experiences. Such understanding is one of the most difficult and necessary efforts of the soul. Shelley compared the skylark, lost in the radiance of the sun, to

a Poet hidden
In the light of thought
Singing hymns unbidden,
Till the world is wrought
To sympathy with hopes and fears it heeded not.

To create such sympathy is one of the deepest functions of poetry, and one of the most bitterly needed.

EXERCISES

Questions

1. Highet indicates five basic uses for poetry to answer his theme question. What are they? Which is the most complex?
2. The organization of this essay is clear and well defined. Outline it. Find the transitions that join each section.
3. The first two uses of poetry, which Highet calls the "pleasures of poetry," are concerned with surface meanings. What are they? How do they become more complex? What poems can you think of to illustrate these first uses of poetry? Are they also pleasures for you?
4. What variations are given to illustrate the didactic poem, the poem to teach? Examine the examples; what do they reveal about the form of didactic (or mnemonic) poetry? Is this a legitimate purpose for poetry? How does the riddling poem fit into this category?
5. In what ways does poetry serve as "aids to life" in expressing "general experience"?
6. The last form of poetry is that "close to magic." Why is it close to magic? What is its special value?
7. What is paradox? Why is it a particularly fitting form for poetry— especially of the riddling or magical types?
8. Why is logic not enough to help us understand our universe? Why is mystical poetry likely to be of more use today than ever before?
9. What is the deepest function of poetry?
10. Evaluate the order of the uses he presents. What controls it?
11. Almost every point in this essay is clarified by illustration. What additional poems can you supply to fit the categories?

Vocabulary

chagrin
didactic
sordid

For Discussion and Writing

1. Interpreting a poem: whose interpretation is right?
2. A poem that has moved me
3. Why some poetry is difficult to understand
4. Why I still hate poetry
5. Why I enjoy poetry

6. Lyrics of popular songs as poetry
7. Writing a poem: articulating the inarticulate
8. The need for poetry today
9. The "use" of music and art

CROSS REFERENCES

CIARDI: "I Met a Man"
MacLEISH: "Thoughts on an Age that Gave Us Hiroshima"
RICH: "Ringo, Paul, Lenny, George, Elvira, Dave, Wolfgang and John"
ROCKEFELLER: "The Governor Lectures on Art"

RECOMMENDED READING

CIARDI, JOHN: *How Does a Poem Mean?* (Houghton Mifflin Co.: 1960)
FROST, ROBERT: "The Figure a Poem Makes," which is the introduction to
  Complete Poems of Robert Frost (Holt, Rinehart & Winston: 1967)

MORTIMER J. ADLER

"WHAT MAKES A BOOK GREAT?"

INTRODUCTION

Mortimer J. Adler (1902–   ) is concerned with great books, great ideas, and the freedom of the mind and spirit that great thinking inevitably leads to. In pursuit of this end, Dr. Adler earned his doctorate in philosophy at Columbia University and then went on to the University of Chicago where he taught for twenty-two years. There, together with Robert Hutchins, he developed the Great Books Program. He has, since then, been director of the Institute for Philosophical Research. Among his books are *What Man Has Made of Man* (1938); *How to Read a Book* (1940); and *The Idea of Freedom*, Vol. I (1958), Vol. II (1961). His most recent book, for which he was an associate editor, is *The Difference of Man and the Difference It Makes* (1968).

TO THE READER

Dr. Adler answers, in several ways, a question often asked by students; each answer provides an additional insight into the value of great books.

Great books are those that contain the best materials on which the human mind can work in order to gain insight, understanding, and wisdom.

Each in its own way raises the recurrent basic questions which men must face. Because these questions are never completely solved, these books are the sources and monuments of a continuing intellectual tradition.

[2]   Carl Van Doren once referred to great books as "the books that never have to be written again." They are the rare, perfect achievements of sustained excellence. Their beauty and clarity show that they are masterpieces of the fine as well as of the liberal arts. Such books are justifiably called great whether they are books of science, poetry, theology, mathematics, or politics.

[3]   The richness of great books shows itself in the many levels of meaning they contain. They lend themselves to a variety of interpretations. This does not mean that they are ambiguous or that their integrity is compromised. The different interpretations complement one another and allow the reader to discover the unity of the work from a variety of perspectives. We need not read other books more than once to get all that they have to say. But we can always go deeper into great books. As sources of enlightenment, they are inexhaustible.

[4]   The interest in many good books is limited to a definite period of history. They do not possess the universal appeal that results from dealing with the fundamental questions which confront men in all times and places and in a way that men in all times and places can understand. Great books, on the contrary, transcend the provincial limits of their origin. They remain as world literature. The ones we are sure are great are the ones men everywhere turn to again and again through the centuries.

[5]   In view of this, it is often said that great books must pass the test of time. This is quite true. But it is not the passage of time that makes the books great. They were great when they were written. An enduring interest in a book merely confirms its greatness. We may consider some contemporary books great, but we cannot be sure. Their excellence still remains to be proved before the tribunal of the ages.

[6]   Mark Twain once remarked that "the great books are the books that everyone wishes he *had* read, but no one *wants* to read." People wish they had read them because they are the indispensable material of a liberal education. They shy away from reading them because these books require thought. And thinking is hard. It is probably one of the most painful things that human beings are called upon to do.

[7]   The great books are not easy to read. No one should expect to understand them very well on a first reading, or even to master them fully after many readings. I have often said that they are the books which are over everyone's head all of the time. That is why they must be read and reread. That is also why they are good for us. Only the things which are over our head can lift us up.

[8]   Like all the other good things in life, what the great books have to offer is hard to get. But it is precisely because great books are difficult that they are more readable and more worth reading than other books. It is precisely

because they raise problems which they do not finally answer that they can provoke us to think, inquire, and discuss. It is precisely because their difficulty challenges our skill in reading that they can help us to improve that skill. It is precisely because they often challenge our accepted prejudices and our established opinions that they can help us to develop our critical faculties.

[9]   The difficulty of these books comes not from the fact that they are poorly written or badly conceived, but rather from the fact that they are the clearest and simplest writing about the most difficult themes that confront the human mind. They deal with these themes in the easiest possible way. Therein lies their greatness.

EXERCISES

Questions

1.   Define great books as Van Doren did. Evaluate his definition.
2.   What is the relationship of the time factor to the greatness of a work? What fallacy is sometimes ascribed to the time factor?
3.   What is the humor of Twain's statement? What is the truth in Adler's interpretation?
4.   What is the impact of the idea "they are the books . . . over everyone's head all of the time"? Evaluate Adler's reasoning.
5.   Why are great books difficult? What is the final test of greatness?

For Discussion and Writing

1.   Great books raise problems which they don't answer
2.   Great books are difficult to read
3.   Great books challenge our accepted prejudices and established opinions

MORTIMER J. ADLER

"HOW TO READ A DIFFICULT BOOK"

TO THE READER

In reading this article, follow Dr. Adler's directions; you will then know how to read a difficult book and also how to read to remember.

The most important rule about reading is one I have told my great books seminars again and again: In reading a difficult book for the first time, read the book through without stopping. Pay attention to what you can understand, and don't be stopped by what you can't immediately grasp. Keep on this way. Read the book through undeterred by the paragraphs, footnotes, arguments, and references that escape you. If you stop at any of these stumbling blocks, if you let yourself get stalled, you are lost. In most cases you won't be able to puzzle the thing out by sticking to it. You have a much better chance of understanding it on a second reading, but that requires you to read the book *through* for the first time.

[2]   This is the most practical method I know to break the crust of a book, to get the feel and general sense of it, and to come to terms with its structure as quickly and as easily as possible. The longer you delay in getting some sense of the over-all plan of a book, the longer you are in understanding it.

From *Great Ideas from the Great Books* by Mortimer J. Adler. Copyright, ©, 1961, 1963, by Mortimer J. Adler. Reprinted by permission of the publisher, Washington Square Press, Inc.

You simply must have some grasp of the whole before you can see the parts in their true perspective—or often in any perspective at all.

[3]   Shakespeare was spoiled for generations of high-school students who were forced to go through *Julius Caesar*, *Hamlet* or *Macbeth* scene by scene, to look up all the words that were new to them, and to study all the scholarly footnotes. As a result, they never actually read the play. Instead, they were dragged through it, bit by bit, over a period of many weeks. By the time they got to the end of the play, they had surely forgotten the beginning. They should have been encouraged to read the play in one sitting. Only then would they have understood enough of it to make it possible for them to understand more.

[4]   What you understand by reading a book through to the end—even if it is only fifty per cent or less—will help you later in making the additional effort to go back to places you passed by on your first reading. Actually you will be proceeding like any traveler in unknown parts. Having been over the terrain once, you will be able to explore it again from vantage points you could not have known about before. You will be less likely to mistake the side roads for the main highway. You won't be deceived by the shadows at high noon, because you will remember how they looked at sunset. And the mental map you have fashioned will show better how the valleys and mountains are all part of one landscape.

[5]   There is nothing magical about a first quick reading. It cannot work wonders and should certainly never be thought of as a substitute for the careful reading that a good book deserves. But a first quick reading makes the careful study much easier.

[6]   This practice helps you to keep alert in going at a book. How many times have you daydreamed your way through pages and pages only to wake up with no idea of the ground you have been over? That can't help happening if you let yourself drift passively through a book. No one ever understands much that way. You must have a way of getting a general thread to hold onto.

[7]   A good reader is active in his efforts to understand. Any book is a problem, a puzzle. The reader's attitude is that of a detective looking for clues to its basic ideas and alert for anything that will make them clearer. The rule about a first quick reading helps to sustain this attitude. If you follow it, you will be surprised how much time you will save, how much more you will grasp, and how much easier it will be.

EXERCISES

Questions

1.   What is the basic rule for the first reading of a great book? How many more readings should then be given?

2. Consider the illustration in paragraph 3 concerning the reading of Shakespeare in high school. How does your own experience compare with Adler's judgment?
3. In what ways is the analogy about the traveler valid? Is it invalid in any way? Why is it a valuable device for understanding?
4. What is the obligation of the reader to a great book? What does Adler offer as a reward to the reader who follows his instructions?

For Discussion and Writing

1. "Great books are books that never have to be written again," a comment by C. Van Doren.
2. (A) great book(s) I have read
3. A book that gave me insight
4. My first encounter with Shakespeare
5. Why I resist reading
6. Why I'd rather read than watch TV
7. A great book I hated

CROSS REFERENCES

ROBINSON: "On Various Kinds of Thinking"
WODEHOUSE: "William Shakespeare and Me"

P. G. WODEHOUSE

"WILLIAM SHAKESPEARE AND ME"

INTRODUCTION

P. G. Wodehouse (1881–   ) long ago introduced to the world a calm, impeccable, and always sensible butler named Jeeves as valet to a silly and foolish young gentleman named Bertie Wooster. The impact was such that he has written literally dozens of Jeeves books for an avid readership. Mr. Wodehouse, born in England, first came to the United States in 1909 and now makes his permanent home on Long Island. Although he is in his eighties, he is still writing. Many of his early books have been recopyrighted and reissued. Some of his titles reveal the seriousness of his work: *The Heart of a Goof* (1926) (1963); *Indiscretions of Archie* (1921) (1963); *The Brinkmanship of Galahad Threepwood* (1965); and *all* those Jeeves books.

TO THE READER

P. G. Wodehouse explores, in fun—but not entirely—a fan's declaration that Wodehouse is better than Shakespeare. He reminds us that comparisons between artists are, at best, tricky.

From *The New York Times*, August 26, 1956. © 1956–1966 by The New York Times Company. Reprinted by permission of The New York Times Company and the author.

Whatwith this summer's activities at Stratford-on-Housatonic,[1] the movie of "Richard the Third" and Orson Welles having a pop at "King Lear," Shakespeare has been a good deal in the news of late. And when I say Shakespeare, do not run away with the idea that I am not perfectly aware that it may have been Shakespere, Shakspere or even Shikspur. Spelling was his weak spot, and to the end of his life he never could get it right. But, as he said himself, what's in a name?

[2] It is too bad that we have so little information about this great writer. Nobody seems to know where he lived, whom he married and what he looked like. He is generally supposed to have married Anne Hathaway, but there is an entry in an existing register relating to the wedding of "William Shakespeare" and "Annam Whately de Temple Grafton." One can only suppose that the clerk was a poorer speller than the bridegroom himself and that this was his plucky, though scarcely successful, attempt at writing "Anne Hathaway." At that, it would not have been at all a bad shot for those times.

[3] As regards his appearance, there are sixteen portraits of him in the book of reference which I have consulted, and except that they are all solid on the fact that he never shaved, each is absolutely different from the others. Of course, it must have been difficult to paint Shakespeare's portrait. He was always working on a new play in the room in the theatre marked "No Admittance," and you had to get the best view of him you could through the keyhole. It is, indeed, possible that, absorbed in his work, he had to have himself painted by the correspondence method, describing by letter what he thought he looked like and leaving the rest to the artist.

[4] The reason I am bringing him up now is that the press-clipping agency to which I subscribe has just sent me an extract from one of the English morning papers which seems to me to open up a rather interesting line of thought. It is a letter to Ye Ed from a woman living in Wortleberry-below-the-Hill, near Market Bumpstead, Salop, and in it she says that she considers Shakespeare "grossly materialistic and much overrated" and "greatly prefers P. G. Wodehouse."

[5] Well, it is not for me to say whether she is right or not. One cannot arbitrate in these matters of taste. Shakespeare's stuff is different from mine, but that is not necessarily to say that it is inferior. There are passages in Shakespeare to which I would have been quite pleased to put my name. That "To be or not to be" thing. Some spin on the ball there. The man may have been grossly materialistic, but he could line them out all right when in midseason form. I doubt, too, if I have ever done anything much better than Falstaff. Let's leave it at this — Bill's good, I'm good. Both good eggs, is the way I look at it. (Still, awfully glad you like my stuff, old thing, and I hope you don't just get it out of the library. Even if you do, 'At-a-girl, and cheers.)

[1]river in Connecticut that empties into Long Island Sound at Stratford, Connecticut

[6]   One of the things people should remember when they compare Shakespeare with me and hand him the short straw, is, that he did not have my advantages. I have privacy, he did not. When I write a novel I sit down on the old trouser-seat and write it. I may have to break off at intervals to let the dog out and let the cat in and let the cat out and let the dog in and interview young men who are working their way through college by selling magazine subscriptions and then let the cat in and let the dog out and go and answer wrong numbers on the telephone, but I don't have Burbage breathing down my neck all the time and asking haven't I for God's sake finished that thing yet.

[7]   Burbage[2] must have been a perpetual pain in the neck to Shakespeare. Even today a dramatic author suffers from managers—Feuer and Martin, for instance, think nothing of grabbing you by the seat of the pants and throwing you out of the theatre—but in the Fifteen Nineties anyone who got mixed up with the writing end was like somebody in a slave camp. Burbage was the fellow who was putting on the show and he felt that that entitled him to treat the Swan of Avon like a juvenile delinquent.

[8]   In those days a good run for a play was one night. Two was sensational, and if you did three *Variety*[3] called it a socko. Shakespeare would dash off "Romeo and Juliet," say, for production on Monday, and on Tuesday morning at 6 o'clock along would come Burbage in a great state of excitement and wake him with a wet sponge.

[9]   "Asleep!" Burbage would say, seeming to address an invisible friend on whose sympathy he knew he could rely. "Six o'clock in the morning and he's still asleep! Six by golly o'clock and still wallowing in hoggish slumber! Don't I get no service or cooperation? Is this a system? Good heavens, Bill, why aren't you up and working?"

[10] Shakespeare sits up and rubs his eyes.

[11] "Oh, hello, Burb. That you? How are the notices?"

[12] "Never mind the notices. Don't you realize we've got to give 'em something tomorrow night?"

[13] "What about 'Romeo'?"

[14] "Came off last night. Hell's bells, how long do you expect these charades to run? If you haven't something to follow, we'll have to close the theatre. Got anything?"

[15] "Not a thing."

[16] "Then what do you suggest?"

[17] "Bring on the bears."

[18] "They don't want bears, they want a play, and stop groaning like that. Groaning won't get us anywhere."

[19] So Shakespeare would heave himself out of bed, and dig down in the box where he kept other people's plots, and by lunchtime, with Burbage

[2]Richard Burbage (1567?–1619), English actor who was an associate of Shakespeare
[3]the newspaper of show business

popping in all the while he would somehow manage to turn out "Othello," and Burbage would skim through it and say "It'll need work," but he supposed it would have to do.

[20] A playwright cannot give of his best under these conditions, and this, I think, accounts for a peculiarity in Shakespeare's work which has escaped the notice of many critics—to wit, the fact that while his stuff sounds all right, it generally doesn't mean anything. There can be little doubt that, when he was pushed for time (and when wasn't he?), William Shakespeare just shoved down anything and trusted to the charity of the audience to pull him through.

[21] "What on earth does 'abroach' mean?" Burbage would ask, halting the rehearsal of "Romeo and Juliet."

[22] "It's something girls wear," Shakespeare would say. "You know. Made of diamonds and fastened with a pin."

[23] "But you say 'Who set this ancient quarrel new abroach?', and it don't seem to me to make sense."

[24] "Oh, it's all in the acting," Shakespeare would say. "Just speak the line quick and nobody will notice anything."

[25] And that would be that, till they were putting on "Pericles, Prince of Tyre" and somebody had to say to somebody else "I'll fetch thee with a wanion." Shakespeare would get around that by pretending that a wanion was the latest court slang for cab, but this gave him only a brief respite, for the next moment they would be asking him what a "geck" was or a "loggat" and wanting to know what he meant by saying a character had become "frampold" or "rawly." It was a wearing life, and though Shakespeare would try to pass it off jocularly by telling the boys at the Mermaid that it was all in a lifetime and the first hundred years were the hardest and all that sort of thing, there can be little doubt that he felt the strain and that it affected the quality of his work.

[26] Nevertheless, I stick to it that he was good. I would definitely place him in the Wodehouse class. I would say that the principal difference between Shakespeare and myself is not that he is grossly materialistic while I, as everybody knows, am so spiritual that it hurts, but purely a matter of treatment. We get our effects differently. Take, for instance, the familiar farcical situation of the man who doesn't know that something unpleasant is standing behind him. Here is how Shakespeare handles it ("The Winter's Tale," Act 3, Scene 3):

> Farewell!
> The day frowns more and more. . . . I never saw
> The heavens so dim by day.
> A savage clamor!
> I am gone for ever!
>   (Exit, pursued by a bear)*

*This is not quite what Shakespeare wrote, but close enough for Wodehouse's purpose. [Editor]

[27] I should have adopted a somewhat different approach. Thus:

[28] I gave the man one of my looks.

[29] "Touch of indigestion, Jeeves?"

[30] "No, sir."

[31] "Then why is your tummy rumbling like that?"

[32] "Pardon me, sir, the noise to which you allude does not emanate from my interior but from that of the animal that has just joined us."

[33] "Animal? What animal?"

[34] "A bear, sir. If you will turn your head, you will observe that a bear is standing in your immediate rear, inspecting you in a somewhat menacing manner."

[35] I pivoted the loaf. The honest fellow was perfectly correct. It was a bear, and not a small bear either. One of the large economy size. And it was certainly giving me an extremely dirty look. One could see at a g. that there was little or no chance of starting a beautiful friendship.

[36] "Advise me, Jeeves," I yipped. "What do I do for the best?"

[37] "I fancy it might be advisable if you were to exit, sir."

[38] I did, closely followed by the dumb chum. And that, boys and girls, is how your grandfather clipped six seconds off Roger Bannister's[4] mile.

[39] Who can say which method is the superior?

EXERCISES

Questions

1. In what ways does Wodehouse indicate Shakespeare is better than he? In what way are they equal? Who does Wodehouse think is better?

2. What does the title suggest? What do the first three paragraphs contribute to the essay? Could it have started just as well with paragraph 4?

3. What information does Wodehouse supply about Shakespeare?

4. How do the two writers compare regarding working conditions? Compare the effect of having Burbage "bother him" and letting dogs and cats in and out. Is there a deeper significance to this?

5. Comment on the "peculiarity in Shakespeare's work" that "while his stuff sounds all right, it generally doesn't mean anything."

6. What do the archaic words mean? Why does Wodehouse bring them into the essay? What cliches can be found in paragraph 25? Why do you think he used them?

7. How many different types of humor can you find in this short piece? Which was funniest? Why?

8. Whose method is superior? What is the point of the comparison?

[4]British athlete and track star

Vocabulary

allude
emanate
jocularly

For Discussion and Writing

1. Shakespeare: an inspired hack
2. Does discomfort produce art?
3. Shakespeare's English
4. Burbage and Shakespeare
5. Art and commerce of art versus commerce?

CROSS REFERENCES

CIARDI: "I Met a Man"
HIGHET: "What Use Is Poetry?"
ROCKEFELLER: "The Governor Lectures on Art"

RECOMMENDED READING

STOPPARD, TOM: *Rosenkrantz and Guildenstein Are Dead* (Grove Press: 1968)
SHAKESPEARE, WILLIAM: *Hamlet,* etc.

ALAN RICH

"RINGO, PAUL, LENNY, GEORGE, ELVIRA, DAVE, WOLFGANG AND JOHN"

INTRODUCTION

Alan Rich (1924–   ) has been involved in the musical world most of his professional life beginning in 1953 as director of the Pacifica Foundation in Berkeley, California, an organization that, among other things, has developed two high fidelity stations on FM radio. In 1961, Mr. Rich came East to be associate music critic of *The New York Times* and from there, in 1963, went over to *The New York Herald Tribune* where he remained until the paper went out of business. Mr. Rich has contributed articles to many magazines such as *High Fidelity, Musical Quarterly,* and *American Record Guide* and has written a book, *Careers and Opportunities in Music* (1964). He is currently associated with *New York,* a magazine begun in 1968. This article was taken from the first issue of *New York.*

TO THE READER

The people named in the title have a lot more in common than almost anyone suspects.

Reprinted from *New York* magazine, April 8, 1968, with the permission of *New York* and the author.

Mozart is in the jukes again, this time disguised as Elvira Madigan. A song from Schumann's *Dichterliebe* sells Ultrabrite Toothpaste, and a snatch of Brahms' *Double Concerto* punctuates scenes of an afternoon soap opera on TV. And yet there are still those who would have you believe in a magic moat that separates popular and serious cultures.

[2]   If such a moat ever existed, we are currently watching it being filled in. The signs are everywhere around us of a two-way infiltration between the two cultures, most of it beneficial and some of it not. Each culture creates its own artifacts[1] from the other.

[3]   A few culture buffs are unhappy that a snatch from Mozart's *Piano Concerto No. 21* got used as background music for *Elvira Madigan;* I was, too, to the extent that a piece of music that happens to mean a great deal to me kept turning up in that very pretty movie to distract my attention, and also that it kept getting shut off before the end. (In a rare, for him, burst of critical insight, B. H. Haggin once described that particular slow movement as one in which listeners are very likely to stop breathing.)

[4]   Yet, I can at least hope that the 15,000 people who have bought the DGG LP of the concerto because of the movie might someday also discover the remarkable way Mozart uses soft trumpets and drums in the first movement, and the subtle and tricky construction of the whole marvelous piece. Likewise, I might hope that anyone using Ultrabrite Toothpaste because of its singing commercial might some day discover the other fine songs in Schumann's cycle.

[5]   But even if these things don't come to pass, we have to live with the realization that nothing on the Olympian slopes is as sacred as it used to be. We have to assume, for example, that the current problems of several symphony orchestras in tying down a permanent conductor is part of the pop conversational picture even among people who might not be caught dead at the Philharmonic. Zubin Mehta says he doesn't choose to run, and that is enough to land him on the cover of *Time.* San Francisco cops Seiji Ozawa, and New York's reaction is like when the Giants moved away. The conversation that goes on about these matters is pretty much on the surface, of course; you have to read the *Time* story rather meticulously to find out whether Mehta is a good conductor or not, but there are plenty of other items in the story to hold the attention. That's partly Lenny's fault, of course, showing how even as august a figure as a symphony conductor can make good journalistic copy. But again, if all those pictures of Bernstein with Jackie Kennedy sold a few records or won a few converts for Mahler, why not?

[6]   The sooner we recognize this dynamic reunion of the pop and nonpop, the closer we may get to a solution of some of the current musical crises. It seems to me, for example, and I mean this only half facetiously, that the

[1]any object made by man, especially with a view toward subsequent use

Philharmonic management could do a lot worse than consider certain accepted pop figures for Bernstein's successor. Would The Beatles be such a bad choice?

[7]   For one thing, there are four of them, which would substantially reduce the work load that all conductors today are complaining about. For another, they would certainly bring in audiences. And for a third, they are — as Bernstein was when he got the Philharmonic job — among the most dynamic, creative spirits in music today. (If you can think of another piece of music created in the last ten years as powerful, immediate, communicative and original as *Sgt. Pepper* I'd like to hear about it.) If we assume, easy enough, the current doldrums in the symphonic repertory, the crying need for some major breakthrough to enliven the experience of concertgoing, the lack of major talent in traditional sources, I give you Ringo, Paul, John and George as a perfectly viable[2] way out, with a few guest conductors now and then for Beethoven. About the only drawback I can see, in fact, is that The Beatles record for Capitol and the Philharmonic is under contract to Columbia, and that's hardly a major hangup.

[8]   To bring about this rapprochement[3] on the orchestral scene would merely parallel the similar crossfeeding that has been going on among composers. Its signs are everywhere around us. A few months ago Columbia brought out a set of no fewer than 17 new LPs devoted to new music, most of it pretty far out and all of it included in what you would call the serious category. Yet, one of the most fascinating aspects of this survey was the constant evidence that serious composers are pulling anything and everything into their music, and usually making it work.

[9]   On one disc, Steve Reich, a young New York composer, builds a whole big electronic piece by taking a spoken phrase (from a Negro boy's testimony at a Civil Rights rally) and letting it spread gradually over a stereophonic setup into a powerful study in musical obsession. Another local boy, Calvin Hampton, creates a big chamber piece out of subtle contrapuntal[4] manipulation of a phrase from an old song called *I'm in Love with Tootsie Oodles.*

[10] And, on the so-called other side, The Beatles and Rolling Stones move steadily toward large-scale pieces involving some of the most sophisticated techniques out of the Princeton and Cologne electronic studios, combined with intensely intricate word-plus-music textures as complex for our time as Mozart's operatic ensembles were for theirs. If this be pop, it's a long way from *The Isle of Capri.* Meanwhile Dave Brubeck, one of the first to infuse jazz idioms with intellectual respectability, has moved easily and gracefully into large-scale serious composition with a big oratorio brought out last month in Cincinnati, which is designed to be performed with an overlay of jazz improvisation.

[2]practical, workable
[3]an establishment of harmonious relations
[4]composed of two or more relatively independent melodies sounded together

[11] Naturally, the hard cores of the two cultures remain relatively integral. There is still plenty of pop music qua pop to tickle the teenies, and plenty of conductors around who still play their Brahms straight. The ferment is at the edges, where these worlds collide.

[12] It is much too soon, of course, to trumpet the thesis that pop culture has ceased to exist, or serious culture, for that matter. But it is far too late to pretend that either side is any kind of pure and unsullied entity. Attempts to preserve this purity, especially on the serious side, are partly responsible for the present stagnation in our musical language, a stagnation which has been clearly propounded this season in the sorry procession of new serious compositions introduced for the Philharmonic's 125th birthday, to cite a single collection of evidence.

[13] It is much too pat to assume that the way out of this stagnation is for every serious composer today, all the way from good ol' Roy Harris to bad ol' Stockhausen, to suddenly start turning out rock symphonies and jazz operas. It is equally absurd to expect every proficient pop musician to work in terms of 40-minute integrated compositions in Bachian counterpoint. All I know is that in that shadowy no man's land where the cultures overlap, the activity is violent and worth the attention of anyone who has ever wondered where music is going.

EXERCISES

Questions

1. State, in one sentence, Rich's thesis as it appears in paragraphs 6 and 13. In what other paragraphs is there a restatement?
2. What signs does Rich cite to support his belief that there is an overlap between pop and serious culture? Can you provide any other examples?
3. What possible advantages lie in the merging of pop and serious forms? Why is it foolish to insist that each form maintain its purity? What disadvantages are there in merging?
4. In what ways might The Beatles be good as directors of the Philharmonic? Would they have any handicaps in that job? Why doesn't Rich mention this?
5. In what ways is serious music ready for The Beatles?
6. What does it suggest about music and culture to note that they do overlap "at the edges"?
7. How does Rich's style combine serious and pop writing even as his article talks about serious and pop music?

Vocabulary

august (adj.)
entity
oratorio

For Discussion and Writing

1. The Beatles' contribution to music
2. Using classical music commercially
3. Where is music going?
4. Electronic music
5. Pop is serious music
6. Serious music is popular
7. What makes music "good"?
8. The music business

CROSS REFERENCES

ADLER: "What Makes a Book Great?"
HIGHET: "What Use Is Poetry?"
ROCKEFELLER: "The Governor Lectures on Art"

ARCHIBALD MacLEISH

"THOUGHTS ON AN AGE THAT GAVE US HIROSHIMA"

INTRODUCTION

Archibald MacLeish (1892–   ) set out to be a lawyer, earned his degree, and practiced law from 1920 to 1923. He abandoned law for poetry, however, and in 1925 released his first book of poems, *The Pot of Earth*. He has had an active career of magazine work, teaching, and government service, serving in the latter as Librarian of Congress from 1939 to 1944 and Assistant Secretary of State from 1944 to 1945 when he helped draw up the constitution of UNESCO. Since 1949, Mr. MacLeish has been at Harvard. He has written several books of poetry, including *Conquistador,* which won the Pulitzer Prize in 1930; some verse plays, including *The Fall of the City,* in 1937, and *J.B.,* in 1958; and his most recent book, *Continuing Journey.*

TO THE READER

In this short speech, delivered in 1967 at the opening of the Lincoln Center (New York) Festival of the Arts, Mr. MacLeish explains that the arts will lead men to peace and that life without the arts is inevitably destructive.

There would be nothing unusual about a festival of the arts at Lincoln Center for the Performing Arts but for one thing: the current standing of

Reprinted by permission of the author.

the arts. Speaking in Washington recently, the composer, William Schuman, who is president of the Center, remarked with some feeling that the Congress of the United States "does not understand the value and the meaning of the arts as a precious national asset." He might have gone further to include the state legislatures of the several states, the city councils of the various cities and more or less every other public agency that undertakes to speak for the American people, not to mention those that speak for the rest of the world as well. For the failure to understand "the value and the meaning of the arts" is not a wholly American characteristic, however much the Europeans may wish it were. It is a defect of the age and as evident in contemporary Paris and contemporary Peking and contemporary Moscow as in contemporary Washington—more evident, perhaps, because in contemporary Moscow the arts are explicitly subordinated to the public business of the State, and in Peking to adolescent mobs the State employs, while in Paris the primacy of politicians is only less notorious than the dictatorship of the political philosophers.

[2]   Man in the electronic age is not a votary[1] of the arts—he has more serious business. He sees himself, whatever his economic system, as a social and scientific animal, the great unraveler of the universe, its potential master, and his tool is not the sculptor's chisel any longer or the brush that paints an image of himself—his tool is technological information. The arts may flourish in new galleries, new concert halls, enormous audiences, princely contributions, but what really matters is the journey to the moon, the voyage within the atom, the automation of industrial enterprises, the instantaneous communication of the message, the miraculous discoveries of medicine, the invention of new foods, new fabrics—a new life.

[3]   It is not remarkable that the arts should take a secondary place in the century of Bohr[2] and Einstein. They took a secondary place, no doubt, when Prometheus brought back fire. But the trouble is, as we are coming more and more to see, that the Promethean life is not enough. Technological information, even the immeasurable stores of technological information we have brought back from the fabulous voyages of discovery in the last few decades, have not produced Utopia even yet. Technological information has given us the electronic age and the electronic age has given us the beginnings of the affluent society and the affluent society has polluted its water, fouled its air, alienated its children, defiled its cities and stumbled and fumbled its way into a series of the most murderous and destructive and degrading wars the world has ever seen.

[4]   What is wrong is not, of course, the great discoveries of science—information is always better than ignorance, no matter what information or what ignorance. What is wrong is the belief behind the information, the belief that information alone will change the world. It won't. Information

---

[1]a person who is devoted or addicted to some subject or pursuit; a devoted follower or admirer

[2]Niels Bohr, a Danish physicist who won the Nobel Prize in 1922

without human understanding is like an answer without its question—
meaningless. And human understanding is only possible through the arts.
It is the work of art that creates the human perspective in which information
turns to truth. The psychological discoveries of the last two generations
have told us more about ourselves, or what we choose to call our selves,
than men before us ever guessed, and yet we still reread the Greeks, who
came to self through art, to learn to understand our nature. Nuclear physics
opened the sources of inexhaustible power to mankind, and that power,
without an understanding of the human meaning of the power, gave us
Hiroshima.

[5]   Information without the intervention, the mediation, of the arts will
always lead to Hiroshima. Which is why a celebration of the arts at this
tragic moment of worldwide darkness and confusion and dismay has a
particular significance. We need to remind ourselves that man cannot exist
as man without an image of himself to question all he knows—and that the
arts alone can create that image. Without those last quartets of Beethoven,
without Oedipus the King, without a Hamlet or a Lear, or Michelangelo's
ceiling, or the Odes of Keats, the electronic age could be a nightmare—a
brighter, louder, more disastrous nightmare than any that has gone before.
With the arts, instructed by the arts, it could become a great, perhaps the
greatest age.

EXERCISES

Questions

1.   What is MacLeish's definition of the meaning or use of the arts? What
does he feel the arts can contribute today?
2.   Why will science or technology without the arts always lead to Hiroshima? Why won't information alone change the world? In what sense
is human understanding possible through the arts?
3.   What is the average man's reaction to the arts? How is he shortchanging
himself? How has the electronic age contributed to this?
4.   Why do we still reread the Greeks? What is the difference between ourselves and our selves?
5.   Comment on MacLeish's statement: "Information is always better than
ignorance, no matter what information or what ignorance."
6.   MacLeish uses comparison and contrast to develop paragraph 2. What
is he contrasting? In what respect does he contrast them?

For Discussion and Writing

1.   A life without art
2.   The art form that brings me the most pleasure

3.   The National Arts Foundation
4.   The arts program at our college
5.   Federal aid to the arts—a boon or an interference?

CROSS REFERENCES

ADLER: "What Makes a Great Book?"
HIGHET: "What Use Is Poetry?"
ROCKEFELLER: "The Governor Lectures on Art"
SEVAREID: "The Dark of the Moon"

RECOMMENDED READING

HERSEY, JOHN: *Hiroshima* (Knopf: 1946)

iv

Two
Private
Issues

"...Sex and violence everywhere!"

ON THE LIMITS OF DISSENT

PLATO

"APOLOGY"

INTRODUCTION

Plato (427–347 B.C.), the great Greek philosopher, recorded and immortalized his teacher, Socrates (469–399 B.C.), and thus the logic and remarkable
insights of both have been passed down through the ages. Socrates is the
subject of or chief logician for many of Plato's greatest works, including *The
Republic, Symposium,* and *Phaedo,* where the death of Socrates is described.
The *"Apology"* was Socrates' argument before the Athenian Senate when he
was placed on trial for his life on charges of heresy and treason.

TO THE READER

Socrates, the philosopher and teacher, was brought before the Senate and
charged with heresy, as "an evildoer, and a curious person, who searches
into things under the earth and in heaven, and [who] makes the worse appear
the better cause," and with teaching his beliefs to the youth of Athens. In
his speech in his own behalf, he explained why he had gone searching for
the truth: an oracle of the god Apollo had said that Socrates was the wisest
of men. His refusal to accept this judgment was partly responsible for the
charge of heresy. He explained that in his search to find who was the wisest
of men and in his many searches for truth, he went among the politicians,
the artists, and the artisans of the city asking questions. He found "that the

From *The Works of Plato,* 3d ed., translated by Benjamin Jowett.

men most in repute were all but the most foolish; and that others less esteemed were really wiser and better." This announcement of his created
many enemies, among them Meletus, one of the men who charged Socrates
with atheism, heresy, and polluting the young. In the "Apology," Socrates
subjected Meletus to close cross-examination to show that the charges were
not only false, but malicious as well.

Socrates concluded from his inquiry into truth that, "He . . . is the
wisest who, like Socrates, knows that his wisdom is in truth worth nothing."
This was not designed to appeal to politicians who wanted the people to
believe in the infallibility of their leaders. But, Socrates would not desist from
his inquiries or his findings.

The section of the "Apology" that follows comes at the conclusion
of his refutation of the specific charges.

Knowing the divisions of the "Apology" should make the reading easier:

Paragraphs 1 to 11 — Statement of his true goal: the pursuit of truth
and integrity

Paragraphs 12 to 15 — His final appeal to the Senate

Paragraphs 16 to 22 — His statement after the judgment

Paragraphs 23 to conclusion — His statement after sentence was passed

I have said enough in answer to the charge of Meletus: any elaborate
defence is unnecessary; but I know only too well how many are the en-
mities which I have incurred, and this is what will be my destruction if I am
destroyed; — not Meletus, nor yet Anytus, but the envy and detraction of
the world, which has been the death of many good men, and will probably
be the death of many more; there is no danger of my being the last of them.
[2]   Some one will say: And are you not ashamed, Socrates, of a course
of life which is likely to bring you to an untimely end? To him I may fairly
answer: There you are mistaken: a man who is good for anything ought not
to calculate the chance of living or dying; he ought only to consider whether
in doing anything he is doing right or wrong — acting the part of a good man
or of a bad. Whereas, upon your view, the heroes who fell at Troy were
not good for much, and the son of Thetis above all, who altogether despised
danger in comparison with disgrace; and when he was so eager to slay
Hector, his goddess mother said to him, that if he avenged his companion
Patroclus, and slew Hector, he would die himself — "Fate," she said, in
these or the like words, "waits for you next after Hector"; he, receiving
this warning, utterly despised danger and death, and instead of fearing them,
feared rather to live in dishonour, and not to avenge his friend. "Let me
die forthwith," he replies, "and be avenged of my enemy, rather than abide
here by the beaked ships, a laughing stock and a burden of the earth."
Had Achilles any thought of death and danger? For whereever a man's
place is, whether the place which he has chosen or that in which he has
been placed by a commander, there he ought to remain in the hour of dan-

ger; he should not think of death or of anything but of disgrace. And this, O men of Athens, is a true saying.

[3]   Strange, indeed, would be my conduct, O men of Athens, if I, who, when I was ordered by the generals whom you chose to command me at Potidaea and Amphipolis and Delium, remained where they placed me, like any other man, facing death—if now, when, as I conceive and imagine, God orders me to fulfill the philosopher's mission of searching into myself and other men, I were to desert my post through fear of death, or any other fear; that would indeed be strange, and I might justly be arraigned in court for denying the existence of the gods, if I disobeyed the oracle because I was afraid of death, fancying that I was wise when I was not wise. For the fear of death is indeed the pretence of wisdom, and not real wisdom, being a pretence of knowing the unknown; and no one knows whether death, which men in their fear apprehend to be the greatest evil, may not be the greatest good. Is not this ignorance of a disgraceful sort, the ignorance which is the conceit that a man knows what he does not know? And in this respect only I believe myself to differ from men in general, and may perhaps claim to be wiser than they are:—that whereas I know but little of the world below, I do not suppose that I know: but I do know that injustice and diso- bedience to a better, whether God or man, is evil and dishonourable, and I will never fear or avoid a possible good rather than a certain evil. And therefore if you let me go now, and are not convinced by Anytus, who said that since I had been prosecuted I must be put to death; (or if not that I ought never to have been prosecuted at all); and that if I escape now, your sons will all be utterly ruined by listening to my words—if you say to me, Socrates, this time we will not mind Anytus, and you shall be let off, but upon one condition, that you are not to enquire and speculate in this way any more, and that if you are caught doing so again you shall die;—if this was the condition on which you let me go, I should reply: Men of Athens, I honour and love you; but I shall obey God rather than you, and while I have life and strength I shall never cease from the practice and teaching of philosophy, exhorting any one whom I meet and saying to him after my manner: You, my friend,—a citizen of the great and mighty and wise city of Athens,—are you not ashamed of heaping up the greatest amount of money and honour and reputation, and caring so little about wisdom and truth and the greatest improvement of the soul, which you never regard or heed at all? And if the person with whom I am arguing, says: Yes, but I do care; then I do not leave him or let him go at once; but I proceed to interrogate and examine and cross-examine him, and if I think that he has no virtue in him, but only says that he has, I reproach him with undervaluing the greater, and overvaluing the less. And I shall repeat the same words to every one whom I meet, young and old, citizen and alien, but especially to the citizens, inasmuch as they are my brethren. For know that this is the command of God; and I believe that no greater good has ever happened

in the State than my service to the God. For I do nothing but go about persuading you all, old and young alike, not to take thought for your persons or your properties, but first and chiefly to care about the greatest improvement of the soul. I tell you that virtue is not given by money, but that from virtue comes money and every other good of man, public as well as private. This is my teaching, and if this is the doctrine which corrupts the youth, I am a mischievous person. But if any one says that this is not my teaching, he is speaking an untruth. Wherefore, O men of Athens, I say to you, do as Anytus bids or not as Anytus bids, and either acquit me or not; but whichever you do, understand that I shall never alter my ways, not even if I have to die many times.

[4]   Men of Athens, do not interrupt, but hear me; there was an understanding between us that you should hear me to the end: I have something more to say, at which you may be inclined to cry out; but I believe that to hear me will be good for you, and therefore I beg that you will not cry out. I would have you know, that if you kill such an one as I am, you will injure yourselves more than you will injure me. Nothing will injure me, not Meletus nor yet Anytus—they cannot, for a bad man is not permitted to injure a better than himself. I do not deny that Anytus may, perhaps, kill him, or drive him into exile, or deprive him of civil rights; and he may imagine, and others may imagine, that he is inflicting a great injury upon him: but there I do not agree. For the evil of doing as he is doing—the evil of unjustly taking away the life of another—is greater far.

[5]   And now, Athenians, I am not going to argue for my own sake, as you may think, but for yours, that you may not sin against the God by condemning me, who am his gift to you. For if you kill me you will not easily find a successor to me, who, if I may use such a ludicrous figure of speech, am a sort of gadfly,[1] given to the State by God; and the State is a great and noble steed who is tardy in his motions owing to his very size, and requires to be stirred into life. I am that gadfly which God has attached to the State, and all day long and in all places am always fastening upon you, arousing and persuading and reproaching you. You will not easily find another like me, and therefore I would advise you to spare me. I dare say that you may feel out of temper (like a person who is suddenly awakened from sleep), and you think that you might easily strike me dead as Anytus advises, and then you would sleep on for the remainder of your lives, unless God in his care of you sent you another gadfly. When I say that I am given to you by God, the proof of my mission is this:—if I had been like other men, I should not have neglected all my own concerns or patiently seen the neglect of them during all these years, and have been doing yours, coming to you individually like a father or elder brother, exhorting you to regard virtue; such conduct, I say, would be unlike human nature. If I had gained anything, or if my exhortations had been paid, there would have been some

[1]a biting insect; a person who repeatedly and persistently annoys others with schemes, ideas, demands, and requests

sense in my doing so; but now, as you will perceive, not even the impudence of my accusers dares to say that I have ever exacted or sought pay of any one; of that they have no witness. And I have a sufficient witness to the truth of what I say — my poverty.

[6]   Some one may wonder why I go about in private giving advice and busying myself with the concerns of others, but do not venture to come forward in public and advise the State. I will tell you why. You have heard me speak at sundry times and in divers places of an oracle or sign which comes to me, and is the divinity which Meletus ridicules in the indictment. This sign, which is a kind of voice, first began to come to me when I was a child; it always forbids but never commands me to do anything which I am going to do. This is what deters me from being a politician. And rightly, as I think. For I am certain, O men of Athens, that if I had engaged in politics, I should have perished long ago, and done no good either to you or to myself. And do not be offended at my telling you the truth: for the truth is, that no man who goes to war with you or any other multitude, honestly striving against the many lawless and unrighteous deeds which are done in a State, will save his life; he who will fight for the right, if he would live even for a brief space, must have a private station and not a public one.

[7]   I can give you convincing evidence of what I say, not words only, but what you value far more — actions. Let me relate to you a passage of my own life which will prove to you that I should never have yielded to injustice from any fear of death and that "as I should have refused to yield" I must have died at once. I will tell you a tale of the courts, not very interesting perhaps, but nevertheless true. The only office of State which I ever held, O men of Athens, was that of senator: the tribe Antiochis, which is my tribe, had the presidency at the trial of the generals who had not taken up the bodies of the slain after the battle of Arginusae; and you proposed to try them in a body, contrary to law, as you all thought afterwards; but at the time I was the only one of the Prytanes who was opposed to the illegality, and I gave my vote against you; and when the orators threatened to impeach and arrest me, and you called and shouted, I made up my mind that I would run the risk, having law and justice with me, rather than take part in your injustice because I feared imprisonment and death. This happened in the days of the democracy. But when the oligarchy of the Thirty was in power, they sent for me and four others into the rotunda, and bade us bring Leon the Salaminian from Salamis, as they wanted to put him to death. This was a specimen of the sort of commands which they were always giving with the view of implicating as many as possible in their crimes; and then I showed, not in word only but in deed, that, if I may be allowed to use such an expression, I cared not a straw for death, and that my great and only care was lest I should do an unrighteous or unholy thing. For the strong arm of that oppressive power did not frighten me into doing wrong; and when we came out of the rotunda the other four went to Salamis and fetched Leon, but I went quietly home. For which I might have lost my

life, had not the power of the Thirty shortly afterwards come to an end.
And many will witness to my words.

[8]   Now, do you really imagine that I could have survived all these years,
if I had led a public life, supposing that like a good man I had always maintained the right and had made justice, as I ought, the first thing? No, indeed, men of Athens, neither I nor any other man. But I have been always
the same in all my actions, public as well as private, and never have I
yielded any base compliance to those who are slanderously termed my
disciples, or to any other. Not that I have any regular disciples. But if any
one likes to come and hear me while I am pursuing my mission, whether
he be young or old, he is not excluded. Nor do I converse only with those
who pay; but any one, whether he be rich or poor, may ask and answer
me and listen to my words; and whether he turns out to be a bad man or
a good one, neither result can be justly imputed to me; for I never taught
or professed to teach him anything. And if any one says that he has ever
learned or heard anything from me in private which all the world has not
heard, let me tell you that he is lying.

[9]   But I shall be asked, Why do people delight in continually conversing
with you? I have told you already, Athenians, the whole truth about this
matter: they like to hear the cross-examination of the pretenders to wisdom;
there is amusement in it. Now, this duty of cross-examining other men has
been imposed upon me by God; and has been signified to me by oracles,
visions, and in every way in which the will of divine power was ever inti-
mated to any one. This is true, O Athenians; or, if not true, would be soon
refuted. If I am or have been corrupting the youth, those of them who are
now grown up and have become sensible that I gave them bad advice in
the days of their youth should come forward as accusers, and take their
revenge; or if they do not like to come themselves, some of their relatives,
fathers, brothers, or other kinsmen, should say what evil their families have
suffered at my hands. Now is their time. Many of them I see in the court.
There is Crito, who is of the same age and of the same deme[2] with myself,
and there is Critobulus, his son, whom I also see. Then again there is Lysanias
of Sphettus, who is the father of Aeschines — he is present; and also there
is Antiphon of Cephisus, who is the father of Epigenes; and there are the
brothers of several who have associated with me. There is Nicostratus the
son of Theosdotides, and the brother of Theodotus (now Theodotus himself
is dead, and therefore he, at any rate, will not seek to stop him); and there
is Paralus the son of Demodocus, who had a brother Theages; and Adeiman-
tus the son of Ariston, whose brother Plato is present; and Aeantodorus, who
is the brother of Apollodorus, whom I also see. I might mention a great
many others, some of whom Meletus should have produced as witnesses
in the course of his speech; and let him still produce them, if he has forgotten
— I will make way for him. And let him say, if he has any testimony of the

---

[2]a district

sort which he can produce. Nay, Athenians, the very opposite is the truth. For all these are ready to witness on behalf of the corrupter, of the injurer of their kindred, as Meletus and Anytus call me; not the corrupted youth only — there might have been a motive for that — but their uncorrupted elder relatives. Why should they too support me with their testimony? Why, indeed, except for the sake of truth and justice, and because they know that I am speaking the truth, and that Meletus is a liar.

[10] Well, Athenians, this and the like of this is all the defence which I have to offer. Yet a word more. Perhaps there may be some one who is offended at me, when he calls to mind how he himself on a similar, or even a less serious occasion, prayed and entreated the judges with many tears, and how he produced his children in court, which was a moving spectacle, together with a host of relations and friends; whereas I, who am probably in danger of my life, will do none of these things. The contrast may occur to his mind, and he may be set against me, and vote in anger because he is displeased at me on this account. Now, if there be such a person among you, — mind, I do not say that there is, — to him I may fairly reply: My friend, I am a man, and like other men, a creature of flesh and blood, and not "of wood or stone," as Homer says; and I have a family, yes, and sons, O Athenians, three in number, one almost a man, and two others who are still young; and yet I will not bring any of them hither in order to petition you for an acquittal. And why not? Not from any self-assertion or want of respect for you. Whether I am or am not afraid of death is another question, of which I will not now speak. But, having regard to public opinion, I feel that such conduct would be discreditable to myself, and to you, and to the whole State. One who has reached my years, and who has a name for wisdom, ought not to demean himself. Whether this opinion of me be deserved or not, at any rate the world has decided that Socrates is in some way superior to other men. And if those among you who are said to be superior in wisdom and courage, and any other virtue, demean themselves in this way, how shameful is their conduct! I have seen men of reputation, when they have been condemned, behaving in the strangest manner: they seemed to fancy that they were going to suffer something dreadful if they died and that they could be immortal if you only allowed them to live; and I think that such are a dishonour to the State and that any stranger coming in would have said of them that the most eminent men of Athens, to whom the Athenians themselves give honour and command, are no better than women. And I say that these things ought not to be done by those of us who have a reputation; and if they are done, you ought not to permit them; you ought rather to show that you are far more disposed to condemn the man who gets up a doleful scene and makes the city ridiculous, than him who holds his peace.

[11] But, setting aside the question of public opinion, there seems to be something wrong in asking a favour of a judge, and thus procuring an acquittal, instead of informing and convincing him. For his duty is, not to

make a present of justice, but to give judgment; and he has sworn that he will judge according to the laws, and not according to his own good pleasure; and we ought not to encourage you, nor should you allow yourselves to be encouraged, in this habit of perjury—there can be no piety in that. Do not then require me to do what I consider dishonourable and impious and wrong, especially now, when I am being tried for impiety on the indictment of Meletus. For if, O men of Athens, by force of persuasion and entreaty I could overpower your oaths, then I should be teaching you to believe that there are no gods, and in defending should simply convict myself of the charge of not believing in them. But that is not so—far otherwise. For I do believe that there are gods, and in a sense higher than that in which any of my accusers believe in them. And to you and to God I commit my cause, to be determined by you as is best for you and me.

[12] There are many reasons why I am not grieved, O men of Athens, at the vote of condemnation. I expected it, and am only surprised that the votes are so nearly equal; for I had thought that the majority against me would have been far larger; but now, had thirty votes gone over to the other side, I should have been acquitted. And I may say, I think, that I have escaped Meletus. I may say more; for without the assistance of Anytus and Lycon, any one may see that he would not have had a fifth part of the votes, as the law requires, in which case he would have incurred a fine of a thousand drachmae.

[13] And so he proposes death as the penalty. And what shall I propose on my part, O men of Athens? Clearly that which is my due. And what is my due? What returns shall be made to the man who has never had the wit to be idle during his whole life; but has been careless of what the many care for—wealth, and family interests, and military offices, and speaking in the assembly, and magistracies, and plots, and parties. Reflecting that I was really too honest a man to be a politician and live, I did not go where I could do no good to you or to myself; but where I could do the greatest good privately to every one of you, thither I went, and sought to persuade every man among you that he must look to himself, and seek virtue and wisdom before he looks to his private interests, and look to the State before he looks to the interests of the State; and that this should be the order which he observes in all his actions. What shall be done to such an one? Doubtless some good thing, O men of Athens, if he has his reward; and the good should be of a kind suitable to him. What would be a reward suitable to a poor man who is your benefactor, and who desires leisure that he may instruct you? There can be no reward so fitting as maintenance in the Prytaneum,[3] O men of Athens, a reward which he deserves far more than the citizen who has won the prize at Olympia in the horse or chariot race,

---

[3] a public building used as a meeting place for the administrative body of the community

whether the chariots were drawn by two horses or by many. For I am in want, and he has enough; and he only gives you the appearance of happiness, and I give you the reality. And if I am to estimate the penalty fairly, I should say that maintenance in the Prytaneum is the just return.

[14] Perhaps you think that I am braving you in what I am saying now, as in what I said before about the tears and prayers. But this is not so. I speak rather because I am convinced that I never intentionally wronged any one, although I cannot convince you—the time has been too short: if there were a law at Athens, as there is in other cities, that a capital cause should not be decided in one day, then I believe that I should have convinced you. But I cannot in a moment refute great slanders; and, as I am convinced that I never wronged another, I will assuredly not wrong myself. I will not say of myself that I deserve any evil, or propose any penalty. Why should I? Because I am afraid of the penalty of death which Meletus proposes? When I do not know whether death is a good or an evil, why should I propose a penalty which would certainly be an evil? Shall I say imprisonment? And why should I live in prison, and be the slave of the magistrate of the year—of the Eleven? Or shall the penalty be a fine, and imprisonment until the fine is paid? There is the same objection. I should have to lie in prison, for money I have none, and cannot pay. And if I say exile (and this may possibly be the penalty which you will affix), I must indeed be blinded by the love of life, if I am so irrational as to expect that when you, who are my own citizens, cannot endure my discourses and words, and have found them so grievous and odious that you will have no more of them, others are likely to endure me. No, indeed, men of Athens, that is not very likely. And what a life should I lead, at my age, wandering from city to city, ever changing my place of exile, and always being driven out! For I am quite sure that wherever I go, there, as here, the young men will flock to me; and if I drive them away, their elders will drive me out at their request; and if I let them come, their fathers and friends will drive me out for their sakes.

[15] Some one will say: Yes, Socrates, but cannot you hold your tongue, and then you may go into a foreign city, and no one will interfere with you? Now, I have great difficulty in making you understand my answer to this. For if I tell you that to do as you say would be a disobedience to the God, and therefore that I cannot hold my tongue, you will not believe that I am serious; and if I say again that daily to discourse about virtue, and of those other things about which you hear me examining myself and others, is the greatest good of man, and that the unexamined life is not worth living, you are still less likely to believe me. Yet I say what is true, although a thing of which it is hard for me to persuade you. Also, I have never been accustomed to think that I deserve to suffer any harm. Had I money I might have estimated the offence at what I was able to pay, and not have been much the worse. But I have none, and therefore I must ask you to proportion the

fine to my means. Well, perhaps I could afford a mina, and therefore I propose that penalty: Plato, Crito, Critobulus, and Apollodorus, my friends here, bid me say thirty minae, and they will be the sureties. Let thirty minae be the penalty; for which sum they will be ample security to you.

[16] Not much time will be gained, O Athenians, in return for the evil name which you will get from the detractors of the city, who will say that you killed Socrates, a wise man; for they will call me wise, even although I am not wise, when they want to reproach you. If you had waited a little while, your desire would have been fulfilled in the course of nature. For I am far advanced in years, as you may perceive, and not far from death. I am speaking now not to all of you, but only to those who have condemned me to death. And I have another thing to say to them: You think that I was convicted because I had no words of the sort which would have procured my acquittal—I mean, if I had thought fit to leave nothing undone or unsaid. Not so; the deficiency which led to my conviction was not of words— certainly not. But I had not the boldness or impudence or inclination to address you as you would have liked me to do, weeping and wailing and lamenting, and saying and doing many things which you have been accustomed to hear from others, and which, as I maintain, are unworthy of me. I thought at the time that I ought not to do anything common or mean when in danger: nor do I now repent of the style of my defence; I would rather die having spoken after my manner, than speak in your manner and live. For neither in war nor yet at law ought I or any man to use every way of escaping death. Often in battle there can be no doubt that if a man will throw away his arms, and fall on his knees before his pursuers, he may escape death; and in other dangers there are other ways of escaping death, if a man is willing to say and do anything. The difficulty, my friends, is not to avoid death, but to avoid unrighteousness; for that runs faster than death. I am old and move slowly, and the slower runner has overtaken me, and my accusers are keen and quick, and the faster runner, who is unrighteousness, has overtaken them. And now I depart hence condemned by you to suffer the penalty of death,—they too go their ways condemned by the truth to suffer the penalty of villainy and wrong; and I must abide by my award—let them abide by theirs. I suppose that these things may be regarded as fated,—and I think that they are well.
[17] And now, O men who have condemned me, I would fain prophesy to you; for I am about to die, and in the hour of death men are gifted with prophetic power. And I prophesy to you who are my murderers, that immediately after my departure punishment far heavier than you have inflicted on me will surely await you. Me you have killed because you wanted to escape the accuser, and not to give an account of your lives. But that will not be as you suppose: far otherwise. For I say that there will be more accusers of you than there are now; accusers whom hitherto I have restrained: and as they are younger they will be more inconsiderate with you, and you will be more offended at them. If you think that by killing men you can pre-

vent some one from censuring[4] your evil lives, you are mistaken; that is not a way of escape which is either possible or honourable; the easiest and the noblest way is not to be disabling others, but to be improving yourselves. This is the prophecy which I utter before my departure to the judges who have condemned me.

[18] Friends, who would have acquitted me, I would like also to talk with you about the thing which has come to pass, while the magistrates are busy, and before I go to the place at which I must die. Stay then a little, for we may as well talk with one another while there is time. You are my friends, and I should like to show you the meaning of this event which has happened to me. O my judges—for you I may truly call judges—I should like to tell you of a wonderful circumstance. Hitherto the divine faculty of which the internal oracle is the source has constantly been in the habit of opposing me even about trifles, if I was going to make a slip or error in any matter; and now as you see there has come upon me that which may be thought, and is generally believed to be, the last and worst evil. But the oracle made no sign of opposition, either when I was leaving my house in the morning, or when I was on my way to the court, or while I was speaking, at anything which I was going to say; and yet I have often been stopped in the middle of a speech, but now in nothing I either said or did touching the matter in hand has the oracle opposed me. What do I take to be the explanation of this silence? I will tell you. It is an intimation that what has happened to me is a good, and that those of us who think that death is an evil are in error. For the customary sign would surely have opposed me had I been going to evil and not to good.

[19] Let us reflect in another way, and we shall see that there is great reason to hope that death is a good; for one of two things—either death is a state of nothingness and utter unconsciousness, or, as men say, there is a change and migration of the soul from this world to another. Now, if you suppose that there is no consciousness, but a sleep like the sleep of him who is undisturbed even by dreams, death will be an unspeakable gain. For if a person were to select the night in which his sleep was undisturbed even by dreams, and were to compare with this the other days and nights of his life, and then were to tell us how many days and nights he had passed in the course of his life better and more pleasantly than this one, I think that any man, I will not say a private man, but even the great king will not find many such days or nights, when compared with the others. Now, if death be of such a nature, I say that to die is gain; for eternity is then only a single night. But if death is the journey to another place, and there, as men say, all the dead abide,[5] what good, O my friends and judges, can be greater than this? If, indeed, when the pilgrim arrives in the world below, he is delivered from the professors of justice in this world, and finds the true judges who are said to give judgment there, Minos and Rhadamanthus and

[4]disapproving, harshly criticizing
[5]a reference to Hades, for the Greeks not a place of punishment but the dwelling place for all souls after death

Aeacus and Triptolemus, and other sons of God who were righteous in their own life, that pilgrimage will be worth making. What would not a man give if he might converse with Orpheus and Musaeus and Hesiod and Homer? Nay, if this be true, let me die again and again. I myself, too, shall have a wonderful interest in there meeting and conversing with Palamedes, and Ajax the son of Telamon, and any other ancient hero who has suffered death through an unjust judgment; and there will be no small pleasure, as I think, in comparing my own sufferings with theirs. Above all, I shall then be able to continue my search into true and false knowledge; as in this world, so also in the next; and I shall find out who is wise, and who pretends to be wise, and is not. What would not a man give, O judges, to be able to examine the leader of the great Trojan expedition; or Odysseus or Sisyphus, or numberless others, men and women too! What infinite delight would there be in conversing with them and asking them questions! In another world they do not put a man to death for asking questions: assuredly not. For besides being happier than we are, they will be immortal, if what is said is true.

[20] Wherefore, O judges, be of good cheer about death, and know of a certainty, that no evil can happen to a good man, either in life or after death. He and his are not neglected by the gods; nor has my own approaching end happened by mere chance. But I see clearly that the time had arrived when it was better for me to die and be released from trouble; wherefore the oracle gave no sign. For which reason, also, I am not angry with my condemners, or with my accusers; they have done me no harm, although they did not mean to do me any good; and for this I may gently blame them.

[21] Still, I have a favour to ask of them. When my sons are grown up, I would ask you, O my friends, to punish them; and I would have you trouble them, as I have troubled you, if they seem to care about riches, or anything, more than about virtue; or if they pretend to be something when they are really nothing,—then reprove them, as I have reproved you, for not caring about that for which they ought to care, and thinking that they are something when they are really nothing. And if you do this, both I and my sons will have received justice at your hands.

[22] The hour of departure has arrived, and we go our ways—I to die, and you to live. Which is better God only knows.

EXERCISES

Questions

1. Paragraphs 2 and 3 state Socrates' basic ethical belief. What is it? What is the philosopher's mission? Relate paragraphs 3 and 15; what is the mission of all men?

2. Why is Socrates not ashamed "of a course of life which is likely to bring . . . [him] to an untimely end"?
3. In what way does Socrates liken himself to the gadfly? In what way does he criticize himself? Why would he not be a politician?
4. How does he make an emotional plea while protesting against such pleas?
5. What is Socrates' view of the judgment after the Senate's vote? Why will he not plead to save his life and accept exile instead?
6. What does Socrates believe might have saved him from the death sentence? Why was this unacceptable to him? What was his prophecy? What is the larger significance of his prophecy?
7. With what words does Socrates comfort his friends? What is his attitude toward death? In what ironic way does his request for his sons establish Socrates' "victory" over the Senate that condemned him?

For Discussion and Writing

1. "The fear of death is . . . the pretense of wisdom and not real wisdom, being a pretense of knowing the unknown, and no one knows whether death, which men in their fear apprehend to be the greatest evil, may not be the greatest good."
2. "The unexamined life is not worth living."
3. "I would rather die having spoken after my manner, than speak in your manner and live."
4. "He, . . . is the wisest, who, like Socrates, knows that his wisdom is in truth worth nothing."

CROSS REFERENCES

BARR: "The Civilization of the Dialogue"
GALBRAITH: "Dissent in a Free Society"
SOLOMON: "Freedom of Speech at Ohio State"
THOREAU: "On the Nature of Civil Disobedience"

RECOMMENDED READING

ANDERSON, MAXWELL: "Barefoot in Athens" (William Morrow & Co.: 1952)
IBSEN, HENRIK: "An Enemy of the People," included in *Six Plays* (New York: Modern Library, 1951) tr. by Eva LeGallienne.

JOHN KENNETH GALBRAITH

"DISSENT IN A FREE SOCIETY"

INTRODUCTION

John Kenneth Galbraith (1908–   ) is probably best known as the author of *The Affluent Society*, published in 1958, which describes the economic condition of the United States. Dr. Galbraith earned his Ph.D. at the University of California in economics, and he has taught in many of the nation's leading universities, including California, Princeton, and Harvard. He has also given many years of government service, most notably as Ambassador to India from 1961 to 1963. Dr. Galbraith has written many books and articles in addition to *The Affluent Society*. Among them are *The Liberal Hour* (1960), and his most recent books, *The New Industrial State* (1967), and *Triumph* (1968), his first novel. The following article is a commencement address made at Annamalai University when he was Ambassador to India.

TO THE READER

Galbraith, viewing dissent as intrinsic to a democratic society, even obligatory under certain conditions, believes it serves to strengthen that society.

The last five paragraphs clearly summarize the speech.

A few days after the resumption of nuclear tests—after the long moratorium, when it seemed that restraint and good sense had arrested

Reprinted by permission of the author.

the terrible contest which the tests signified — I had a talk with an old friend in Washington. He asked me what would have happened if the United States had been the first to take this grim and fateful step. He answered his own question: a multitude of critics would everywhere have condemned the action.

[2]   "Why," he inquired, "is the United States government so much more subject to criticism than the governments of other countries?"

[3]   There is a related question which is frequently asked of me in India. It is, "Why are your papers and your political leaders so severe in their treatment of India?" Surely, it is suggested, there are more iniquitous[1] objects of attack than this mild and friendly land. "Why do you search so assiduously for our faults? Why do you pick on Mr. Nehru?"

[4]   Any satisfactory answer to these questions must deal with the peculiar and often paradoxical[2] role of criticism in the open society, in that society which not only accords opportunity but offers encouragement to a plurality of views, and in which it is assumed that every persuasively argued idea can have an influence, however marginal, on the march of events.

[5]   Let me say at the outset that I am not much inclined to efforts to gloss over or explain the unexplainable. There have been some aspects of recent critical comment which do not seem to me entirely encouraging or defensible. I detect a certain tendency to conclude that if it is necessary to rebuke one of the two great powers, something fairly stern must also be said about the other. Morality, I think we may agree, is not always in the middle. In the case of the nuclear test resumption, the United States was pressing actively and in good faith for a treaty at the time the tests were resumed. A diligent effort to end the tests and a unilateral step to resume them are not open to equal criticism.

[6]   There is another tendency in criticism which I doubt that anyone would condone. Some countries, never without effort, have schooled themselves to a tolerant response when attacked. They do not strike back; certainly they do not respond with threats or sanctions. It would be unfortunate if any of us, in our natural and inevitable desire to mend the manners and behavior and policies of others, were to concentrate on the safest and most amiable targets. Perhaps this does not happen very often; I believe that we should be on guard against the temptation. Let me turn now to a more agreeable and constructive role of criticism, which it is equally important that we understand.

[7]   The peculiarities and paradoxes of criticism in the open society can initially be illustrated by examining recent American comment on public education. In the United States we have the world's oldest system of universal primary education. We also have the world's most diverse and imaginative and, in many respects, most highly developed system of secondary

[1]wicked, unjust
[2]a seemingly self-contradictory statement that in reality expresses a truth

education. American colleges and universities were the first in the world to make higher education a democratic right. Until they did so, university education had always been the privilege of a minute intellectual, aristocratic, or financial elite. Yet, not even the most diligent student of the recent literature on American education would have been aware of these virtues. I am obliged to tell you that he would not have been aware of them from my own rather lengthy writings on the subject, and in composing the foregoing brief encomiums,[3] I felt strangely out of character. The reason is that we have been seeking in these last years to improve our educational system. The first step toward improvement was a rigorous exposure of what was wrong. Nor was it considered entirely wise to admit that anything was right.

[8]   In such matters criticism is the engine of change. The individual with no children or prospect of procreation and more than a little concerned about his taxes contends that the schools are fine. That is his defense of the status quo. The concerned citizen shuns identification with such praise; for him it is the language of contentment, even of reaction. He must say that the schools are overcrowded if he is to make the case for new schools. He must say that the teachers are grossly underpaid if he is to persuade anyone that the pay of teachers must be increased. He must picture the pupils as a major menace to law and order if he is to argue that their playgrounds should be enlarged. In recent years the American educational reformer has found the Soviet Union his most valuable ally. The core of all modern criticism of our education is the claim that the Soviets are doing much better. With this they helpfully agree. The paradox, one on which we rarely reflect, is that the best friend of our schools, colleges, and universities is ordinarily the man who makes out the worst case, absolutely or by comparison with others, for their current performance.

[9]   Elsewhere in American social life, change similarly waits upon criticism. We raise the minimum wage for workers only by noting that the income of those affected is extremely inadequate. We improve the position of the aged only after enlarging on the poverty imposed by their present pensions. We can hope for the renewal and rebuilding of our cities only if we first publicize the noisome qualities of our slums. We win support for artistic and cultural activities only by warning of our tendency toward narrow materialism. One of the best publicized states of the American union in the last year or so has been West Virginia. This mountain region is not our showpiece; on the contrary, it contains our poorest communities. And that is the reason for its fame. By drawing attention to the plight of the miners in this unfortunate part of the country, we have won measures — increased supplies of free food, steps to rehabilitate the economic life of derelict regions — which it is hoped will be a partial remedy.

[10]   It is not essential that the criticism which wins change be valid. Much

---

[3] a formal expression of high praise

of it has a ritual quality. Our trade unions win increases in pay only after appearing to affirm the classic prediction of Marx that workers under capitalism undergo progressive immiserization.[4] Things are not quite that bad. There is a Chinese proverb which holds that even the prickly mimosa is an adequate defense against a naked man armed only with a just cause. Our armed services win appropriations from the United States Congress only after establishing both their nakedness and the appalling prickliness of the opposing mimosa. If farm legislation in the United States is to pass, the American farmer must be pictured as the most oppressed of agriculturists. He has indeed suffered certain vicissitudes in recent years, but he remains by quite a margin the most opulent[5] tiller in all the world.

[11] Since social criticism is an engine of change, its employment has become a matter of political controversy. In the United States, as elsewhere, political division turns on attitudes toward change. On the one hand are those who by temperament, inertia, vested interest, or nostalgia are disposed to protect the present or retrieve the past. And on the other side are those who by compassion, disposition, or from discontent seek change, in the conviction that it will mean improvement. To the first group, social criticism is unwelcome, save perhaps as it serves to recover the past. For those who seek change, criticism is an essential instrument of political action. To the first group, criticism is gratuitous, unwise, and even defamatory. To the second group, it is a welcome resort to truth. These are not minor differences. The last presidential campaign in the United States was fought largely over the issue of social criticism. Should we make a point of our faults and shortcomings in the hope that this might be an inducement to improvement? Should we avoid mention of them lest this be taken as an admission before the world of weaknesses in the American society? There were some who thought this a rather slight issue. I am not so sure. It concerned, I think, one of the central characteristics of the open society.

[12] All open societies employ criticism as an instrument of change. No close observer of the habits and customs of Indian journalists and political leaders can imagine that Indian society is in any way retarded in this respect. A desire for improvement, whether it be in integration of linguistic groups, in the rate of economic growth, the performance of public-sector plants, the efficiency of the civil service, the discipline of students, the effectiveness of the Congress Party, the availability of housing, the quality of urban housekeeping, the supply of electric power, or, one suspects, the excesses of the monsoon, begins with a severe condemnation of what exists.

[13] One is regularly asked in the United States about the slow progress of Indian agricultural development, the shortcomings in the management of public-sector plants, or the inadequacy of the population policy. The source and documentation for this concern, without exception, are the criticisms

[4]intended as a translation of the German word meaning "act of making or state of becoming miserable," especially impoverishment

[5]wealthy, affluent

of Indian scholars and journalists. Their comments, like American comments on education, come from those who most want improvement.

[14] This use of criticism as an engine of change is, in short, common to all open societies. It is also, more than incidentally, a recurrent source of error in assessing their strength. These societies wear their faults on their sleeves. Or, more accurately, they inscribe them on their banners, for this is fundamental to their mechanism of reform. The society that does not have a similar need to publicize its shortcomings may be thought by superficial men to have no shortcomings. In fact, it may merely be leaving them uncorrected. During World War II, those of us who were concerned with industrial mobilization in the United States and the United Kingdom were made constantly and painfully aware of the inadequacy of our performance. Our shortcomings were a source of joy to all journalists. In time, even those of us who were best situated to appreciate our own virtues came to agree. This was the sort of thing that democracies did very badly. Their governments lacked the powers of decision; their people were reluctant to give up their accustomed luxuries; their tendency was to do too little too late. I do not recall that we ever went so far as to blame ourselves as individuals.

[15] All of these things were true. The wartime performance of the democracies was far from perfect. But others were imperfect as well. Mussolini looked well in prospect and rather less well in retrospect. In the closing months of the war and thereafter, it became my task to unravel the procedures by which Germans had employed their totalitarian authority to wage the war. In many respects the Germans had been even more dilatory than we. Most German factories had remained on a single shift throughout the conflict; women were never mobilized; luxury consumption was preserved until rather late in the war; the leaders had been very cautious about imposing sacrifices on a people whom they did not trust. And where we had been forced to improve our ways under the relentless criticism of the public and press, the German authorities had suffered no such onslaught. They had not been forced by public criticism to mend their course. The façade they presented to the world seemed imposing and efficient. So, in some degree, it seemed to the Nazi leaders themselves. In fooling the world, they had also fooled each other.

[16] I am not especially sanguine[6] about the improvability of man, and I have even graver doubts about his chances for redemption after he assumes public office. But I am persuaded that official inadequacy is something that can be enjoyed only in silence. Often, during the course of my own public experience, I have noted my first reaction to some sin of omission or commission. Invariably my initial reaction is to hope that the mistake won't be found out. Consideration of how the matter might be corrected comes somewhat later. We may lay it down as a law that, without public criticism, all governments look much better and are much worse.

[6]cheerful, hopeful, or confident

[17] I come now to a further point. We rely on criticism to bring change in the open society. But this instrument is not narrowly limited by national boundaries. Nothing confines the individual in the use of this instrument to his own government. There is a convention that no citizen interferes with the government of another state. The accepted modern practice, by contrast, is one of constant intervention. The citizens of every open society are constantly concerned with altering the policies of other such societies.

[18] Specifically, when they see something in the actions of another government which does not meet with their approval, they resort to the same instrument they employ at home. They react with criticism precisely as they do to disapproved behavior by their own government. They may have less hope that they will be able to alter the actions of the other government. Their instinct is still to try.

[19] And their instinct is sound. The open society is so described because it is open to the influence of any idea. Its decisions are not taken in accordance with an ordained and settled system of doctrine which it is pointless for any person or group to hope to alter. And influential ideas can come from anywhere; no exclusive license for criticism is issued with a passport. It would be silly to suggest that external criticism is as influential as that which is reinforced by the sanction of the franchise. But a remarkable number of factors combine with natural receptivity to ideas to ensure the overseas critic a hearing. Domestic critics of a policy regularly draw reinforcement from attacks by friendly foreigners. If something induces an angry uproar abroad, many will take it as an indication of mismanagement or error. In an interdependent world a critical press may eventually have an adverse effect on something important—on trade, aid, votes in the United Nations, or the rooms accorded to tourists. The opinion of people in other countries owes some of its influence to the simple circumstance that people have been taught to think it is important. Thomas Jefferson began the most famous of American proclamations by observing that it was called forth by "a decent respect to the opinions of mankind."

[20] In consequence of this use of criticism as an instrument of internal government, the open societies are vigorous critics of each other. Indian journalists, commentators, and political leaders attack the United States on racial integration, military alliances, Far Eastern policy, the movies, and a host of other sins. This is not the mark of a misanthropic nature, even among the journalists. The criticism we have long observed comes with greatest vigor from our most devoted friends. This is to be expected. One's friends are most concerned to correct policy which seems to them in error. Nor are they without success. It was, for example, the drumfire of criticism with which Indian journalists attacked various theses on the evils of neutralism in the last decade which was influential in their early abandonment.

[21] And the reaction with which we are dealing is reversible. When the American journalist, commentator, or congressman looks similarly askance at India's economic organization, agricultural system, United Nations pos-

ture, or some internal social or religious institutions, he is similarly assuming that his words will be influential, for it is his faith that any argument must be influential.

[22] I do not wish to carry these matters to extremes. At all times some men will speak out of antagonism. Some, as I said at the outset, will criticize as the result of calculation, not conviction. But, as between the open societies, it is very likely that men will speak out of the conviction that what they criticize can be changed.

[23] This peculiar role of criticism, we should observe, operates in substantial measure only as between open societies. It is another of the paradoxes of social criticism that, although we may be much less enamored of the behavior of a closed society, we will usually be much less comprehensive in our criticism of that behavior. The closed system, being closed, is unresponsive to our influence. This we sense, so we do not bang hopelessly on the blank wall. We reserve our arguments and even, on occasion, our anger for more responsive and malleable[7] societies.

[24] During World War II, any superficial observer could easily have supposed from reading the American newspapers that the real enemy of the American people was still the British. And the inadequacies of the Americans enlivened many a long evening of English conversation. No German general came in for nearly so much adverse American comment as Montgomery. Nor did the British accord nearly so much critical scrutiny to any enemy leader as to Eisenhower. Neither of the open societies was nearly so harsh on the Soviets as it was on the other. The reason was not that the government of Marshal Stalin was regarded with particular approval in Britain and the United States, although no one would deny it the admiration it earned for its resistance. People did not criticize the Soviet government, for the simple reason that no one supposed that such criticism would have much effect.

[25] Some simple guides to everyday action and reaction emerge from the foregoing, and let me specify them.

[26] First, and most obvious, we must recognize that criticism is essential in the intercourse of open societies. We should expect it. We should expect on occasion to be angered by it. Anger is one of the responses to ideas which all skilled purveyors seek, for it is the mark of a peculiarly penetrating impact.

[27] Second, we ought to remember that the open society, by its nature, puts its worst foot forward. This is the way it improves itself. If this is not kept in mind, we will have a highly distorted view of the achievements of these societies, especially in comparison with other systems. The United States maintains in India a rather substantial organization with the function, among others, of defending our society from its critics. The critics are mostly Americans.

[28] Third, we must remember that, although criticism is sometimes an instrument of conflict, it is more often an index of fraternity. Formal and dull men say that one does not criticize a friendly government. They should know that it is friendly governments that one does criticize. Evil by one's

---

[7]adaptable

antagonists is assumed. Lapses from virtue by one's friends call for immediate corrective comment.

[29] Fourth, we must recognize that, as between the open societies, criticism represents, in effect, an extension of franchise, in a most valuable form. We have been told by every prophet of the commonplace that this is a small and highly interrelated world. Actions of the United States Congress have a bearing on the rate of Indian economic development and well-being. Decisions by the Indian government substantially condition American foreign policy. Is it surprising that we should have developed ways of influencing the decisions by which we are affected? On the contrary, it was natural and desirable. And it was inevitable that criticism, the principal instrument by which the citizen brings influence to bear in the open society, should be internationally employed.

[30] Finally, we must not equate criticism as between the open societies with criticism as between the open and closed systems. One does no service, here or elsewhere, by establishing overly exclusive categories. I doubt that any national community is wholly unresponsive to the influence of ideas. Yet, the formal acceptance of a ruling ideology and the formal alignment of expressed opinion therewith enormously modify the impact of both internal and external opinion, and, indeed, are designed to do so. The result is of extreme importance. Since criticism does not appreciably affect the policy of such communities, its deployment is not rewarding. This is soon discovered or sensed. The critics then concern themselves with those societies they have found responsive. It is not the most unwelcome policy that arouses the most objection. Rather, it is the one that seems most susceptible to the influence of criticism, and hence most subject to change. Criticism, no less than the lambs and the calves, soon develops an instinct for the greener pasture.

EXERCISES

Questions

1. Galbraith's theme appears in paragraph 11. What is the most distinguishing feature of dissent in an open society? Why is it a matter of political controversy? Summarize the two sides that are contrasted.
2. The introductory remarks about nuclear testing rather date the article. Can you supply a more recent American action that would invite similar criticism?
3. What two tendencies of social criticism does Galbraith reject?
4. What is the paradox of the criticism of American education? Why is the paradox necessary and justifiable? In what other areas does Galbraith illustrate this peculiar functioning? Why is the exaggerated quality of criticism justifiable?
5. Which is the stronger society—the openly critical or the silent? Why? What is the equation he draws about governments and criticism?

6. On what basis does social criticism operate between countries? Why? Consider nonstudents participating in college demonstrations in the light of this concept.
7. What are the key points concerning dissent that Galbraith stresses?
8. What does Galbraith mean by "criticism . . . soon develops an instinct for the greener pasture"?
9. Most of the ideas in this essay are developed by comparison and contrast or by illustration. Find examples of each.
10. In what paragraphs does Galbraith relate his remarks to his Indian audience? In what ways does he find American and Indian societies comparable?

Vocabulary

askance	moratorium
assiduously	procreation
defamatory	sanctions
deployment	totalitarian
derelict	vicissitudes
misanthrope	

For Discussion and Writing

1. Dissent on our campus
2. Dissenters on our campus
3. Dissent and disruption
4. Student power: organ for change
5. Dissent and higher education

CROSS REFERENCES

FARRELL: "Today's Disobedience Is Uncivil"
KELMAN: "When Civil Disobedience Is Justifiable"
KENNEDY: "Inaugural Address"
PLATO: "Argument"
THOREAU: "On the Duty of Civil Disobedience"

RECOMMENDED READING

BOWEN, CATHERINE DRINKER: *Yankee from Olympus: Justice Holmes and his Family,* (Atlantic Monthly Press: 1944).

ERIC SOLOMON

"FREE SPEECH
AT OHIO STATE"

INTRODUCTION

Eric Solomon tells us in his article that he is a Ph.D. from Harvard and was and English professor at Ohio State. Now he is at San Francisco State College. What he doesn't tell us is that when serving in World War II, he became interested in war literature, which resulted in a book, *The Faded Banners—A Treasury of 19th Century Civil War Fiction*, published in 1960. The title of that book gives a clue to his other special interest in literature, Stephen Crane. To date, Dr. Solomon has published two books on Crane, *Stephen Crane in England* (1964), and *Stephen Crane: from Parody to Realism* (1966).

TO THE READER

The title is as sarcastic as the tone of much of the article.

When you go out into the real world, for God's sake don't start every second sentence with the words, 'At Harvard, we—'" I think I did a pretty fair job of attending to this advice from the late Hyder Rollins when I took my first job in 1958, teaching English at the Ohio State University. And ten years of Harvard didn't seem to incapacitate me for teaching in a state university. There were, certainly, some differences in discussing Mark Twain with a class in Cambridge, Massachusetts, and in Columbus, Ohio; in Cambridge, a rhetorical[1] question as to who, in our world, has ever taken a raft down the Mississippi would not bring forth a complacent freshman raising his hand. But I taught my classes, published my articles, drank Jim Beam at faculty cocktail parties, received promotions, raises, tenure, research grants, administrative posts. I liked and admired my colleagues, was satisfied with the library, was more than satisfied with my chairman, lived inexpensively and well in the elm-shaded streets of Columbus. Nevertheless (sorry, Mr. Rollins), at Harvard, we had freedom of speech.

[2]   When I left Ohio State after six years, in the wake of almost one third of my department who had, for a variety of reasons, taken other appointments, and after I had helped to initiate a lawsuit against the president and board of trustees, I had learned that good salaries, light teaching loads, and air-conditioned offices are no substitutes for a full measure of academic freedom. During years of arguments about who should be free to speak on the campus, the university administration defiantly asserted that there existed no interference with an instructor's freedom in the classroom. Yet for me, and for many of my colleagues, what we considered the necessity to spend incredible amounts of time in clandestine[2] meetings, in preparing speeches, in responding to attacks — in politics, actually — meant that our classroom performances, the measure of our preparations, in fact, *were* being interfered with. When a community and a board of trustees seem to be forcing a teacher to his knees, even an English teacher realizes that the metaphor has gone astray: one can pray in that position, but one cannot teach.

[3]   I now think that the free speech battles at Ohio State in the early 1960s were, like those at Berkeley, symptoms of a more widespread disease affecting the academic body and the community. The tempests at Ohio State were inevitable, given the nature of the society in which we — those whom Governor DiSalle once told me the university president had described as a "few unfortunate appointments we made from Eastern schools" — found ourselves. First, Columbus is one of the three most reactionary[3] cities in the United States. The John Birch Society seems middle-of-the-road in Franklin County, far outdistanced to the right by long-entrenched groups such as the Navy League or (my favorite) the Watch Washington Society. Second, Columbus is not really urban. Although it prides itself on its near 100 percent population of native-born Americans, the more than 600,000 citizens of greater Columbus form themselves into loosely connected groups of communities. There is little heavy industry, a weak trade union tradition, a

[1]used for or concerned with mere effect or style
[2]secret or concealed
[3]political movement in the direction of conservatism or extreme rightism

large floating group of indigent Negroes on their way out of the Deep South. Third, Columbus has a very tightly controlled power structure consisting of a few families, a few banks, and one newspaper. Physically, there are two newspapers, the morning Scripps-Howard being the liberal one; its role is compromised by the fact that it uses the evening *Dispatch* advertising and printing departments. Fourth, Columbus is the state capital. And finally, it is the home of one of the largest educational institutions in the world.

[4]   When these social ingredients were joined by one new force after World War II, a much larger influx of students and faculty from outside Franklin County, from outside Ohio, even from outside the Midwest, some kind of conflict was preparing. The community was simply the wrong size and nature to assimilate what I think of as "creeping universitism," the quiet and steady arrival of men whose backgrounds were wide-ranging, whose views were varied, and whose commitments were to the general sophisticated intellectual community as well as to the local campus. Had Columbus been as large as Chicago or Los Angeles, say, the university and its doings might have been lost in the multitude of public and private colleges; had the city been as small as Bloomington or Urbana, the university might have been able to dominate the community. But Columbus is in the middle range, and the legislature is directly on the scene.

[5]   When intellectuals from Harvard, Berkeley, Michigan, the Sorbonne settled into Franklin County, it was unavoidable that eventually they would question certain local codes and customs. So when I arrived in Columbus in 1958, the ink still wet on my Ph.D., I came to a city complacent in its great agricultural-cum-engineering institution that had turned out crushing Rose Bowl champions with awesome efficiency; but unbeknown to the bankers and boosters, "their" university had for years been steadily attracting humanists and scientists who did not consider themselves only state employees —similar to elevator operators, as a *Dispatch* editorial once put it. I came to Ohio State to teach; I remained to spend much too much time in politics.

[6]   A classic example of how community-university relations worked in Columbus occurred when the faculty council, the elected representative body for the entire faculty, voted not to send the football team to the Rose Bowl even if they won the Big Ten championship as was their wont.[4] The issues involved were complex, but basically, those opposed to the Rose Bowl game argued that it was detrimental to the main job of the university, education, because too many students traveled to California and returned late to classes. Also it was felt that the game was purely a business venture. The main thrust against the Rose Bowl came from arts and sciences faculty plus a few administrators primarily concerned with curriculum. I stress this lineup because during the later troubles, essentially the same lines would be drawn. In favor of the Rose Bowl as a necessary and deserved reward for fine young athletes were the board of trustees, the top administration, in-

[4]custom, habit

cluding the president, Novice G. Fawcett, and faculty drawn largely from agriculture, medicine, and engineering.

[7]   What fascinated those of us new to Ohio State was not the closeness of the vote, or the rioting students who smashed the doors of the faculty club, but the community response, a wild bellow of rage that these upstart employees of the state (the faculty) should presume to attack the city's most beloved and prestigious institution. Those faculty members most prominent as anti-Rose Bowl received the traditional all-night obscene-phone-call treatment. The *Dispatch* assisted in this process by telephoning each member of the council, asking how he voted, and then on the first night after the vote, printing on the front page the name, address, and phone number of all those who had either admitted to voting against the Rose Bowl or who had not informed the newspaper how they voted. On the second evening appeared names, addresses, phone numbers, and salaries. On the third night, names and so forth, plus amount of money spent by each dissenting professor on out-of-state travel—relevant since these men denied the athletes their trip. The frustration of the newspapers was particularly intense because only Big Ten rules regarding faculty control of athletics kept the administration from overturning the vote. It was shortly overturned anyway, but the team has not been winning.

[8]   Telephone violence was a fairly normal part of Columbus living. When I was chairman of the Central Ohio chapter of the American Civil Liberties Union (I'd never even heard of the ACLU before coming to Columbus; for me, as for others, the community was a great teacher of civil liberties), I learned to anticipate and hang up on the first curse. To be fair to Columbus, I recall only one genuine threat of violence to a faculty member, and this was understandable because his wife had come out publicly in favor of peace and the United Nations. After a group attacked his house, cut his phone wires, and smeared his windows with horse manure (rural values prevail), my colleague was rather disturbed for his family's safety, particularly as one of the right-wing radio stations continued to broadcast his wife's name and address and call her organization "Communist." Because the police were uninterested, for five nights a group of faculty guarded his house armed with baseball bats and cameras. Odd weapons, but our defense was organized by a former Union official who insisted that we get our assailants' photos; fortunately we were disturbed only by a few mysterious cars.

[9]   As in the Rose Bowl case, "unfortunate" faculty appointments continued to plague the community and the university in all sorts of unexpected places. A few socialists formed a Dissent Forum; another group sprang up, Students for Liberal Action. The Student Senate Human Relations committee blew the whistle on the university's involvement in segregated off-campus housing; some law school professors joined this one, and the dean of students was outspoken in his opposition to faculty meddling. We were disconcerted by the sense of interlocking directorates: a university president on the same bank board of directors as the newspaper owner and the chairman of the trustees; a dean of students active in the real estate profession.

[10] It was foreseeable, then, that when a major clash came, it would be over the issue of free speech, of the rights of students and faculty to invite into the community, onto the campus—property which is tax-supported by the very people whose values would be threatened—speakers from outside Columbus who might, almost assuredly would, question the accepted local way of life, and by doing so, influence for the worse the receptive, tender minds of the future citizens of the community, the students.

[11] Ohio State had an ugly history of free speech contradictions during the 1950s. A notorious "gag rule," which denied access to the campus to any speaker not acceptable to the administration, was finally—or so most faculty and students thought—done away with, and student organizations, with faculty advisers' consent, were given the right to invite a speaker to address a group.

[12] That the rule was still vague, confusing, and open to contradictory interpretations became clear in the spring of 1961, when a California-based scholar of Soviet contemporary history, William Mandel, was barred from the campus. He was invited to speak by a young faculty member who had enjoyed his refutations of the House Un-American Activities Committee in the film *Operation Abolition*. On a technicality, since the inviter was only an assistant instructor, the invitation was held to be invalid. When a student organization then stepped into the breach and invited Mandel, a monumental brouhaha[5] took place over whether the faculty adviser had to *want* the speaker or simply agree that his talk might be educational.

[13] The rule was sufficiently unclear so that two law professors, of differing political persuasions, could in good faith come up with opposite interpretations. The administration chose the reading it preferred. Mandel spoke in Columbus, but in the muddy backyard of his original sponsor. (An ironic sidelight to this affair was that while Ohio State did not punish the instructor, the receipt of a number of hostile *Dispatch* articles in reference to his activities in this case led a Nebraska state college to revoke his contract for the following year; the AAUP[6] has since blacklisted the college for its conduct. Although there were some objections in high places, Ohio State did give the man an additional year of teaching in place of the withdrawn job.)

[14] The faculty council struggled during the autumn of 1961 to write a clear rule that both faculty and trustees would accept—a task that has not yet been satisfactorily accomplished—and a number of disturbed faculty members took to holding weekly dinners in order to discuss our fears about the direction in which the university seemed to be heading. We were mostly younger men and women, drawn primarily from the departments of English, history, philosophy, and psychology, as well as from the law school. There was no formal organization; we simply invited people worried about academic freedom who would bring their friends, and we exchanged horror

[5]excited public discussion, as the clamor attending some sensational event
[6]American Association of University Professors

stories. These little meetings had two rather important consequences, however. From them sprang the idea that the Student Senate sponsor a symposium on the Idea of a University,[7] in order to persuade the administration that a free society called for an open campus. The students were enthusiastic; four of us wrote personal letters to friends in academic life, who literally fought their way through snowstorms to provide, under Cardinal Newman's title, some brilliant defenses of the historical concepts of the university as an open forum. The administration and trustees managed to ignore the event, despite the contributions of such leaders of American intellectual life as Howard Mumford Jones, Stringfellow Barr, Fred Harvey Harrington, and Henry Steele Commager.

[15] One other result of these dinners was that when the battle really opened in the spring of 1962, we had a nucleus; we were ready to start instantly the innumerable round of meetings, day and night, lunch and dinner, noon and midnight, at first in private houses, then as more and more senior and respected professors joined us, in empty law school classrooms, always seeking ways out, ways to respond to the encroachments upon our sense of academic freedom without simply withdrawing irresponsibly.

[16] What happened in 1962 was simple. A student group invited three speakers from the Emergency Civil Liberties Union, according to all the rules and with the full support of the faculty adviser. One of these men, a former OSU graduate student named Philip Luce, was particularly obnoxious to the administration, both personally and politically, while the other two, Clark Foreman and an undergraduate from Berkeley active in anti-HUAC activities, were not exactly welcome guests. But the students *had* followed the new rule. And, literally at the eleventh hour, while substantial crowds were milling around a locked law school auditorium, the president, unable to persuade the faculty adviser to rescind the invitation, ordered him to cancel the meeting. This was done; the men spoke in a police-covered backyard, this time the yard of a rooming house, whose boarders had named it Rosa Luxembourg House.

[17] That night our dinner group, expanded by some faculty who had been withdrawn from politics since the McCarthy days, held an emergency meeting. The next day there were speeches and protests all over the campus. With two other professors, I spoke to a crowd of 500 students (off campus, on the steps of the Wesley Foundation). Resolutions were passed; the *Dispatch* hailed the president's action; John Bricker[8] for the board of trustees invited any professor who didn't like the way things were run at Ohio State to move on. The AAUP met and condemned the president's intransigence.[9] One of the most moving aspects of this whole protest was the way more and more senior faculty members, high in rank, prestige, years of service, and

[7] the title of an essay by John Henry Cardinal Newman who developed the idea of the university as the site for the pursuit of truth

[8] former Republican Senator from Ohio of conservative persuasion

[9] inflexibility, an uncompromising attitude

love of the university, sprang to the defense of the ideals involved. They were doubly motivated; they sought to defend free speech and, equally important, to preserve Ohio State University, to make it a place where the younger faculty, lacking total commitment to the campus, would want to stay. They deplored, influenced, pressured, and stood up to be counted.

[18] The climax of the faculty unrest was the calling of a faculty meeting, the *whole* faculty in its many (no one was quite sure how many) hundreds. There had been only one such meeting in a decade, but an antiquated rule, since changed, allowed forty faculty signatures (we gathered over 300) to call such a meeting. A number of students who were eager to demonstrate, picket, riot, were restrained by their faculty friends' passionate pleas to leave it in our hands; I shall never be sure whether, if we had not done so, the outcome might have been very different; the sit-in was not yet a common-place, however. We were convinced that among the teaching faculty, we possessed the votes to censure President Novice G. Fawcett's actions. What we did not know was who made up the official faculty of Ohio State University.

[19] Although the exact figures were often disputed, it turned out that the faculties of arts and sciences, of law, of education, of engineering, and so forth, were in the minority in the university, where nearly 800 agricultural extension workers, county agents, and the like had faculty appointments, where hundreds of private M.D.'s who taught as little as one hour a week in a clinic — often to qualify for football seats, since the 83,000-seat stadium was always sold out — were voting faculty. The word went out; the campus was filled with strangers asking the way to the auditorium.

[20] It was in many ways the most remarkable meeting I have ever attended, with more than 1500 faculty members on the floor, and the gallery packed with noisy students. The president presided, even though his actions were under consideration, and he insisted that each speech or motion be tape-recorded, a rather inhibiting move. (One of my students, majoring in radio-TV, I believe, ran the machine, and later bootlegged me a tape of the meeting in its entirety, the only one in existence outside the administration's hands; I treasure it.) There were speeches in favor of the president's action and attacking the private life of Philip Luce. The president recognized his own supporters first, and a motion to praise his action was on the floor: thus those who wished to censure him had to key their speeches to that motion, for, as we expected; only one vote would occur. A voice vote was taken, clearly in support of the president's position. Out of some kind of hubris,[10] perhaps a confidence that he had the support of the entire faculty and that the voices against him had come from the students, the president called for a head count.

[21] More than 1000 men stood in favor of the president. But the 500 who stood to oppose his action, while the students cheered, included nearly the

[10]excessive pride

entire heart of the teaching faculty, many chairmen, even some deans, and the entire English department, for example. As I watched the smile fade from President Fawcett's face, I realized the meaning of the term "poleaxed" for the first time. The rest of the meeting—of the year, of the academic-freedom battle, really—was anticlimax. A swift vote to adjourn passed by a similar 2 to 1 margin.

[22] Some of the younger faculty, while disturbed by the rather cynical conduct of the meeting, could accept this as, after all, power politics. But the attitude of a few of our senior colleagues was disheartening. They had been clobbered ruthlessly, and yet they were wildly exultant in the size of the vote against the president. I felt then that these men, some of whom I still admire as much as any in the profession, were punchy from too many defeats over the years; a technical knockout seemed scarcely distinguishable from a victory. Of course, the vote negated any possibility of national AAUP interest, for the faculty will had been heard. The year dribbled to an end with more speeches, consultations, promises of negotiations for a new rule. "Free Speech Now" badges appeared. Some students conceived a fine plan for an airplane to circle around the graduation ceremonies while hauling a free speech banner. Money was raised, the plane hired, and many of us who had never attended a graduation sweated in the hot sun of the stadium, waiting for the plane that never appeared. The speaker was Curtis LeMay; the CAB grounded the airplane.

[23] During the next year, while faculty advisory committees strove to devise a speaker rule that would avoid the administration's new demands that a room be applied for well in advance, that the prospective speaker's name be given, and that he be required to sign a loyalty oath before being officially invited, there were some interesting academic innovations. One event was the formation of a group effort unique, as far as I know, in the history of American education: the Committee for the Study of Alternatives. The inspiration behind this organization came from the same faculty that had ruefully dined out the preceding year, our ranks greatly strengthened by professors appalled by the administration's steamroller tactics. The idea was simple: since Columbus was a one-newspaper town, where even national television programs had to pass through local selectors, since speakers representing alternative viewpoints were to be barred from the campus, and since as busy teachers we could not really start our own newspaper, we would raise money and place a full-page advertisement in the student newspaper regularly every two weeks presenting alternative answers to the questions then being answered in only one manner. Two or three faculty members would prepare an ad, sometimes drawing from the locally feared New York *Times* a reported speech or quoting from a published book, sometimes writing an original statement, in order to present alternatives on various issues: free speech, Columbus' tax structure, or nuclear disarmament, for example. The academic community was pleased or angered, according to its politics, but some discussion seeped onto the campus. The *Dispatch*,

in its report on the formation of Alternatives, inadvertently got its front-page typesetting mixed, and ran the story, without even a comma in separation, directly into a report of the Attorney General's calling a New York group a Communist front.

[24] Much time was spent in the search for a formula to knit together a campus becoming progressively split along left-right lines. Lunch at the faculty club was in the nature of a conspiracy, with people looking on, re-marking on who sat with whom and why. Some teachers, men prominent enough to receive yearly job offers, were saying to hell with all these ac-tivities, who needs Ohio State? And they took Senator Bricker's advice. The administration was bland: thirty or forty professors didn't make much dif-ference to a faculty of nearly 2000. And so President Fawcett barred Frank Wilkinson, a vigorous foe of HUAC, from speaking on the campus — after a good many speakers representing the opposite viewpoint had appeared.

[25] More meetings, protests, wails, and another fascinating novelty, a lawsuit. This suit, which is still in the courts, accuses the president, the board, and a dean of denying the members of the student group who issued the invitation and the barred speaker their constitutional rights under the First Amendment, arguing that freedom of speech involves the right to listen. When finally decided, this case may ensure that state campuses should be as free as other public property.

[26] For more than four years the question of free speech has been argued at Ohio State. But the administrative line has been held. Last spring, students dramatized the continued restrictions on free speech at Ohio State by invit-ing the Marxist historian, Herbert Aptheker, to stand *silently* on a stage while a large crowd applauded the nonspeaker whom the university had for-bidden to speak. After his departure, a professor read from Aptheker's books, borrowed from the university library. Protest marches and satiric broadsides keep this conflict alive; but even a compromise on this issue cannot relieve the academic community's sense of alienation.

[27] I think I reflect the feelings of many of my former colleagues — now at Duke, Stanford, Riverside, La Jolla, Buffalo, Connecticut, Massachu-setts, Wisconsin, Indiana — when I express my own sense of loss and nos-talgia as well as anger. Certainly, such administrative stupidity still moves me to rage; but I learned a great deal from my years in Columbus, and I know what to look for in a college, and what to fight for.

EXERCISES

Questions

1. Solomon states his theme in paragraph 2. What is it? How is the rest of the article related to that statement?
2. What was the "nature of the society" in Columbus that led "inevitably"

to the problem at the University? How many of these conditions are widespread? Why was Ohio State suddenly willing and able to create such a controversy?

3. What is the significance of the Rose Bowl decision in terms of academics and in terms of the sides for and against sending the team to California?

4. Paragraph 9 lists other points of conflict between faculty and administration. Some of these also affected students. Which ones?

5. Why does Solomon introduce the historical background in paragraphs 11 to 15? What were the effects of Mandel's being prevented from speaking? How is it related to the 1962 incident regarding three speeches?

6. In what ways was the faculty meeting a turning point? Was it a victory or a defeat? What is the significance of the phrase "stood up to be counted" that ends paragraph 17?

7. What illegal and immoral actions took place at the legally called meeting of the whole faculty?

8. What is the significance of the last sentence of paragraph 22? of Herbert Aptheker's silent appearance? of the exodus of professors from Ohio State?

9. An undercurrent tone of sarcasm runs through the essay. Find examples of it.

Vocabulary

encroachments
incapacitate
indigent
prestigious
refutation

For Discussion and Writing

1. The right to hear what's wrong
2. Free speech at my college
3. Heckling: its legitimacy
4. Nazis and Communists: their right to be heard
5. When the free press is a monopoly

CROSS REFERENCES

BARR: "The Civilization of the Dialogue"
GALBRAITH: "Dissent in a Free Society"
LAMPELL: "I Think I Ought to Mention I Was Blacklisted"
ROVERE: "The Most Gifted and Successful Demagogue This Country Has Ever Known"
SPITZ: "The Timken Edition of Lenin"

RECOMMENDED READING

AAUP: *Joint Statement on Rights and Freedoms of Students,* 1968
AAUP statement on academic freedom for faculty

JAMES T. FARRELL

"TODAY'S DISOBEDIENCE IS UNCIVIL"

INTRODUCTION

James T. Farrell (1904–   ) is considered to have written one of the three best novels of the thirties, his trilogy *Studs Lonigan*. (The two other best books of that period are by authors also in this volume, John Steinbeck and John Dos Passos.) It is a story of a young tough raised in the slums of Chicago. Mr. Farrell has had a long and distinguished career as a novelist and short story writer. He also edited books on Theodore Dreiser and H. L. Mencken. One of his earliest books, *New Year's Eve* (1929), was reissued in 1967. His two most recent novels are *Lonely for the Future* (1966) and *A Brand New Life* (1968).

TO THE READER

Farrell opposes current practices of civil disobedience by denying that they are civil. In doing this, he reminds dissenters of some of their obligations.

Civil disobedience is only a temporary political means of struggle and resistance. If a campaign of civil disobedience attains its goal, it will be followed by the imposition of law and authority. And law, as Chief Justice Harlan F. Stone defined it, "amounts to those rules of behavior which society makes mandatory."

[2]   The late Mohandas Gandhi organized civil disobedience, called *satyagraha,* in opposition to British rule over India. However, Gandhi, whose political sense of timing was expert and whose capacity for leadership was genius, was very clear on the limits and the aims of civil disobedience.

[3]   The first time that he called for *satyagraha,* there was rioting. Gandhi immediately called off *satyagraha.* He told his followers, in effect, that [they] were not yet worthy or ready for civil disobedience.

[4]   This was leadership. Without it, *satyagraha* can be tragic and dangerous. Those who practice nonviolence are helpless in the face of those who resort to violence.

[5]   The limits of civil disobedience are not easily defined. Here, I must state that the limits and the sources of justification are relative, depending upon concrete circumstance. Concerning the war in Vietnam, is there anyone who does not welcome sound and rational criticism? I personally do not like any war; and I am reluctant to give support to any war. But I am not a pacifist.

[6]   The practice of civil disobedience here in relationship to the Administration's policy in Vietnam has, to a considerable extent, been unworthy. It has been accompanied by obscenities hurled against the President. Insults against his wife. I live near the United Nations. In walking by pickets, peacefully and without any thought of infringing on their rights to picket, I have been called an "Ignorant Fascist," "a Daily News Reader" because I did not say "Yes," or "Amen" or whatever vocal agreement seemed to be necessary. The opportunity for critics of the Administration's policies to express their views and to organize has been more than ample. There is no need to resort to angry civil disobedience.

[7]   I and many others predicted a war such as the Vietnam war in 1954 after the Geneva Conference. And again in 1956. Is it any wonder that we look with a weary eye upon those who describe it as a current crime being committed by the current Administration? Where were the not-so-young advocates of civil disobedience then?

[8]   You ask for a statement on civil disobedience. I answer with a question. What civil disobedience? Have we reached the point in history where civil disobedience is writing dirty words on a fence about the President of the country? Or calling members of his Administration names? I support the policy of the United States in its present commitment. And for my polit-

ical views, I have been insulted by mail and by students during lectures. All of whom are terribly concerned about the freedom of people all over the world—unless they have another view, obviously.

EXERCISES

1.   Farrell does not state his theme; he implies it. State it in your own words.
2.   What does he think of the idea of civil disobedience as practiced by Mohandas Gandhi? What is the key to *satyagraha*?
3.   How does Farrell define civil disobedience? How adequate is this definition?
4.   What do the more vocal practitioners of civil disobedience do to make it "uncivil"?
5.   Evaluate his criticism of "not-so-young advocates of civil disobedience" back in 1954–1956.
6.   What are the responsibilities of those who practice civil disobedience?
7.   What is the tone of the article? What is its relationship to the content?

For additional "Exercises" and for "Recommended Reading" see Kelman: "When Civil Disobedience Is Justifiable," pp. 325–328.

HERBERT C. KELMAN

"WHEN CIVIL DISOBEDIENCE IS JUSTIFIABLE"

INTRODUCTION

Herbert C. Kelman (1927–   ) holds his Ph.D. in psychology from Yale University. He has been both a teacher and a researcher at universities and mental health centers literally from coast to coast. He worked at one time at the Center of Advanced Study of the Behavioral Sciences (1954–1955) at Stanford, California, and was Resident Psychologist at the National Institute for Mental Health in Bethesda, Maryland. Currently, he teaches at the University of Michigan. Some of his publications reveal Dr. Kelman's interest in the social aspects of psychology—an article "Research Approaches to the Study of War and Peace" and a book he edited with others in his field, *International Behavior* (1965).

TO THE READER

The component parts of the term "civil disobedience" must be looked at to understand the whole.

In the current debate about proper forms of protest, the term "civil disobedience" is often applied loosely to a wide range of activities. I shall use it more narrowly to refer to a deliberate, open, and announced violation of a law or a rule which is seen as immoral, unjust, or in other ways inconsistent with some basic values of the society — and hence as illegitimate and no longer binding on the citizen.

[2]　Civil disobedience is a form of protest peculiar to a democratic society, in which authority is justified and limited by the consent of the governed and used in the pursuit of policies that represent the wishes, purposes and aspirations of the population. Insofar as these conditions are met, the actions of the Government are legitimate. Civil disobedience is justified — and, in fact, obligatory in terms of the highest principles of citizenship — when legitimate processes break down in a system that is otherwise basically democratic. There are two interrelated components in such a breakdown of legitimate processes which, when they occur jointly, set the stage for civil disobedience:

[3]　**(1)** The Government takes or condones actions that are inconsistent with certain important values on which the society and its political system are built, and that thus violate the basic assumptions on which the Government's legitimacy rests. This has been true, for example, in American society's treatment of the Negro population. The prevailing policies, laws and practices have been unjust in that they have discriminated against one segment of the population and allowed advantages to some groups at the expense of and through the suppression of others.

[4]　**(2)** There are no adequate legitimate procedures available for individuals and groups to avoid complicity in these illegitimate actions of their Government and to work effectively for change in the policies, laws and practices that they find abhorrent. In the struggle for racial equality, for example, effective legitimate procedures were unavailable because, in many parts of the country, Negroes were excluded from the political process. . . .

[5]　A good citizen engages in civil disobedience only when he is morally repelled by a law or policy and when its objectionable features touch on the core of his identity. He assumes that the values prompting him to engage in civil disobedience are widely shared in the society, even though they may be latent at the moment, and that they will become awakened in a majority of the population once they are dramatically called to their attention.

[6]　Civil disobedience does not represent a dissociation from society, but is, rather, an act of profound commitment to it. It is a *civil* act — that is, the act of a citizen manifesting his citizenship, not the act of an outsider. It is an act of *disobedience* — that is, a deliberate and often symbolic or even ritualistic violation of a specific rule, rather than a rejection of the system as a whole.

[7]　The term "disobedience," in fact, has meaning only if one assumes

that, in general, the system is entitled to obedience. Unlike revolution, which denies the legitimacy of the very system itself, civil disobedience merely denies the legitimacy of certain specific laws, policies, or practices of a specific administration, within the framework of the existing system. Those who engage in civil disobedience are usually more deeply committed to the values and procedures on which the system is built than those who always obey without question. They regard certain actions as illegitimate precisely because they see them as inconsistent with these values and procedures. By engaging in civil disobedience they are working toward a restoration of the system's legitimacy and integrity, and expressing a faith in the society's capacity to be true to its own values.

[8]   In challenging government policies and practices that increasingly deviate from the basic values and procedures of the society, civil disobedience helps to revitalize these values and procedures in the face of changing circumstances. Moreover, it helps to re-establish the basis of law and order in the voluntary support of the population rather than in the coercive power of the state.

[9]   To fulfill these functions effectively, civil disobedience must be based, as I have pointed out, on moral repulsion rather than mere personal dislike of a law or policy. The line between these two cannot be sharply drawn and, thus, the justifiability of civil disobedience in any given case must remain, in part, a matter of subjective choice.

[10] Nevertheless, there are some broad criteria for choosing the occasion and form of civil disobedience that can readily distinguish it from "taking the law into your own hands." These include strict adherence to nonviolence, readiness to accept punishment, as close a connection as possible between the action and the object of protest, the minimal alienation of the wider community. It must be remembered that, in the final analysis, civil disobedience is a form of persuasion whose success depends on awakening latent moral forces in the society.

EXERCISES

Questions

1.   What is Kelman's definition of civil disobedience, of each word in turn, and the collective term? Compare this with Farrell's definition.
2.   Why is civil disobedience peculiar to a democratic society? When is civil disobedience justified and even obligatory?
3.   What are the two conditions that justify civil disobedience? How have these conditions been present in the struggle for racial equality?
4.   What does civil disobedience deny? What does it confirm? What should its effect be on society?
5.   What is the relationship of civil disobedience to morality?

6.   What are the obligations and responsibilities of those who would practice civil disobedience?

For Discussion and Writing

Apply Kelman's criteria (paragraphs 3 and 4) or Farrell's to:
1.   Protesting the draft
2.   Protesting Dow Chemical Company
3.   Protesting war
4.   Protesting the university administration
5.   Protesting police brutality
6.   Protesting the protests

CROSS REFERENCES

FARRELL: "Today's Disobedience Is Uncivil"
GALBRAITH: "Dissent in a Free Society"
THOREAU: "On the Duty of Civil Disobedience"

RECOMMENDED READING

KATOPE, CHRISTOPHER G., and ZOLBROD, PAUL G.: *Beyond Berkely:
A Sourcebook in Student Values* (World: 1966).

ON VIOLENCE

JONATHAN SWIFT

"A MODEST PROPOSAL
for Preventing
the Children of Ireland
from Being a Burden
to Their Parents
or Country"

INTRODUCTION

Jonathan Swift (1667–1745) was an Anglican clergyman who rose to be Dean of St. Patrick's Cathedral in Dublin, Ireland. He is best known for his great work, *Gulliver's Travels,* which when abridged is read by children, but in its original form is strictly for adults. It is a scathing satire on mankind, satire being Swift's dominant mode of writing. He also composed his own epitaph, and his tomb bears these words: "Where savage indignation no longer lacerates the heart." In "A Modest Proposal . . . " we see both the indignation and the tears of his epitaph.

TO THE READER

Swift created a narrator here who makes a modest but unacceptable proposal, which he then supports with excellent logic.

You will realize this immoral work is really profoundly moral when you distinguish the modest proposal from the real proposal.

It is a melancholy object to those who walk through this great town or travel in the country, when they see the streets, the roads, and cabin-doors crowded with beggars of the female sex, followed by three, four, or six children, all in rags, and importuning every passenger for an alms. These mothers instead of being able to work for their honest livelihood, are forced to

330

employ all their time in strolling to beg sustenance for their helpless infants, who, as they grow up, either turn thieves for want of work, or leave their dear native country, to fight for the Pretender in Spain, or sell themselves to the Barbadoes.

[2]   I think it is agreed by all parties, that this prodigious number of children in the arms, or on the backs, or at the heels of their mothers, and frequently of their fathers, is in the present deplorable state of the kingdom a very great additional grievance; and therefore whoever could find out a fair, cheap, and easy method of making these children sound and useful members of the common-wealth, would deserve so well of the public as to have his statue set up for a preserver of the nation.

[3]   But my intention is very far from being confined to provide only for the children of professed beggars; it is of a much greater extent, and shall take in the whole number of infants at a certain age, who are born of parents in effect as little able to support them, as those who demand our charity in the streets.

[4]   As to my own part, having turned my thoughts, for many years, upon this important subject, and maturely weighed the several schemes of other projectors, I have always found them grossly mistaken in their computation. It is true, a child just dropt from its dam,[1] may be supported by her milk for a solar year with little other nourishment, at most not above the value of two shillings, which the mother may certainly get, or the value in scraps, by her lawful occupation of begging; and it is exactly at one year old that I propose to provide for them in such a manner, as, instead of being a charge upon their parents, or the parish, or wanting food and raiment for the rest of their lives, they shall, on the contrary, contribute to the feeding and partly to the clothing of many thousands.

[5]   There is likewise another great advantage in my scheme, that it will prevent those voluntary abortions, and that horrid practice of women murdering their bastard children, alas! too frequent among us — sacrificing the poor innocent babes, I doubt, more to avoid the expense than the shame — which would move tears and pity in the most savage and inhuman breast.

[6]   The number of souls in this kingdom being usually reckoned one million and a half, of these I calculate there may be about two hundred thousand couple whose wives are breeders; from which number I subtract thirty thousand couples, who are able to maintain their own children, although I apprehend there cannot be so many, under the present distresses of the kingdom; but this being granted, there will remain an hundred and seventy thousand breeders. I again subtract fifty thousand, for those women who miscarry, or whose children die by accident or disease within the year. There only remain an hundred and twenty thousand children of poor parents annually born: The question therefore is, How this number shall be reared, and provided for? which, as I have already said, under the present situation of affairs, is utterly impossible by all the methods hitherto proposed; for we can

[1] a female parent (used especially of four-footed animals)

neither employ them in handicraft or agriculture; we neither build houses, (I mean in the country) nor cultivate land: They can very seldom pick up a livelihood by stealing till they arrive at six years old, except where they are of towardly parts, although, I confess, they learn the rudiments much earlier; during which time they can however be properly looked upon only as probationers; as I have been informed by principal gentleman in the county of Cavan, who protested to me, that he never knew above one or two instances under the age of six, even in a part of the kingdom so renowned for the quickest proficiency in that art.

[7]   I am assured by our merchants, that a boy or a girl before twelve years old, is no saleable commodity, and even when they come to this age, they will not yield above three pounds, or three pounds and half a crown at most, on the exchange; which cannot turn to account either to the parents or kingdom, the charge of nutriment and rags having been at least four times that value.

[8]   I shall now therefore humbly propose my own thoughts, which I hope will not be liable to the least objection.

[9]   I have been assured by a very knowing American of my acquaintance in London, that a young healthy child well nursed is at a year old a most delicious, nourishing, and wholesome food, whether stewed, roasted, baked, or boiled; and I make no doubt that it will equally serve in a fricassee, or ragout.

[10]   I do therefore humbly offer it to publick consideration, that of the hundred and twenty thousand children, already computed, twenty thousand may be reserved for breed, whereof only one fourth part to be males; which is more than we allow to sheep, black cattle, or swine; and my reason is that these children are seldom the fruits of marriage, a circumstance not much regarded by our savages; therefore one male will be sufficient to serve four females. That the remaining hundred thousand may, at a year old, be offered in the sale to the persons of quality and fortune through the kingdom; always advising the mother to let them suck plentifully in the last month, so as to render them plump and fat for a good table. A child will make two dishes at an entertainment for friends; and when the family dines alone, the fore or hind quarter will make a reasonable dish, and seasoned with a little pepper or salt will be very good boiled on the fourth day, especially in winter.

[11]   I have reckoned upon a medium that a child just born will weigh 12 pounds, and in a solar year, if tolerably nursed, increaseth to 28 pounds.

[12]   I grant this food will be somewhat dear, and therefore very proper for landlords, who, as they have already devoured most of the parents, seem to have the best title to the children.

[13]   Infants' flesh will be in season throughout the year, but more plentiful in March, and a little before and after; for we are told by a grave author, an eminent French physician, that fish being a prolific diet, there are more children born in Roman Catholic countries about nine months after Lent than at any other season; therefore, reckoning a year after Lent, the markets will be more glutted than usual, because the number of popish infants is at

least three to one in this kingdom: and therefore it will have one other collateral advantage, by lessening the number of papists among us.

[14] I have already computed the charge of nursing a beggar's child (in which list I reckon all cottagers, laborers, and four-fifths of the farmers) to be about two shillings per annum, rags included; and I believe no gentleman would repine to give ten shillings for the carcass of a good fat child, which, as I have said, will make four dishes of excellent nutritive meat, when he hath only some particular friend or his own family to dine with him. Thus the squire will learn to be a good landlord, and grow popular among his tenants; the mother will have eight shilling net profit, and be fit for work till she produces another child.

[15] Those who are more thrifty (as I must confess the times require) may flay the carcass, the skin of which artificially dressed will make admirable gloves for ladies, and summer boots for fine gentlemen.

[16] As to our city of Dublin, shambles[2] may be appointed for this purpose in the most convenient parts of it, and butchers we may be assured will not be wanting; although I rather recommend buying the children alive and dressing them hot from the knife, as we do roasting pigs.

[17] A very worthy person, a true lover of his country, and whose virtues I highly esteem, was lately pleased in discoursing on this matter to offer a refinement upon my scheme. He said that many gentlemen of this kingdom, having of late destroyed their deer, he conceived that the want of venison might be well supplied by the bodies of young lads and maidens, not exceeding fourteen years of age nor under twelve; so great a number of both sexes in every country being now ready to starve for want of work and service; and these to be disposed of by their parents if alive, or otherwise by their nearest relations. But with due deference to so excellent a friend, and so deserving a patriot, I cannot be altogether in his sentiments; for as to the males, my American acquaintance assured me from frequent experience, that their flesh was generally tough and lean, like that of our schoolboys, by continual exercise, and their taste disagreeable, and to fatten them would not answer the charge. Then as to the females, it would, I think with humble submission, be a loss to the publick, because they soon would become breeders themselves: And besides it is not improbable that some scrupulous people might be apt to censure such a practice (although indeed very unjustly) as a little bordering upon cruelty, which, I confess, hath always been with me the strongest objection against any project, how well soever intended.

[18] But in order to justify my friend, he confessed that this expedient was put into his head by the famous Psalmanazar, a native of the island Formosa, who came from thence to London, above twenty years ago, and in conversation told my friend, that in his country when any young person happened to be put to death, the executioner sold the carcass to persons of quality, as

[2] a slaughterhouse

a prime dainty, and that, in his time, the body of a plump girl of fifteen, who was crucified for an attempt to poison the Emperor was sold to his Imperial Majesty's prime minister of state, and other great mandarins of the court, in joints from the gibbet, at four hundred crowns. Neither indeed can I deny, that if the same use were made of several plump young girls of this town, who, without one single groat to their fortunes, cannot stir abroad without a chair, and appear at a play-house and assemblies in foreign fineries which they never will pay for, the kingdom would not be the worse.

[19] Some persons of a desponding spirit are in great concern about that vast number of poor people, who are aged, diseased, or maimed, and I have been desired to employ my thoughts what course may be taken, to ease the nation of so grievous an encumbrance. But I am not in the least pain upon that matter, because it is very well known, that they are every day dying, and rotting, by cold, and famine, and filth, and vermin, as fast as can be reasonably expected. And as to the younger labourers, they are now in almost as hopeful a condition. They cannot get work, and consequently pine away for want of nourishment, to a degree, that if at any time they are accidentally hired to common labour, they have not strength to perform it, and thus the country and themselves are happily delivered from the evils to come.

[20] I have too long digressed, and therefore shall return to my subject. I think the advantages by the proposal which I have made are obvious and many, as well as of the highest importance.

[21] For *first*, as I have already observed, it would greatly lessen the number of papists, with whom we are yearly over-run, being the principal breeders of the nation, as well as our most dangerous enemies, and who stay at home on purpose with a design to deliver the kingdom to the Pretender, hoping to take their advantage by the absence of so many good Protestants, who have chosen rather to leave their country, than stay at home, and pay tithes against their conscience to an Episcopal curate.

[22] Secondly, the poorer tenants will have something valuable of their own, which by law may be made liable to distress and help to pay their landlord's rent, their corn and cattle being already seized, and money a thing unknown.

[23] Thirdly, whereas the maintenance of an hundred thousand children, from two years old and upward, cannot be computed at less than ten shillings apiece per annum, the nation's stock will be thereby increased fifty thousand pounds per annum, besides the profit of a new dish introduced to the tables of all gentlemen of fortune in the kingdom who have any refinement in taste. And the money will circulate among ourselves, the goods being entirely of our own growth and manufacture.

[24] Fourthly, the constant breeders, beside the gain of eight shillings sterling per annum[3] by the sale of their children, will be rid of the charge of maintaining them after the first year.

[3]year (Latin)

[25] Fifthly, this food would likewise bring great custom to taverns, where the vintners will certainly be so prudent as to procure the best receipts for dressing it to perfection, and consequently have their houses frequented by all the fine gentlemen who justly value themselves upon their knowledge in good eating; and a skillful cook, who understands how to oblige his guests, will contrive to make it as expensive as they please.

[26] Sixthly, this would be a great inducement to marriage, which all wise nations have either encouraged by rewards or enforced by laws and penalties. It would increase the care and tenderness of mothers toward their children, when they were sure of a settlement for life to the poor babes, provided in some sort by the public, to their annual profit instead of expense. We should soon see an honest emulation among the married women, which of them could bring the fattest child to the market. Men would become as fond of their wives during the time of their pregnancy as they are now of their mares in foal, their cows in calf, their sows when they are ready to farrow; nor offer to beat or kick them (as is too frequent a practice) for fear of a miscarriage.

[27] Many other advantages might be enumerated. For instance, the addition of some thousand carcasses in our exportation of barreled beef, the propagation of swine's flesh, and improvement in the art of making good bacon, so much wanted among us by the great destruction of pigs, too frequent at our tables; which are no way comparable in taste or magnificence to a well-grown, fat, yearling child, which roasted whole will make a considerable figure at a lord mayor's feast or any other public entertainment. But this and many others I omit, being studious of brevity.

[28] Supposing that one thousand families in this city would be constant customers for infants' flesh, besides others who might have it at merry meetings, particularly at weddings and christenings, I compute that Dublin would take off annually about twenty thousand carcasses; and the rest of the kingdom (where probably they will be sold somewhat cheaper) the remaining eighty thousand.

[29] I can think of no one objection that will possibly be raised against this proposal, unless it should be urged that the number of people will be thereby much lessened in the kingdom. This I freely own, and 'twas indeed one principal design in offering it to the world. I desire the reader will observe that I calculate my remedy for this one individual kingdom of Ireland, and for no other that ever was, is, or, I think, ever can be upon earth. Therefore let no man talk to me of other expedients: of taxing our absentees at five shillings a pound: of using neither clothes, nor household furniture, except what is of our own growth and manufacture: of utterly rejecting the materials and instruments that promote foreign luxury: of curing the expensiveness of pride, vanity, idleness, and gaming in our women: of introducing a vein of parsimony,[4] prudence and temperance: of learning to love our country, where in

---

[4]extreme or excessive economy, stinginess

we differ even from Laplanders, and the inhabitants of Topinamboo: of quitting our animosities, and factions, nor act any longer like the Jews, who were murdering one another at the very moment their city was taken: of being a little cautious not to sell our country and consciences for nothing: of teaching landlords to have at least one degree of mercy towards their tenants. Lastly, of putting a spirit of honesty, industry, and skill into our shop-keepers, who, if a resolution could now be taken to buy only our native goods, would immediately unite to cheat and exact upon us in the price, the measure, and the goodness, nor could ever yet be brought to make one fair proposal of just dealing though often and earnestly invited to it.

[30] Therefore I repeat, let no man talk to me of these and the like expedients,[5] till he hath at least some glimpse of hope, that there will ever be some hearty and sincere attempt to put them in practice.

[31] But as to my self, having been wearied out for many years with offering vain, idle, visionary thoughts, and at length utterly despairing of success, I fortunately fell upon this proposal, which as it is wholly new, so it hath something solid and real, of no expense and little trouble, full in our own power, and whereby we can incur no danger in disobliging England. For this kind of commodity will not bear exportation, the flesh being of too tender a consistence, to admit a long continuance in salt, although perhaps I could name a country, which would be glad to eat up our whole nation without it.

[32] After all, I am not so violently bent upon my own opinion, as to reject any offer, proposed by wise men, which shall be found equally innocent, cheap, easy, and effectual. But before something of that kind shall be advanced in contradiction to my scheme, and offering a better, I desire the author or authors, will be pleased maturely to consider two points. *First,* as things now stand, how they will be able to find food and raiment for a hundred thousand useless mouths and backs. And *Secondly,* there being a round million of creatures in human figure throughout this kingdom, whose whole subsistence put into a common stock would leave them in debt two millions of pounds sterling, adding those who are beggars by profession, to the bulk of farmers, cottagers and labourers, with their wives and children, who are beggars in effect; I desire those politicians, who dislike my overture, and may perhaps be so bold to attempt an answer, that they will first ask the parents of these mortals, whether they would not at this day think it a great happiness to have been sold for food at a year old, in the manner I prescribe, and thereby have avoided such a perpetual scene of misfortunes as they have since gone through, by the oppression of landlords, the impossibility of paying rent without money or trade, the want of common sustenance, with neither house nor clothes to cover them from the inclemencies of the weather, and the most inevitable prospect of entailing the like or greater miseries upon their breed for ever.

[5]fit or suitable ideas for the purpose

[33] I profess, in the sincerity of my heart, that I have not the least personal interest in endeavoring to promote this necessary work, having no other motive than the public good of my country, by advancing our trade, providing for infants, relieving the poor, and giving some pleasure to the rich. I have no children by which I can propose to get a single penny; the youngest being nine years old, and my wife past child-bearing.

EXERCISES

Questions

1. In paragraph 10 Swift presents his theme, his proposal. What is the underlying assumption? In what earlier paragraphs does Swife allude to it to work up the reader's curiosity? Describe your initial reaction to the proposal and explain why you felt as you did.
2. Since the speaker is not Jonathan Swift, draw a character portrait of the maker of the proposal as he sees himself and as you see him.
3. What were the conditions in Ireland that needed remedying? What was the specific problem with the children?
4. What is Swift's stated objective? Examine his title and paragraph 3.
5. The first hint of Swift's attitude is in paragraph 4: "dropt from its dam." Why are these words significant? What other examples of animal analogies can you find? How do such words and phrases contribute to his theme?
6. Against whom is his anger really directed? What paragraphs reveal his real target?
7. What purpose can you find for the digression of paragraphs 17 to 19?
8. What are the many advantages Swift offers for adopting his proposal? Why does the list of advantages contribute to the horror with which we read the essay?
9. What comment has he implied about the motives of human behavior in paragraph 26?
10. What are his real solutions to the problems of the Irish?
11. Which paragraph most reveals Swift's basic humanity?
12. What is the purpose of the last paragraph? Why is it a fitting culmination for the essay?
13. How are morality and dissent combined in this essay?

Vocabulary

collateral
deference
flay
gibbet

importuning
prodigious
towardly
vintners

For Discussion and Writing

1. Facing the inhumanity in man
2. When a moral principle clashes with a moral principle
3. When a moral principle clashes with a legal principle
4. Means and ends — can they violate each other?
5. Welfare: a modest proposal
6. Violence as a solution

CROSS REFERENCES

HARRINGTON: "The American Experience: Historically Violent"
STEINBECK: "America and Americans"
THURBER: "The Trouble with Man Is Man"
WERTHAM: Epilogue from *The Show of Violence*
WOODWARD: "America: Part of an International Culture of Violence"

JOHN STEINBECK

"AMERICA AND AMERICANS"

INTRODUCTION

John Steinbeck (1902–1968) was one of America's best writers and one of its most popular—a combination that does not go together as often as it should. He wrote for about forty years and his two favorite subjects seem to have been America in general and individual Americans in particular. Mr. Steinbeck's classic novel is *The Grapes of Wrath,* 1939, a story about migrants, which some people believe to be the most influential social novel of the century. His other major books are *East of Eden,* and *The Winter of Our Discontent* for which he was awarded the Nobel Prize for Literature in 1962. He has also written a host of shorter works. His last books included *Travels with Charlie* and *America and Americans,* from which these excerpts have been taken.

TO THE READER

There is no central thesis here as Steinbeck speculates on American (im) morality, past and present.

The key to this essay is paradox: a sharp contrast, frequently an apparent contradiction; it is sometimes between what we remember and what actually was or between two currently existing conditions.

I t is customary (indeed, at high-school graduations it is a require-
ment) for speakers to refer to America as a "precious inheritance" — our
heritage, a gift proffered like a sandwich wrapped in plastic on a plastic
tray. Our ancestors, so it is implied, gathered to the invitation of a golden
land and accepted the sacrament of milk and honey.

[2]   This is not so. In the beginning we crept, scuttled, escaped, were driven
out of the safe and settled corners of the earth, to the fringes of a strange and
hostile wilderness, a nameless and hostile continent. Far from welcoming us,
it resisted us. This land was no gift. The firstlings worked for it, fought for it,
and died for it. They stole and cheated and double-crossed for it, and when
they had taken a little piece, the way a fierce-hearted man ropes a wild mus-
tang, they had then to gentle it and smooth it to make it habitable at all.

[3]   We built America, and the process made us Americans — a new breed,
rooted in all races, stained and tinted with all colors, a seeming ethnic[1] an-
archy.[2] Then in a little, little time, we became more alike than we were
different — a new society; not great, but fitted by our very faults for greatness:
E Pluribus Unum.

[4]   The whole thing is crazy. Every single man in our emerging country
was out for himself against all others — for his safety, his profit, his future.
When his family grew up about him, he set it against all other families. When
communities arose, each one defended itself against other communities.
The surges of the new restless, needy, and strong — grudgingly brought in for
purposes of hard labor and cheap wages — were resisted, resented, and only
accepted when a new and different wave came in.

[5]   All that was required to release the mechanism of oppression and
sadism was that the newcomers be meek, poor, weak in numbers, and un-
protected — although it helped if their skin, hair, eyes were different, and if
they spoke some language other than English, or worshiped in some church
other than Protestant. The Pilgrim Fathers took out after the Catholics, and
both clobbered the Jews; the Germans clotted for self-defense until the Irish
took the resented place; the Irish became "Americans" against the Poles;
the Slavs against the Italians. On the West Coast the Chinese ceased to be
enemies only when the Japanese arrived; and they, in the face of the in-
vasions of Hindus, Filipinos and Mexicans.

[6]   It occurs to me that this very cruelty toward newcomers might go far
toward explaining the speed with which the ethnic and national strangers
merged with the "Americans." In spite of all the pressure the old people
could bring to bear, the children of each ethnic group denied their background and their ancestral language. Despite the anger, the contempt, the
jealousy, the self-imposed ghettos and segregation, something was loose in

---

[1]sharing a cultural, racial, religious, or language tradition
[2]a theory that regards the absence of direct or coercive government as a political ideal
and that proposes the cooperative and voluntary association of individuals and groups as the
principal mode of organized society

this land called America. The new generations wanted to be Americans more than they wanted to be Poles, or Germans, or Hungarians, or Italians, or British. And in one or two, certainly not more than three generations, each ethnic group has clicked into place in the union without losing the *pluribus.*

•   •   •   •   •   •

[7]   One of the generalities most often noted about Americans is that we are a restless, a dissatisfied, a searching people. We spend our time searching for security, and hate it when we get it. For the most part we are an intemperate[3] people: We eat too much when we can, drink too much, indulge our senses too much. Even in our so-called virtues we are intemperate: A teetotaler is not content not to drink—he must stop all the drinking in the world; a vegetarian among us would outlaw the eating of meat. We work too hard, and many die under the strain; and then to make up for that we play with a violence just as suicidal. The result is that we seem to be in a state of turmoil all the time, both physically and mentally. We are able to believe that our Government is weak, stupid, overbearing, dishonest, and inefficient, and at the same time we are deeply convinced that it is the best Government in the world, and we would like to impose it upon everyone else.

[8]   Americans overindulge their children and do not like them; the children in turn are overly dependent and full of hate for their parents. Americans are remarkably kind and hospitable and open with both guests and strangers; and yet they will make a wide circle around a man dying on the pavement rather than become involved. Fortunes are spent getting cats out of trees and dogs out of sewer pipes; but a girl screaming for help in the street draws only slammed doors, closed windows and silence.

[9]   Americans seem to live and breathe and function by paradox; but in nothing are we so paradoxical as in our passionate belief in our own myths.[4] We truly believe ourselves to be natural-born mechanics and do-it-yourselfers. We spend our lives in motorcars, yet most of us—a great many of us at least—do not know enough about a car to check the gas tank when the motor fails. Our believed myths are everywhere: We shout that we are a nation of laws, not men—and then proceed to break every law we can if we can get away with it. From puberty we are preoccupied with sex; but our courts, our counselors, and our psychiatrists are dealing constantly with cases of sexual failure or charges of frigidity or impotence, which amounts to the same thing.

•   •   •   •   •   •

[10] The dreams of a people either create folk literature or find their way into it; and folk literature, again, is always based on something that happened. Our most persistent folktales—constantly retold in books, movies, and television shows—concern cowboys, gun-slinging sheriffs and Indian

---

[3]not moderate regarding indulgence of appetite or passion

[4]an unproved collective belief that is accepted uncritically and is used to justify a social institution, as belief in the biological inferiority of slaves is used to support a slave society

fighters. These folk figures existed — perhaps not quite as they are recalled nor in the numbers indicated, but they did exist; and this dream persists. Even businessmen in Texas wear the high-heeled boots and big hats, though they ride in airconditioned cars and have forgotten the reason for the high heel. All of our children play cowboy and Indian. The brave and honest sheriff who with courage and a six-gun brings law and order and civic virtue to a Western community is perhaps our most familiar hero, no doubt descended from the brave, mailed knight of chivalry who battled and overcame evil with lance and sword. Even the recognition signals are the same: white hat, white armor — black hat, black shield. And in these moral tales, so deep-set in us, virtue does not arise out of reason or orderly process of law — it is imposed by violence and maintained by the threat of violence. I wonder whether this folk wisdom is the story of our capability. Are these stories permanent because we know within ourselves that only the threat of violence makes it possible for us to live together in peace?

[11] A national dream need not, indeed may not, be clear-cut and exact. For Americans it is called "The American Way of Life." No one can define it or point to any one person or group who lives it, but it is very real nevertheless.

[12] I have often wondered at the savagery and thoughtlessness with which our early settlers approached this rich continent. They came at it as though it were an enemy, which of course it was. They burned the forests, they swept the buffalo from the plains, blasted the streams, and ran a reckless scythe through the virgin and noble timber. Perhaps they felt that the land could never be exhausted, that a man could move on to new wonders endlessly. They pillaged the country as though they hated it, as though they held it temporarily and might be driven off at any time.

[13] This tendency toward irresponsibility persists in very many of us today — our rivers are poisoned by reckless dumping of sewage and toxic industrial wastes, the air of our cities is filthy and dangerous to breathe from the belching of uncontrolled products from combustion of coal, coke, oil and gasoline. Our towns are girdled with wreckage and the debris of our toys — our automobiles and our packaged pleasures.

• • • • • •

[14] Since the river-polluters, the air-poisoners are not criminal or even bad people, we must presume that they are heirs to the early conviction that sky and water are unowned and that they are limitless. In the light of our practices here at home it is interesting to read of the care taken with the carriers of our probes into space, to make utterly sure that they are free of pollution of any kind. We would not think of doing to the moon what we do every day to our own country.

• • • • • •

[15] In nothing are the Americans so strange and set apart from the rest of the world as in their attitudes toward the treatment of their children. Americans did not always fear, hate, and adore their children; in our early days a

child spent its helpless and pre-procreative days as a child, and then moved naturally into adulthood. This was true across the world. I have studied the children in many countries and I find nothing to approximate the American sickness. Where could it have started, and is it a disease of the children or of the parents? One thing we know: children seem to be able to get over it; parents rarely. . . .

[16] Our child-sickness has developed very rapidly in the last 60 years, and it runs parallel, it would seem, with increasing material plenty and the medical conquest of child-killing diseases. Suddenly it was no longer acceptable that the child should be like his parents and live as they did; he must be better, live better, know more, dress more richly, and if possible change from his father's trade to a profession. This dream became touchingly national. Since it was demanded of the child that he be better than his parents, he must be gaited, guided, pushed, admired, disciplined, flattered and forced. But since the parents were and are no better than they are, the rules they propounded were not based on their experience but on their wishes and hopes.

[17] If the hope was not fulfilled—and it rarely was—the parents went into a tailspin of guilt, blaming themselves for having done something wrong or at least something not right. This feeling of self-recrimination on the part of the parents was happily seized upon by the children, for it allowed them to be failures through no fault of their own. Laziness, sloppiness, indiscipline, selfishness and general piggery, which are the natural talents of children and were once slapped out of them, if they lived, now became either crimes of the parents or sickness in the children, who would far rather be sick than be disciplined.

[18] Into this confusion the experts entered, and American parents put their troubles, and their children, in the hands of the professionals—doctors, educators, psychologists, neurologists, even psychoanalysts. The only trouble was and is that few of the professionals agreed with one another except in one thing: It was the consensus that the child should always be the center of attention—an attitude which had the full support of the children.

[19] The open warfare between adults and teen-agers becomes constantly more bitter. It doesn't occur to the adult that he has allowed the rules of warfare to be rigged against him; that he has permitted himself to be bound, defanged and emasculated.[5] I do not blame the youth; no one has ever told him that his tricks are obvious, his thoughts puerile,[6] his goals selfish, his art ridiculous. Psychoanalysts constantly remind their little patients that they must find the real "me." The real "me" invariably turns out to be a savage, self-seeking little beast.

•   •   •   •   •   •

[20] I find I have been putting off writing about the most serious problem

[5]deprived of strength or vigor, weakened
[6]childishly foolish, immature, or trivial

Americans are faced with, both as a people and as individuals. We discuss it constantly, and yet there is not even a name for it. Immorality does not describe it, nor does lack of integrity, nor does dishonesty. Many people, not able to face the universal spread and danger of the cancerous growth, split off a fragment of the whole to worry about or to try to cure. But I begin to think that the evil is one thing, not many, that racial unrest, the emotional crazy quilt that drives our people in panic to the couches of the psychoanalysts, the fallout, dropout, copout insurgency of our children and young people, the rush to stimulant as well as hypnotic drugs, the rise of narrow, ugly and vengeful cults of all kinds, the distrust and revolt against all authority, political, religious or military, the awful and universal sense of apprehension and even terror—and this in a time of plenty such as has never been known—I think all of these are manifestations of one single cause.

> •   •   •   •   •   •

[21] I'm not going to preach about any good old days. By our standards of comfort they were pretty awful. What did they have then that we are losing or have lost? Well, for one thing they had rules—rules concerning life, limb, and property, rules governing deportment, manners, conduct, and finally rules defining dishonesty, dishonor, misconduct and crime. The rules were not always obeyed, but they were believed in, and a breaking of the rules was savagely punished. . . . It was necessary not only to punish the bad, or natural, but to reward the good people who lived by the rules. And since it was impractical to make these rewards in physical form, more and more of the payments were put over into a future life.

[22] Over the millennia most of us have learned to obey the rules or suffer punishment for breaking them. But most important, even the rule-breaker knew he was wrong and the other right; the rules were understood and accepted by everyone. At intervals in our history, through unperceived changes, usually economic, the rules and the enforcing agents have ceased to work. Inevitably the result has been a wild and terrible self-destructive binge, a drunken horror of the spirit giving rise to the unspeakable antics of crazy children. This dark mania has continued until rules were reapplied, rewritten or reenforced.

[23] Adlai Stevenson, speaking of a politician of particularly rancid practices, once said, "If he were a bad man, I wouldn't be so afraid of him. But this man has no principles. He doesn't know the difference." Could this be our difficulty, that gradually we are losing our ability to tell the difference? The rules fall away in chunks, and in the vacant place we have a generality: "It's all right because everybody does it." This is balanced with another cry of cowardice. In the face of inequity, dishonesty in government, or downright plundering, the word is "Go fight City Hall!" The implication, of course, is that you can't win. And yet in other times we did fight City Hall, and often we won.

[24] The American has never been a perfect instrument, but at one time

he had a reputation for gallantry, which to my mind is a sweet and price-less quality. It must still exist, but it is blotted out by the dust cloud of self-pity. The last clear statement of gallantry in my experience was one I heard in a recidivist state prison, a place of two-time losers, all lifers. In the yard an old and hopeless convict spoke as follows: "The kids come up, and they bawl how they wasn't guilty, or how they was framed, or how it was their mother's fault, or their father was a drunk. Us old boys try to tell 'em— 'Kid, for Christ's sake do your *own* time and let us do ours.'" In the present climate of whining self-pity, of practiced sickness, of professional gold-bricking, of screaming charges about whose fault it is, one hears of very few who do their own time, who take their rap and don't spread it around. It is as though the quality of responsibility had atrophied.[7]

[25] Americans, very many of them, are obsessed with tensions. Nerves are drawn tense and twanging. Emotions boil up and spill over into violence largely in meaningless or unnatural directions. In the cities people scream with rage at one another, taking out their unease on the first observable target. The huge reservoir of the anger of frustration is full to bursting. The legal and criminal distribution of sleeping pills and pep pills is astronomical, the first kind offering escape into sleep and the second, access to a false personality, a biochemical costume in which to strut. Kicks increasingly take the place of satisfaction. Of love, only the word, bent and bastard-ized, remains.

●   ●   ●   ●   ●   ●

[26] But now we have food and shelter and transportation and the more terrible hazard of leisure. I strongly suspect that our moral and spiritual disintegration grows out of our lack of experience with plenty. Once, in a novel, I wrote about a woman who said she didn't want a lot of money. She wanted just enough. To which her husband replied that "just enough" doesn't exist. There is no money or not enough money. Even a billionaire hasn't enough money.

[27] But we are also poisoned with things. Having many things seems to create a desire for more things, more clothes, houses, automobiles. Think of the pure horror of Christmases when children tear open package after package and then, when the floor is heaped with wrappings and presents, say—"Is that all?" And two days later the smashed and abandoned "things" are added to our national trash pile, and perhaps the child, having got in trouble, explains, "I didn't have anything to do." And he means exactly that—nothing to do, nowhere to go, no direction, no purpose, and worst of all, no needs. Wants he has, yes, but for more bright and breakable "things." We are trapped and entangled in things.

[28] In my great-grandmother's time things were important. I know, be-cause I have read her will, and the things she found important enough to

[7]declined, decreased, or wasted away

bequeath by legal instrument we would have thrown away — such things as four pewter spoons, one broken in the handle, the square of black cotton lace. I had from Grandmama the little box of leaves from the Mount of Olives, a small bowl carved from one piece of onyx and beautiful to see, 12 books and eight sheets of music. These were valuable things.

[29] It is probable that the want of things and the need of things have been the two greatest stimulants toward the change and complication we call progress. And surely we Americans, most of us starting with nothing, have contributed our share of wanting. Wanting is probably a valuable human trait. It is the means of getting that can be dangerous.

[30] When students cheat in examinations, it may be bad for them as individuals, but for the community it means that the graduate is traveling with false papers and very shortly the papers — in this case the college degree — lose their value. When military cadets cheat it is a kind of treason, for it means they have not learned to do the things they will be assigned to do. John Kennedy said his famous lines, "Ask not what your country can do for you; ask what you can do for your country," and the listening nation nodded and smiled in agreement. But he did not say it because it might happen, but because it *is* happening, and in increasing volume. And it is historically true that a nation whose people take out more than they put in will collapse and disappear.

[31] The evil that threatens us came quickly and quietly, came from many directions and was the more dangerous because it wore the face of good. Almost unlimited new power took the place of straining muscles and bent backs. Machinery took the heavy burden from our shoulders. Medicine and hygiene cut down infant mortality almost to the vanishing point, and at the same time extended our life span. Automation began to replace our workers. Whereas the majority of our people used to work the land, new developments in machines and chemistry enabled a precious few to produce more food than we needed or could possibly use. Leisure, which again had been the property of heaven, came to us before we knew what to do with it, and all of these good things falling on us unprepared constitute calamity.

[32] We have the things and we have not had time to develop a way of thinking about them. We struggle with our lives in the present and our practices in the long and well-learned past. We had a million years to get used to the idea of fire and only 20 to prepare ourselves for the productive-destructive tidal wave of atomic fission. We have more food than we can use and no way to distribute it. Our babies live, and we have no work for their hands. We retire men and women at the age of their best service for no other reason than that we need their jobs for younger people. To allow ourselves the illusion of usefulness we have standby crews for functions which no longer exist.

[33] And finally we can come back to the subject of morals.

[34] Ethics, morals, codes of conduct, are the stern rules which in the

past we needed in order to survive—as individuals, as groups, as nations. Now, although we give lip service to survival, we are embarrassed and beginning to be smothered by our own numbers. Americans, who are makers and lovers of statistics, are usually puzzled and irritated when it is suggested that we are a statistic. But neither the sleeping pill, the Church, nor the psychiatrist can long hide from us the fact that economic laws apply to ourselves, that increased supply causes a drop in value; that we already have too many people and are in process of producing *far* too many.

•   •   •   •   •   •

[35] Perhaps one can judge the health of a society by the nature as well as the incidence of crimes committed against it. Consider us today not only in the cities but in small towns and country as well. There are, of course, the many crimes against property, but increasingly they are destructive rather than gainful. The greatest increase, however, is in crimes against people, against the physical bodies of people. The rapes have little to do with sexuality and much to do with destructive murder. The mugging in the streets, the violence which has turned our parks into jungles, has little to do with robbery; its purpose and its drive seem to be destructive—the desire to hurt, to maim, to kill. And even when need for money is the motive of the violence, the reason is again sad and sick and destructive, this time self-destructive—the need for drugs to abolish consciousness or for stimulants to give shape and substance to a schizoid[8] twin, hallucinatory aids in the creation of another world to take the place of this hated one. This too is a kind of murder—the surrender to what is known as kicks, the whipping of reluctant nerves, the raising of savage specters that even the witchcraft of the Middle Ages could not evoke. It is a murder of the self that might be called upon for responsibility.

[36] These things are true of the actual aggressors, but how about the bystanders? Remember the windows slammed against a girls' cry for help in the night? How often have you seen a man collapse in the street, and the passersby hurry on lest they be involved? People seeing or hearing a violence look away, walk away, refuse to talk to the police. Life is indeed cheap, and moreover it is becoming hateful. We act as though we truly hated one another and silently approved the removal of one among us.

[37] Could it be that below the level of thought, our people sense the danger of the swarming, crowding, invasion of America by Americans? Starvation, pestilence, plague, which once cut us down, are no longer possible. And war? Well, during the *last* war with all its slaughter, the world's population increased. Are people genuinely afraid of the bomb, or do they look to it to do the job we have eliminated from nature?

[38] It is probable that here is where morals—integrity, ethics, even charity—have gone. The rules allowed us to survive, to live together and to increase. In our written, remembered, and sensed history, there has always

---

[8]characterized by or suggestive of a split personality

been more work than we could ever do. Our needs were greater than their possible fulfillment. But if our will to survive is weakened; if our love of life, our memories of a gallant past and faith in a shining future are removed — what need is there for morals or rules?

[39] Why are we on this verge of moral and hence nervous collapse? I believe it is because we have reached the end of a road and have discovered no new path to take, no duty to carry out and no purpose to fulfill. I think we will find a path to the future, but its direction may be unthinkable to us now. When it does appear, however, and we move on, the path must have direction, it must have purpose — and the journey must be filled with a joy of anticipation, for the boy today, hating the world, creates a hateful world and then tries to destroy it and sometimes himself as well.

[40] Something happened in America to create the Americans. Now we face the danger which in the past has been most destructive to the human: success, plenty, comfort, and ever-increasing leisure. No dynamic people has ever survived these dangers. If the anesthetic of self-satisfaction were added to our hazards, we would not have a chance of survival — as Americans.

[41] If I inspect my people and study them and criticize them, I must love them if I have any self-love, since I can never be separate from them and no more objective about them than I am about myself. I am not young, and yet I wonder about my tomorrow. How much more, then, must my wonder be about the tomorrow of my people, which is a young people. My questioning is compounded of some fear, more hope, and great confidence.

[42] I have named the destroyers of nations: comfort, plenty, and security — out of which grow a bored and slothful cynicism, in which rebellion against the world as it is, and myself as I am, is submerged in listless self-satisfaction. A dying people tolerates the present, rejects the future, and finds its satisfactions in past greatness and half-remembered glory. A dying people arms itself with defensive weapons and with mercenaries against change. When greatness recedes, so does belief in greatness. A dying poet invariably concedes that poetry has gone, that beauty has withered away. Then mountains do not rise up as they once did against the sky, and girls are not as pretty. Ecstasy fades to toleration, and agony subsides to a dull aching. Vision dims like the house lights in a theater — and the world is finished. As it is with a poet, so it is with a people.

[43] It is in the American negation of these symptoms of extinction that my hope and confidence lie. We are not satisfied. Our restlessness, perhaps inherited from the hungry immigrants of our ancestry, is still with us. Young Americans are rebellious, angry, searching like terriers near a rat's nest. The energy pours out in rumbles, in strikes and causes, even in crime; but it is energy. Wasted energy is only a little problem, compared with the lack of it.

[44] The world is open as it has never been before, and for the first time in human experience we have the tools to work with. Three fifths of the world and perhaps four fifths of the world's wealth lie under the sea, and we can get to it. The sky is open at last, and we have the means to rise into it. Revolt

is in the air—in the violence of the long, hot summer; in the resentment against injustice and inequality, and against cynical cruelty. There is blind anger against delay, against the long preparation for the long journey—perhaps the longest, darkest journey of all, with the greatest light at the end of it.

[45] We are in the perplexing period of change. We seem to be running in all directions at once—but we are running. And I believe that our history, our experience in America, has endowed us for the change that is coming. We have never sat still for long; we have never been content with a place, a building—or with ourselves. Americans do not lack places to go and new things to find. We have cut ourselves off from the self-abuse of war by raising it from a sin to an extinction. Far larger experiences are open to our restlessness—the fascinating unknown is everywhere.

[46] How will the Americans act and react to a new set of circumstances for which new rules must be made? We know from our past some of the things we will do. We will make mistakes; we always have. But from our beginning, in hindsight at least, our social direction is clear. We have moved to become one people out of many. We have failed sometimes, taken wrong paths, paused for renewal, filled our bellies and licked our wounds; but we have never slipped back—never.

EXERCISES

Questions

1. In what ways does Steinbeck attack the myth about America being the warm and welcoming "Statue of Liberty land" in his opening six paragraphs? What positive values does he present?

2. In paragraph 7, Steinbeck says Americans are "a restless, a dissatisfied, a searching people." How does he illustrate this? What are the excesses he charges to us? These are broad generalizations. Can you support or attack them with facts?

3. In paragraph 10, Steinbeck refers to a key paradox in American morality—virtue and violence. What is the paradox? Give other examples and discuss.

4. How does Steinbeck explain our apparent irresponsibility with our natural resources? How does paragraph 14 relate to Sevareid's viewpoint?

5. What is the source of our "child sickness"? What are the effects? In what ways are the "rules of warfare . . . rigged against" the adult? against the youth? Is there any relationship between this "child sickness" and the "don't-trust-anyone-over-30" attitude of many teenagers?

6. The transitional paragraph 20 begins the meat of the essay. What does Steinbeck feel held Americans together in the past? What does he fear is happening today?

7.   What is the paradox of having "things"? In what ways is this good? In what ways is this bad? What needs to be done now?
8.   What is the nature of recent crime? What seems to be the source of this? How is this related to our attitude toward "things"? How does this contribute to the growth of violence in our country?
9.   How is our attitude toward things and the nature of recent crime related to morals? What is implied about our attitude toward life?
10.   What is the problem of Americans today? What is Steinbeck's solution? What is his outlook, his warning, and his faith?

Vocabulary

consensus
gaited
millennia
recidivist
specters

For Discussion and Writing

1.   Violence: how integral to the American scene?
2.   The heroic strongmen: Popeye, Superman, the cowboy
3.   The tyranny of the teen-ager
4.   The need for rules
5.   Cheating on campus
6.   Everybody cheats: why shouldn't I?
7.   Graft in high places and low
8.   Stealing our own resources

CROSS REFERENCES

FULBRIGHT: "The Cold War in American Life"
HARRINGTON: "The American Experience: Historically Violent"
KENNEDY: "Inaugural Address"
KING: "I Have a Dream"
MINER: "Body Ritual among the Nacirema"
WOODWARD: "America: Part of an International Culture of Violence"

RECOMMENDED READING

CARSON, RACHEL: *The Sea Around Us*
STEINBECK, JOHN: *Travels with Charlie*

C. VANN WOODWARD

"AMERICA: PART OF AN INTERNATIONAL CULTURE OF VIOLENCE"

INTRODUCTION

C. Vann Woodward (1908–   ) began his long career by teaching English for a year at a small southern college; he then switched to history and law for his graduate work and his career thereafter. He has taught at many colleges in the south and on the eastern seaboard and, since 1961, has been Sterling Professor of History at Yale University. Dr. Woodward has written several books, among them: *The Battle for Leyte Gulf* (1947); *The Origins of the New South* (1877–1913) (1951), for which he won the Bancroft Prize; *The Strange Career of Jim Crow* (1955); and his most recent, *The Comparative Approach to American History* (1968).

TO THE READER

Woodward considers whether America, while historically violent, is as violent as many other nations.

From *The New York Times Magazine,* April 28, 1968. © 1968 by The New York Times Magazine Company. Reprinted by permission of The New York Times Magazine Company and the author.

I would say that America is part of an international culture of violence to which we have made distinctive contributions. The nations belonging to this culture differ much in the style and character as well as in the quality of violence they contribute. In addition to her obvious contributions to the technology and weaponry of violence, America might claim an innovative role in the style and variety of violence. Henry James described the business scene of his time as the "boundless ferocity of battle." Labor struggles in America have set international records of violence. Racial conflict, so far, has not. The brutality of success-at-any-price, however, the national cult of "making it," the escalation in verbal and literary violence, and the progress of the mass media in communicating violence owe much to American know-how. This is not to deny to other countries — Germany, Russia, China, Indonesia and India, for example — their legitimate claims to distinctive contributions in both style and quantity of violence.

[2]   While assessments of national violence make sense only in comparative terms, it is a mistake to overlook striking internal variations in the character and amount of violence. For example, the homicide rate for blacks is far higher than among whites in all regions of the country, while the Negro suicide rate is only about one-third that for whites. Yet in spite of the low suicide rate, black violence is in another sense largely self-inflicted — in the sense that black people are its main victims. As Malcolm X so graphically illustrated in his "Autobiography," the principal victim of "crime in the streets" is the Negro. The same is true of the ghetto riots.

[3]   Granting the significance of internal variations in violence, one should never overlook some national differences of vital importance. Obviously there is much in American culture and environment that tolerates, encourages, and even rewards violent behavior. As appallingly common as acts of violence are, however, they are mainly the deeds of individuals. Where they are the work of groups, even large groups, they are most often "spontaneous," done in "the heat of passion." Conspiracy, ideology, religion and calculation have had relatively small parts.

[4]   So far, America, apart from the War for Southern Independence, has escaped great holocausts of internal violence. There is nothing in her record to compare with the political bloodbath in Russia before the Second World War, the horrors of genocide in Germany during the war, and the tragic mass killings between the Islamic and Hindu people of India after the war. The corpses in each country ran into the millions. More recently the domestic bloodbaths in Indonesia, Sumatra and Borneo have reckoned their corpses in the hundreds of thousands.

[5]   Race prejudice is itself a form of violence, and its expression is now the greatest threat, of a cataclysmic and hitherto foreign scale of violence in America. Race riots are not new to America. The worst occurred in New York City in 1863, a week after the Battle of Gettysburg. The number killed

was never known, but the most reliable estimate is about 70. No one of the riots from Watts to the present has claimed so many lives. The 125 cities that suffered disturbances in the week after Martin Luther King's assassination counted 43 dead. These killings are a disgrace to our country — but they are not numbered in the hundreds, the thousands or the millions.

[6]   No special providence spares America from such an escalation. It is a source of wonder that in the many opportunities for tipping the scale from race riot to race war the tipping point has not been reached. There will be more opportunities.

[7]   It is obvious that we are going to have to live with racism and violence for some time to come. It is also clear that violence will continue to figure in foreign as well as in domestic disputes. We do not have to abandon hope of diminishing violence in both areas in order to acknowledge the desperate importance of preventing escalation to the holocaust stage in either.

EXERCISES

Questions

1. Woodward's theme appears in paragraph 1. What is it? What does he imply about violence in America? Which examples of violence refer to actual physical confrontations? Which are nonphysical?
2. What significance can you derive from the comparison of homicide-suicide rates among blacks and whites? What is the significance of this in relation to his theme?
3. What seems to be the motive for individual acts of violence? for groups? Is it true that conspiracy, ideology, religion, and calculation have had a small part?
4. How does American violence differ from that of Russia? Germany? India, Indonesia, Sumatra and Borneo? How different are these from our Civil War?
5. What evidence is presented concerning American racial violence? What keeps our racial strife from expanding?
6. What warning is implied about our racial violence? Woodward offers no solution to violent behavior. Can you?

Vocabulary

cataclysmic
genocide
holocausts
innovative

For Discussion and Writing

See HARRINGTON: "The American Experience: Historically Violent," p. 358.

CROSS REFERENCES

HARRINGTON: "The American Experience: Historically Violent"
STEINBECK: "America and Americans"
THURBER: "The Trouble with Man Is Man"
WERTHAM: "Epilogue" from *The Show of Violence*
WOLFE: "Clean Fun at Riverhead"

MICHAEL HARRINGTON

"THE AMERICAN EXPERIENCE: HISTORICALLY VIOLENT"

INTRODUCTION

Michael Harrington(1928–   ), possibly more than any other man in the United States, was responsible for stirring popular concern over the conditions of the poor. His book *The Other America,* 1963, has been declared a direct cause in the formulation of the Johnson Administration's war on poverty. Mr. Harrington, who took his degrees at Holy Cross and the University of Chicago, has long been involved in working with the poor and oppressed. As an editor of such papers as the *Catholic Worker* and *New America,* as a consultant for the Fund for the Republic, and as a member of the national executive committee of the Socialist Party, he has been an articulate spokesman for the rights of the deprived. Two more recent books by Mr. Harrington are *The Accidental Century,* 1965, and *Toward a Democratic Left: A Radical Program for a New Majority,* 1968.

TO THE READER

Harrington contends that violence only gets the corrective attention it is due when it cuts across class lines, but that it is and has always been integral to American life.

Let me begin with an accurate cliché: The American experience has been, and is, particularly violent.

[2]   In the beginning there were the vigilante justice of the frontier, the genocidal[1] campaigns against the Indians, the restless mobility of a society in which many men asserted their identity rather than inheriting it and a gun was called The Great Equalizer. Later, after the West was pacified, the killing took new forms. The labor history of the United States is probably the bloodiest to be found in an industrialized nation and the most recent massacre, at Republic Steel on Memorial Day, 1937, is only 31 years behind us. I sometimes think that this intensity of the American class struggle is a function of the relative weakness of the American class consciousness. Workers and bosses did not confront one another as members of cohesive[2] classes with distinct traditions but as egalitarian individuals in a grudge fight.

[3]   Our legacy of violence persists to the present day. Until the very recent changes in our censorship laws, the contrast between French and American policy in this area was most revealing. In Paris, young people were forbidden to see our gory films but permitted to view nudity; in New York, we were appalled by naked bodies and completely tolerant of mayhem.

[4]   After World War II, a number of factors gave new impetus to this American trait. The society was becoming almost completely urbanized, and traditional institutions, like the family and the church, cracked under the strain. At the same time, the maturing of the postwar baby boom vastly increased the crime-prone age group of 18 to 24. But, as in almost all things American, the violence provoked by this rapid change and ethical incertitude[3] hurt some people more than others. More precisely, the poor — above all, the black poor packed into deteriorating ghettos — were the chief victims.

[5]   Crimes against the person, the President's Commission on Law Enforcement demonstrated a little more than a year ago, occur most often in the impoverished central city and least often in the affluent suburbs. This is part of the routine violence which this society visits upon its worst-off. As long as it stays in the ghetto, it is ignored; when it threatens the white middle class, it becomes a national problem.

[6]   But this everyday brutality of slum life, which grows out of poverty and despair, is not to be confused with riots. For the riots are a communal expression of the ghetto's anguish rather than individual tragedies induced by social conditions. These risings, the Kerner Commission[4] documented, are not made by the most destitute but by young people, often employed in dead end jobs, who see the society moving away from them despite their hard work. The Government bears a responsibility for this angry disenchantment, for Washington has, in recent years, promised boldly and performed

[1]descriptive of the deliberate and systematic extermination of a national or racial group
[2]characterized by the act or state of unity, sticking together
[3]uncertainty, doubtfulness, insecurity
[4]the National Advisory Commission on Civil Disorders

timidly. The "unconditional" war on poverty was proclaimed more than four years ago; yet last January the Council of Economic Advisers announced that there had been an increase in substandard housing in the central cities. It is dangerous to raise up people's hopes and then dash them down.

[7]   To complicate matters further, there is not even an easy way to "buy off" these riots. For as people begin to make gains, they do not become satisfied and complacent, but rather, quite often, more demanding. It should not be a surprise that riots erupted in Detroit and New Haven with their socially-conscious municipal administrations. It is precisely when people are making progress, but not as fast as they want, that they explode.

[8]   Finally, there is the assassin, the man who kills a John F. Kennedy or a Martin Luther King. In times of extraordinary change, like ours, there is always the possibility of a paranoid response: Unable to understand the kaleidoscopic facts, a man sees in them the occult[5] pattern of a conspiracy that justified killing a deceitful leader. This psychology is most often met on the political right but, as Oswald may show, it has its left-wing variants as well. This demented vision can possess an isolated individual or it can inspire a terrorist group or even movement (Europeans recognize only the politically conscious, organized forms of the disease; they do not understand that Americans are as individualistic about their psychoses as about anything else).

[9]   If my analysis is correct, much of the violence in this society is unnecessary. If the slums were abolished within 5 to 10 years there would likely be a marked decrease in the commonplace homicides, rapes and assaults which the poor are driven to inflict upon one another. If the turbulent change in American society could be democratically subjected to social control there would perhaps be less incitement to paranoia. And if the nation actually honored its promises the disillusionment which brings people to riot could be wiped out.

[12]   With so many complex variables involved, it would be foolish to suggest simple solutions. Yet one might well ponder an incident from the life and times of Dr. King. In Montgomery during the bus boycott there were no special sermons on personal conduct, yet there was a marked decrease in crime among Negroes. The people had discovered a dignity and purpose within themselves and by changing their society they changed themselves. What the Montgomery Improvement Association could do, the United States of America could try to do.

[5]mysterious, secret

EXERCISES

Questions

1. What evidence does Harrington present to support the first part of his theme, that the American experience has been violent? Which of these has or have been incorporated into our folklore? Which has or have been largely forgotten and ignored?
2. How has a lack of class consciousness increased the American class struggle?
3. What is the difference between the French target for censorship and our own? What is revealed about the two nations?
4. What post World War II conditions "gave new impetus" to American violence? Who was most affected by it? Consider his ironic comment that violence is ignored until it strikes the middle class. Is this true?
5. What are the causes of uprisings in the cities? Why is it significant that uprisings have occurred in socially progressive municipalities?
6. What kind of violence is responsible for most assassinations? Why is this, too, so much a reflection of today?
7. Compare the themes of paragraphs 7 and 9. Is there a contradiction in Harrington's assertions?
8. What does Harrington believe are the most important measures to be taken now?
9. What is the significance of the response to the Montgomery bus boycott?

Vocabulary

egalitarian
kaleidoscope
paranoid
variant

For Discussion and Writing

1. Gang clashes: ethnic wars on a small scale
2. Success-at-any-price as a contributor to violence
3. Traffic deaths: violence on the highways
4. The N.R.A.: defender of weaponry
5. The paradox of hope: a cause of violence
6. Bringing violence home: TV's role
7. Controlling the violence in myself
8. The need for gun control
9. Toy guns and war games: fun or training?
10. The draft riots of the Civil War
11. Homicide in the U.S. — a comparison with other nations
12. Student violence: the Sorbonne, Columbia, Berkeley, and so on
13. Watts, Detroit, or Chicago: a study of a race riot

CROSS REFERENCES

CAMUS: "The Spirit of Algiers"
FULBRIGHT: "The Cold War in American Life"
MINER: "Body Ritual among the Nacirema"
STEINBECK: "America and Americans"
WERTHAM: Epilogue from *The Show of Violence*
WOLFE: "Clean Fun at Riverhead"
WOODWARD: "America: Part of an International Culture of Violence"

RECOMMENDED READING

The Kerner Commission Report, *Report of the National Advisory Commission on Civil Disorders*
The U.S. Riot Commission Report
President's Commission to Report on Violence in America
WERTHAM, FREDRIC: *The Seduction of the Innocent*

V

The Hope
and the
Reassurance

"What do you think, Professor? Is it a laser, a maser,
a quasar or just a little ray of hope for all mankind?"

JOHN F. KENNEDY

"INAUGURAL ADDRESS"

INTRODUCTION

John F. Kennedy (1917–1963) was our 35th President. Since his assassination, and that of his brother, the legend about him has grown. The legend has, unfortunately, tended to distort history and, in many ways, has been a disservice to the man. Kennedy was more than a political leader; he was a historian and a writer of distinction. While still a student at Harvard, he wrote *While England Slept* (1940), and later, when hospitalized with a back injury, *Profiles in Courage* (1955), for which he won the Pulitzer Prize. A man may be best known by his own words. Kennedy's Inaugural Address is considered one of his finest documents.

TO THE READER

Although Kennedy was very much a man of this century, he continuously ties the past to the present.

Most of us know the famous lines of paragraph 25: "Ask not what your country can do for you — ask what you can do for your country." Kennedy uses this kind of balance throughout the speech.

From *Inaugural Addresses of the Presidents of the United States from George Washington, 1789, to John F. Kennedy, 1961.* (87th Congress, 1st Session, House Doc. 218. Washington, D.C., 1961.)

We observe today not a victory of party but a celebration of freedom — symbolizing an end as well as a beginning — signifying renewal as well as change. For I have sworn before you and Almighty God the same solemn oath our forebears prescribed nearly a century and three-quarters ago.

[2] The world is very different now. For man holds in his mortal hands the power to abolish all forms of human poverty and all forms of human life. And yet the same revolutionary beliefs for which our forebears fought are still at issue around the globe — the belief that the rights of man come not from the generosity of the state but from the hand of God.

[3] We dare not forget today that we are the heirs of that first revolution. Let the word go forth from this time and place, to friend and foe alike, that the torch has been passed to a new generation of Americans — born in this century, tempered by war, disciplined by a hard and bitter peace, proud of our ancient heritage — and unwilling to witness or permit the slow undoing of those human rights to which this nation has always been committed, and to which we are committed today at home and around the world.

[4] Let every nation know, whether it wishes us well or ill, that we shall pay any price, bear any burden, meet any hardship, support any friend, oppose any foe to assure the survival and the success of liberty.

[5] This much we pledge — and more.

[6] To those old allies whose cultural and spiritual origins we share, we pledge the loyalty of faithful friends. United, there is little we cannot do in a host of new cooperative ventures. Divided, there is little we can do — for we dare not meet a powerful challenge at odds and split asunder.

[7] To those new states whom we welcome to the ranks of the free, we pledge our word that one form of colonial control shall not have passed away merely to be replaced by a far more iron tyranny. We shall not always expect to find them supporting our view. But we shall always hope to find them strongly supporting their own freedom — and to remember that, in the past, those who foolishly sought power by riding the back of the tiger ended up inside.

[8] To those peoples in the huts and villages of half the globe struggling to break the bonds of mass misery, we pledge our best efforts to help them help themselves, for whatever period is required — not because the Communists may be doing it, not because we seek their votes, but because it is right. If a free society cannot help the many who are poor, it cannot save the few who are rich.

[9] To our sister republics south of our border, we offer a special pledge — to convert our good words into good deeds — in a new alliance for progress — to assist free men and free governments in casting off the chains of poverty. But this peaceful revolution of hope cannot become the prey of hostile powers. Let all our neighbors know that we shall join with them to oppose aggression or subversion anywhere in the Americas. And let every other power know that this hemisphere intends to remain the master of its own house.

[10] To that world assembly of sovereign states, the United Nations, our

last best hope in an age where the instruments of war have far outpaced the instruments of peace, we renew our pledge of support — to prevent it from becoming merely a forum for invective — to strengthen its shield of the new and the weak — and to enlarge the area in which its writ may run.

[11] Finally, to those nations who would make themselves our adversary, we offer not a pledge but a request: that both sides begin anew the quest for peace, before the dark powers of destruction unleashed by science engulf all humanity in planned or accidental self-destruction.

[12] We dare not tempt them with weakness. For only when our arms are sufficient beyond doubt can we be certain beyond doubt that they will never be employed.

[13] But neither can two great and powerful groups of nations take comfort from our present course — both sides overburdened by the cost of modern weapons, both rightly alarmed by the steady spread of the deadly atom, yet both racing to alter that uncertain balance of terror that stays the hand of mankind's final war.

[14] So let us begin anew — remembering on both sides that civility is not a sign of weakness, and sincerity is always subject to proof. Let us never negotiate out of fear. But let us never fear to negotiate.

[15] Let both sides explore what problems unite us instead of belaboring those problems which divide us.

[16] Let both sides, for the first time, formulate serious and precise proposals for the inspection and control of arms — and bring the absolute power to destroy other nations under the absolute control of all nations.

[17] Let both sides seek to invoke the wonders of science instead of its terrors. Together let us explore the stars, conquer the deserts, eradicate disease, tap the ocean depths and encourage the arts and commerce.

[18] Let both sides unite to heed in all corners of the earth the command of Isaiah — to "undo the heavy burdens . . . [and] let the oppressed go free."

[19] And if a beachhead of cooperation may push back the jungles of suspicion, let both sides join in creating a new endeavor — not a new balance of power, but a new world of law, where the strong are just and the weak secure and the peace preserved.

[20] All this will not be finished in the first 100 days. Nor will it be finished in the first 1,000 days, nor in the life of this Administration, nor even perhaps in our lifetime on this planet. But let us begin.

[21] In your hands, my fellow citizens, more than mine, will rest the final success or failure of our course. Since this country was founded, each generation of Americans has been summoned to give testimony to its national loyalty. The graves of young Americans who answered the call to service surround the globe.

[22] Now the trumpet summons us again — not as a call to bear arms, though arms we need — not as a call to battle, though embattled we are — but a call to bear the burden of a long twilight struggle year in and year out, "rejoicing in hope, patient in tribulation" — a struggle against the common enemies of man: tyranny, poverty, disease and war itself.

[23] Can we forge against these enemies a grand and global alliance, north and south, east and west, that can assure a more fruitful life for all mankind? Will you join in that historic effort?

[24] In the long history of the world, only a few generations have been granted the role of defending freedom in its hour of maximum danger. I do not shrink from this responsibility — I welcome it. I do not believe that any of us would exchange places with any other people or any other generation. The energy, the faith, the devotion which we bring to this endeavor will light our country and all who serve it — and the glow from that fire can truly light the world.

[25] And so, my fellow Americans: ask not what your country can do for you — ask what you can do for your country.

[26] My fellow citizens of the world: ask not what America will do for you, but what together we can do for the freedom of man.

[27] Finally, whether you are citizens of America or citizens of the world, ask of us here the same high standards of strength and sacrifice which we ask of you. With a good conscience our only sure reward, with history the final judge of our deeds, let us go forth to lead the land we love, asking His blessing and His help, but knowing that here on earth God's work must truly be our own.

EXERCISES

Questions

1. Which paragraph states the theme of this address? What is the function of paragraph 5? Where else do you find references to liberty and freedom in this speech?

2. The structure of this speech is simple. Construct an outline for it. Note how the structure uses balance and repetition. What similarities do you find in paragraphs 6–11? and in paragraphs 14–19? 25–27?

3. Closely examine paragraph one and see how it establishes the tone, language, content, and theme of the piece.

4. The Kennedy style is known for its balance. Examine paragraphs 8 and 14 for examples of parallelism. What other examples can be found?

5. Paragraph 10 shows a fine example of Kennedy's use of repetition and antithesis (a stylistic device in which contrasting or opposing phrases are placed close to each other) in "the instruments of war . . . the instruments of peace." Find other examples.

6. Note his use of the series (see paragraphs 3, 4, and 17) to build a cumulative effect. Are there other examples? Be sure to check the last paragraph, the three "asks."

7. Kennedy's opening words refer to American history. Where else does he refer to history in his speech? Where is the Bible referred to?

8. By specific reference, show what kind of world he envisioned. See especially paragraphs 15 and 17. What progress has been made toward this world since Kennedy made this speech?
9. How did he draw you, the reader, in? What devices did he use to persuade you to "join in that historic effort"? (Paragraph 23)
10. What do you think of the idea expressed in the last sentence of paragraph 8?
11. What do you think of the message of paragraph 14, particularly of sentence one?

For Discussion and Writing

Answering Kennedy's call:
1. A project I can follow for my country
2. My role in the freedom of man
3. Student participation in politics
4. What I can do for peace

CROSS REFERENCES

FULBRIGHT: "The Cold War in American Life"
KING: "I Have a Dream"
MINER: "Body Ritual among the Nacirema"
WHITE: "The Meaning of Democracy"

RECOMMENDED READING

WHITE, THEODORE: *The Making of the President, 1960* (Atheneum: 1961)

MARTIN LUTHER KING, JR.

"I HAVE A DREAM"

INTRODUCTION

Martin Luther King, Jr. (1929–1968) won the Nobel Prize in 1965 as a fitting recognition for a lifetime dedicated to the brotherhood of man. As preparation for his life work, Dr. King earned two advanced degrees: his Ph.D. and his Doctor of Divinity both from Boston University. His work as a Civil Rights leader started modestly enough with a bus boycott in Montgomery, Alabama, when he was president of the Montgomery Improvement Association but continued until he won international recognition. A follower of Thoreau and Gandhi, Dr. King believed in nonviolence and Christian principles. His sudden death was a violation of all he stood and spoke for. Two books in which he expresses his beliefs are *Stride Toward Freedom* (1958) and *Why We Can't Wait* (1964). Dr. King was an eloquent and moving speaker; the following speech was delivered to the enormous crowd assembled for the historic march on Washington in August 1963.

TO THE READER

The message is inspirational because it reminds all citizens of the very tenets of American belief, but the language is also inspirational in its poetic use of imagery and metaphor and its magnificent rhythm. Read sections aloud to get the full effect.

Five score years ago, a great American, in whose symbolic shadow we stand today, signed the Emancipation Proclamation. This momentous decree came as a great beacon of light and of hope to millions of Negro slaves who had been seared in the flames of withering injustice. It came as a joyous daybreak to end the long night of their captivity.

[2]   But one hundred years later, the Negro still is not free. One hundred years later, the life of the Negro is still sadly crippled by the manacles of segregation and the chains of discrimination.

[3]   One hundred years later, the Negro lives on a lonely island of poverty in the midst of a vast ocean of material prosperity. One hundred years later, the Negro is still languished in the corners of American society and finds himself an exile in his own land. So we have come here today to dramatize a shameful condition.

[4]   In a sense we have come to our nation's capital to cash a check. When the architects of our republic wrote the magnificent words of the Constitution and the Declaration of Independence, they were signing a promissory note to which every American was to fall heir. This note was a promise that all men, yes, black men as well as white men, would be granted the inalienable rights of life, liberty, and the pursuit of happiness.

[5]   It is obvious today that America has defaulted on this promissory note insofar as her citizens of color are concerned. Instead of honoring this sacred obligation, America has given the Negro people a bad check, which has come back marked "insufficient funds."

[6]   But we refuse to believe that the bank of justice is bankrupt. We refuse to believe that there are insufficient funds in the great vaults of opportunity of this nation. So we have come to cash this check—a check that will give us upon demand the riches of freedom and the security of justice.

[7]   We have also come to this hallowed spot to remind America of the fierce urgency of now. This is no time to engage in the luxury of cooling off or to take the tranquilizing drug of gradualism.[1] Now is the time to make real the promises of democracy. Now is the time to rise from the dark and desolate valley of segregation to the sunlit path of racial justice. Now is the time to lift our nation from the quicksands of racial injustice to the solid rock of brotherhood. Now is the time to make justice a reality for all of God's children.

[8]   It would be fatal for the nation to overlook the urgency of the movement and to underestimate the determination of the Negro. This sweltering summer of the Negro's legitimate discontent will not pass until there is an invigorating autumn of freedom and equality. 1963 is not an end but a beginning. Those who hope that the Negro needed to blow off steam and will now be content will have a rude awakening if the nation returns to business as usual.

[1]the principle or policy of achieving some goal by gradual steps rather than by drastic change

[9]   There will be neither rest nor tranquility in America until the Negro is granted his citizenship rights. The whirlwinds of revolt will continue to shake the foundations of our nation until the bright day of justice emerges.
[10]   But there is something that I must say to my people who stand on the warm threshold which leads into the palace of justice. In the process of gaining our rightful place we must not be guilty of wrongful deeds.
[11]   Let us not seek to satisfy our thirst for freedom by drinking from the cup of bitterness and hatred. We must forever conduct our struggle on the high plane of dignity and discipline. We must not allow our creative protest to degenerate into physical violence. Again and again we must rise to the majestic heights of meeting physical force with soul force.
[12]   The marvelous new militancy which has engulfed the Negro community must not lead us to a distrust of all white people, for many of our white brothers, as evidenced by their presence here today, have come to realize that their destiny is tied up with our destiny and they have come to realize that their freedom is inextricably bound to our freedom. This offense we share mounted to storm the battlements of injustice must be carried forth by a bi-racial army. We cannot walk alone.
[13]   And as we walk, we must make the pledge that we shall always march ahead. We cannot turn back. There are those who are asking the devotees of civil rights, "When will you be satisfied?" We can never be satisfied as long as the Negro is the victim of the unspeakable horrors of police brutality.
[14]   We can never be satisfied as long as our bodies, heavy with the fatigue of travel, cannot gain lodging in the motels of the highways and the hotels of the cities. We cannot be satisfied as long as the Negro's basic mobility is from a smaller ghetto to a larger one.
[15]   We can never be satisfied as long as our children are stripped of their selfhood and robbed of their dignity by signs stating "for whites only." We cannot be satisfied as long as a Negro in Mississippi cannot vote and a Negro in New York believes he has nothing for which to vote. No, we are not satisfied, and we will not be satisfied until justice rolls down like waters and righteousness like a mighty stream.
[16]   I am not unmindful that some of you have come here out of excessive trials and tribulation. Some of you have come fresh from narrow jail cells. Some of you have come from areas where your quest for freedom left you battered by the storms of persecution and staggered by the winds of police brutality. You have been the veterans of creative suffering. Continue to work with the faith that unearned suffering is redemptive.
[17]   Go back to Mississippi; go back to Alabama; go back to South Carolina; go back to Georgia; go back to Louisiana; go back to the slums and ghettos of the Northern cities, knowing that somehow this situation can, and will be changed. Let us not wallow in the valley of despair.
[18]   So I say to you, my friends, that even though we must face the difficulties of today and tomorrow, I still have a dream. It is a dream deeply rooted in the American dream that one day this nation will rise up and live

out the true meaning of its creed—we hold these truths to be self evident, that all men are created equal.

[19] I have a dream that one day on the red hills of Georgia, sons of former slaves and sons of former slave-owners will be able to sit down together at the table of brotherhood.

[20] I have a dream that one day, even the state of Mississippi, a state sweltering with the heat of injustice, sweltering with the heat of oppression, will be transformed into an oasis of freedom and justice.

[21] I have a dream my four little children will one day live in a nation where they will not be judged by the color of their skin but by the content of their character. I have a dream today!

[22] I have a dream that one day, down in Alabama, with its vicious racists, with its governor having his lips dripping with the words of interposition[2] and nullification,[3] that one day, right there in Alabama, little black boys and black girls will be able to join hands with little white boys and white girls as sisters and brothers. I have a dream today!

[23] I have a dream that one day every valley shall be exalted, every hill and mountain shall be made low, the rough places shall be made plain, and the crooked places shall be made straight and the glory of the Lord will be revealed and all flesh shall see it together.

[24] This is our hope. This is the faith that I go back to the South with.

[25] With this faith we will be able to hew out of the mountain of despair a stone of hope. With this faith we will be able to transform the jangling discords of our nation into a beautiful symphony of brotherhood.

[26] With this faith we will be able to work together, to pray together, to struggle together, to go to jail together, to stand up for freedom together, knowing that we will be free one day. This will be the day when all of God's children will be able to sing with new meaning—"my country 'tis of thee; sweet land of liberty; of thee I sing; land where my fathers died, land of the pilgrim's pride; from every mountain side, let freedom ring"— and if America is to be a great nation, this must become true.

[27] So let freedom ring from the prodigious hilltops of New Hampshire.

[28] Let freedom ring from the mighty mountains of New York.

[29] Let freedom ring from the heightening Alleghenies of Pennsylvania.

[30] Let freedom ring from the snow-capped Rockies of Colorado.

[31] Let freedom ring from the curvaceous slopes of California.

[32] But not only that.

[33] Let freedom ring from Stone Mountain of Georgia.

[34] Let freedom ring from Lookout Mountain of Tennessee.

[35] Let freedom ring from every hill and molehill of Mississippi, from every mountainside, let freedom ring.

[36] And when we allow freedom to ring, when we let it ring from every

---

[2]the doctrine that an individual state may oppose any federal action it believes encroaches on its sovereignty

[3]failure of a state to aid in enforcement of federal laws within its limits

village and hamlet, from every state and city, we will be able to speed up that day when all of God's children—black men and white men, Jews and Gentiles, Catholics and Protestants—will be able to join hands and to sing in the words of the old Negro spiritual. "Free at last, free at last; thank God Almighty, we are free at last."

EXERCISES

Questions

1. King presents his theme in paragraph 18. What is his dream? Paraphrase paragraphs 18 to 23. Read your paraphrase and King's words out loud to recognize the force of the original. How is his theme related to the idea, expressed in the last paragraph, that then all will sing "Free at last"?

2. How many metaphors can you find in the first three paragraphs? What is their contribution to the speech's introduction?

3. What three reasons does King offer for the presence of the marchers in Washington that August day? What underlying cause does he refer to?

4. Discuss the symbol of the check and the promissory note. Is the analogy fitting? Why is it effective? Is it consistent with his dream?

5. What three cautions does he suggest? To whom are they directed? How do the first two relate to the last paragraph?

6. What sentences can you find that invoke Biblical phrases or diction? What sentences use diction relevant to our national heritage or patriotism?

7. The conclusion, beginning in paragraph 27, is almost a prose poem. Find the words that give it its tone of exaltation. What lines convey imagery? What lines use alliteration? In what lines does King bring together the religious and patriotic symbolism of the entire speech?

8. Reread paragraph 7 for style. How many different metaphors has he used? How does the word "now" at the end of the first sentence function for the rest of the paragraph? Here King introduces the parallel "now is the time" emphasized by its repetition.Find other instances of this paralleling and repetition.

9. Comment on his observation "unearned suffering is redemptive." How is this different from using religion as an "opiate"?

Vocabulary

prodigious
redemptive
tribulation

For Discussion and Writing

1. Why Negroes can't wait
2. Separate and unequal

3.   Is America a racist society?
4.   The Northern ghetto
5.   The marches on Washington
6.   The relationship of dreams to hope to action
7.   Civil Rights legislation in my state

CROSS REFERENCES

FULBRIGHT: "The Cold War in American Life"
KENNEDY: "Inaugural Address"
THOREAU: "On the Duty of Civil Disobedience"

RECOMMENDED READING

The Kerner Commission Report, *Report of the National Advisory Commission on Civil Disorders* (Bantam: 1968)

HENRY THOREAU

AN EXCERPT FROM "ON THE DUTY OF CIVIL DISOBEDIENCE"

INTRODUCTION

Henry Thoreau (1817–1862) was a quiet peaceful man of strong ethical convictions. He rarely left home (which was Concord, Massachusetts); he led no movements; and he was largely unread during his own lifetime. Yet his influence, based largely on only two works, the full-length *Walden* and the essay "On the Duty of Civil Disobedience," has been felt around the world. Mahatma Gandhi, who led India to independence via passive resistance, credited Thoreau's writings. Martin Luther King, Jr., spoke of the influence of Thoreau and Gandi on his thinking. The somewhat isolated, nature-observing Thoreau who "traveled much in Concord" has traveled via his pen much further in the world.

TO THE READER

There have been many untrue stories of Thoreau's jailing; this is the true one.
It is important to know why Thoreau went to jail. Though not an abolitionist, he strongly opposed slavery. He further opposed the Mexican War which he believed would extend slavery. The refusal to pay the poll tax was

his protest; it was his way of saying "I will not support any state that supports slavery." In his words:

"I know this well, that if one thousand, if one hundred, if ten men I could name, — if ten *honest* men only, — ay, if *one* HONEST man, in this State of Massachusetts, *ceasing to hold slaves,* were actually to withdraw from this co-partnership, and be locked up in the county jail therefor, it would be the abolition of slavery in America. For it matters not how small the beginning may seem to be: what is once well done is done forever."

He decided to be that "*one* HONEST man."

I have paid no poll-tax[1] for six years. I was put into a jail once on this account, for one night; and, as I stood considering the walls of solid stone, two or three feet thick, the door of wood and iron, a foot thick, and the iron grating which strained the light, I could not help being struck with the foolishness of that institution which treated me as if I were mere flesh and blood and bones, to be locked up. I wondered that it should have concluded at length that this was the best use it could put me to, and had never thought to avail itself of my services in some way. I saw that, if there was a wall of stone between me and my townsmen, there was a still more difficult one to climb or break through before they could get to be as free as I was. I did not for a moment feel confined, and the walls seemed a great waste of stone and mortar. I felt as if I alone of all my townsmen had paid my tax. They plainly did not know how to treat me, but behaved like persons who are underbred. In every threat and in every compliment there was a blunder; for they thought that my chief desire was to stand the other side of that stone wall. I could not but smile to see how industriously they locked the door on my meditations, which followed them out again without let or hindrance, and *they* were really all that was dangerous. As they could not reach me, they had resolved to punish my body; just as boys, if they cannot come at some person against whom they have a spite, will abuse his dog. I saw that the State was half-witted, that it was timid as a lone woman with her silver spoons, and that it did not know its friends from its foes, and I lost all my remaining respect for it, and pitied it.

[2]   Thus the State never intentionally confronts a man's sense, intellectual or moral, but only his body, his senses. It is not armed with superior wit or honesty, but with superior physical strength. I was not born to be forced. I will breathe after my own fashion. Let us see who is the strongest. What force has a multitude? They only can force me who obey a higher law than I. They force me to become like themselves. I do not hear of *men* being *forced* to live this way or that by masses of men. What sort of life were that

---

[1] a tax, the payment of which is sometimes required to vote (This tax has since been declared unconstitutional by the United States Supreme Court.)

[2] probably a county seat

to live? When I meet a government which says to me, "Your money or your life," why should I be in haste to give it my money? It may be in a great strait, and not know what to do: I cannot help that. It must help itself; do as I do. It is not worth the while to snivel about it. I am not responsible for the successful working of the machinery of society. I am not the son of an engineer. I perceive that, when an acorn and a chestnut fall side by side, the one does not remain inert to make way for the other, but both obey their own laws, and spring and grow and flourish as best they can, till one, perchance, overshadows and destroys the other. If a plant cannot live according to its nature, it dies; and so a man.

[3]   The night in prison was novel and interesting enough. The prisoners in their shirtsleeves were enjoying a chat and the evening air in the doorway, when I entered. But the jailer said, "Come, boys, it is time to lock up"; and so they dispersed, and I heard the sound of their steps returning into the hollow apartments. My room-mate was introduced to me by the jailer as "a first-rate fellow and a clever man." When the door was locked, he showed me where to hang my hat, and how he managed matters there. The rooms were whitewashed once a month; and this one, at least, was the whitest, most simply furnished, and probably the neatest apartment in town. He naturally wanted to know where I came from, and what brought me there; and, when I had told him, I asked him in my turn how he came there, presuming him to be an honest man, of course; and, as the world goes, I believe he was. "Why," said he, "they accuse me of burning a barn; but I never did it." As near as I could discover, he had probably gone to bed in a barn when drunk, and smoked his pipe there; and so a barn was burnt. He had a reputation of being a clever man, had been there some three months waiting for his trial to come on, and would have to wait as much longer; but he was quite domesticated and contented, since he got his board for nothing, and thought that he was well treated.

[4]   He occupied one window, and I the other; and I saw that if one stayed there long, his principal business would be to look out the window. I had soon read all the tracts that were left there, and examined where former prisoners had broken out, and where a grate had been sawed off, and heard the history of the various occupants of that room; for I found that even here there was a history and a gossip which never circulated beyond the walls of the jail. Probably this is the only house in the town where verses are composed, which are afterward printed in a circular form, but not published. I was shown quite a long list of verses which were composed by some young men who had been detected in an attempt to escape, who avenged themselves by singing them.

[5]   I pumped my fellow-prisoner as dry as I could, for fear I should never see him again; but at length he showed me which was my bed, and left me to blow out the lamp.

[6]   It was like traveling into a far country, such as I had never expected to behold, to lie there for one night. It seemed to me that I never had heard the

town clock strike before, nor the evening sounds of the village; for we slept with the windows open, which were inside the grating. It was to see my native village in the light of the Middle Ages, and our Concord was turned into a Rhine Stream, and visions of knights and castles passed before me. They were the voices of old burghers that I heard in the streets. I was an involuntary spectator and auditor of whatever was done and said in the kitchen of the adjacent village inn—a wholly new and rare experience to me. It was a closer view of my native town. I was fairly inside of it. This is one of its peculiar institutions; for it is a shire[2] town. I began to comprehend what its inhabitants were about.

[7]   In the morning, our breakfasts were put through the hole in the door, in small oblong-square tin pans, made to fit, and holding a pint of chocolate, with brown bread, and an iron spoon. When they called for the vessels again, I was green enough to return what bread I had left; but my comrade seized it, and said that I should lay that up for lunch or dinner.Soon after he was let out to work at haying in a neighboring field, whither he went every day, and would not be back till noon; so he bade me good-day, saying that he doubted if he should see me again.

[8]   When I came out of prison—for some one interfered, and paid that tax—I did not perceive that great changes had taken place on the common, such as he observed who went in a youth and emerged a tottering and gray-headed man; and yet a change had to my eyes come over the scene—the town, and State, and country—greater than any that mere time could effect. I saw yet more distinctly the State in which I lived. I saw to what extent the people among whom I lived could be trusted as good neighbors and friends; that their friendship was for summer weather only; that they did not greatly propose to do right; that they were a distinct race from me by their prejudices and superstitions, as the Chinamen and Malays are; that in their sacrifices to humanity they ran no risks, not even to their property; that after all they were not so noble but they treated the thief as he had treated them, and hoped, by a certain outward observance and a few prayers, and by walking in a particular straight though useless path from time to time, to save their souls. This may be to judge my neighbors harshly; for I believe that many of them are not aware that they have such an institution as the jail in their village.

[9]   It was formerly the custom in our village, when a poor debtor came out of jail, for his acquaintances to salute him, looking through their fingers, which were crossed to represent the grating of a jail window, "How do ye do?" My neighbors did not thus salute me, but first looked at me, and then at one another, as if I had returned from a long journey. I was put into jail as I was going to the shoemaker's to get a shoe which was mended. When I was let out the next morning, I proceeded to finish my errand, and, having put on my mended shoe, joined a huckleberry party, who were impatient

---

[2]probably a county seat

to put themselves under my conduct; and in half an hour—for the horse was soon tackled—was in the midst of a huckleberry field, on one of our highest hills, two miles off, and then the State was nowhere to be seen.
[10] This is the whole history of "My Prisons."

[11] I have never declined paying the highway tax, because I am as desirous of being a good neighbor as I am of being a bad subject; and as for supporting schools, I am doing my part to educate my fellow-countrymen now. It is for no particular item in the tax bill that I refuse to pay it. I simply wish to refuse allegiance to the State, to withdraw and stand aloof from it effectually. I do not care to trace the course of my dollar, if I could, till it buys a man or a musket to shoot one with—the dollar is innocent—but I am concerned to trace the effects of my allegiance. In fact, I quietly declare war with the State, after my fashion, though I will still make what use and get what advantage of her I can, as is usual in such cases.
[12] If others pay the tax which is demanded of me, from a sympathy with the State, they do but what they have already done in their own case, or rather they abet injustice to a greater extent than the State requires. If they pay the tax from a mistaken interest in the individual taxed, to save his property, or prevent his going to jail, it is because they have not considered wisely how far their private feelings interfere with the public good.
[13] This, then, is my position at present. But one cannot be too much on his guard in such a case, lest his action be biased by obstinacy or an undue regard for the opinions of men. Let him see that he does only what belongs to himself and to the hour.

EXERCISES

Questions

1. According to Thoreau, what is the state doing by imprisoning him? How was he free? What was the most dangerous part of himself?
2. When Thoreau says, in paragraph 2, "If a plant cannot live according to its nature, it dies, and so a man," he is referring to man's highest, his most moral and ethical nature, not his biological drives. Is the analogy he makes apt? How does a man "die" if he does not live morally?
3. Notice how paragraphs 3, 6, and 8 begin with a topic sentence. How do the paragraphs develop those topics? How many specific details does he bring in to support his themes.
4. How apt is the metaphor that a night in jail was like "traveling into a far country"? (See paragraph 6.) This is an example of Thoreau's traveling much in Concord. How does the paragraph illustrate the kind of mind Thoreau had?
5. In paragraph 8, Thoreau reflects on his nonconformity, on how he is different from his neighbors. How is he different from his neighbors? Dis-

cuss his comment on them as representative of all American citizens —
as people more concerned with property and individual well-being than
with mankind.

6. The tone of the excerpt is casual, even amused. How is it deceptive? In
    what paragraphs and statements do we become aware of Thoreau's real
    feelings?

7. Thoreau's "declaration of war" has been called the quietest in history.
    How is the tone of Thoreau's "declaration of war" in keeping with the
    tone of the rest of the excerpt?

8. Compare Thoreau's attitude toward freedom in jail with Sartre's toward
    freedom in a dictatorship.

For Discussion and Writing

1. Comment on: "I saw that, if there was a wall of stone between me and
    my townsmen, there was a still more difficult one to climb or break
    through before they could get to be as free as I was."

2. The following quotations are from other parts of "Civil Disobedience."
    Comment.

    a. "I think that we should be men first, and subjects afterward. It is
        not desirable to cultivate a respect for the law so much as for the
        right."

    b. "There is little virtue in the action of masses of men."

    c. "A man has not everything to do, but something; and because he
        cannot do *everything*, it is not necessary that he should do *something*
        wrong."

    d. "Unjust laws exist; shall we be content to obey them, or shall we
        endeavor to amend them, and obey them until we have succeeded,
        or shall we transgress them at once? . . . if [the law] is of such a na-
        ture that it requires you to be the agent of injustice to another, then,
        I say, break the law."

    e. "You must live within yourself, and depend on yourself always
        tucked up and ready for a start . . ."

CROSS REFERENCES

FARRELL: "Today's Disobedience Is Uncivil"
GALBRAITH: "Dissent in a Free Society"
KELMAN: "When Disobedience Is Justifiable"
KING: "I Have a Dream"
PLATO: "Apology"
SARTRE: "The Republic of Silence"
THOREAU: *"On the Duty of Civil Disobedience"*

RECOMMENDED READING

KING, JR., MARTIN LUTHER: *"Letter from Birmingham Jail,"* Chapter 5 in
  Why We Can't Wait (New York: Harper & Row, 1964)
KRUTCH: "The Meaning of Thoreau"

JEAN PAUL SARTRE

"THE REPUBLIC OF SILENCE"

INTRODUCTION

Jean Paul Sartre (1905–   ) is more closely associated with existentialism than perhaps any other writer of the twentieth century. While primarily a philosopher, he is also a novelist and a playwright. *No Exit,* 1944, and *The Respectful Prostitute,* 1946, are two of his better-known plays. His major philosophical work is *Being and Nothingness,* while *Nausea,* 1938, is probably his most widely read novel. Perhaps he is best known as the first, and to date only, man who has ever turned down the Nobel Prize for Literature. That was in 1964. That same year, he published his autobiography, *Words.*

TO THE READER

Sartre presents his definitions of freedom and responsibility and shows the relationship between the two.

Note Sartre's stress on the individual *alone* and how many ways and words he uses to enforce the idea of loneliness.

W̲e were never more free than during the German occupation. We had lost all our rights, beginning with the right to talk. Every day we were

insulted to our faces and had to take it in silence. Under one pretext or another, as workers, Jews, or political prisoners, we were deported EN MASSE.
Everywhere, on billboards, in the newspapers, on the screen, we encountered the revolting and insipid picture of ourselves that our oppressors
wanted us to accept. And, because of all this, we were free. Because the
Nazi venom seeped even into our thoughts, every accurate thought was a
conquest. Because an all-powerful police tried to force us to hold our
tongues, every word took on the value of a declaration of principles. Because we were hunted down, every one of our gestures had the weight of a
solemn commitment. The circumstances, atrocious as they often were,
finally made it possible for us to live, without pretense of false shame, the
hectic and impossible existence that is known as the lot of man. Exile, captivity, and especially death (which we usually shrink from facing at all in happier times) became for us the habitual objects of our concern. We learned
that they were neither inevitable accidents, nor even constant and exterior
dangers, but that they must be considered as our lot itself, our destiny, the
profound source of our reality as men. At every instant we lived up to the full
sense of this commonplace little phrase: "Man is mortal!" And the choice
that each of us made of his life and of his being was an authentic choice because it was made face to face with death, because it could always have
been expressed in these terms; "Rather death than. . . ." And here I am not
speaking of the élite among us who were real Resistants, but of all Frenchmen who, at every hour of the night and day throughout four years, answered
NO. But the very cruelty of the enemy drove us to the extremities of this
condition by forcing us to ask ourselves questions that one never considers
in time of peace. All those among us — and what Frenchman was not at one
time or another in this situation — who knew any details concerning the Resistance[1] asked themselves anxiously, "If they torture me, shall I be able to
keep silent?" Thus the basic question of liberty itself was posed, and we
were brought to the verge of the deepest knowledge that man can have of
himself. For the secret of a man is not his Oedipus complex or his inferiority
complex: it is the limit of his own liberty, his capacity for resisting torture
and death.

[2]   To those who were engaged in underground activities, the conditions
of their struggle afforded a new kind of experience. They did not fight
openly like soldiers. In all circumstances they were alone. They were hunted
down in solitude, arrested in solitude. It was completely forlorn and un-
befriended that they held out against torture, alone and naked in the presence of torturers, clean-shaven, well-fed, and well-clothed, who laughed
at their cringing flesh, and to whom an untroubled conscience and a boundless sense of social strength gave every appearance of being in the right.
Alone. Without a friendly hand or a word of encouragement. Yet, in the

[1]an underground organization composed of groups of private individuals working as an
opposition force in a conquered country to overthrow the occupying power, usually by acts of
sabotage (here, the French against the Nazis in World War II)

depth of their solitude, it was the others that they were protecting, all the others, all their comrades in the Resistance. Total responsibility in total solitude — is this not the very definition of our liberty? This being stripped of all, this solitude, this tremendous danger, were the same for all. For the leaders and for their men, for those who conveyed messages without knowing what their content was, as for those who directed the entire Resistance, the punishment was the same — imprisonment, deportation, death. There is no army in the world where there is such equality of risk for the private and for the commander-in-chief. And this is why the Resistance was a true democracy: for the soldier as for the commander, the same danger, the same forsakenness, the same total responsibility, the same absolute liberty within discipline. Thus, in darkness and in blood, a Republic was established, the strongest of Republics. Each of its citizens knew that he owed himself to all and that he could count only on himself alone. Each of them, in complete isolation, fulfilled his responsibility and his role in history. Each of them, standing against the oppressors, undertook to be himself, freely and irrevocably. And by choosing for himself in liberty, he chose the liberty of all. This Republic without institutions, without an army, without police, was something that at each instant every Frenchman had to win and to affirm against Nazism. No one failed in this duty, and now we are on the threshold of another Republic. May this Republic about to be set up in broad daylight preserve the austere virtues of that other Republic of Silence and of Night.

EXERCISES

Questions

1. What is the significance of the title? What was the Republic of Silence?
2. The essay opens with a paradox that the next few sentences support. What is the paradox? Why were men more free? Is there anything else paradoxical in this essay?
3. The essay has two paragraphs. Could or should there be more? Where would you make one or more other divisions?
4. How many words can you find that are synonyms for *alone* or for the quality of loneliness? How does this reiteration of words relate to the central theme?
5. Sartre writes many cause-and-effect sentences such as "and because of all this, we were free." Notice also how the halves are about the same length. Can you find other examples of this type of sentence?
6. What is Sartre's definition of liberty? How does a man reach the secret of knowing himself? Citing details, show how the various acts of the oppressors "freed" the Frenchmen.
7. What made the Resistance a true democracy? How was the responsibility of individuals related to the well-being of the group?

8. Why is a choice made "face to face with death" an authentic choice?
9. In the light of current history, is there any irony in the last sentence?
10. Comment on the oppressor whose "untroubled conscience and . . . boundless sense of social strength gave every appearance of being in the right." Can an individual be right if everyone else says no? Can a group possibly be wrong if it is a large majority?

For Discussion and Writing

1. The military as an undemocratic society
2. Finding courage in a crisis
3. Sophocles and Sartre: liberty and death
4. Answering NO to what is morally wrong if legally right
5. Thoreau and Sartre: the freedom of choice
6. Conscientious objection to military service

CROSS REFERENCES

GALBRAITH: "Dissent in a Free Society"
LAMPELL: "I Think I Ought to Mention I Was Blacklisted"
PLATO: "Apology"
THOREAU: "On the Duty of Civil Disobedience"

RECOMMENDED READING

CAMUS, ALBERT: *The Stranger* (New York: Knopf, 1946)
MALAMUD, BERNARD: *The Fixer* (New York: Farrar, Straus & Giroux, 1966)

WILLIAM FAULKNER

"NOBEL PRIZE ACCEPTANCE SPEECH"

INTRODUCTION

William Faulkner (1897–1962) won the Nobel Prize for Literature in 1949, confirming international recognition of his genius. He is considered by some critics to be the greatest American writer of the twentieth century, although he was, and is, still not as widely read as many less significant writers. Among his great works are *The Sound and the Fury* (1929); *Light in August* (1932); and *Intruder in the Dust* (1948). Many films have been made based on his works, such as *The Long Hot Summer* and *Sanctuary*.

Faulkner's style is difficult (it is not hard to believe that he flunked freshman English at the University of Mississippi) with page-long sentences, erratic punctuation, even sentences and paragraphs that begin with small letters; but his penetrating view of mankind is worth examining despite the fact that it sometimes involves extra effort on the reader's part.

TO THE READER

Notice Faulkner's views on the artist's responsibility to man and Faulkner's belief in the endurance of mankind.

Reprinted from *The Essays, Speeches, and Public Letters of William Faulkner,* © 1966, Random House, Inc., by permission of the publisher.

I feel that this award was not made to me as a man but to my work—a life's work in the agony and sweat of the human spirit, not for glory and least of all for profit, but to create out of the materials of the human spirit something which did not exist there before. So this award is only mine in trust. It will not be difficult to find a dedication for the money part of it commensurate[1] with the purpose and significance of its origin. But I would like to do the same with the acclaim, too, by using this moment as a pinnacle from which I might be listened to by the young men and women already dedicated to the same anguish and travail, among whom is already that one who will some day stand here where I am standing.

[2]   Our tragedy today is a general and a universal physical fear so long sustained by now that we can even bear it. There are no longer problems of the spirit. There is only the question: when will I be blown up? Because of this, the young man or woman writing today has forgotten the problems of the human heart in conflict with itself which alone can make good writing because only that is worth writing about, worth the agony and the sweat.

[3]   He must learn them again. He must teach himself that the basest of all things is to be afraid; and, teaching himself that, forget it forever, leaving no room in his workshop for anything but the old verities and truths of the heart, the old universal truths lacking which any story is ephemeral[2] and doomed—love and honor and pity and pride and compassion and sacrifice. Until he does so he labors under a curse. He writes not of love, but of lust, of defeats in which nobody loses anything of value, of victories without hope and worst of all without pity or compassion. His griefs grieve on no universal bones, leaving no scars. He writes not of the heart but of the glands.

[4]   Until he relearns these things, he will write as though he stood among and watched the end of man. I decline to accept the end of man. It is easy enough to say that man is immortal simply because he will endure; that when the last ding-dong of doom has clanged and faded from the last worthless rock hanging tideless in the last red and dying evening, that even then there will still be one more sound: that of his puny, inexhaustible voice, still talking. I refuse to accept this. I believe that man will not merely endure: he will prevail. He is immortal, not because he alone among creatures has an inexhaustible voice, but because he has a soul, a spirit capable of compassion and sacrifice and endurance. The poet's, the writer's, duty is to write about these things. It is his privilege to help man endure by lifting his heart, by reminding him of the courage and honor and hope and pride and compassion and pity and sacrifice which have been the glory of his past. The poet's voice need not merely be the record of man, it can be one of the props, the pillars to help him endure and prevail.

[1]corresponding in amount or degree
[2]lasting a very short time

EXERCISES

Questions

1. Faulkner is dealing with two main points: man's fears and how to handle them; and the writer's job, how to help mankind. What is the chief fear? How must man handle fear? What is the artist's job?
2. State the theme of the speech in a sentence or two. Is there a single sentence in the speech that states the theme?
3. What transitional devices has Faulkner used to tie the paragraphs to each other? to link the sentences?
4. Note the language and imagery of the last paragraph, particularly the sentence beginning "It is easy enough . . ." How different is this sentence from poetry?
5. In paragraph 3, note the list of nouns joined by the conjunction "and"; this is typical of Faulkner's style. Can you find another example?
6. What is the difference between man enduring and man prevailing?
7. How much is the behavior of each of us affected by the great fear of being blown up (paragraph 5)?
8. How does Faulkner define the difference between love and lust?
9. Do you agree with Faulkner that the only true subject of good writing is "the problems of the human heart in conflict . . ." (paragraph 2)? Does this and the statement in paragraph 3 help you to separate good and bad writing?

Vocabulary

pinnacle
travail
verities

For Discussion and Writing

1. *"This is the way the world ends Not with a bang but a whimper."*—
    T. S. Eliot, "The Hollow Men"*
2. "Man will not merely endure: he will prevail."
3. The world will end with a sigh of relief.
4. The artist's responsibility to man.

CROSS REFERENCES

CIARDI: "I Met a Man"
HIGHET: "What Use Is Poetry?"
ROCKEFELLER: "The Governor Lectures on Art"
SCHWARTZ: "Why Write a Book?"

*Reprinted from *Collected Poems 1909–1962* by T. S. Eliot, by permission of Harcourt, Brace & World, Inc.

BERTRAND RUSSELL

PROLOGUE TO *THE AUTOBIOGRAPHY OF BERTRAND RUSSELL*

INTRODUCTION

Bertrand Russell (1872–   ) can be described in many ways, but two are most significant. As an intellectual, he is one of the great minds of the twentieth century, having achieved worldwide recognition in mathematics, philosophy, sociology, and literature, for which he won the Nobel Prize in 1950. As a controversial figure, he has shocked and upset generations of people by his advanced views on religion, politics, and pacifism. Whether one agrees with Russell or not, however, one must always concede him to be a man whose life has been dictated by his principles, accepting public scorn, even jail, for his ideas. He has stood for what he believed concerning peace and love.

TO THE READER

In this short introduction to Russell's *Autobiography,* there is almost perfect organization and balance. Note how this man who is an avowed atheist shows his strong religious convictions.

Three passions, simple but overwhelmingly strong, have governed my life: the longing for love, the search for knowledge, and unbearable pity for the suffering of mankind. These passions, like great winds, have blown me hither and thither, in a wayward course, over a deep ocean of anguish, reaching to the very verge of despair.

[2]   I have sought love, first, because it brings ecstasy—ecstasy so great that I would often have sacrificed all the rest of life for a few hours of this joy. I have sought it, next, because it relieves loneliness—that terrible loneliness in which one shivering consciousness looks over the rim of the world into the cold unfathomable lifeless abyss. I have sought it, finally, because in the union of love I have seen, in a mystic miniature, the prefiguring vision of the heaven that saints and poets have imagined. This is what I sought, and though it might seem too good for human life, this is what—at last—I have found.

[3]   With equal passion I have sought knowledge. I have wished to understand the hearts of men. I have wished to know why the stars shine. And I have tried to apprehend the Pythagorean[1] power by which number holds sway above the flux. A little of this, but not much, I have achieved.

[4]   Love and knowledge, so far as they were possible, led upward toward the heavens. But always pity brought me back to earth. Echoes of cries of pain reverberate in my heart. Children in famine, victims tortured by oppressors, helpless old people a hated burden to their sons, and the whole world of loneliness, poverty, and pain make a mockery of what human life should be. I long to alleviate the evil, but I cannot, and I too suffer.

[5]   This has been my life. I have found it worth living, and would gladly live it again if the chance were offered me.

EXERCISES

Questions

1.   Russell states his thesis in the first paragraph. Note how the next three paragraphs develop the thesis. How does he relate his conclusions to the rest of the material?
2.   His five simple paragraphs are closely linked. What words has he repeated to tie them together?
3.   Russell makes use of metaphor to illuminate his writing. What metaphors can you find? How effective are they?
4.   The language of this piece is very simple and most of the sentences are quite short. What devices of sentence structure are used to create variety?

[1] a geometric theory devised by the Greek mathematician Pythagoras

5. In paragraph 1, what is the effect of calling those three forces in life "passions"? What do you think of his three passions as motivating forces of life? What do such passions reveal of the character of the man?

6. Why do these passions drive him to the verge of despair? Why does he not despair?

7. In paragraph 4, has Russell omitted any source of pain you consider important?

8. Russell replaces divine love with the power of human love. (See paragraph 2.) How do you feel about this? Also note what he says of the function of love. Do you agree?

For Discussion and Writing

1. Man's inevitable "terrible loneliness"

2. Love and knowledge as balances for the "unbearable pity for the suffering of mankind"

3. The forces that govern my life

CROSS REFERENCES

MacLEISH   "Thoughts on an Age That Gave Us Hiroshima"
PLATO: "Apology"
SARTRE: "The Republic of Silence"
SEVAREID: "The Dark of the Moon"
WERTHAM: "Epilogue" from *The Show of Violence*

Afterword

FREDRIC WERTHAM

"EPILOGUE" FROM *THE SHOW OF VIOLENCE*

INTRODUCTION

Fredric Wertham (1895–   ) was born in Germany, was educated internationally, and has spent almost his entire professional career as a psychiatrist working in the United States. Dr. Wertham has long been interested in
violence — its causes and its manifestations. Among his many appointments is
that of physician in charge of the psychiatric clinic for the Court of General
Sessions of New York City. This has allowed him to study the case histories
of those arrested and brought to trial for violent crimes. He has written several books: *Dark Legend: A Study in Murder,* 1942; *The Show of Violence,*
1949, from which this "Epilogue" is taken; *The Seduction of the Innocent,*
1955, an attack on comic books in their glorification of violence as sadistic
corrupters of children; and *An Exploration of Human Violence,* 1966.

Since ancient times there have been many interpretations of the
meaning of Cain's story. Theologians have said that Cain was just evil and
Abel righteous. Or they speculated that there may have been two Eves, the
first one who gave Adam the apple and was cast out of the Garden of Eden

and the second one who was the mother of Cain and Abel; Cain and Abel quarreled because both wanted the first Eve.

Poets have tried to re-create the figure of Cain and have made him explain himself:

> A dreary dream
> Had madden'd me

The philosophers have speculated that Cain was ill-tempered and did not act on a plan but on a sudden impulse. They have given Cain a legalistic defense: since he had never seen or heard of a slain person, he did not know that striking his brother would kill him.

The psychologists have analyzed Cain and found "sibling rivalry," an Oedipus complex, or "rejection" by a parent.

Sociologists point out that the conflict was between the shepherd and the man who first tilled the soil; or between communal property and the first man who, rejected by the group, established private property. And that Cain and Abel were not the names of individuals but of *gentes* or clans.

Maybe for us today the meaning of the legend is a simple direct answer to Cain's question, to be acted upon in our everyday life.

"Am I my brother's keeper?" The answer is yes.